# THE SEARCH FOR STRATEGY

**Recent Titles in**
**Contributions in Military Studies**

The Soviet Military and the Future
*Stephen J. Blank and Jacob W. Kipp, editors*

Soviet Military Doctrine from Lenin to Gorbachev, 1915–1991
*Willard C. Frank and Philip S. Gillette, editors*

Soviet Military Reform in the Twentieth Century: Three Case Studies
*Raymond J. Swider, Jr.*

The Laws of Land Warfare: A Guide to U.S. Army Manuals
*Donald A. Wells*

Raiders or Elite Infantry? The Changing Role of the U.S. Army Rangers from Dieppe to Grenada
*David W. Hogan, Jr.*

The U.S. Military
*John E. Peters*

Unconventional Conflicts in a New Security Era: Lessons from Malaya and Vietnam
*Sam C. Sarkesian*

"Mad Jack": The Biography of Captain John Percival, USN, 1779–1862
*David F. Long*

Military Helicopter Doctrines of the Major Powers, 1945–1992: Making Decisions about Air-Land Warfare
*Matthew Allen*

Joint Military Operations: A Short History
*Roger A. Beaumont*

Iron Brigade General: John Gibbon, A Rebel in Blue
*Dennis S. Lavery and Mark H. Jordan*

Looking Back on the Vietnam War: A 1990s Perspective on the Decisions, Combat, and Legacies
*William Head and Lawrence E. Grinter, editors*

# THE SEARCH FOR STRATEGY

## *Politics and Strategic Vision*

Edited by
*Gary L. Guertner*

Foreword by Major General William A. Stofft

PUBLISHED UNDER THE AUSPICES OF THE STRATEGIC STUDIES INSTITUTE OF THE U.S. ARMY WAR COLLEGE

Contributions in Military Studies, Number 143

Greenwood Press
Westport, Connecticut • London

**Library of Congress Cataloging-in-Publication Data**

The Search for strategy : politics and strategic vision / edited by
Gary L. Guertner ; foreword by William A. Stofft.
p. cm. — (Contributions in military studies, ISSN 0883–6884 ;
no. 143)
"Published under the auspices of the Strategic Studies Institute of the
U.S. Army War College."
Includes bibliographical references and index.
ISBN 0–313–28881–X (alk. paper)
1. United States—Military policy. 2. Strategy. I. Guertner,
Gary L. II. Series.
UA23.S394 1993
355′.0335′73—dc20 92–35916

British Library Cataloguing in Publication Data is available.



Library of Congress Catalog Card Number: 92–35916
ISBN: 0–313–28881–X
ISSN: 0883–6884

First published in 1993

Greenwood Press, 88 Post Road West, Westport, CT 06881
An imprint of Greenwood Publishing Group, Inc.

Printed in the United States of America

The paper used in this book complies with the
Permanent Paper Standard issued by the National
Information Standards Organization (Z39.48–1984).

10 9 8 7 6 5 4 3 2 1

**Copyright Acknowledgment**

The author and publisher gratefully acknowledge permission to quote extracts from the following:

Karl von Clausewitz, *On War*, ed. and trans. Michael Howard and Peter Paret. Copyright © 1976 by Princeton University Press. Used with permission of PUP.

*To Colonel Karl Robinson,*
*whose career has demonstrated that strategy*
*ultimately depends on leaders with wisdom,*
*courage, compassion, and the natural ability to*
*motivate others to action.*

# Contents

Figures ix

Foreword *by Major General William A. Stofft* xi

Acknowledgments xiii

Introduction xv

**PART I: STRATEGY AS POLITICS**

1 Why Is Strategy Difficult?
*David Jablonsky* 3

2 The National Security Strategy: Documenting Strategic Vision
*Donald M. Snider* 46

3 The National Military Strategy
*Harry E. Rothmann* 57

4 Strategy and Management in the Post–Cold War Pentagon
*Robert J. Art* 71

5 The New Politics of the Defense Budget
*Gordon Adams* 98

6 The Armed Forces in a New Political Environment
*Gary L. Guertner* 121

**PART II: STRATEGY AS CREATIVE CONCEPTS AND APPLICATION: THE FUTURE OF DETERRENCE**

7 Deterrence before Hiroshima: The Past as Prologue
*George H. Quester* 131

8 The Future of Deterrence in a New World Order
*Robert P. Haffa, Jr.* 147

9 A Conventional Force Dominant Deterrent
*Gary L. Guertner* 166

**PART III: STRATEGY AS CREATIVE CONCEPTS AND APPLICATION: TECHNOLOGICAL SUPERIORITY**

10 Compensating for Smaller Forces through Technology
*Anthony H. Cordesman* 181

11 Prospects and Risks of Technological Dependency
*James Blackwell* 200

12 Deterring Regional Threats from Weapons Proliferation
*Leonard S. Spector* 217

13 Conventional Arms Transfers: Exporting Security or Arming Adversaries?
*Michael T. Klare* 239

**PART IV: STRATEGY AS CREATIVE CONCEPTS AND APPLICATION: COLLECTIVE SECURITY AND COLLECTIVE DEFENSE**

14 Collective Security after the Cold War
*Inis L. Claude, Jr.* 255

15 Security Structures in Asia
*Sheldon W. Simon* 272

16 Reconciling Alliances, Coalitions, and Collective Security Systems in Post–Cold War Europe
*Douglas T. Stuart* 290

Conclusions: The Strategy Paradigm versus the Political Paradigm 305

Index 311

About the Contributors 325

# Figures


| | | |
|---|---|---|
| 1.1 | The Policy Continuum | 5 |
| 1.2 | The Remarkable Trinity | 7 |
| 1.3 | The Impact of Technology | 7 |
| 1.4 | The Continuum of War | 12 |
| 1.5 | National Strategy: The Horizontal Plane | 13 |
| 1.6 | National Strategy and the Vertical Continuum of War | 13 |
| 1.7 | Strategic Vision | 33 |
| 3.1 | National Military Objectives | 58 |
| 3.2 | Military Strategy Concepts | 60 |
| 3.3 | Force Composition | 62 |
| 3.4 | Base Force Packages and Supporting Capabilities | 63 |
| 9.1 | Conventional Deterrence and International Stability | 168 |
| C.1 | The Strategy Paradigm | 306 |
| C.2 | The Political Paradigm | 307 |
| C.3 | The Permanency of Strategy | 308 |

# Foreword

This book brings together the papers presented at the U.S. Army War College during the February 1992 Strategy Conference. Its authors have made an extraordinary contribution to the professional understanding of the national security policy process in particular and national and military strategy in general.

Strategy is the calculated relationship of ends and means. In a generic sense this definition is practiced every day, whether it be the housewife determining what to buy at the local store or the small unit military leader responding to the inevitable cry of "What would you do in this situation?" However, at the highest level of decision making concerned with a nation's security, the process so briefly mentioned in the definition of strategy becomes infinitely more complex. This book describes that complexity in detail, emphasizing the inevitable conflict in democratic societies between the "ideal" strategic vision and the political process required to fund and execute it.

An exceptional group of scholars and practitioners have contributed their work to this volume. Their collective analysis of the substance and process of strategy formulation should be required reading for staff officers, their civilian counterparts throughout the national security bureaucracies, and for the new members of the Clinton Administration who have inherited a transitional period of history no less dramatic and uncertain than the early Cold War years bequeathed to Harry Truman. Like Truman, they face the task of building a new strategic consensus.

Victory in hot or cold wars is often fragile and tragically temporary. Victory is a phase line in a permanent struggle to promote and defend our national interests. The contributors to this volume explicitly make this argument as a reminder for the national leadership to avoid what the late Barbara Tuchman described as the American dislike for war demonstrated by a "desperate attachment to three principles—unpreparedness until the eleventh hour; the quickest feasible strategy for victory regardless of political aims; and instant demobilization, no matter how inadvisable, the moment hostilities are over."

Nothing, however, is inevitable or predetermined. We, as a nation, are capable of learning and applying the lessons of history and politics. As professionals, the nation's military and civilian leadership have the obligation to prevent the nation and the next generation from having to, in the words of Philip Caputo, "fight its wars, endure the same old experiences, suffer the loss of illusion, and learn the same old lessons on its own."

William A. Stofft
Major General, U.S. Army
Commandant
U.S. Army War College

# Acknowledgments

Every book is the product of intense labor, much of which is never visible to the reader. First, because their labor initiated this project, I would like to thank Colonel John Auger and Major Kathy Ward for their assistance, creativity, and perseverance in organizing the Army War College Strategy Conference from which this text evolved.

Second, neither the conference nor the book would have been possible without the support of Mr. Andrew Marshall, Director of the Office of Net Assessment. His encouragement and funding of the conference created a forum for creative thinkers and innovative ideas at a time when our country desperately needs both.

Marianne Cowling patiently assisted in editing the text. My secretary, Pat Bonneau, produced waves of revisions unequaled outside the discipline of Soviet history. Readers will also be relieved to know that Lawrence Miller and Daniel Barnett proved the adage that pictures save thousands of words. Their skill in creating the artwork for the figures add substantially to the originality and clarity of the text.

Last, but certainly not least, I am deeply indebted to the contributors, who diligently met deadlines with insightful and original contributions to the study and process of national security strategy.

# Introduction

The search for national security strategy periodically opens major policy debates that push us in new, sometimes revolutionary directions. The collapse of the Soviet Union and the end of the Cold War have reopened a national debate unmatched since the end of World War II. Dramatic changes in the international system have forced us to reevaluate old strategies and look for new focal points amidst the still unsettled debris of the bipolar world. At issue for strategists are the role of the United States in a new world order and our capabilities to defend and promote our national interests in a new environment where threats are both diffuse and uncertain, where conflict is inherent, yet unpredictable.

The strategy paradigm comprised of "ends, ways, and means" has almost universal applicability. It defines objectives, identifies courses of action to achieve them, and provides the resources to support each course of action. The relationships among these elements of strategy allow for planning and the debating of alternative strategic visions and calculations. This paradigm and its application to national strategy and to military strategy is taught to senior military officers at every service college.[1]

The creative core of strategy is the calculated relationship of ends and means. But in the complex decision-making structures of a modern nation-state, who defines the ends, who provides the means, and who is responsible for the calculated relationships between the two? Strategy as a rational, calculating process is possible only when a single vision dominates or is shared at every stage of the paradigm. In a politically fragmented system in which decision-making authority is constitutionally separated from the process of resource allocation, the search for strategy is more difficult. It is not a scientific enterprise wherein success depends solely on expertise and the systematic analysis of data. Instead, multiple strategic visions compete for influence and resources. Under the best of circumstances (a consensus on interests, objectives, and threats), strategy formulation is an intensely political process, heavily influenced by parochial interests, conflict, bargaining, and ultimately compromise. We do what we can agree to do; rational decision making in a democracy is the ability to harmonize competing strategic visions and interests. That assumption forms the major thesis of this book: *The dominant factor in the search for strategy is the domestic political environment.*

Part I applies this thesis to a series of studies that describe the *process* of strategy formulation in the post–Cold War political environment of the United States. Part II focuses specifically on national military strategy, isolating those strategic concepts that have the greatest potential synergistic value to a nation that is confronting domestic constraints on defense resources and challenges to its future role as the sole surviving superpower in a new world order.

## PART I: STRATEGY AS POLITICS

Part I begins with a theoretical tour de force by David Jablonsky, who raises and answers the question, "Why Is Strategy Difficult?" His answers begin with the review of early efforts to make strategy formulation a "scientific" process. Clausewitz plays a pivotal role in Jablonsky's analysis, for it was his theory of war that clearly established the primacy of politics over science in strategy and war. This is described in the context of Clausewitz's "remarkable trinity"—the government, the army, and the people. Any theory of war or grand strategy that ignores any one of these, Clausewitz warned, was certain to fail.

Clausewitz did not discuss bureaucratic politics or the separation of power in a constitutional democracy. He did, however, systematically anticipate the requirements to harmonize competing interests and achieve strategic consensus at home before victory in war was possible. By extrapolation, Jablonsky builds on this concept, applying it to the formulation of grand strategy in an environment in which the confluence of strategic vision and decisive authority to implement that vision are rare and short-lived. The dilemma is in maintaining a strategic consensus that minimizes the natural tension in national security affairs between domestic and foreign policy objectives. The solution is never easy to achieve, but the most successful means of consensus building is through strategic vision and strategies that are based on interests rather than threats.

In Chapter 2, Donald Snider describes the related problem of developing and documenting strategic vision in the President's Annual Report on National Security Strategy. In theory, this formal presentation of grand strategy was intended to lend coherence to the budgeting process: A clear statement of interests, objectives, and concepts for achieving them would give Congress a clear idea of the resources required to support the President's strategy.

In practice, presidents have been reluctant or unable to articulate a detailed strategic vision in an annual document that plays a role in a political process as highly charged as resource allocation. Consequently the document has been written at the level of the lowest common denominator to achieve consensus and minimize controversy. The details of strategic vision and strategy preferences have been communicated through personal testimonies by administration officials before committees and by presidential speeches or episodic documents designed for wider appeal and political support. One can argue that the greatest benefit derived from the requirement to formalize the national security strategy, no matter how bland it may appear to some, is to make political appointees and executive bureaucracies aware that they, like the President, need long-range plans that are integrated and coordinated with those of other agencies and departments.

The process of coordination within the Department of Defense is described by Harry Rothmann in Chapter 3. Rothmann's analysis centers on the unclassified *National Military Strategy* document published by the Chairman of the Joint Chiefs of Staff. This document outlines how the armed forces intend to implement the defense requirements contained in the President's *National Security Strategy* and the Secretary of Defense's policies spelled out in the classified *Defense Planning Guidance.*

The *National Military Strategy* document represents the calculations of objectives, strategic concepts, and resources by the nation's military leadership. The process depends not only on the Chairman's strategic vision but also on the informal personal relationships that cut through interservice rivalry and parochialism, building consensus by persuasion and compromise.

The Chairman's vision and political skills must, at the same time, play a critical role in linking the president's national security strategy, supporting military strategy, and the Congress's willingness to provide resources. The last challenge is the true test for the cohesion and effectiveness of the nation's military strategy.

In Chapter 4 Robert Art explores two fundamental and interrelated questions about the new military strategy. First, how well suited is the strategy to the needs of the post–Cold War world? Second, does the top political and military leadership of the Pentagon have sufficient control over the defense bureaucracy to make its decisions stick?

The answer to the first question is that crucial correctives need to be taken before the national military strategy can be fully effective. Two of the four fundamental strategic concepts of the Cheney-Powell strategy are seriously flawed, according to Art. Although forward presence and crisis response are ideally suited to both our fiscal capabilities and the most probable threat scenarios in the post–Cold War world, strategic defense and a reconstitution capability for global war are beyond the scope of our resources as well as any conceivable threats on the horizon.

Space-based interceptors are expensive to deploy, and the technology is by no means proven. Space-based systems will not be effective against missile attacks by regional rivals that threaten U.S. allies, because these missiles will have depressed trajectories well below the range of U.S. space-based interceptors. The United States can better protect its allies from such regional threats by deploying theater-based defensive systems.

Similarly, the Pentagon's strategy for a global reconstitution capability is not well-founded. The Pentagon intends reconstitution to deter any potential adversary from attempting to build forces capable of posing a global challenge to the United States and, if deterrence fails, to provide a global war-fighting capability. Providing for some reconstitution capability is sensible, if by that one means the ability to quickly accelerate the output of existing production lines and to mobilize the reserves of trained manpower in a crisis. But this is a surge capability for a limited regional crisis, not a reconstitution capability for all-out global war.

In answering his second question, which relates management to strategy, Art argues that as a result of the 1986 Defense Reorganization Act, Pentagon management is superior to its strategy. The Secretary of Defense and the Chairman of the Joint Chiefs of Staff now possess the requisite management tools to get what they want from the bureaucracies they oversee. Art's optimism for the future of the Defense Reorganization Act is based on his analysis of progress in four actions since 1989: (1) the development of the Base Force and the new military strategy; (2) the balance that has been planned over the next five years among modernization, readiness, and force size; (3) the military conduct of the war in the Persian Gulf; and (4) the current status of the roles and missions disputes among the services.

Art concludes from these cases that Goldwater-Nichols has not and will not end interservice disputes, but rather has successfully created an institutional force within the military to wage constant war against it. The true test will be whether the emphasis on joint duty will begin to produce officers truly capable of putting the coherence of the national military strategy above service parochialism.

Gordon Adams demonstrates in Chapter 5 how difficult the military's job will be in the Congress if they fail to speak with a single voice. The unraveling of Cold War military architecture and the budgets that sustained it have exposed conflicts of interest in the defense planning, decision-making, and budgeting process. The interplay among the armed services, industry, special interests, and the Congress is nothing new. However, that interplay was arguably somewhat less visible during much of the 1950s–80s, since peacetime defense budgets remained relatively stable, as did the specific, major military threat to the United States.

By contrast, as the United States enters the post–Cold War world the defense policy process faces a more complex political environment: severe fiscal constraints; a need to redefine military roles and missions, as well as the forces, hardware, and budgets that go with them; all in the context of a congressional and public debate over the pace of defense reductions and the uses of savings from a smaller military budget. The defense plans, programs, and budgets of the twenty-first century will be shaped by the interaction of these forces. Moreover, each of the factors that has an impact on defense is changing. The first observable change was fiscal, as the debate over defense budgets shifted from the turf of the threat to the turf of the deficit.

That the debate becomes political is made all the more possible by the fact that *the budget is not delivered to Congress in the framework of a national strategy*. The "titles" in the budget are devoid of any strategic meaning or measure of military output: Military Personnel, Operations and Maintenance, Procurement, Research and Development, and Family Housing. These broad structural categories tend to decouple resource allocation decisions from the strategic goals of national security policy. As a consequence, the political debate over the defense budget tends to be dominated by line-items. The incentives for elected representatives, moreover, have not favored debate over strategy, since their primary concern is reelection. When it comes to defense matters, the priorities of constituents are typically focused on the level and location of spending, not its strategic rationale. The congressional politics of defense is thus likely to become more prominent as resources decline. Combined with the absence of a perceived threat, bureaucratic in-fighting, and resource limitations, the struggle for the defense budget will be played out more visibly in the congressional arena, an arena in which short-term political exigencies dominate and often unravel the best of strategic visions.

In Chapter 6, Gary Guertner further describes the new domestic political environment in which the armed forces must compete for resources to implement the national military strategy. Popular passions can demobilize armies as rapidly as they can mobilize them, and the armed services, therefore, have an uphill battle in the competition for resources needed to solve serious and widespread domestic problems. Reallocation of resources from defense to domestic programs is justified, but a coherent military strategy requires planned, phased cuts and a degree of fiscal stability.

The best way to achieve stability in the defense budget is to relate it to the interests of the American public. These interests remain largely unchanged. They include (1) our own economic vitality, which is in turn linked to the stability of the industrial centers of Europe and Northeast Asia; and (2) free access to vital resources. Promoting these interests in peacetime does not require the United States to be the world's policeman. It does assume, however, that if a clear choice is given, the national pride of the American people will support its status as a superpower, capable of promoting or defending these interests, albeit with more of the burdens of power shared by our allies.

Promoting interests nearly always involves friends and allies who are more inclined to develop long-term, mutually beneficial economic and political relations if they are confident that the United States can promote those interests in peace and defend them in war. The leverage of U.S. military power remains a vital component of national strategy.

## PARTS II, III, AND IV: STRATEGY AS CREATIVE CONCEPTS AND APPLICATION

Part I demonstrates that the search for strategy is an intensely political process in which the natural tensions between domestic and foreign policy requirements threaten the essential balance in the ends-ways-means paradigm. Imbalances between ends and means create risks. Living with risk is a natural state of affairs in the lives of individuals as well as nations. Few strategies have resources sufficient for complete assurance of success. When there is a consensus that the risks to national security are unacceptable, strategy is revised. How the commitments-capabilities mismatch is resolved depends on the political process just described. The options include:

- Accepting risks;
- Redefining objectives;
- Increasing resources; or
- Identifying new, more cost-effective strategic concepts.

Parts II, III, and IV identify the strategic concepts that appear to be the most prudent choices for the world's remaining superpower. Global and domestic stability depend on our ability to adjust national strategy by shifting resources from defense to economic instruments of power. These shifts, already well under way, require unprecedented creativity in the formulation of military strategy. Where objectives are likely to remain constant and where resources are declining, we are left with the creative core of the strategy paradigm—strategic concepts. Here the originality, imagination, and creativity of the strategist can play a decisive role.

The current *National Military Strategy* document assumes that regional conflicts are the major forseeable threats to U.S. global interests. The strategic concepts, or ways to meet these threats, are to maintain a forward presence, prepare for crisis response, be able to reconstitute larger forces, and provide a credible strategic deterrence and defense. These core concepts are supported by eight subordinate and somewhat redundant concepts: (1) Readiness, (2) Collective Security, (3) Arms Control, (4) Maritime and Aerospace Superiority, (5) Strategic Agility, (6) Power Projection, (7) Technological Superiority, and (8) Decisive Force.[2]

Parts II, III, and IV identify what appear to be the most integrating, cost-effective, and mutually supporting of these strategic concepts:

- Strategic Deterrence and Defense, but with an emphasis on conventional deterrence;
- Technological Superiority; and
- Collective Security.

These choices were made on the assumption that resources and the size of the Base Force will fall below the levels described in the current *National Military Strategy*. Whatever the "final" Base Force may be, U.S. military strategy will require the underpinnings of credible deterrence, technological superiority, and partnership in a collective security/collective defense regime.

## The Future of Deterrence

Part II examines the future of deterrence. Chapters by George Quester, Robert Haffa, and Gary Guertner identify theories and strategies of nuclear deterrence that appear transferable to conventional deterrence in a multipolar world. Quester examines the lessons of conventional deterrence before the Cold War; Haffa develops a detailed theory of extended conventional deterrence for the future; and Guertner builds a case for its application.

Their first analytical obstacle is semantic. The simultaneous rise of the Cold War and the nuclear era gave rise to a body of literature and a way of thinking in which deterrence became virtually synonymous with nuclear weapons. In fact, deterrence has always been pursued through a mix of nuclear and conventional forces. The force mix changed throughout the Cold War in response to new technology, anticipated threats, and fiscal constraints. There have been, for example, well-known cycles in both U.S. and Soviet strategy in which their respective strategic concepts evolved from nuclear-dominant deterrence (Eisenhower's massive retaliation and its short-lived counterpart under Khrushchev) to the more balanced deterrence (Kennedy to Reagan) of flexible response, which linked conventional forces to a wide array of nuclear capabilities in a "seamless web" of deterrence that was "extended" to our NATO allies.

Early proponents of nuclear weapons tended to view nuclear deterrence as a self-contained strategy, capable of deterring threats across a wide spectrum of threat. By contrast, the proponents of conventional forces have always argued that there are thresholds below which conventional forces pose a more credible deterrent. Moreover, there will always be nondeterrable threats to U.S. interests that will require a response, and that response, if military, must be commensurate with the levels of provocation. A threat to use nuclear weapons against a Third World country, for instance, would put political objectives at risk because of worldwide reactions and the threat of horizontal escalation.

The end of the Cold War has dramatically altered the seamless web of deterrence and decoupled nuclear and conventional forces. Nuclear weapons have a declining political-military utility once one moves below the threshold of deterring a direct nuclear attack against the territory of the United States. As a result, the post–Cold War period is one in which stability and the deterrence of war are likely to be measured by the capabilities of conventional forces. Ironically, the downsizing of U.S. and Allied forces is occurring simultaneously with shifts in the calculus of deterrence that call for conventional domination of the force mix. In the past, conventional deterrence theories and strategies were severely undermined by their subordination to a bipolar strategic nuclear competition. Conditions now exist, the authors argue, for a coherent concept of general, extended conventional deterrence.

## Technological Superiority

The future of deterrence is tied inextricably to technology and our ability to integrate its benefits without excessive costs and mismanagement, but also without excessive reliance. This challenge is addressed in Part III by Anthony Cordesman, James Blackwell, Leonard Spector, and Michael Klare. Their chapters provide detailed sets of guidance for the development and integration of technology in support of the post–Cold War national military strategy.

Tony Cordesman's comprehensive approach to strategy and technology is a sober reminder that technology is not always a panacea, and if costs are not controlled, its multiplier effect will be less than 1.0. Cordesman lists the "iron laws" of the effective use of technology in war. These, he reminds us, are the basic starting points for research, development, and procurement decisions. The methods for integrating technology and strategy are, however, easier to identify than to manage in a highly politicized environment in which guarding vested professional and economic interests in the "top line" of the defense budget are often more important than abstract concepts like optimizing the force-multiplying effects of technology.

Because technologies have a more positive force multiplier effect when they interact, Cordesman concludes that we should plan a broad mix of technologies that are specifically integrated in a concept of operations. Under these conditions, technology could be decisive against most Third World threats.

James Blackwell assesses the prospects and risks of integrating technology and military strategy. We must, he cautions, simultaneously embrace technology while avoiding dependency on it as a panacea for every future crisis or war. The study examines two distinct aspects of technological dependency. The first is a national military strategy that depends on resources (R&D) and technological innovation to compensate for a radically reduced force structure. The second is dependency on foreign sources of technology.

Blackwell cautions that an investment strategy to achieve technological superiority should be balanced against the needs for efficiency and flexibility. In the future, there will be no political support for costly "silver bullets" that concentrate resources, denying the industrial base its needed hedge to expand production against threats that are greater than expected. In some cases our technological lead may be so far ahead of potential adversaries that we can afford to maintain existing inventories already paid for during the Cold War.

A subset of technological dependency involves foreign technology. This compounds both potential benefits and risks. Blackwell draws upon research from general economic theory and from the defense sector to propose a balanced policy that maintains access to foreign technology while minimizing (not eliminating) the risks of both dependency on foreign sources and the unwanted diffusion of U.S. technological advantages. On balance, it is better to exploit opportunities for access to foreign developments than to maintain high walls of protection around our own laboratories and factories.

Both Cordesman and Blackwell describe the value of technology and come to the same conclusion—that its true value is determined only in the larger context of a military strategy that places an equal value on people, training, operational concepts, and doctrine.

Technology is a double-edged sword. It may act as a force multiplier, but the laws of science and math apply equally to our potential adversaries. Leonard Spector and Michael Klare remind us of this unfortunate fact and emphasize the importance of concurrent political strategies that may be effective in preempting threats to our interests from the proliferation of military technology.

The most prominent shift in the national military strategy is from the global Soviet threat to a new focus on regional contingencies. No threat looms larger in these contingencies than the proliferation of nuclear weapons and ballistic missiles. Leonard Spector examines proliferation trends and proposes a predominately diplomatic strategy for containing the problem. He identifies three "waves" of nuclear proliferation: (1) The first comprises the five states with declared weapons and doctrine—the United States, Russia, Great Britain, France, and China. (2) The second wave includes a less visible group that has developed a covert capability without testing weapons or declaring a doctrine of "deterrence"—for example, Israel, India, and probably Pakistan. (3) A third wave of would-be proliferators includes so-called radical states like Iraq, Iran, Libya, and North Korea. Spector's political approach is based on the common interests of "wave" one and two states to prevent further proliferation. Political-economic incentives have already worked in the cases of Brazil, Argentina, Taiwan, and South Africa—states that appear to have abandoned their nuclear weapons programs.

Spector does not rule out the option of military force. Force, especially under international sanctions, can be a powerful tool to back diplomatic efforts. Many regional crises may be precipitated by nuclear proliferation. The U.S. strategy will require a delicate balance not to increase incentives to that very threat. Use of force, therefore, remains a last resort.

Michael Klare expands the problem of proliferation to include conventional arms. His chapter examines the dichotomy in the U.S. response to conventional and unconventional arms proliferation. There is a widespread belief that nuclear/biological/chemical (NBC) proliferation is inherently destabilizing no matter who the recipient might be, while transfers of conventional arms can enhance stability if they are provided to friendly powers.

With the end of the Cold War, however, this long-standing dichotomy in U.S. responses to conventional and unconventional proliferation has begun to change. Although the spread of NBC munitions continues to be seen as an especially significant peril requiring stepped-up nonproliferation efforts, many policymakers now view conventional arms transfers as a similar problem, with a comparable requirement for international controls. In recognition of the threat posed by the uncontrolled commerce in conventional arms, U.S. policymakers have begun to view such traffic as both a legitimate and an important concern for arms control.

However, it has been difficult to develop a consistent policy and strategy because of competing pressures and demands: On the one hand, there is pressure to follow through on pledges to establish international controls on conventional arms traffic; on the other, pressure exists to preserve long-standing military relationships with friendly foreign governments.

Klare maintains that despite the Administration's efforts to balance competing demands, there will be a growing contradiction between selling arms to allies and pursuing multilateral constraints on arms transfers. The United States cannot pursue both objectives and expect to accomplish its stated policy goals of regional stability in a world in which long-standing loyalties and alliances are breaking down and in which every nation is scrambling to advance its own national interests.

Klare concludes from this that in today's uncertain and chaotic world, it is safer to view most arms transfers as a potential proliferation risk rather than as an assured asset for U.S. national security. Implicit in Klare's analysis is the assumption that solutions to the problem must ultimately be multilateral because the history of unilateral restraint in conventional arms transfers has often been rewarded by the loss of a commercial market and political influence to others. The policy dilemmas posed by conventional arms proliferation are also directly related to Part IV, which examines collective security and collective defense.

### Collective Security and Collective Defense

Collective security is incorporated in the 1992 *National Military Strategy* document. As a strategic concept, its historical roots run deep. Each of the three great conflicts in the twentieth century—World War I, World War II, and the Cold War—transformed the international system, and each was accompanied at the end by the hope for a collective security system that could prevent or at least contain future conflict. The Gulf War reinforced the hopes of those who see collective security as the successor to the Cold War.

Part IV makes the case that collective security is a viable concept that can contribute to the success of our national military strategy provided that (1) a clear, conceptual distinction is made between collective security and collective defense; (2) the two concepts are viewed as reinforcing rather than antithetical; and, therefore, (3) collective security and collective defense can be integrated to form transregional security linkages through existing multinational organizations—a seamless web of collective action.

Collective security in its purest form is an idealistic, almost utopian notion on which no nation could reliably place its survival. In theory, collective security means establishing organizational structures and legal commitments to guarantee that aggression by one state against any other would be resisted by the collective action of other members. Aggression is deterred by the credible promise of overwhelming collective resistance. A pure collective security system is the alternative to competitive military alliances (collective defense).

Collective security includes the activities sanctioned by the United Nations ranging from peacekeeping operations to active military intervention or sanctions short of war. Collective security also includes the activities of regional organizations like the Conference on Security and Cooperation in Europe (CSCE), which may in the future legitimize and set in motion a similar range of collective actions in an expanding European theater.

In reality, no nation can be relied upon consistently to put collective interests above its national interests. Collective security, therefore, fails the test of its central assumptions that nations perceive each threat in the same way and are prepared to take identical risks while bearing the costs of military action.

Thus, there are limits to collective security and a continuing need to supplement it with collective defense. What is unique about the post–Cold War period is that there is both a need and an opportunity at every level of political-military planning to coordinate the structures and functions of collective security and collective defense in ways that can make both more effective, mutually supportive instruments for security.

Military intervention sanctioned by the United Nations (collective security) requires coalition forces. Coalitions are temporary agreements for a specified common action. They may be ad hoc or drawn from alliance systems like NATO that have formal, long-term defense obligations and structures for their execution (collective defense). The Gulf War was an example of the cooperative linkage between collective security and collective defense that can and should be promoted as a force multiplier in U.S. national military strategy.

The three chapters in Part IV provide policymakers and military planners with the strategic context in which coordination can occur. In the first, Inis Claude challenges the academic literature that treats collective security and collective defense as antithetical. The founders of the United Nations deliberately structured its members' obligations to preclude unwanted participation in collective security. During the Cold War, the loose obligation to collective security legitimized collective defense and created a tenuous coexistence between the two. In the post–Cold War world, this coexistence is being replaced by collective security's unambiguous dependency on U.S. leadership and its ability to assemble limited, ad hoc coalitions that are legitimized by the United Nations and other international bodies.[3] The future of collective security is inextricably linked to U.S. leadership. Ironically, as U.S. leadership in collective security has grown, its dominant role in traditional collective defense arrangements (NATO) has declined.

Providing U.S. leadership of a collective security system does not mean being the world's policeman. The United States and its allies seem committed to a policy of "selective anti-aggression"; military action is attractive only if other sanctions are ineffective and if the United States is able to mobilize ad hoc coalitions to replace the more formalized collective defense systems of the Cold War. In a more general sense, the *collective deterrent* value of the United Nations may contribute even more to stability than *collective security* through its functional roles of negotiations, cooperation, central services (peacetime engagement), and the global transparency of these activities that help vulnerable states to resist coercion.

The U.S. leadership and its ability to fashion ad hoc coalitions in support of collective security will depend on the degree to which bilateral and multilateral defense agreements can be maintained, albeit in radically reduced form. Forward presence, whether defined as limited, joint cooperation[4] with allies or the forward deployment of combat units, provides the catalyst for U.S. power projections and crisis response in support of both collective security and collective defense.

Sheldon Simon's chapter on Asian security assesses this requirement and the reasons why an Asian regional security regime akin to the Conference on Security and Cooperation in Europe is unlikely. Instead, both U.S. interests and Asian stability depend on continued U.S. presence negotiated through a series of bilateral defense agreements, all of which are capable of supporting broad-based collective security (United Nations) or an ad hoc regional coalition (collective defense) against a regional hegemon.

Implicit in Simon's analysis is recognition that the architecture and application of collective security and collective defense will be substantially different in Asia than it is in Europe. Cultural and historic links and the "collectiveness of interests" are not the same. As strategy in the new world order moves from the more concrete structure and substance of collective defense and forward *deployment* to the more trusting and idealist concepts of collective security and forward *presence*, these differences between European and Asian allies may become more apparent, requiring skillful diplomacy as much as military strategy.

Douglas Stuart's chapter on European security also builds upon the functional distinctions between collective defense and collective security as they apply to Europe. These distinctions are fundamental to the creation of a new security architecture and the relative power of its European and transatlantic pillars.

Stuart views the competitive institutional struggles among NATO, EC-WEU (European Community-Western European Union), and the CSCE as actually strengthening NATO in the long run, resulting in a three-tiered organization that provides an overlapping web of security functions ranging from collective security to collective defense.

A three-tiered NATO is based on the assumptions that:

1. The November 1991 Rome Declaration commits the alliance to management of crises and conflict prevention anywhere in Europe. The allies have also created a new North Atlantic Cooperation Council (NACC) as a forum for confidence building and consultation between NATO and former members of the Warsaw Pact. The NACC has the potential to preempt many of the CSCE's areas of responsibility, pushing the Cold War defensive perimeter outward, and thus toward collective security functions in place of traditional collective defense against a single, common threat.
2. NATO can and should preserve its core of members committed to collective defense against a single external threat or coalition, even if that threat is currently ill-defined.
3. NATO can stand firmly between Europe and the United Nations as a pan-European peacekeeping organization. The alliance would also be available to respond to requests by the UN Security Council for out-of-area collective security missions just as it did during the Gulf War.

A U.S. military presence and full political commitment are required for NATO to broaden its mandate to include commitments to both collective defense and collective security. A U.S. leadership in the UN Security Council and its continued commitment to NATO and European security make NATO the ideal security broker that combines old collective defense missions with new collective security requirements that have grown out of the political rubble of the Soviet empire.

NATO may also serve as a significant force multiplier during a period of defense reductions in every NATO capital. It is perhaps unique in history that a single organization can serve both the functions of collectively securing an extended community of states and providing for credible collective defense against threats outside that community.

Finally, it is worth noting the new vigor of the United Nations that has been demonstrated not only in Desert Storm but also through its peacekeeping forces currently deployed on eleven fronts. The size of UN "armies" is growing—22,000 in Cambodia and 14,000 in Yugoslavia.[5] As forces increase, the knowledge and skill required for joint action at the operational level will increase the importance and the value of existing collective defense structures in making collective security a credible option in the new world order. Readers should be mindful, however, of two factors that will most affect the value of collective security in the future.

First, in the context of national military strategy, no strategic concept can be evaluated in isolation. The synergistic effects of all strategic concepts applied to achieving military and political objectives must be weighed as part of the strategy formulation process. The potential value of collective security is especially difficult to establish because it requires one nation to link its security to the military capabilities and political will of others. This affects force structure decisions in both the quantitative and qualitative sense and, in turn, determines capabilities for power projection and crisis response. Its potential must always be balanced against the risks that collective security may require significant limitations on unilateral action.

Second, and intimately related, the American public shows little enthusiasm for an active role as the single, global superpower. Opinion polls reflect an introspective national mood created by domestic problems, especially economic issues, many of which are being attributed to the sacrifices required to win the Cold War.[6] During cycles of national introversion, the risks inherent in collective security as an alternative to unilateralism are well worth taking. Greater dependency on allies is politically essential for sharing not only the military burden but also the increasingly salient political and fiscal responsibilities. In Western Europe and Japan, burden sharing in the context of collective security and collective defense is also an essential deterrent to the nationalization of defense and all of its potentially destabilizing effects.

## CONCLUSIONS

The *Search for Strategy* concludes that in a democracy there will inevitably be conflicts between the ideal strategy paradigm and the political process.

Nevertheless, three steps are recommended to minimize the obstacles to coherent strategy formulations. First, strategic vision must be articulated at the top to galvanize the bureaucracy and the Congress. Second, both the American public and policymakers need to reexamine the concept of "victory" as an end state. Victory in hot wars or cold ones connotes that our responsibilities have ended and that our interests are secure. Good strategy does not recognize the concept of victory. There are no victories; there are only phase lines in a permanent struggle to promote and defend our national interests.

Finally, the American concept of victory as an end state feeds the natural tension between domestic and foreign policy resources. A comprehensive approach to strategy recognizes the interdependence of foreign and domestic interests and coordinates political, economic, and military power in the pursuit of those interests.

## NOTES

1. This includes the National Defense University; the Army, Air and Naval War Colleges; and their equivalent Command and Staff Colleges.

2. Colin L. Powell, *The National Military Strategy 1992*, Office of the Joint Chiefs of Staff, January 1992, pp. 6–10. The ends-ways-means paradigm is somewhat obscured in this document by the division of strategic concepts (ways) into two categories labeled "foundations" and "strategic principles."

3. "Ad hoc" used with "coalition" is redundant. Nevertheless, Part IV emphasizes that distinguishing between coalitions and alliances is just as important as distinguishing between collective security and collective defense. An alliance is a formal, long-term agreement with specified structure and obligations. A coalition is a short-term alliance that builds a consensus and coordinates common action against a specific objective. Alliances are essential to collective defense; coalitions are essential to collective security. This study advocates linking both to future collective security missions.

4. In contrast to forward deployments of military forces, forward presence may take the form of periodic deployments, joint exercise, or training. Its contribution to collective security and collective defense will rest on its ability to signal U.S. interests and commitments. The credibility of the signal will depend on the viability of other strategic concepts, most notably the power projection capabilities of the United States and its allies.

5. Paul Lewis, "As the U.N.'s Armies Grow, the Talk Is of Preventing War," *The New York Times*, March 1, 1992, p. E2.

6. These data are discussed in Chapter 6.

# PART I

# STRATEGY AS POLITICS

# 1

# Why Is Strategy Difficult?

*David Jablonsky*

Colonel (Ret.) Arthur Lykke has taught an entire generation of U.S. Army War College students that strategy at any level consists of ends or objectives, ways or concepts, and means or resources. This three-element framework is nothing more than a reworking of the traditional definition of strategy as the calculated relationship of ends and means. Yet the student response is always overwhelmingly favorable, with Lykke's framework invariably forming the structure for subsequent seminar problems on subjects ranging from the U.S. Civil War to nuclear strategy. This is due, in part, to the fact that students weaned on the structural certitude of the five-paragraph field order and the Commander's Estimate naturally find such structure comforting in dealing with the complexities of strategy. But those students also know from their experience in the field that there are limits to the scientific approach when dealing with human endeavors. As a consequence, they can also appreciate the art of mixing ends, ways, and means, using for each element the part subjective, part objective criteria of suitability, feasibility, and applicability—the essence of strategic calculation.[1]

The ends-ways-means paradigm also provides a structure at any level of strategy to avoid confusing the scientific product with the scientific process. The former involves production propositions that are logically related and valid across time and space. The search for these immutable principles over the centuries by students of war failed, because they looked on classical strategy as something like physical science that could produce verities in accordance with certain regularities. This was further compounded by military thinkers who made claims for scientific products without subjecting those products to a scientific process. Both Jomini and Mahan, for instance, ignored evidence in cases that did not fit their theories or principles of strategy.[2] The strategic paradigm, then, serves as a lowest common denominator reminder that a true scientific product is not possible from the study of strategy. At the same time, however, that paradigm provides a framework for the systematic treatment of facts and evidence—the very essence of the scientific process. In this regard, Admiral Wylie has pointed out:

> I do not claim that strategy is or can be a "science" in the sense of the physical sciences. It can and should be an intellectual discipline of the highest order, and the strategist should prepare himself to manage ideas with precision and clarity and imagination.... Thus, while strategy itself may not be a science, strategic judgment can be scientific to the extent that it is orderly, rational, objective, inclusive, discriminatory, and perceptive.[3]

All that notwithstanding, the limitations of the strategic paradigm bring the focus full circle back to the art involved in producing the optimal mix of ends, ways, and means. Strategy, of course, does depend on the general regularities of that paradigm. But strategy does not always obey the logic of that framework, remaining, as the German Army Regulations *Truppenführung* of 1936 described it, "a free creative activity resting upon scientific foundations."[4] The purpose of this chapter is to demonstrate why, despite increasingly scientific approaches to formulation and implementation, strategy remains principally an art rather than a science, and why within that art the "creative activity" of blending the elements in the strategic paradigm has become progressively more difficult over the centuries.

## FROM REVOLUTIONS TO TOTAL WAR

In the wake of the Napoleonic Wars, there was a growing recognition of the increased complexity of strategy, summarized in Karl von Clausewitz's warning that "there can be no question of a *purely military* evaluation of a great strategic issue, nor of a purely military scheme to solve it."[5] At the tactical level, the Prussian philosopher wrote, "the means are fighting forces trained for combat; the end is victory." For the strategic, however, Clausewitz concluded that military victories were meaningless unless they were the means to obtain a political end, "those objects which lead directly to peace."[6] Thus, strategy was "the linking together (*Verbindung*) of separate battle engagements into a single whole, for the final object of the war."[7] And only the political or policy level could determine that objective. "To bring a war, or any one of its campaigns to a successful close requires a thorough grasp of national policy," he pointed out. "On that level strategy and policy coalesce."[8] For Clausewitz, this vertical continuum (see Figure 1.1) was best exemplified by Frederick the Great, who embodied both policy and strategy and whose Silesian conquests of 1741 he considered to be the classic example of strategic art by demonstrating "an element of restrained strength,... ready to adjust to the smallest shift in the political situation."[9]

**Figure 1.1**
**The Policy Continuum**

With his deceptively simple description of the vertical continuum of war, Clausewitz set the stage for the equivalent of a Copernican shift in the strategic ends-ways-means paradigm. Now that paradigm was more complex, operating on both the military and policy levels with the totality of the ends, ways, and means at the lower levels interconnected with the political application at the policy level of those same strategic elements. This connection was the essence of Clausewitz's description of war as a continuation of political intercourse (*Verkehr*) with the addition of other means. He explained that

> We deliberately use the phrase "with the addition of other means" because we also want to make it clear that war in itself does not suspend political intercourse or change it into something entirely different.... The main lines along which military events progress, and to which they are restricted, are political lines that continue throughout the war into the subsequent peace.... War cannot be divorced from political life; and whenever this occurs in our thinking about war, the many links that connect the two elements are destroyed and we are left with something pointless and devoid of sense.[10]

## The Industrial and French Revolutions

This growing complexity in dealing with the strategic paradigm was compounded by two upheavals. Clausewitz was profoundly aware of one, the French Revolution; he was totally ignorant of the other, the industrial/technological revolution. Prior to the French Revolution, eighteenth-century rulers had acquired such effective political and economic control over their people that they were able to create their war machines as separate and distinct from the rest of society. The Revolution changed all that with the appearance of a force "that beggared all imagination" as Clausewitz described it,

> Suddenly, war again became the business of the people—a people of thirty millions, all of whom considered themselves to be citizens. There seemed no end to the resources mobilized; all limits disappeared in the vigor and enthusiasm shown by governments and their subjects.... War, untrammelled by any conventional restraints, had broken loose in all its elemental fury. This was due to the peoples' new share in these great affairs of state; and their participation, in its turn, resulted partly from the impact that the Revolution had on the internal conditions of every state and partly from the danger that France posed to everyone.[11]

For Clausewitz, the people greatly complicated the formulation and implementation of strategy by adding "primordial violence, hatred and enmity, which are to be regarded as a blind natural force" to form with the army and the government what he termed *the remarkable trinity* (see Figure 1.2). The army he saw as a "creative spirit" roaming freely within "the play of chance and probability," but always bound to the government, the third element, in "subordination, as an instrument of policy, which makes it subject to reason alone."[12]

It was the complex totality of this trinity that, Clausewitz realized, had altered and complicated strategy so completely.

> Clearly the tremendous effects of the French Revolution . . . were caused not so much by new military methods and concepts as by radical changes in policies and administration, by the new character of government, altered conditions of the French people, and the like.... It follows that the transformation of the art of war resulted from the transformation of politics.[13]

But while that transformation had made it absolutely essential to consider the elements of the Clausewitzian trinity within the strategic paradigm, the variations possible in the interplay of those elements moved strategy even farther from the realm of scientific certitude. "A theory that ignores any one of them or seeks to fix an arbitrary relationship between them," Clausewitz warned in this regard, "would conflict with reality to such an extent that for this reason alone it would be totally useless."[14]

Like most of his contemporaries, Clausewitz had no idea that he was living on the eve of a technological transformation born of the Industrial Revolution. But that transformation, as it gathered momentum throughout the remainder of the nineteenth century, fundamentally altered the interplay of elements within the Clausewitzian trinity, further complicating the for-

**Figure 1.2**
**The Remarkable Trinity**

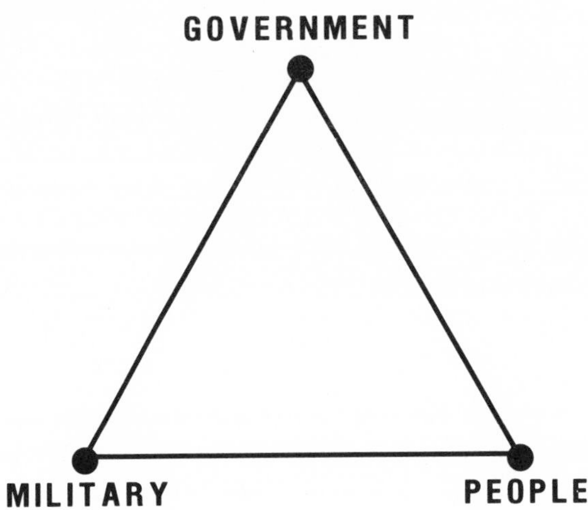


**Figure 1.3**
**The Impact of Technology**

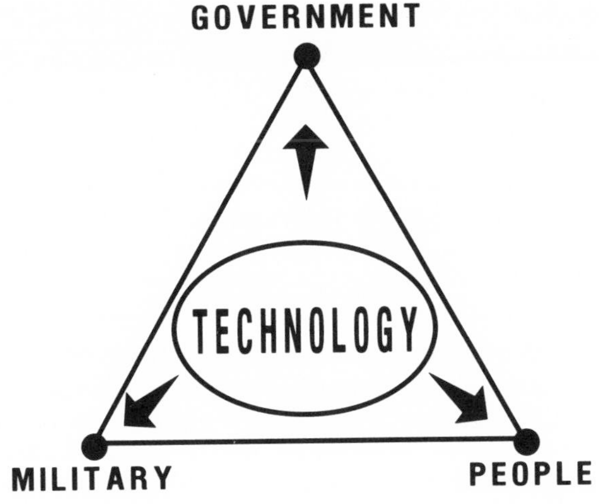


mulation and application process within the strategic paradigm (see Figure 1.3).

In terms of the military element, technology would change the basic nature of weapons and modes of transportation, the former stable for a hundred years, the latter for a thousand. Within a decade of Clausewitz's death in

1831, that process would begin in armaments with the introduction of breech-loading firearms and in transportation with the development of the railroads.[15]

Technology had a more gradual effect on the role of the people. There were, for example, the great European population increases of the nineteenth century as the Industrial Revolution moved on to the continent from Great Britain. This trend led, in turn, to urbanization: the mass movement of people from the extended families of rural life to the "atomized," impersonal life of the city. There, the urge to belong, to find a familial substitute, led to a more focused allegiance to the nation-state manifested in a new, more blatant and aggressive nationalism.

This nationalism was fueled by the progressive side effects of the Industrial Revolution, particularly in the area of public education, which meant, in turn, mass literacy throughout Europe by the end of the nineteenth century. One result was that an increasingly literate public could be manipulated by governments as technology spawned more sophisticated methods of mass communications. On the other hand, those same developments also helped democratize societies, which then demanded a greater share in government, particularly over strategic questions involving war and peace. In Clausewitz's time, strategic decisions dealing with such matters were rationally based on *Realpolitik* considerations to further state interests, not on domestic issues. By the end of the nineteenth century, the Rankeian *Primat der Aussenpolitik* was increasingly challenged throughout Europe by the need of governments for domestic consensus—a development with far-reaching implications for the conduct of strategy at the national level within the basic ends-ways-means paradigm.[16]

During much of that century, as the social and ideological upheavals unleashed by the French Revolution developed, military leaders in Europe generally attempted to distance their armed forces from their people. Nowhere was this more evident than in the Prussian cum German military, where the leaders worked hard over the years to prevent the adulteration of their forces by liberal ideas. "The army is now our fatherland," General von Roon wrote to his wife during the 1848 revolutions, "for there alone have the unclean and violent elements who put everything into turmoil failed to penetrate."[17] The revolutions in industry and technology, however, rendered this ideal unattainable. To begin with, the so-called *Technisierung* of warfare meant the mass production of more complex weapons for ever larger standing military forces. The key ingredients for these forces were the great population increases and the rise of nationalism as well as improved communications and governmental efficiency—the latter directed at general conscription of national manhood, which, thanks to progress in railroad development, could be brought to the battlefield in unlimited numbers.

At the same time, this increased interaction between the government/military and the people was also tied to other aspects of the impact of technology on the Clausewitzian trinity. Technological innovations in weaponry during this period, for example, were not always followed by an understanding of their implications, societal as well as military. Certainly, there was the inability on the part of all European powers to perceive the growing advantage of defensive over offensive weapons demonstrated in the Boer and Russo-Japanese wars. That inability was tied in with a trend in Europe at the time to combine élan with a military focus on moral force, bloodshed, and decisive battles. The result was that the military leaders of France, Germany, and Russia all adopted offensive military doctrines in some form.[18]

The fact that these doctrines led to the self-defeating offensive strategies of World War I ultimately had to do with the transformation of civil-military relations within the Clausewitzian trinity in their countries. In France, as an example, the officer corps distrusted the trend by the leaders of the Third Republic toward shorter terms of military service, which it believed threatened the army's professional character and tradition. Adopting an offensive doctrine and elevating it to the highest level was a means to combat this trend, since there was general agreement that an army consisting primarily of reservists and short-term conscripts could only be used in the defense. "Reserves are so much eyewash," one French general wrote at the time, "and take in only short-sighted mathematicians who equate the value of armies with the size of their effectives, without considering their moral value."[19] Although these were setbacks for those who shared this sentiment in the wake of the Dreyfus Affair and the consequent military reforms, it only required the harsher international climate after the Agadir crisis of 1911 for General Joffre and his young Turks to gain the ascendancy. Their philosophy was summed up by their leader, who explained that in planning for the next war he had "no preconceived idea other than a full determination to take the offensive with all my forces assembled."[20]

Under these circumstances, French offensive doctrine became increasingly unhinged from strategic reality as it responded to the more immediate demands of domestic and intragovernmental politics. The result was France's ill-conceived strategic lunge in 1914 toward its former possessions in the East, a lunge that almost provided sufficient margin of assistance for Germany's Schlieffen Plan, another result of military operational doctrine driving policy. In the end, only the miracle of the Marne prevented a victory for the Germans as rapid and complete as that of 1870.[21]

There were other equally significant results as the full brunt of technological change continued to alter the relationship between the elements of the Clausewitzian trinity in all the European powers. The larger, more complex armies resulted in the growing specialization and compartmentalization of the military—a trend that culminated in the emulation of the German General Staff system by most of the European powers. It is significant that Clausewitz had ignored Carnot, the "organizer of victory" for

Napoleon, when considering military genius. Now with the increase in military branches as well as combat service and combat service support organizations, the age of the "military-organizational" genius had arrived. All this in turn affected the relationship in all countries between the military and the government. For the very increase in professional knowledge and skill caused by technology's advance in military affairs undermined the ability of political leaders to understand and control the military, just as technology was making that control more important than ever by extending strategy from the battlefield to the civilian rear, thus blurring the difference between combatant and noncombatant.[22]

At the same time, the military expansion in the peacetime preparation for war began to enlarge the economic dimensions of conflict beyond the simple financial support of Clausewitz's era. As Europe entered the twentieth century, new areas of concern began to emerge ranging from industrial capacity and the availability and distribution of raw materials to research and development of weapons and equipment. All this, in turn, increased the size and role of the European governments prior to World War I—with the result, as William James perceptively noted, that "the intensely sharp competitive preparation for war by the nation is the real war, permanently increasing, so that the battles are only a sort of public verification of mastery gained during the 'peace' intervals."[23]

Nevertheless, the full impact of the government's strategic role in terms of national instruments of power beyond that of the military was generally not perceived in Europe, despite some of the more salient lessons of the American Civil War. In that conflict, the South lost because its strategic means did not match its strategic ends and ways. Consequently, no amount of operational finesse on the part of the South's great captains could compensate for the superior industrial strength and manpower that the North could deploy. Ultimately, this meant for the North, as Michael Howard has pointed out, "that the operational skills of their adversaries were rendered almost irrelevant."[24] The Civil War also illustrated another aspect of the changes within the strategic paradigm: the growing importance of the national will of the people in achieving political as well as military strategic objectives. That social dimension of strategy on the part of the Union was what prevented the early southern operational victories from being strategically decisive and what ultimately allowed the enormous industrial-logistical potential north of the Potomac to be realized.

## The Revolutions Joined: The Age of Total Wars

Strategy changed irrevocably with the full confluence in World War I of the trends set in train by the Industrial and French revolutions. In particular, the technology in that war provided, as Hanson Baldwin has pointed out, "a preview of the Pandora's box of evils that the linkage of science with industry in the service of war was to mean."[25] How unexpected the results of that linkage could be was illustrated by a young British subaltern's report to his commanding general after one of the first British attacks in Flanders. "Sorry sir," he concluded. "We didn't know it would be like that. We'll do better next time."[26]

But of course there was no doing better next time, not by British and French commanders in Flanders, not by Austrian troops on the Drina and Galician fronts in 1914, not by the Russian officers on the Gorlice-Tarnow line in 1915. The frustration at this turn of events was captured by Alexander Solzhenitsyn in his novel *August 1914.* "How disastrously the conditions of warfare had changed," he wrote, "making a commander as impotent as a rag doll! Where now was the battlefield . . . , across which he could gallop over to a faltering commander and summon him to his side?"[27] It was this milieu that demonstrated the inadequacy of classical strategy to deal with the intricacies of modern warfare. Napoleon had defined that strategy as the "art of making use of time and space."[28] But the dimensions of these two variables had been stretched and rendered more complex by the interaction of technology with the elements of the Clausewitzian trinity. And that very complexity, augmented by the lack of decisiveness at the tactical level, impeded the vertical continuum of war outlined in Clausewitz's definition of strategy as the use of engagements to achieve policy objectives.

Only when the continuum was enlarged, as the Great War demonstrated, was it possible to restore warfighting coherence to modern combat. And that, in turn, required the classical concept of strategy to be positioned at a midpoint, an operational level, designed to orchestrate individual tactical engagements and battles in order to achieve strategic results (see Figure 1.4). Now, a military strategy level, operating within the ends-ways-means paradigm on its own horizontal plane, was added as another way station on the vertical road to the fulfillment of policy objectives. This left the concept of strategy, as it had been understood since the time of Clausewitz, transformed into:

> the level of war at which campaigns and major operations are planned, conducted and sustained to accomplish strategic objectives. . . . Activities at this level link tactics and strategy. . . . These activities imply a broader dimension of time or space than do tactics; they provide the means by which tactical successes are exploited to achieve strategic objectives.[29]

At the same time, the full impact of technology on the Clausewitzian trinity in each of the combatant states during World War I substituted the infinitely more complex concept of national strategy for that of policy. To begin with, the growing sophistication and quantity of arms and munitions, as well as the vast demands of equipment and supply made by the armies, involved the national resources of industry, science, and agriculture—var-

**Figure 1.4**
**The Continuum of War**

iables with which the military leaders were not prepared to deal. To cope with these variables, governments were soon forced to transform the national lives of their states in order to provide the sinews of total war.

Looking back over fifty years later on the totality of this change in what Clausewitz had termed *policy*, Admiral Eccles defined the concept of national strategy that emerged in World War I as "the comprehensive direction of all the elements of national power to achieve the national objectives."[30] The U.S. Department of Defense (DoD) is more explicit, defining the new level of strategy that emerged at the national level after 1914 as the "art and science of developing and using the political, economic, and psychological powers of a nation, together with its armed forces during peace and war, to secure national objectives."[31]

National strategy, then, involves all the elements of national power. Those elements, in turn, can be conveniently broken down on a horizontal plane into the categories described in the DoD definition of national strategy: political, economic, psychological, and military (see Figure 1.5).

The linchpin in this horizontal design is the military instrument of power at the national strategic level—the apex, as we have seen emerging in World War I, of the vertical continuum of war (see Figure 1.6).

Thus, the mix of ends, ways, and means at the national military strategic level will directly affect (and be affected by) the same paradigm operating at each level of the vertical continuum. Adding to the complexity is the

**Figure 1.5**
**National Strategy: The Horizontal Plane**

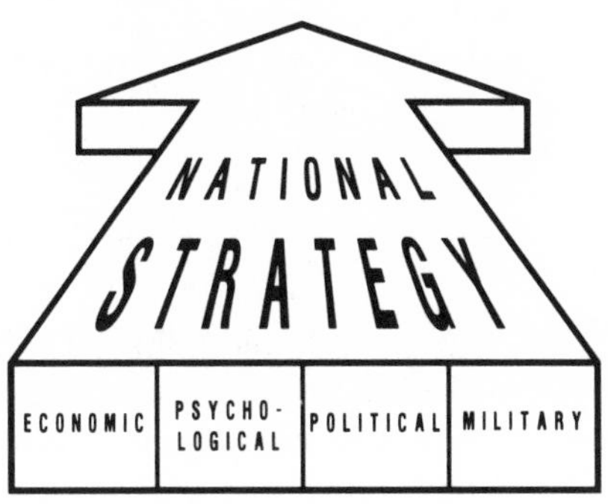


**Figure 1.6**
**National Strategy and the Vertical Continuum of War**

interplay on the horizontal plane of national military strategy with the other strategies derived from the elements of national power, each operating within its own strategic paradigm and all contributing to the grand design of national strategy, as that strategy evolves within its own overall mix of ends, ways, and means. That this horizontal and vertical interplay has rendered the formulation and implementation of strategy at every level more difficult has become increasingly obvious. "Because these various elements of power cannot be precisely defined, compartmented, or divided," Admiral Eccles concluded about the "fog" of strategy, "it is normal to expect areas of ambiguity, overlap, and contention about authority among the various elements and members of any government."[32]

## THE COLD WAR: STRATEGY IN THE AGE OF LIMITED WARS

At the end of World War II, technology in the form of atomic bombs changed the nature of warfare and thus further complicated the process of mixing the elements of the strategic paradigm on both the horizontal plane of national strategy and the vertical continuum of war. To begin with, nuclear technology moved Clausewitz's definition of absolute war from a Platonic ideal to a physical possibility in which strategy in war could consist of, in his words, "a single short blow."[33] In Clausewitz's day, human effort was expended to transcend the limitations imposed on the conduct of war by the constraints of what he called "the world of reality."[34] After 1945, the primary focus of that effort was to impose such limits. For without limitations on the new technology, the Clausewitzian connection would be broken between military strategy at the apex of the vertical continuum and policy represented by the sum total of national strategy on the horizontal plane. Victory in such circumstances of total war could have "an unacceptedly high cost" for the Prussian philosopher; for Bernard Brodie in the new nuclear age, it was a meaningless concept.[35] As a consequence, the strategic paradigm was twisted and stretched, as that new age proceeded, to include the concept of deterrence: the art of fashioning ways so as not to use means in order to avoid war.[36]

A major reason for all this was the beginning of the Cold War rivalry between the Soviet Union and the United States that would deliberately place policy limitations on warfare reminiscent of Clausewitz's era. This 45-year twilight war with its conflict-during-peace dynamic involving all the elements of national power transformed the purely wartime concept of national or grand strategy. For the Soviet Union, the transformation had long since taken place because of the influence of the holistic and universalist Marxist-Leninist ideology. As a consequence, Soviet strategic thinking from the beginning did not perceive a major "break" between war and peace, each of which was merely a phase in the larger construct of a belief system that viewed all politics, society, economics, and even warfare from the standpoint of class struggle. That this early focus did not give Soviet national strategy a distinct advantage of continuity and coherence over the decades was due to the Marxian hope of global conversion to its own image, a goal that, when achieved, would mean that the traditional power instruments of national strategy would fade away. Because of that hope, as Condoleezza

Rice has pointed out, "Soviet leaders have had to grapple with the problems of statecraft with one eye riveted on their legitimizing myth—pursuit of the international victory of the proletariat."[37]

For the United States, however, the transformation in strategy occurred in the rapidly unfolding events immediately after World War II with the adjustment not only to international involvement in peacetime, but to the mantle of global leadership as well. National strategy, as we have seen in the DoD definition, now emerged as something infinitely more complex and multilayered for American leaders, involving all national elements of power to form long-term domestic and foreign policies. Those policies would act as a guide for years or, as they had in the case of the Roman Empire, for centuries. In that context, national or grand strategy was not something that came into existence when a war began or automatically ceased upon conflict termination.[38]

As a consequence the strategic paradigm was extended into another dimension, which further complicated the art of balancing ends, ways, and means. It was no longer enough for American leaders to ensure that in wartime the nonmilitary elements along the horizontal plane of national strategy were not neglected, as they had been in Germany during both world wars. Now, it was also incumbent upon these leaders to ensure that the military element of power was not neglected in peace by preparing a national or grand strategy that, as Edward Mead Earle presciently observed in 1943, "so integrates the policies and armaments of the nation that the resort to war is either rendered unnecessary or is undertaken with the maximum chance of victory."[39] For the first time in its history, the United States would be forced to deal with the essential paradox of grand strategy faced by the Roman Empire and other great powers in the intervening centuries: *Si vis pacem, para bellum* (If you want peace, prepare war).

## The Government

"Since 1947," Aaron Friedberg has pointed out, "every Administration has made at least one attempt, and in some cases several, to define a comprehensive national strategy for the United States."[40] At the same time, there has been a steady evolution of institutions and procedures designed to rationalize the processes associated with peacetime formulation and implementation of national strategy. The results range from the National Security Act of 1947 to the Defense Reorganization Act of 1986, the latter requiring the President to submit an annual national strategy to Congress. This document, the President's so-called *National Security Strategy*, consciously uses the strategic paradigm and a strategic thought process that has generally evolved over the years since 1945. In the 1991 strategy, for example, there are discussions of enduring national interests and objectives derived from core values, an outline of changing threats and opportunities affecting those interests, and separate sections on the elements of national power, each specifically tied to the strategic paradigm, for example, "Relating Means to Ends: An Economic Agenda for the 1990s."[41]

The apparent rational and scientific aspects of the document, however, conceal basic problems in terms of the strategic paradigm. Generally, for example, there are four enduring American interests calling for survival as a free and independent nation, a healthy and growing economy, good relations with allied and friendly nations, and a stable and secure world. But a national strategy requires more detail, particularly in terms of prioritization. For example, the distinction between derivative vital and peripheral interests is not easy to make and may change, as in the case of Korea in 1950, because of the nature of events and perceived damage to national credibility, the latter always important in an age dominated by the concept of deterrence. Vital interests, one former Secretary of Defense has pointed out in this regard, are "easily debased coinage. Everything becomes a vital interest, and we must be able to distinguish between those things that are truly critical and those things that are only desirable."[42] Moreover, agreement on threats to national interests is never easy in peacetime and can be further complicated, as NSC–68 demonstrated at the height of the Cold War, when the process is reversed and interests are made a function of the threat.

Even when national strategic ends are agreed upon, the ways and means within the strategic paradigm can prove enormously variable on the horizontal plane. There was, for example, general national consensus for forty-five years concerning the objectives of containing the Soviet Union on its post–World War II portion of the Eurasian land mass. Yet, as John Lewis Gaddis has demonstrated, the national strategic ways of the United States oscillated throughout the Cold War. On the one hand, there was the indiscriminate approach to containment with its assumption of undifferentiated interests and unlimited means. On the other, a more eclectic approach emphasized the dangers that generation of unlimited means in pursuit of Cold War victory could have in terms of distorting the American economy and society.[43]

In addition, as the United States has learned since 1945, it is extremely difficult at the national strategic level to establish clear cause and effect ties between means application and ends advancement. That problem is further complicated by the fact that opponents obviously have no wish to clearly indicate the conditions under which they are coerced, deterred, or even influenced. Thus, the strategic concepts for reconciling means with ends are often formulated at the national strategic level without full knowledge of the adversary's or potential adversary's cost/risk/benefit calculations.

That this can have major strategic impact is demonstrated by contrasting the two Mideast wars of 1967 and 1973. In 1967, the Israeli victories were due in large part to an understanding of the political and culturally based military weakness of the Arab opponents ranging from the disjointedness of alliance politics to a disinclination for fighting at night. In 1973, the situation was reversed with the success of the Egyptian surprise attack that launched the Yom Kippur War. That success was due to the correct Israeli conclusion that Egypt could not expect to win a war militarily and thus to the false assumption that Egypt would not attack. But for Egyptian president Sadat, even an unsuccessful war on the vertical continuum would provide enormous political and economic benefits in the horizontal dimension of national strategy.

And if this were not enough, the policy elites in the United States have to craft and implement national strategy within a political system in which power is shared, authority is fragmented, and strategic consensus only rarely achieved. In particular, the constitutional divide between the legislative and executive branches of the government, the key rational facilitator in the Clausewitzian trinity, vastly complicates all aspects of working within the strategic paradigm in peacetime. The executive branch is primarily responsible for establishing ends and ways to achieve those ends, while the legislative branch combines authorizing legislation and budgeting authority to give it primary control of the means. Moreover, those means must be translated by the executive branch into the elements of national power, the complex interplay of which defies any formula. In modern national strategy, Admiral Eccles has pointed out in this regard,

> the attempt to take a strictly quantified systemic approach is doomed to failure because the most important elements in the complex relations between usable military power, economics, and international and domestic political factors cannot be measured at any one time with the degree of accuracy necessary to make estimates of relative power in other than very general terms.[44]

The very complexity in all this, as President Reagan pointed out in his 1988 *National Security Strategy*, requires "a cooperative endeavor" between both branches. Certainly that will be essential if the United States is to return to an approach like that of the period up through 1965 when external national strategic objectives were pursued with general consistency. That consistency was possible because Congress delegated much authority in foreign policy to the President on account of at least two interrelated factors. To begin with, there was an overall consensus for the twenty years following World War II in terms of political, economic, and military policies focused on containment. Moreover, the institutional arrangements that concentrated congressional power in the hands of a relatively small number of key figures made the process of consultation and coordination much easier between that body and the executive branch. As a consequence, nothing more was necessary for sustainment of executive policies on strategic matters than to gain the support of a small group of committee chairmen.

All that changed during and after the Vietnam conflict when internal reforms caused a dispersion of congressional power marked by the end of the seniority system, the proliferation of subcommittees, and the expansion of supporting staffs. The result was more independence for congressional members in the foreign policy aspects of national strategy, which in turn only exacerbated executive-legislative friction. For the military, the increased friction meant an ever deeper involvement by Congress in examining and modifying even the most minute details of the annual defense budget, beginning with congressional requirements in the 1960s for annual authorizations concerning weapons procurements and then spreading to other key parts of the budget. In the next decade, this micromanagement increased because of growing dissatisfaction with what was perceived as an "imperial presidency," accompanied by an anti-defense mood in the wake of Vietnam, and by the massive increase in the staffs of defense committees. This trend, as Robert Art has demonstrated, served to divert the attention of Congress, and thus of DoD, away from the macro ends, ways, and means considerations of national military strategy to the constant struggle over the minutia of the next year's budget. "The overwhelming focus on the annual budget to the neglect of the longer-term," he wrote, "occurred in the Pentagon to a large extent because it happened first in Congress. The Pentagon had no choice but to focus only on the next fiscal year because Congress' actions required it."[45]

Ideally in all this, the making of national strategy within the executive branch would be accomplished by highly rationalized procedures within a functionally defined structure. But despite the fact that the agencies in that branch are organized in a hierarchical manner with clear lines of responsibility and authority, the actual process of dealing with national strategy in peacetime is generally similar to other inefficient types of public policymaking. At the top, of course, are the President, his staff, and his principal advisers who oversee the bureaucracies associated with national strategy. Overlaying this formal structure are myriad ad hoc and permanent committees and interagency groups through which the major participants formulate and implement parts of the national strategy. At best, the system is difficult to manage because of its pluralistic nature and because it operates in peacetime within a political framework oriented on bargaining and compromise—all of which normally produce only narrow, incremental change.

The result is that a truly comprehensive U.S. national strategy or national security strategy is not likely to emerge in peacetime. The ironic fact is that the United States can only produce a national strategy—that is, one that truly incorporates more than a military strategy across the horizontal plane—when the country is at war or when war is perceived as imminent. When these conditions do not obtain, only the defense and intelligence communities remain fully involved with the concerns of national security and strategy. Other agencies, whether Commerce and Treasury or Energy and Agriculture, simply have other priorities in peacetime and resist strategy or strategies that normally overlap the functional power areas of national strategy. In the end, the pluralistic, decentralized U.S. government lacks the institutional wherewithal to bring its bureaucracies together in support of a focused grand strategy in peacetime.[46]

### The Military

The fact that a peacetime strategy at the national level in the United States is more a heuristic device than a grand national plan creates problems for the U.S. military establishment, which requires certitude in planning within the strategic paradigm at each level of the vertical war continuum. For most of U.S. history, such certitude was not necessary. Like Great Britain, which could afford through much of its existence to remain aloof from the continental wars that mandated strong monarchies and standing armies, the United States could allow central authority and the army to wither behind the shield of maritime power after gaining independence. Ironically for the British, the consequence was that their anti-military tradition took root and flourished in the new republic. Nowhere was this more apparent than in the initial reaction of the Founding Fathers to the concept of a standing army, which they found more repellent than did the Whigs of England. "I believe," Madison wrote in this regard, "there was not a member in the Federal Convention who did not feel indignation at such an institution."[47]

All this was undermined by the relentless progress of technology. Until the twentieth century, the sea provided a barrier not only of space but of time as well. And even during the first half of that century, the United States in the manner of Great Britain could afford to build up its strength and readiness after entering a war unprepared. Thus it was that the nuclear revolution combined with the advent of the Cold War marked the first time in U.S. history in which it was necessary to maintain a large standing peacetime military force. It was that force, increasingly more complex and powerful, that operated over the decades after 1945 under the military strategic concepts of forward deployment, collective security, and strategic mobility—all designed for nuclear and conventional extended deterrence and assurance under the overarching objective of containment.

As this military force grew during the Cold War, there were attempts to impose order and certitude from within the U.S. defense establishment on the vertical continuum by such procedural approaches as the Joint Strategic Planning System (JSPS) and the Planning, Program, and Budgeting System (PPBS). That a system like PPBS could not substitute for the lack of truly comprehensive peacetime national strategic guidance was illustrated by Henry Kissinger's scathing judgment of Robert McNamara and his subordinates:

He overemphasized the quantitative aspects of defense planning; by neglecting intangible psychological and political components he aimed for a predictability that was illusory and caused needless strains to our alliances. His eager young associates hid their moral convictions behind a seemingly objective method of analysis which obscured that their questions too often predetermined the answers and that these answers led to a long-term stagnation in our military technology.[48]

The 1986 Goldwater-Nichols DoD Reorganization Act addressed the vertical and horizontal dimensions of the interface of national military strategy with national strategy. On the horizontal plane, the tasks of both the Secretary of Defense and the Chairman of the Joint Chiefs of Staff in coordinating the functional divisions of the military structure have been eased considerably. The Chairman is now the principal military advisor to the President and the Secretary, the National Command Authorities, and has overall responsibility for providing strategic direction to the armed forces as well as for the formulation and review of mid- and near-term plans. There is also an iterative coordination between the Chairman and the Secretary, as the Secretary provides guidance on budgets and programs as well as on contingency plans.

On the vertical continuum, the Commanders-in-Chief (CINCs) of unified and specified commands have been provided much more authority not only over their commands but in their interaction back up the hierarchical scale to the national strategic level. The services, of course, still retain administrative and support responsibility for their forces regardless of the combatant command. But the Chairman now advises the Secretary on the degree of conformity between service budget proposals and the priorities established by the CINCs. Moreover, those commanders at the theater strategic level can inform the Secretary directly if they consider their authority over, or the control of components in, their command to be insufficient.

The congressional aspect of this significant military reform, however, is also a major reason why this interface is so problematic. Simply put, the U.S. military is caught in a strategic dilemma created by the Constitution. To begin with, the military is committed to apolitical professionalism as it focuses on the purely military aspects of blending the optimal mix of ends, ways, and means at the national military strategic level. That type of professionalism is possible, in theory, because of the orientation of the profession on the Constitution—best expressed by General MacArthur, who, in the wake of his dismissal by President Truman, denounced:

a new and heretofore unknown and dangerous concept that the members of our Armed Forces owe primary allegiance or loyalty to those who temporarily exercise the authority of the Executive Branch of Government rather than to the country and its Constitution which they are sworn to defend. No proposition could be more dangerous.[49]

But it is the Constitution that undermines this type of professionalism and skews the military's relationship with the other two-thirds of the trinity, particularly the government. As we have seen, the approach by the framers of that document to civil-military relations reflected the heritage of military power distribution in eighteenth-century Great Britain. In the ensuing century and a half, however, there emerged a fundamental difference. On the one hand, the evolution of British government under its unwritten constitution resulted in the centralization within the Cabinet of all authority over the military—a clear-cut line of control from the government to the armed forces. On the other hand, in this particular regard, the U.S. Constitution has remained essentially frozen in its eighteenth-century form, primarily due to the inflexible, written character of that document as well as the general lack of concern with military affairs that marked much of U.S. history.

The consequence of all this in the United States, despite the widespread belief to the contrary, is the lack of clear-cut, objective civilian control of the armed forces that makes a clear distinction between political and military responsibilities. Instead, as Samuel Huntington has pointed out, "the Constitution . . . mixes political and military functions, interjecting politics into military affairs and military affairs into politics."[50] For example, the clauses of the Constitution that are normally referred to as the basis of direct civilian control of the military actually provide for almost precisely the opposite by dividing high-level civilian responsibility for military affairs while simultaneously fostering the direct access by military authorities to these civilian elites. The result is at least a two-fold complication for the interrelationship of the U.S. military and government in the rational application of ends, ways, and means at the level of national strategy.

The first complication stems from the separation of power within the national government, which divides control of the nation's military forces between the President and Congress. Thus, Article II, Section 2 of the Constitution stipulates that the "President shall be Commander-in-Chief of the Army and the Navy of the United States." But that same document also contains a clear reminder that the U.S. military is an extension of the people when in Article I, Section 8 it places the very existence of those armed forces in the hands of Congress, "the representatives," in Alexander Hamilton's words, "of the people, periodically elected."[51] Despite this separation, however, there occurs what has been called "the iron law of institutional survival," which simply means that the "power to govern cannot be . . . divided. If each branch is to share in it, each branch must exercise it at every opportunity. The separation of powers thus leads inevitably to the duplication of function."[52]

That duplication catches the U.S. military squarely in between two institutional poles, further complicating the formulation and implementation of strategy in the United States. It was not always so, of course. Prior to World War II, Congress was more interested in the disbursing aspects of the military than its warfighting side. As a consequence, most military interactions with that body were conducted by the civilian supply and logistics elements in the armed forces, whether it was the Ordnance Service of the army or the Bureaus of Yards and Docks in the navy. Moreover, military policy issues were just not important in that period to the American public. This plus the relative disinterest of Congress in such issues allowed the Service Chiefs in their infrequent dealings with Capitol Hill to act primarily as spokesmen for the executive branch. "In the Budget we are presenting," General MacArthur pointed out in 1935, "we are merely the agent of the President."[53]

With the expansion of the peacetime standing armed forces during the Cold War, the primary focus of congressional relations with the U.S. military shifted from the technical services and bureaus to the Service Chiefs and their military strategies and policies. As a result, Congress began to demand the same independent professional military advice given to the President. Caught in a two-way governmental squeeze, the chiefs often oscillated between extremes. At one end were the leaders of the so-called 1949–50 "revolt of the admirals," almost all actively campaigning against executive policies on unification and the development of the B–36 bomber. At the other extreme, there was General Bradley defending the President's FY51 budget, which was not in keeping with his professional judgment. "I have come to the point where I do not accept them as experts," Senator Taft declared that year, "particularly when General Bradley makes a foreign policy speech. I suggest that the Joint Chiefs of Staff are absolutely under the control of the Administration."[54]

The second complication for the military-government interface in the United States is the fact that within the total federal system, there are constitutional clauses that divide control over the militia between the national and state governments. Until 1903 this dual control existed only in war, with the militia remaining under state control in peacetime. Beginning that year, the situation was reversed, with the National Guard remaining under dual control in time of peace and national control in time of war. This division has impeded control of the militia by the national policymakers ever since. For example, the National Guard under these arrangements is a part civilian, part military hybrid that can never be completely subordinated to national military control nor completely removed from political involvement. At the same time, the part state, part national status of the Guard also means that it is heavily involved in the conflicting interests of the federal system.

This military federalism is part of the American political process that adds to the complexity of the strategic process, with the modern influence of the militia dependent on its peacetime dual control and its identification with the hallowed constitutional symbols of the citizen soldier and states' rights. Congress, of course, could destroy this dual status by abrogating its power under the militia clauses in peacetime as it did in the nineteenth century, leaving neither federal supervision nor effective federal support for the National Guard. Conversely, Congress could federalize the Guard in peacetime and make it an exclusively national force under the Constitution's army clause. Neither is likely to happen because of the political influence the Guard has by virtue of being placed between two competing authorities.

Nor are there likely to be any changes to the separation of powers, the major constitutional impediment to a fully rational link in the American system between two key elements of the Clausewitzian trinity in the national strategy process. That separation cannot be altered short of constitutional change; and even if such fundamental change were possible, it is highly questionable if it would be worth the price. "There are values other than civilian control and military professionalism," Samuel Huntington has pointed out in this regard, "and these were the values the Framers had in mind when they wrote the Constitution. Foreign countries have more effective systems of civilian control but no country has as effective a system of restraints upon arbitrary political power or such a unique balance of executive unity and legislative diversity."[55]

## The People

The national strategy of the United States or any democratic nation must harmonize with the strategic culture of the people it seeks to serve. The basis for that culture is the generally shared attitudes in the society-at-large concerning the nature and requirements of national security, the conditions of peace and war, and the utility of and restrictions on force. This type of national consensus generally obtained throughout the Cold War in terms of the overall objective of containment. But the nuclear technology that helped precipitate the era also ushered in an age of limited wars, which ultimately destroyed that consensus in terms of the national ways and means in the nation's strategic paradigm.[56]

In the end, it was the public passions that had a moderating effect on the two principal limited conflicts of the Cold War: Korea and Vietnam. This was contrary not only to the experiences of both world wars, but, as we have seen, to the expectations of Clausewitz as well. Nevertheless, the Prussian philosopher would probably have understood. Every era, he remarked in *On War*, "had its own kind of war, its own limiting conditions, and its own peculiar preconceptions.... It follows, therefore, that the events of every age must be judged in the light of its own peculiarities."[57]

Many of these "peculiarities" in the decades after 1945 had to do with the massive impact of technology on American lives. The nuclear revolution created a threat to national survival for the first time in U.S. history. This, in turn, caused an increased interest on the part of the American people over the years in national security affairs—a trend reflected in Congress during that period. At the same time, technological advances in areas ranging from health and education to mass communication were producing a more strategically aware electorate, increasingly articulate and vociferous in its involvement in the political process that determined U.S. national strategy. As a consequence, when disconnections appeared between the horizontal plane of that strategy and the efforts of the U.S. military on the vertical continuum during the Korean and Vietnam conflicts, it was this third part of the Clausewitzian trinity that was ultimately decisive.

Vietnam was particularly instructive in this regard. The French experience in Algeria and Vietnam had already demonstrated that for weaker states struggling for national existence, it was not necessary to fight to win against democracies, but to fight in order not to lose. This two-edged aspect of the psychological element of power in national strategy was demonstrated once again by the U.S. experience in Vietnam. The results of that prolonged war of attrition were transmitted in living color back to the American people. At the same time for the majority of the population, there was an increasingly less discernible linkage of this human cost to achievable ends at the theater strategic level. Without a public perception of this basic operational linkage, the scattered tactical battles and engagements in Vietnam appeared more and more isolated within their own ends, ways, and means construct. The consequent erosion of national will further skewed the horizontal-vertical strategic relationship to the extent that the U.S. operational victory of TET 68 succeeded only at the political level of bringing down the Johnson Administration.

The Vietnam conflict caused the American people to reexamine the fundamental relationship between foreign and domestic policy in national security affairs. In dealing with both environments, values derived from America's geophysical strategic advantage had long worked against an external peacetime national focus. In the wake of Vietnam, this only fueled a growing tendency on the part of the American public to place foreign and defense programs into an almost zero-sum relationship with domestic programs. Certainly for the majority of that public as the Cold War proceeded, there was increased awareness that control of the external environment under containment was intended to enhance the state's security and, thereby, the national quality of life, whether political, economic, or psychological. Simply put, security was a means to an end, not an end in itself—that in fact, as President Eisenhower had pointed out in another era, any quest for absolute security could undermine the fundamental values and institutions that the national strategy was seeking to maintain. "Should we have to resort to anything resembling a garrison state," he warned, "then all that we are striving to defend would be weakened and, if being subjected to this kind of control, could disappear."[58]

Allied to all this was a general questioning of the utility of military power—a perception of war in some instances not as a continuation of policy in the Clausewitzian sense, but as a breakdown.[59] With this trend came public skepticism concerning what constituted vital interests and military threats to those interests—an inclination to accept Lord Salisbury's famous aphorism: "If you believe the doctors, nothing is wholesome; if you believe the theologians, nothing is innocent; if you believe the soldiers, nothing is safe."[60]

For government and military elites, the role of the people in Vietnam left two major lessons. The first was that if action is decided upon, there should be clear purposes and definable military objectives. "No one starts a war," Clausewitz pointed out in this regard, "...without first being clear in his mind what he intends to achieve by that war and how he intends to conduct it."[61] The second lesson was that if ends are clear, means must serve them without succumbing to gradualism, as occurred in Vietnam. That conflict confirmed Clemenceau's observation that war is too serious to be left to generals in the Clausewitzian sense that military means must be governed by the political ends to which they are applied. But Vietnam also added the codicil for the American people that war is too serious to be left to the politicians in the sense that when ends are established, the military means must be used in professional and decisive ways.[62]

Equally important, Vietnam imparted a feeling that national strategy had strayed too far from the strategic culture of the people, thus adversely affecting the normal symbiotic relationship inherent in America's unique version of the Clausewitzian trinity. This is why President Nixon issued a doctrine in 1969 that made a quantum retreat from the Kennedy global "blank check," which had been issued less than a decade before. "We shall furnish military and economic assistance when requested and as appropriate," Nixon stated, "but we shall look to the nation directly threatened to assume primary responsibility of providing the manpower for its own defense."[63] This is why Congress, backed by the American public, overrode the President's veto on the War Powers Resolution in 1973. But it was left to a Secretary of Defense in 1984 to provide an official reminder of the centrality of the people in any consideration of moving from the horizontal dimension of national strategy to the vertical continuum of war. "Before the United States commits combat forces abroad," a key provision of the so-called Weinberger Doctrine read, "there must be some reasonable assurance we will have the support of the American people and their elected representatives in Congress."[64]

## STRATEGY AND THE POST–COLD WAR WORLD

Throughout much of its history, the United States seldom had to subordinate domestic concerns to foreign policy objectives because of its relative immunity from external danger. All that began to change with global leadership and the Cold War, as U.S. policy elites increasingly focused on the realm of foreign policy and the need, in Walter Lippmann's words, to bring "into balance with a comfortable surplus of power in reserve, the nation's commitments and the nation's power."[65] Many of those commitments and the corresponding distribution of assets around the world were due to historical accident or the immediacy of the moment. Thus, as an example, there was the decision by the Truman Administration in 1946, as Soviet-Turkish relations declined, to send the recently deceased Ambassador of Turkey from the United States back to his homeland on the battleship *Missouri*. Since then, U.S. ships have never left the Mediterranean. "Of course each of us," James Schlesinger facetiously testified to Congress in this regard, "when serving as Secretary of Defense provide you annually with a document that explains the present necessity of those assets being in whatever place they are."[66]

In the wake of the Cold War, such explanations are no longer sufficient. The reasons lie in the confluence of four deficits: (1) the budget deficit with the concomitant political imperative of reducing government spending; (2) the trade deficit and the ever more obvious attendant need to make U.S. industry competitive in the world market; (3) the social deficit visible in every congressional district from problems in education, law enforcement, and drug use to the need for health care, housing, and new capital infrastructure; and finally (4) the threat deficit, which coincides with the upswing in domestic demands on resources caused by the other deficits.

Without a major international crisis, the shift of public focus to domestic issues occasioned by these four deficits, as well as a lingering recession, will continue to dominate in the coming years. Moreover, this shift also coincides with significant demographic changes in U.S. politics that suggest it will endure. Among these changes are the increased participation of women and minorities in politics as well as the fact that the "baby-boomer" generation will dramatically enlarge the retirement cohort by the end of the century. In all these groups, when specifically isolated by public opinion polls, there is a strong preference for domestic over foreign policy issues, supported in turn by voting patterns in favor of members of Congress identified with these issues.[67]

## The Military Dilemma

The resultant tensions in national security affairs between domestic and foreign policies complicate the formulation of U.S. national strategy and pose severe problems for the U.S. military establishment. The tensions are symptomatic of a lack of strategic consensus, similar to that which occurred between 1945 and 1950. As a consequence, that period was marked by a disconnection between national strategy and national military strategy as military demobilization continued apace with the Truman Doctrine and its apparent open-ended commitment to contain the Soviet Union on a global basis. That pattern reached its logical denouement on the Pusan Perimeter in June 1950.

The potential for similar disconnections on the horizontal plane of U.S. strategy will increase as the Cold War recedes into history. Even before the end of that twilight conflict, there were growing arguments for economically driven U.S. retrenchment from global commitments as a superpower—to concentrate, as William Hyland described it, "on America's own problems, even at the expense of international obligations and commitments."[68] One group claimed that the United States had entered into persistent and harmful fiscal imbalances because of excessive overseas commitments.[69] Another argued that the United States was hindered in its competition with other industrialized states because those states were not burdened with the extended strategic posture and large defense budgets that encumbered the United States in the post–World War II era. For the most influential purveyor of this argument, it was simply a matter of recognizing that great powers, like people, must face up to old age. "If they spend too much on armaments," Paul Kennedy wrote, "—or, more usually, upon maintaining at growing cost the military obligations they had assumed in a previous period—they are likely to overstrain themselves, like an old man attempting to work beyond his natural strength."[70]

For the American people, as we have seen, such arguments in the post–Cold War era have had increasing impact under the full bludgeoning of the four deficits. The budget deficit is particularly important in this regard. The balanced budget rule, one economist has pointed out, "is so deeply rooted in the nation's political culture that neither full-employment economics nor the presence of the huge deficits created during the Reagan presidency have shaken American politics free from its constraining influence."[71] Consequently, the prospect of greater deficits than ever before only fuels the growing feeling on the part of the American people that the primary threats to U.S. national security are not international but domestic, whether in the form of illicit drugs, inner city rot, the savings and loan fiasco, or the national debt. Added to all this is the wide public perception that defense expenditures have not only caused the budget deficits but the myriad domestic problems as well. For an increasing amount of Americans, J. H. Elliott's description of the decline of seventeenth-century Spain could touch a responsive chord. "Heirs to a society which had over-invested in empire," the noted historian has written, "and surrounded by the increasingly shabby remnants of a dwindling inheritance, they could not bring themselves to surrender their memories and alter the antique pattern of their lives."[72]

The upshot is that there is no strategic consensus that can protect the defense budget in Congress against transfer pressures. In the best of times, there are always such pressures in Congress. This will be exacerbated in the future by growing deficits and shrinking budget margins—all of which mean less discretionary spending. Added to this is the so-called entitlements explosion, driven by recent demographic and economic factors, which is primarily responsible for current budget deficits. The problem is that it is political suicide for Congress to touch these entitlements, particularly Social Security, Medicare, and Medicaid. As a result, only discretionary spending can really be adjusted, forcing an almost zero-sum struggle in this category between domestic programs and those associated with defense. "The question today is not whether we reduce military spending," Senator Nunn warned in the spring of 1990. "That is inevitable. The question is whether we reduce military spending pursuant to a sensible military strategy that meets the threats of today and tomorrow."[73]

The answer was positive from the executive branch. A budget agreement with Congress the following summer called for a steady but slow decline of approximately 25 percent in the current defense budget by 1995. Equally important, in August 1990 President Bush outlined a new military strategy for the United States in a speech at Aspen that focused on shaping U.S. defense capabilities to what he termed "these changing strategic circumstances." "In a world less driven by an immediate threat to Europe and the danger of global war," the President concluded, "—in a world where the size of our forces will be increasingly shaped by the needs of regional contingencies and peacetime presence—we know that our forces can be smaller."[74]

The shift to a military strategy focused on regional contingencies seemed natural enough under a national strategy that still called for the same degree of global involvement by the United States as there had been during the Cold War. The Gulf War, however, demonstrated that the new strategy faces significant problems. To begin with, that conflict proved that the U.S. military establishment is both politically and logistically dependent upon friends and allies. The option of "going it alone" without a substantial degree of assistance from other nations simply does not exist except for minor operations. Moreover, there still remains the increasingly difficult problem of obtaining domestic legitimacy, however masterfully accomplished during the Gulf War. Finally, there is the simple fact that the reduction in the defense budget and the force structures of the armed forces over the next five years will produce a U.S. military force that may not be able to accomplish in 1995 what the U.S. military did in the Gulf War.[75]

All this notwithstanding, even as Desert Shield/Storm proceeded, the Joint Chiefs established a base force for the new military strategy, a minimum force structure that could feed into a political rationale for a controlled builddown of the U.S. armed forces. In the wake of the Gulf conflict, however, public pressure has resulted in new congressional calls for more military cuts over and above that in the budget agreement. Equally important, the traditional congressional political link to the Reserve Component has also placed pressure on the military strategy. That strategy continues much of the "come as you are" Active Component emphasis from the Cold War for two-thirds of the new operational continuum stretching from peacetime engagement through crisis response to global war. Thus, there is the traditional focus on the concepts of deterrence and collective security, with the addition of new or refurbished concepts oriented on regional conflicts such as power projection, forward presence, and reconstitution.

It is a picture of the future much different from that held by the Reserve Component which generally prefers the traditional U.S. mobilization strategy to that of the "come as you are" variety as the strategic landscape changes. As a consequence, the political process has entered the force structure picture with Congress resisting the proposed DoD five-year cuts in the Reserve Component even as the proposed Active Component cuts proceed apace. "If the Department of Defense is prevented from cutting Guard and Reserve personnel, as Congress has proposed," the Secretary of Defense informed that body, "approximately *20 billion dollars* will be expended through 1997 on units *which have no mission.... Such wastefulness will create hollow forces*."[76]

The possible loss of political legitimacy for the base force and the strategy it supports is a serious matter, as the Chairman well realizes. "We'll be fighting a legislative war this year," he recently stated, "instead of one with people getting killed and injured."[77] Nevertheless, the danger of a controlled builddown turning into a resource free-fall is a very real possibility, particularly in an election year. This illustrates the complications of the strategic process for the U.S. military, which is attempting to walk the fine line of establishing a military strategy appropriate both for a builddown and for a national strategy of global activism.[78]

The problems with the base force are symptomatic of the more fundamental one in U.S. politics: the lack of a strategic consensus in the post–Cold War era. Without that consensus, the national strategy of the United States will grow increasingly disconnected from its military strategy. The dilemma was captured unwittingly by the Chairman in his testimony in February 1991 before the House Armed Services Committee. "Our national strategy," General Powell stated, "is founded on the premise that America will continue to provide the leadership needed to preserve global peace and security. Consequently, our military strategy continues to rely on the basic elements that made possible the historic success of containment."[79]

The most basic of those elements is still the concept of U.S. extended deterrence. That concept in a nuclear sense is no longer credible in regional conflicts since it is difficult to imagine any such war today singly threatening the United States. Consequently, the traditional focus on credibility and capability has moved in terms of extended deterrence in regional conflicts to the threat of conventional military force. That threat, in turn, is bound up with the interrelated strategic concepts of power projection and forward presence for regional crisis response throughout the world. Power projection is intended to compensate for the reduction of globally forward deployed

U.S. forces. The resultant U.S. "forward presence" may take the form of reduced garrisons or, depending on the regions, anything from peacetime training teams to combined exercises. The major point, however, is that even while these strategic concepts are sorted out, the reduction of U.S. forward deployed forces and power projection capability will continue, directed more by U.S. domestic budgetary pressures than by overall national strategic guidance.[80]

Those pressures, as we have seen, are not likely to let up, thus further complicating the already complex concept of extended deterrence. With only a U.S. forward presence instead of forward deployed forces, extended conventional deterrence by denial is more likely to fail. And without a credible U.S. power projection capability, extended conventional deterrence by punishment is also more likely to fail. In regard to the latter, the extended U.S. buildup in the Gulf War with all its unique domestic, allied, and enemy circumstances is already perceived as an anomaly.

In any event, one major lesson from that war is that deterrence, for whatever reasons, will fail sometime, somewhere in the future. When that happens, a weakened military can only have an adverse synergistic effect on the other elements of power in the horizontal application of grand strategy—the ultimate result of being willing to settle for a national strategy of global activism without paying for the military power to sustain it. In such circumstances, the inevitable hard choices of abandoning or escalating a commitment will be made only harder by the fundamental split between policy and strategy. And although that split is due to a lack of strategic consensus within the unique American workings of the Clausewitzian trinity, the Prussian philosopher would still recognize the results:

> Only if statesmen look to certain military moves and actions to produce effects that are foreign to their nature do political decisions influence operations for the worse. In the same way as a man who has not fully mastered a foreign language sometimes fails to express himself correctly, so statesmen often issue orders that defeat the purpose they are meant to serve.[81]

## Strategic Consensus and Vision

The decline of the Soviet threat that animated an overall American strategic consensus for over forty years creates a situation that has been repeated many times in history, particularly for the military. "We are somehow fated to enjoy the favour of the gods in larger measure when warring than when at peace," Cincinnatus declared in the same year in which the Athenians kept the Persian Empire at bay at Marathon.[82] In 1883, General Sherman observed that "the army is in reasonably good condition, considering the fact that peace and politics are always more damaging than war."[83] The current concern by that army is not to repeat the traditional and disastrous hollow state that normally follows a builddown in the wake of victory—best expressed in the cry of "No More Task Force Smiths" that currently has found its way into army strategic briefings. The danger inherent in such a cry is in associating only the dispatch of an unprepared, ill-equipped force with a disconnection between national strategy and the vertical continuum of war. In the future under such conditions, the dispatch of a superbly trained ready force, bolstered by the most modern equipment and weapons, may still not be enough against increasingly stronger regional, Third World military forces. In the absence of full and immediate follow-on power projection, for example, the Division Ready Brigade of the 82nd Airborne Division might find itself alone at some future date facing a vastly larger regional force that, if deterrence should fail, could prove the old adage that quantity has a quality all its own.[84]

On a larger scale, the decline of the Soviet threat has produced national strategic problems for the United States not unlike those faced by France and the United Kingdom after World War I. Prior to that conflict, the primary threat that motivated the national strategies for both countries was Imperial Germany. After 1918, of course, that threat initially disappeared. At the same time, as the 1920s progressed, there was increased multipolarity with more players involved with larger roles in global affairs. This led, in turn, to a more problematical, less dependable aspect of traditional allies for both France and Great Britain.

Above all in the wake of World War I, there was the role of the people in the two democracies. The public in both countries was overwhelmingly convinced that a great power war would never reoccur. The costs had simply grown too great in terms of manpower and finances; weapons had become too horrible. As a result, both governments focused upon the social and economic aspects of national security, ranging from education, housing, and health care needs to trade competitiveness and the alleviation of structural unemployment. Defense spending declined precipitously, causing the loss (and in many cases, the disappearance) of manufacturers from the "military-industrial complex" in both countries. At the same time, there was no reduction by either country in foreign commitments and obligations. This lack of military balance in the national strategic calculus played an important role in the appeasement policies of France and Britain in the 1930s as new and unanticipated threats emerged.[85]

The key to maintaining that balance today in the U.S. national strategic calculus is to create a strategic consensus that counteracts the centrifugal forces playing on the elements of the American version of the Clausewitzian trinity. Even then, national consensus is by no means a panacea. Certainly, as the experience in Vietnam demonstrated, the Cold War consensus did not always produce foreign policy success. Moreover, many successes in those years were also due in large measure to advantages no longer enjoyed by the United States. Nevertheless, it was the general strategic consensus that kept the United States oriented during the Cold War, avoiding the situation described by Seneca over a millennium before. "When you don't know what port you're sailing towards," the Roman philosopher warned, "all winds are foul."[86]

The pre-Vietnam strategic consensus was not restored in the Reagan years, contrary to some observations at the time. What President Reagan did succeed in doing was to restore a sense of national self-respect by healing the nation's psychic malaise that grew out of the Vietnam War. This spirit of "feeling good" about America, however, did not constitute a return to the earlier Cold War consensus. Equally important, the President also failed to restore the spirit of sacrifice evoked by that consensus for so many years; indeed, the ultimate message from his tenure in office was that the United States might aspire to great ends without enduring hardships in conjuring up the means. In terms of national security strategy, then, the Reagan years resulted to a large extent in a severance of the connection between ends and means in the realm of foreign policy. Paradoxically, it was this very disjuncture in the strategic paradigm that over the years formed the basic element in President Reagan's reconstituted domestic base by promising so much while demanding so little of the public. In the end, as Robert Tucker has pointed out, the Reagan years "transformed what had been a disposition not to pay for the American position in the world into something close to a fixed resolve not to do so."[87]

That resolve is still there for those like Charles Krauthammer who see a unipolar world in the wake of the Soviet collapse in which U.S. national strategy must focus on global leadership. "Americans are endlessly resourceful," he has written in this regard, "in trying to escape the responsibilities that history has placed on their shoulders." To this, from the opposite extreme, are the questions posed by Pat Buchanan. "What doth it profit a nation," he has asked, "if it gain the whole world, and lose its own soul?"

> What are we getting for $15 billion in foreign aid? Why, 46 years after World War II, are we defending Germany and Japan while they steal our markets? Why must we pacify the Persian Gulf when women walking dogs in Central Park are slashed to death by bums?

As for the post–Cold War global role for the United States, Buchanan had a more direct answer for those who accept Krauthammer's position. "If America does not wish to end her days in the same nursing home as Britannia," he concluded, "she had best can this Beltway geo-babble about 'unipolarity' and 'our responsibility to lead.' "[88]

National consensus in such a milieu will not be easy to attain, but as John Steinbruner has noted, it is an absolute necessity for any workable national strategy. "Impressive as they are, the powers of the presidency do

**Figure 1.7**
**Strategic Vision**

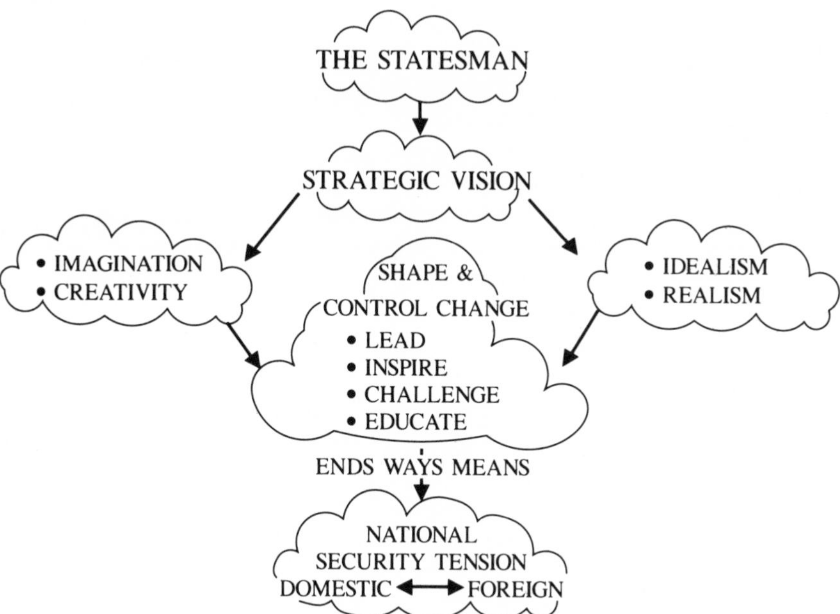


not by themselves confer the capacity to formulate a statement of strategy that will have enduring practical effect," he testified to a Senate committee. "If it is to organize the actions of our deliberately divided government and our competitive political process, such a statement must reflect or inspire a broad consensus of opinion and must also fit the evolving realities of international life."[89] The key to such a consensus of opinion is strategic vision, that image of future change desired by governmental elites (see Figure 1.7). It is by means of this vision that the statesman shapes and controls projected change instead of simply reacting to the forces and trends that swirl without direction into the future. He accomplishes this by dint of imagination and creativity and by balancing realism with realism.

Such leaders in times of upheaval and great change can inspire, challenge, and educate in terms of their image of the future. Education is particularly important, since statesmen have to bridge the gap between their vision and the experiences of their people, between their intuition and national tradition. It is not an easy process. As a result, there are few periods in history in which the confluence of strategic vision and decisive authority to implement that vision has lasted for very long.

During the post–Cold War era, the achievement of this confluence will depend in the United States on the ability of statesmen to resolve the natural tensions in national security affairs between foreign and domestic policy. This will require, in turn, the expert manipulation of ends, ways, and means at the national strategic level. How well those elements of the strategic paradigm are used will determine not only the quality of the strategic vision but the length of time that vision is bolstered by decisive authority.[90] At stake is the middle ground between isolationism and global activism. Thus, the major task of any new vision will be to convince the public, increasingly focused on domestic threats to its national security, that minimizing costs in foreign policy still maximizes real risks to U.S. national security interests as it did for forty-five years. At the same time, the statesmen will have to demonstrate that the United States can differentiate between vital and peripheral interests in the international arena, without succumbing to psychological insecurities that create a perception of threats to U.S. credibility in every international incident.

The U.S. military establishment can help in the process. To begin with, it can establish its relevancy in terms of combating domestic problems—generally perceived by the public as the dominant threat to U.S. national security. The Defense Department, after all, has an enormous reservoir of managerial, organizational, and scientific talent that could be imaginatively put to use in roles and missions that further the links between the military and the people, and by extension, the Congress. Many of these new missions have already been undertaken and are not necessarily mutually exclusive with the goal of maintaining a trained and ready force. For example, there are border patrols and other air and sea interdiction operations against drugs and illegal aliens. Moreover, in addition to aid for nation-building in Third World countries, the logistical, medical and organizational support of the armed forces could be focused on impoverished areas in the United States. In those areas in the coming years, the U.S. military could find innovative ways to wage war on crime, poverty, drugs, and urban rot.[91]

The U.S. armed forces should take the lead in such initiatives and avoid digging in its heels to defend the exclusive focus on what have become traditional missions in the post–World War II era. It is not a new role for the U.S. military. West Point, for instance, was founded in part to provide a cadre of engineers to help settle the frontier. And throughout U.S. history, the armed forces have been used on such projects as the delivery of mail, the construction of roads, and the operation of the Civilian Conservation Corps.

In the same context, there is the technology that is revolutionizing warfare, whether it be in precision guided weapons and stealth delivery systems or advanced sensor systems and battle management platforms. All that is the result of defense research and development (R&D), which has been traditionally associated with high costs by the American taxpayer, who is ever more conscious of the simultaneous decline in U.S. industrial competitiveness. There is great potential, in this regard, in the growing commonality between technologies critical to this civilian economic competitiveness and to military advanced weapon systems. In the future, it is not too farfetched to foresee extensive dual use of defense R&D linking the economic and strategic postures of the United States, thus further strengthening the bonds of national power across the horizontal plane of national strategy. New information technologies, for example, combined with bio-technologies and other innovations will offer enormous opportunities for dramatic progress not only in national defense but equally, if not more significantly for the American public, in the fields of transportation, medicine, energy, telecommunications, and the environment.[92]

In all this, innovation is the key—the willingness on the part of the defense establishment to avoid incremental approaches and, above all, what Lord Salisbury considered the most common error, that of "sticking to the carcasses of dead policies."[93] Such innovations focused on the military link to the people might include entirely new ways to incorporate the Reserve Component into U.S. military strategy—a recognition of the essentially political nature of the relationship. Or it might include a new approach to the all-volunteer force. "It is not that the Army needs the draft or conscription," Harry Summers has pointed out in this regard. "I think the nation needs it. We have lost something of great value if we break the connection between the common defense and the average person."[94]

Innovation, however, does not mean pandering to the public. There is never any guarantee that the prevailing domestic opinion will be consistent with international realities, and in fact it normally is not. Complete consistency of this sort is only rarely a feature of the human condition. Normally, the hard choices caused by conflicts between desirable objectives are denied in public opinion up to the point at which the lessons of harsh experience render them unmistakable. In a similar manner, intense and narrowly focused opinions often dominate broader, more judicious judgments in the American political process until experience once again imposes a corrective.[95]

It is in this area that the U.S. military can also help the statesman in the process of education to ensure that a vision for U.S. national strategy will not only balance foreign and domestic requirements but be bolstered by decisive authority for implementation as well. Thus, while it demonstrates its awareness of the immediacy of the myriad domestic threats to national security, the military must also help convince the American people that the United States cannot pull back from its global leadership responsibilities and that concomitantly military power will remain a requisite ingredient of national strategy. A new multipolar world of rampant nationalism and proliferation of weapons of mass destruction is a Hobbesian one and is likely to grow more so. "Covenants without swords are but words," was one of Hobbes's most basic and depressing truths of political science.[96] The disappearance of the Soviet threat, the public must understand, has not eliminated the barbarians. Like the Romans, the United States is faced with permanent struggle in the international arena.

In all this, the defense establishment will have to consider all elements of the Clausewitzian trinity and think beyond the military aspect of national strategy. If it does not demonstrate an awareness of all the components of this national strategy even as the decline of the Soviet threat affects policy priorities as well as public and congressional opinion, the military elites may seem as out of touch as the British and French General Staffs were in the 1920s. On the other hand, innovation must be tempered by the dangers inherent in making long-term changes in national security based upon the events of the moment. For example, when Theodore Roosevelt was Assistant Secretary of the Navy in the late nineteenth century, he complained that it required two years to build a battleship. There is now a nuclear aircraft carrier in the U.S. fleet named for Roosevelt that took nine years to construct. "You simply do not turn around . . . quality military capability in a matter of days or weeks," Secretary Cheney has pointed out in this regard.[97]

In the future, as U.S. military means decline, the interaction of national military strategy and national strategy will grow more complex. In particular, the reduction of military forces will mean less margin for error in the application of military power along with other national means. This, in turn, will require an increase and a "thickening" of the iterative interaction between political and military elites in order that the former understand the risks inherent in the application of military power as part of the grand strategic ends, ways, and means. As a result, the U.S. military must be prepared to take into account the other areas along the horizontal dimension of national strategy and go beyond Samuel Huntington's "professional military function" of simply advising on "the military needs necessary to carry out adopted policies, and directing the military forces in the implementation of national policy."[98]

## CONCLUSION

The United States is entering an era in which the strategic landscape has changed and is continuing to change. Nevertheless, the core problems that make strategy so difficult for a global power remain essentially the same as they did for earlier powers ranging from Rome to Great Britain. To begin with, there are challenges to U.S. interests throughout the globe. In a constantly changing strategic environment, however, it is difficult in many cases to distinguish which of those interests are vital, not to mention the nature of the challenge or threat to them. In any case, there are never enough armed forces to reduce the risk everywhere; strategic priorities have to be established.

In addition, like the leaders of earlier great powers, U.S. governmental elites have to grapple with the paradox of preparing for war even in peacetime if they wish to maintain the peace. The dilemma in the paradox that makes strategy in any era so difficult is that to overdo such preparations may weaken the economic, psychological, and political elements of power in the long run. The solution is to so balance the total ends, ways, and means that the natural tension in national security affairs between domestic and foreign policy is kept to a minimum while still securing the nation's vital interests with a minimum of risk. This solution, as the leaders of the great global powers of the past would assuredly agree, is not easy to achieve. In an ever more interdependent world in which variables for the strategist within the ends-ways-means paradigm have increased exponentially, strategists are no nearer to a "Philosopher's Stone" than they ever were. Strategy remains the most difficult of all art.[99]

The key to this art in a democratic society, as we have seen, is consensus. In pursuing that consensus, however, it is important not to stray too far from the fundamental strategic culture. "We must consider first and last the American national interest," Walter Lippmann wrote in 1943. "If we do not, if we construct our foreign policy on some kind of abstract theory of rights and duties, we shall build castles in the air. We shall formulate policies which in fact the nation will not support with its blood, its sweat, and its tears."[100]

This does not mean that the strategic culture cannot be adjusted as it was in the United States after World War II. The solution is to produce a strategic vision that does not so far outrun the experience of the American people that it fails to achieve the necessary domestic consensus for decisive authority, however wise the vision. That, in turn, requires the right mixture of leadership and education. Above all, it requires the ability to inspire and challenge, to demonstrate that there can be greater collective national aspirations. "A higher commander," Field Marshall Slim wrote in this regard in the military realm, "must think 'big.' "[101]

It was in this sense that Churchill responded in June 1939 when Walter Lippmann informed him that Ambassador Joseph Kennedy had stated that Great Britain would lose the war that inevitably would come. The British statesman replied that he did not believe it for a moment, but that if it occurred, his nation would go down fighting. "It will then be for you," he concluded, "for the Americans, to preserve and to maintain the great heritage of the English-speaking peoples. It will be for you to think imperially, which means to think always of something higher and more vast than one's own national interests."[102]

If there is no such vision and, as a consequence, the gap between the U.S. national strategy and the U.S. national military strategy grows larger, it will not be enough in the long run to reshape U.S. national strategy only marginally. If extended conventional deterrence is not a viable military strategic concept due to a consensus that rejects the fundamental utility and thus the sinews of military power, then in a radically reshaped security environment, the United States cannot afford to have the type of disconnection between the two strategies that existed for the first five years after World War II. If that disconnection proceeds apace in the coming years, the United States may win the Morgenthau Prize, named after the plan by the U.S. Treasury Secretary in the closing years of World War II to "pastoralize" Germany by removing all of that defeated nation's industry. As a consequence, the prize, as described by its creator, Graham Allison, is for "the most cockamamie approach to national strategy in the wake of a great victory."[103]

To avoid that prize will not be easy because the formulation and implementation of strategy in the modern era is not easy. The basic fact is that the profound strategic issues most likely to affect the fates of nations most deeply are precisely those that do not lend themselves to scientific analysis. On the other hand, as we have seen, within the broad parameters of the strategic paradigm, the art of mixing ends, ways, and means to develop national strategy has, if anything, become more exacting. In summing up the complexities of the strategic paradigm, Fred Ikle has noted that

> In the development of security strategy the contradictions outweigh the harmonies, the uncertainties overwhelm the established facts, the proofs remain utterly incomplete, and yet the stakes exceed all earthly objectives. The strategist has to incorporate into his work the rich and precise facts of physics, engineering, geography, and logistics; he has to allow for the swirling currents and blurred edges of psychology, political science, and history; and he needs to fit all this into the dynamic of international conflict among nations—a dynamic of opposing objectives and clashing forces that is driven as much by human stubbornness as by human error.[104]

## NOTES

1. Arthur F. Lykke, "Defining Military Strategy," *Military Review* 69, No. 5 (May 1989), pp. 2–8, and his testimony before the Senate Armed Services Committee, *National Security Strategy*, hearings before the Committee on Armed Services, United States Senate, One Hundredth Congress, First Session (Washington, DC: USGPO, 1987), pp. 140–145. See also *Sound Military Decision* (Newport, RI: Naval War College, 1942), pp. 32, 34, 164, 165; and Henry E. Eccles, *Military Power in a Free Society* (Newport, RI: Naval War College Press, 1979), p. 73.

2. John Shy, "Jomini," pp. 173–175, and Philip Crowl, "Mahan," p. 454—both in *Makers of Modern Strategy*, ed. Peter Paret (Princeton, NJ: Princeton University Press, 1986). See also Stephen M. Walt, "The Search for a Science of Strategy," *International Security* 12, No. 1 (Summer 1987), pp. 144–145, and John I. Alger, *The Quest for Victory* (Westport, CT: Greenwood Press, 1982). Admiral J. C. Wylie, *Military Strategy: A General Theory of Power Control* (Westport, CT: Greenwood Press, 1980), p. 20.

3. Wylie, *Military Strategy*, p. 10.

4. Martin van Creveld, "Eternal Clausewitz," in *Clausewitz and Modern Strategy*, ed. Michael I. Handel (London: Frank Cass, 1986), p. 41. The formulation of strategy is the creative act of choosing a means, an end, a way to relate a means to

an end." Carl H. Builder, *The Masks of War: American Military Styles in Strategy and Analysis* (Baltimore: Johns Hopkins University Press, 1989), p. 50.

5. Original emphasis. Carl von Clausewitz, *Two Letters on Strategy*, ed./trans. Peter Paret and Daniel Moran (Carlisle, PA: U.S. Army War College, 1984), p. 9.

6. Karl von Clausewitz, *On War*, ed. Michael Howard and Peter Paret (Princeton, NJ: Princeton University Press, 1976), pp. 142–143.

7. Michael Howard, *Clausewitz* (New York: Oxford University Press, 1986), p. 16; Clausewitz, *On War*, pp. 127–132.

8. Clausewitz, *On War*, p. 111. "In the highest realms of strategy . . . there is little or no difference between strategy, policy and statesmanship." Ibid., p. 178. Winston Churchill relearned these lessons in World War I. "The distinction between politics and strategy," he wrote at that time, "diminishes as the point of view is raised. At the summit true politics and strategy are one." Winston S. Churchill, *The World Crisis 1915* (New York: Charles Scribner's Sons, 1929), p. 6.

9. Clausewitz, *On War*, p. 179.

10. Ibid., p. 605.

11. Ibid., pp. 592–593.

12. Ibid., p. 89.

13. Ibid., pp. 609–610.

14. Ibid., p. 89.

15. Michael I. Handel, *War, Strategy and Intelligence* (London: Frank Cass, 1989), p. 63; Howard, *Clausewitz*, pp. 3–4; and van Creveld, "Eternal Clausewitz," p. 36.

16. Handel, *War*, p. 82. See also Dennis E. Showalter, "Total War for Limited Objectives: An Interpretation of German Grand Strategy," in *Grand Strategies in War and Peace*, ed. Paul Kennedy (New Haven, CT: Yale University Press, 1991), pp. 110–111.

17. Gordon A. Craig, *The Politics of the Prussian Army 1640–1945* (New York: Oxford University Press, 1956), p. 107; Michael Howard, "The Armed Forces as a Political Problem," in *Soldiers and Governments*, ed. Michael Howard (Westport, CT: Greenwood Press, 1978), p. 16.

18. Martin van Creveld, "Caesar's Ghost: Military History and the Wars of the Future," *The Washington Quarterly*, Winter 1980, p. 81. See also Michael Howard, "Men against Fire: The Doctrine of the Offensive in 1914," in *Makers of Modern Strategy*, p. 521; and Handel, *War*, pp. 21, 64–68.

19. Howard, "Armed Forces as a Political Problem," p. 17. See also Jack Snyder, "Civil Military Relations and the Cult of the Offensive, 1914–1984," *International Security*, Summer 1984, p. 109.

20. Theodore Ropp, *War in the Modern World* (New York: Collier Books, 1962), p. 229. Snyder, "Civil Military Relations," pp. 110–111, 130, 132–133.

21. The French military elite made a mirror image of their disdain for reservists in their estimates of German strength. The German General Staff made extensive use of German reservists, however, and instead of the 68 German divisions that had been expected in the implementation of French Plan XVII, there were 83. Howard, "Armed Forces as a Political Problem," p. 17. Joffre's failure to use French reservists more fully in 1914 proved to be, as Douglas Porch has pointed out, "like going to war without your trousers on." See Porch, "Arms and Alliances: French Grand Strategy and Policy in 1914 and 1940," in *Grand Strategies in War and Peace*,

p. 142. See also Snyder, "Civil Military Relations," pp. 108, 133. It is true, of course, that had the French Army remained on the defensive instead of plunging into Alsace, it could have brought its full weight to bear on the German Army at the French frontier. Stephen Van Evera, "The Cult of the Offensive and the Origins of the First World War," *International Security*, Summer 1984, p. 89. It is also true, however, that the French offensive ultimately caused Moltke to weaken the right flank that was supposed to "brush the channel with its sleeve." Moreover, as Michael Howard has pointed out, the general concept behind Plan XVII—that France should take the strategic initiative rather than passively await the German offensive—did provide the flexibility that enabled General Joffre to recover rapidly from his opening reverses and redeploy his forces for the battle of the Marne. Howard, "Men against Fire," pp. 522–523.

22. Handel, *War*, pp. 60, 79. "The interchangeability between the statesman and the soldier," General Wavell stated later in summarizing these developments, "passed forever . . . in the last century. The Germans professionalized the trade of war, and modern inventions, by increasing its technicalities, have specialized it." Archibald Wavell, *Generals and Generalship* (London: Macmillan, 1941), pp. 33–34.

23. Handel, *War*, p. 58.

24. Michael Howard, "The Forgotten Dimensions of Strategy," *Foreign Affairs*, Summer 1979, p. 977. See also Gordon A. Craig, "Delbruck: The Military Historian," in *Makers of Modern Strategy*, p. 345.

25. Hanson W. Baldwin, *World War I: An Outline History* (New York: Harper & Row, 1962), p. 159.

26. Gordon A. Craig, *War, Politics and Diplomacy* (New York: Frederick A. Praeger, 1966), p. 197.

27. Alexander Solzhenitsyn, *August 1914* (New York: Bantam Books, 1974), pp. 330–331.

28. David G. Chandler, *The Campaigns of Napoleon* (New York: Macmillan, 1966), p. 161.

29. *JCS Pub 1–02, Department of Defense Dictionary of Military and Associated Terms* (Washington, DC: USGPO, December 1, 1989), p. 264.

30. Henry E. Eccles, *Military Power in a Free Society* (Newport, RI: Naval War College Press, 1979), p. 70.

31. *JCS Pub 1–02*, p. 244. This is what Andre Beaufre long ago termed *total strategy*: "the manner in which all—political, economic, diplomatic, and military—should be woven together." Andre Beaufre, *An Introduction to Strategy* (New York: Praeger, 1965), p. 30.

32. Eccles, *Military Power*, p. 70.

33. Clausewitz, *On War*, p. 79.

34. Ibid.

35. Ibid., p. 91. "Of future total wars we can say that winning is likely to be less ghastly than losing, but whether it be by much or by little we cannot know." Bernard Brodie, *Strategy in the Missile Age* (Princeton: Princeton University Press, 1959), p. 409; Howard, *Clausewitz*, p. 70.

36. "Much of what has been written on strategy is obsolescent—I stress 'obsolescent' not 'obsolete,' " James Schlesinger testified regarding the effects of the nuclear age. Senate Hearings, *National Security Strategy*, p. 221; Handel, *War*, p. 85.

37. Condoleezza Rice, "The Evolution of Soviet Grand Strategy," in *Grand Strategies in War and Peace*, p. 146.

38. Paul Kennedy, "Grand Strategy in War and Peace: Toward a Broader Definition," in *Grand Strategies in War and Peace*, p. 4.

39. Edward Mead Earle, ed., *Makers of Modern Strategy* (Princeton, NJ: Princeton University Press, 1943), p. viii. Paul Kennedy, "American Grand Strategy, Today and Tomorrow: Learning from the European Experience," in *Grand Strategies in War and Peace*, p. 169.

40. Aaron Friedberg, "Appendix C, "History of U.S. Strategic Planning Efforts," *Committee on Integrated Long Term Strategy: Sources of Change in the Future Security Environment* (Washington, DC: USGPO, 1988), p. 164.

41. George Bush, *National Security Strategy 1991* (Washington, DC: USGPO, 1991). "National strategy" and "national security strategy" are used synonymously in this chapter in keeping with the definition of national security as "that part of government policy having as its objective the creation of national and international political conditions favorable to the protection or extension of vital national interests against existing and potential adversaries." Frank N. Trager and Frank L. Simonie, "An Introduction to the Study of National Security," in *National Security and American Society: Theory, Process, and Policy*, eds. Frank N. Trager and Philip S. Kronenberg (Lawrence: University of Kansas Press, 1973), p. 36.

42. James Schlesinger's testimony, *National Security Strategy*, p. 223.

43. John Lewis Gaddis, "Containment and the Logic of Strategy," *The National Interest*, No. 10 (Winter 1987/1988), pp. 27–38; and John Lewis Gaddis, *Strategies of Containment: A Critical Appraisal of Postwar American National Security Policy* (New York: Oxford University Press, 1982), particularly pp. 352–353.

44. Eccles, *Military Power*, p. 701.

45. Robert Art, "Congress and the Defense Budget: Enhancing Policy Oversight," in *Reorganizing America's Defense*, eds. Robert Art, Vincent Davis, Samuel Huntington (New York: Pergamon-Brassey's, 1985), p. 425. See also Aaron L. Friedberg, "Is the United States Capable of Acting Strategically?" *The Washington Quarterly* 14, No. 1 (Winter 1991), pp. 14, 17.

46. Samuel Huntington has pointed out that beginning with the Nixon-Kissinger years, the principal national strategic documents of the U.S. Administrations have focused almost completely on military issues. Samuel Huntington, "The Evolution of U.S. National Strategy," in *U.S. National Security Strategy for the 1990s*, eds. Daniel J. Kaufman, David S. Clark, Kevin P. Sheehan (Baltimore: Johns Hopkins University Press, 1991), pp. 12–13.

47. Louis Smith, *American Democracy and Military Power* (Chicago: University of Chicago Press, 1951), p. 19. Howard, "Armed Forces as a Political Problem," pp. 13–14.

48. Henry Kissinger, *White House Years* (Boston: Little, Brown, 1979), p. 296.

49. D. Clayton James, *The Years of MacArthur, Vol. 7: Triumph and Disaster 1945–1964* (Boston: Houghton Mifflin, 1985), p. 644.

50. Samuel Huntington, *The Soldier and the State* (Cambridge, MA: Harvard University Press, 1957), p. 163.

51. Harry Summers's testimony, *National Security Strategy*, p. 715.

52. Huntington, *Soldier and the State*, p. 402.

53. Elias Huzar, *The Purse and the Sword: Control of the Army by Congress*

*through Military Appropriations, 1933–1950* (Ithaca, NY: Cornell University Press, 1950), p. 147. See also the testimony of the Army Chief of Finance at this time: "I think when the Budget has once been approved by the President and transmitted to Congress, it is his budget estimate and no officer or official of the War Department would have any right to come up here and attempt to get a single dollar more than is contained in that estimate." Mark S. Watson, *Chief of Staff: Prewar Plans and Preparations* (Washington, DC: USGPO, 1950), pp. 21–22.

54. Huntington, *Soldier and State*, p. 386.

55. Ibid., p. 191, also pp. 169, 175, 177.

56. Robert S. Wood's testimony, *National Security Strategy*, p. 146.

57. Clausewitz, *On War*, p. 593.

58. Gaddis, *Strategies of Containment*, p. 136.

59. Clausewitz is often quoted as asserting that "war is a continuation of policy by other means." The problem, however, lies with earlier translations and not with Clausewitz, who maintained "that war is simply a continuation of political intercourse with the addition of other means." *On War*, p. 605. As Admiral Wylie has pointed out, war is, of course, a continuation of the basic policy of national survival in one sense or another for a nonaggressor nation. But other than this and unlike the large element of continuity between the prewar and war policy of communists in Vietnam, war for the United States in anything more specific than ultimate survival is actually a nearly complete collapse of policy. Wylie, *Military Strategy*, pp. 79–81. See also Edward A. Thibault, "War as a Collapse of Policy: A Critical Evaluation of Clausewitz," *Naval War College Review*, May-June 1973, pp. 42–56; and Carl J. Friedrich, "War as a Problem of Government," in *The Critique of War*, ed. Robert Ginsberg (Chicago: H. Regnery, 1969), pp. 165–166, who concludes: "In a very real sense war is not the *continuation* of politics but rather its *abandonment* in favor of violence." Original emphasis.

60. Howard, "Armed Forces as a Political Problem," p. 24.

61. Clausewitz, *On War*, p. 579.

62. Alexander M. Haig, Jr., "Gulf Analogy: Munich or Vietnam?" *The New York Times*, December 10, 1990, p. A19.

63. Richard Nixon, *U.S. Foreign Policy for the 1970s: A New Strategy for Peace* (Washington, DC: USGPO, February 18, 1970), p. 6.

64. Caspar W. Weinberger, "The Uses of Military Power," *Defense 85* (Washington, DC: USGPO, 1985), p. 10.

65. Walter Lippmann, *American Foreign Policy: Shield of the Republic* (Boston: Little, Brown, 1943), p. 9.

66. Schlesinger's testimony, *National Security Strategy*, p. 223.

67. Gary Guertner, "The Army in a New Domestic Political Environment," *SSI Occasional Paper* (Carlisle, PA: U.S. Army War College, 1991).

68. William G. Hyland, "Setting Global Priorities," *Foreign Policy* 3, No. 73 (Winter 1988/89), p. 25.

69. For instance, David Calleo, *Beyond American Hegemony: The Future of the Atlantic Alliance* (New York: Basic Books, 1987).

70. Paul Kennedy, *The Rise and Fall of the Great Powers: Economic Change and Military Conflict from 1500 to 2000* (New York: Random House, 1987), p. 540. See also ibid., pp. 444–445. See also Robert Gilpin, *War and Change in World Politics* (New York: Cambridge University Press, 1981), pp. 158–159. For various

types of counterarguments, see Joseph S. Nye, Jr., *Bound to Lead* (New York: Basic Books, 1990); Samuel P. Huntington, "The U.S.—Decline or Renewal?" *Foreign Affairs* 67, No. 2 (1988/89), pp. 76–96; and Aaron Friedberg, "The Political Economy of U.S. National Security Policy," in *U.S. National Security Strategy for the 1990s*, ed. Kaufman et al., p. 68, who argues: "The United States can put its budgetary house in order without drastic reductions in defense spending, and it may even be able to do so without radical tax increases or extensive cuts in existing social programs. Solvency and world power are not necessarily incompatible."

71. James D. Savage, *Balanced Budgets and American Politics* (Ithaca: Cornell University Press, 1988), pp. 235–236.

72. J. H. Elliott, "Managing Decline: Olvares and the Grand Strategy of Imperial Spain," in *Grand Strategies in War and Peace*, p. 87.

73. Sam Nunn, *Nunn 1990: A New Military Strategy* (Washington, DC: Center for Strategic and International Studies, 1990), p. 41. Nunn pointed out that one definition of military strategy is "the art of looking for danger, finding it everywhere, diagnosing it inaccurately, and prescribing the wrong remedy." Ibid., p. 41. See also Dennis S. Ippolito, *Uncertain Legacies: Federal Budget Policy from Roosevelt through Reagan* (Charlottesville: University Press of Virginia, 1990).

74. George Bush, "In Defense of Defense," Appendix E, Secretary of Defense, *Annual Report to the President and the Congress* (Washington, DC: USGPO, January 1991).

75. James Blackwell, Michael J. Mazart, and Don M. Snider, *The Gulf War: Military Lessons Learned* (Washington, DC: Center for Strategic and International Studies, 1991), pp. 5, 45. But see the Secretary of Defense's October 31, 1991, paper on defense issues, p. 3, in which he addresses the force after the 25 percent reduction: "The goal is to have smaller, well-trained and well-equipped Armed Forces that can be as effective in the future as the force deployed in Operation Desert Storm."

76. Original emphasis. Secretary of Defense, October 31, 1991, paper on defense needs, p. 7. See also Richard Cheney, "DoD Has Responded Dramatically to World Changes," *Defense Issues* 6, No. 48 (October 30, 1991).

77. Eric Schmitt, "A New Battle Is Ahead for Powell: The Budget," *The New York Times*, January 17, 1992, p. A16.

78. Blackwell, Mazart, and Snider, *The Gulf War: Military Lessons Learned*, p. 47. "One can no more construct a new strategy from canceled defense programs," Fred Ikle has warned in this regard, "than one can build a house from woodshavings." Fred C. Ikle, "The Ghost in the Pentagon: Rethinking America's Defense," *The National Interest*, No. 19 (Spring 1990), p. 13.

79. Colin L. Powell, "Emerging Realities, Enduring Realities," *Defense Issues* 6, No. 5 (February 7, 1991), p. 3.

80. McGeorge Bundy, "Nuclear Weapons and the Gulf," and Carl Kaysen, Robert S. McNamara, and George W. Rathjens, "Nuclear Weapons after the Cold War," both in *Foreign Affairs* 70, No. 4 (Fall 1991). Don M. Snider and Gregory Grant, "The Future of Conventional Warfare and U.S. Military Strategy," *The Washington Quarterly* 15, No. 1 (Winter 1992), pp. 219, 223–224. But see Walter B. Slocombe's thesis in terms of Europe in "The Continued Need for Extended Deterrence," *The Washington Quarterly* 14, No. 4 (Autumn 1991).

81. Clausewitz, *On War*, p. 608. On deterrence by denial and punishment, see

Glen Snyder, *Deterrence and Defense* (Princeton, NJ: Princeton University Press, 1961).

82. Stringfellow Barr, *Consulting the Romans: An Analogy between Ancient Rome and Present-Day America* (Santa Barbara, CA: Center for the Study of Democratic Institutions, 1967), p. 7.

83. Professor Jay Luvaas, Department of National Security and Strategy, U.S. Army War College (USAWC), Carlisle, PA.

84. Major-General Stofft, USAWC Commandant, has pointed out that Task Force Smith resulted from an army led during the initial five post–World War II years by a pantheon of American military heroes ranging from Eisenhower, Bradley, and Collins at the strategic level to MacArthur at the theater level. In terms of Korea, of course, there is some mitigation since at least according to Secretary of State Acheson's National Press Club address in January 1950, U.S. policy did not include Korea as a vital interest. Only when credibility came to be seen as a vital interest in the wake of the North Korean attack was the national strategic policy reversed.

85. Kennedy, "American Grand Strategy, Today and Tomorrow," p. 178.

86. Summers's testimony, *National Security Strategy*, p. 716.

87. Robert W. Tucker, "Reagan's Foreign Policy," *Foreign Affairs, America and the World 1988/89* 68, No. 1 (Winter 1988/89), p. 27.

88. All quotes in the paragraph from Patrick J. Buchanan, "Now That Red Is Dead, Come Home, America," *The Washington Post*, September 8, 1991, p. C1. See also Charles Krauthammer, "The Unipolar Movement," *Foreign Affairs* 70, America and the World Edition, 1991.

89. John D. Steinbruner's testimony, *National Security Strategy*, p. 1074.

90. It is striking how many witnesses on national security strategy before the Senate Armed Services Committee emphasized the need for strategic vision. For example, W. Bruce Weinrod, Director of Foreign Policy and Defense Studies at the Heritage Foundation, stressed that "a President who has a clear policy vision, governs wisely, manages well, and chooses subordinates who share his policy agenda, can at least to some extent devise and implement a national strategy; a President who does not do these things will inevitably end up with an incoherent or contradictory strategy." *National Security Strategy*, p. 1086. On the domestic aspect of national security, see Peter G. Peterson and James K. Sebenius, "The Primacy of the Domestic Agenda," in *Rethinking America's Security: Beyond Cold War to New World Order*, eds. Graham Allison and Gregory F. Treverton (New York: W. W. Norton & Company, 1992), pp. 57–93.

91. Bernard E. Trainor and William Rosenau, "Repositioning the Military for the New World Market," *Government Executive*, November 1991, p. 55. As another example, humanitarian aid was a principal focus in 1991, beginning with the American-led provision of food, water, and shelter to 500,000 Kurds in northern Iraq and Turkey. "Americans appeared to take it for granted," Representative Les Aspin commented in this regard, "that the U.S. military forces would play a similar role after a cyclone struck Bangladesh and a volcano erupted in the Philippines." Eric Schmitt, "U.S. Forces Find Work as Angels of Mercy," *The New York Times*, January 12, 1991, p. E3.

92. A key aspect of dual use R&D is that it furthers integrated civil and military production operations, thus providing an efficient and effective way to guarantee a rapid surge in defense production during a crisis without paying for great amounts

of excess capacity. Jacques S. Gansler, "In Search of Spinoffs," *The Washington Post*, January 5, 1992, p. C2.

93. Kenneth Bourne, *The Foreign Policy of Victorian England, 1830–1902* (Oxford: Clarendon Press, 1970), p. 409.

94. Summers's testimony, *National Security Strategy*, p. 737. See also Ikle, "Ghost in the Pentagon," p. 14, who points out that "Washington's national security establishment continues to see the world in terms of the 1947 mindset. By regarding the basic strategy as an unchanging core, it recognizes improvements only at the edges."

95. Steinbruner's testimony, *National Security Strategy*, p. 1075.

96. Thomas Hobbes, *Leviathan*, ed. Michael Oakeshatt (Oxford: Oxford University Press, 1952), p. 109. But see Robert Jervis, "The Future of World Politics: Will It Resemble the Past?" *International Security* 16, No. 3 (Winter 1991/1992), pp. 39–73.

97. Richard Cheney, "Helping the Soviet Union, but Protecting Ourselves," *Defense Issues* 6, No. 45 (August 29, 1991), p. 4. See also Kennedy, "American Grand Strategy: Today and Tomorrow," p. 179.

98. Huntington, *Soldier and the State*, p. 428.

99. Kennedy, "Grand Strategy in War and Peace: Toward a Broader Definition," p. 7. During the Roman Republic, for example, Roman foreign policy was affected by the distrust and fear felt by the ruling patricians for the plebians of Rome on the domestic front. Barr, *Consulting the Romans*, p. 6.

100. Patrick J. Buchanan, "America First, and Second, and Third," *The National Interest*, No. 19 (Spring 1990), pp. 81–82.

101. W. J. Slim, *Conduct of War* (London: The War Office, February 15, 1950), p. 22.

102. Harold Nicolson, *Diaries and Letters 1930–1939*, ed. Nigel Nicolson (New York: Atheneum, 1966), p. 403.

103. Graham Allison's address to the 1992 class of the U.S. Army War College.

104. Fred Ikle, "The Role of Character and Intellect in Strategy," in *On Not Confusing Ourselves: Essays on National Security Strategy in Honor of Albert and Roberta Wohlsteller*, ed. Andrew W. Marshall, J. J. Martin, and Henry S. Rowen (Boulder, CO: Westview Press, 1991), p. 312.

# 2

# The National Security Strategy: Documenting Strategic Vision

*Donald M. Snider*

**SEC. 603. ANNUAL REPORT ON NATIONAL SECURITY STRATEGY**

Sec. 104. (a)(1) The President shall transmit to Congress each year a comprehensive report on the national security strategy of the United States . . .

(2) The national security strategy report for any year shall be transmitted on the date on which the President submits to Congress the budget for the next fiscal year under section 1105 of title 31, United States Code.

(b) Each national security strategy report shall set forth the national security strategy of the United States and shall include a comprehensive description and discussion of the following:

(1) The worldwide interests, goals, and objectives of the United States that are vital to the national security of the United States.

(2) The foreign policy, worldwide commitments, and national defense capabilities of the United States necessary to deter aggression and to implement the national security strategy of the United States.

(3) The proposed short-term and long-term uses of the political, economic, military, and other elements of national power of the United States to protect or promote the interests and achieve the goals and objectives referred to in paragraph (1).

(4) The adequacy of the capabilities of the United States to carry out the national security strategy of the United States, including an evaluation of the balance among the capabilities of all elements of national power of the United States to support the implementation of the national security strategy.

(5) Such other measures as may be helpful to inform Congress on matters relating to the national security strategy of the United States.[1]

By this language, a small section of a much larger reform package known as the Goldwater-Nichols Department of Defense Reorganization Act of 1986, the Congress amended the National Security Act of 1947 to require annually a written articulation of grand strategy from each succeeding President. In so doing, Congress was attempting to legislate a solution to what it, and many observers, believed to be a legitimate and significant problem of long standing in our governmental processes—an inability within the executive branch to formulate, in a coherent and integrated manner, with judicious use of resources drawn from all elements of national power, the mid- and long-term strategy necessary to defend and further those interests vital to the nation's security.

Few in the Congress at that time doubted that there existed a grand strategy, that the nation had been following "containment" in one form or another for over forty years. What they doubted, or disagreed with, was its *focus* in terms of values, interests, and objectives; its *coherence* in terms of relating means to ends; its *integration* in terms of the elements of power; and its *time* horizon. In theory, at least to the reformers, a clearly written strategy would better inform the Congress on the needs for resources to execute the strategy, thus facilitating the annual authorization and appropriation processes, particularly for the Department of Defense.

Four such reports have now been published, two during the second Reagan Administration (1987 and 1988) and three during the Bush Administration (1990–1992). The author of this chapter was responsible for preparation of the 1988 report; this chapter was written in coordination with the official who was responsible for the 1990 and 1991 reports.[2] We have drawn on our experiences to provide insights into the process as well as the individual products.

## THE POLITICAL CONTEXT

Before discussing the individual reports, we must understand the context in which these reports are produced. First, the requirement for the reports did not originate solely, or even mainly, within the Congress. In fact, at that time Congress was much more interested in reforming the Department of Defense; what was reformed east of the Potomac was of much less interest.[3]

Like most pieces of legislation, the idea for a presidential statement of grand strategy had been percolating for several years in many locations—from think tanks, from public-minded citizens, from former government officials, from professional associations, from the academic literature, and from specific interest groups formed for the express purpose of fostering the requirement for such a report. As can be expected from an open, pluralistic process, each proponent had its own purposes for desiring such a statement, resulting in differing expectations of what the structure, content, and use of the final report would be. In retrospect, it is clear that inclusion of the requirement for such a report in the final Goldwater-Nichols bill followed one of the better-known maxims of the policy community: If we can agree on what we want, let's not try to agree on why we want it.

Second, there is always the issue of imprecise language. Just what is national security strategy, as opposed to grand strategy, or defense strategy, or even national military strategy? What are the distinguishable elements of power of the United States and the boundaries between? How can national security strategy subsume foreign policy, as the act seems to imply by its language? Obviously, there was—and is—no real consensus on the language either in academia, where the public servants in Washington took their training, or in Washington, where they practice their arts.

But language does make a difference, particularly within the executive branch where authorities and responsibilities represent power. Even more so, within the interagency arena where responsibilities for preparation of this particular report were viewed as giving direct access to the President's overall agenda and thus as highly desirable, there initially existed little consensus on the components of a national security strategy and what represented coherence. Imprecision in the language of the strategic art compounded the problem even among who wanted a quality product.

The flip side of this positive, "I want to be part of the process" view was the recognition within the executive branch that it was not the only, the principal, or even the most desirable means for the President to articulate his strategic vision. What President in a fast-paced, media-oriented world wants to articulate in a static, annual, written report a detailed statement of his forward-looking strategic vision? If ever there was a surefire means of insuring that your boss would be "hoisted on his own petard," this was it to many of the President's closest political advisors. To influence resource allocations it was considered far better to report mushy "globaloney" to Congress in written form and to depend instead on current, personal testimonies by Administration officials before the Committees, supported by presidential speeches as part of a coherent and widespread campaign of public diplomacy to the electorate of the United States.

The writer must also provide, for context, a feel for the political atmosphere within which the early reports were prepared. My tenure on the staff of the National Security Council (NSC) began just after the Iran-Contra fiasco and during the implementation of the Tower Commission recommendations.[4] To say that White House/congressional relations were at absolute gridlock would be true but would also vastly understate the passion, hostile intensity, and hyper-legalistic approach being taken by both sides on almost every item of the mutual agenda. Whether it be war powers, strategic modernization, strategic defenses, or regional foreign and defense policies, there was a pervasive modus vivendi of little quarter being asked, and only rarely any given.

The tasks before Ambassador Carlucci, General Powell, and other early rebuilders of the NSC process were therefore appropriately focused on rebuilding trust and confidence, and on getting the wheels of government moving again on pressing issues of current policy and their implementation. Recruiting for and reorganizing the NSC staff and its supervision of interagency processes implemented this effort, consuming significant organizational energy. Further, the requirement for the strategy report was not legislated until the fall of 1986, leaving little time for preparation of the initial submission. Therefore, a decision was made that the initial report would document "where we are, strategically" in a comprehensive way but would not go beyond that point. No classified version would be prepared.

Finally, given the existing political context just described, the first task facing one responsible to prepare such a report is to determine from the Assistant to the President for National Security Affairs (APNSA)—or, better, from the President directly—just what the purpose of the document really is. What it is *not* is a neutral, strategic planning document, though many academics and even some in government would prefer it to be. Rather, it was to serve five primary functions.

First, it was agreed that the primary, external purpose of the report was to communicate strategic vision to Congress and thus legitimate a rationale for resources. Second, it was to communicate the same vision to a number of other quite different constituencies. Some of these were foreign, and extensive distributions through the United States Information Agency subsequently proved most effective at communicating changing U.S. intentions to the governments of many nations not on our summit agendas. Third, other audiences were domestic, often political supporters of the President who wanted to see their particular issue prominently displayed under presidential signature; others were more public-minded, wanting to see coherence and farsightedness in the security policies of their government.

Fourth, there was the internal constituency of those in the executive branch who recognized from the beginning the process of creating the document would be of immense substantive value. It is simply impossible to document a strategy where none exists! It became clear that few things educate political appointees faster in terms of their own strategic sensings, or in terms of the qualities and competencies of the "permanent" government in the executive bureaucracies they lead, than to have to commit in writing to the President their agency's plans for the future and how they are to be integrated, coordinated, and otherwise shared with other agencies and departments. The ability to forge consensus on direction, priorities, and pace, getting important players down three political levels "on board," was recognized early as an invaluable, if not totally daunting, opportunity.

Last, any presidential document, regardless of originating requirement, was always viewed in the context of how it contributed to the overall presentation of the President's agenda. Unfortunately, Congress unwittingly insured that the document would be submitted in a low-profile manner: It is required early in January with the budget submission—just before one of the President's premier communication events of the year, the State of the Union address. If they are well coordinated, the two activities can be mutually supportive; but to date the State of the Union address is normally, and appropriately, dominant.

Thus, with these five purposes in mind (all legitimate and necessary, but understood to be almost a zero-sum game in their completion), one sets out in the name of the President to task the Cabinet officials and their strategy-minded lieutenants to articulate the preferred national security strategy for the United States. What followed was an iterative, interagency process of some months' duration, culminating in multiple drafts and several high-level meetings, including the NSC, to resolve differences or approve the final document.

## The 1988 National Security Strategy Report

As noted earlier, the 1987 report was prepared in a very limited period of time and reflected the intent to document current strategic thinking. In its two major sections, one each on foreign policy and defense policy, the document reflected (1) the strong orientation toward Cabinet government, and (2) the strong emphasis on military instruments of power, almost to the exclusion of the others. The section on integrating elements of power referred to the NSC system as the integrator, rather than documenting current strategies toward nations or regions. Of course, the document taken as a whole portrayed a comprehensive strategic approach toward the Soviet Union. The NSC system in the Reagan Administration had produced by then over 250 classified national security decision directives (NSDD). These represented at any point a set of substrategies "effective in promoting the integrated employment of the broad and diverse range of tools available for achieving our national security objectives."[5]

Two major changes from the 1987 format were introduced in the 1988 report. With twin deficits and trade issues prominent on the domestic agenda, the first change was to emphasize all the elements of national power, particularly the economic element, which scarcely had been discussed in the previous report. This led to the second adjustment, which was to explicitly present strategies for integration of the various instruments of power at the regional level. Both efforts probably rate an A for idea and effort and no more than a C for results as seen on the printed page. Behind the printed page, however, I am confident that those who participated in the interagency process are much more inclined to appreciate and to seek a coordinated approach to current and future policy toward a region or subregion.

### The 1990 National Security Strategy Report

The 1990 report was prepared in a vortex of global change. The Bush Administration began with a detailed interagency review of security strategy in the spring of 1989. This effort—and the natural turbulence of a new Administration shaking out its personnel and procedures, notably the Tower nomination—had pushed the preparation of the 1989 report into the early fall. Then, events in Eastern Europe made obsolete certain sections of the draft prose, if not the underlying policy. The original legislation had implicitly assumed a fairly steady state in the international environment; the annual report articulated incremental changes to both our perceptions of and responses to that environment. The pace of change throughout the last half of 1980 pushed the publication of the next report into March 1990.

In content, the 1990 report attempted to fully embrace the reality of change in the Soviet Union and especially in Eastern Europe. However, the response to that change as discussed in the report was cautious. At least one critic described the document as schizophrenic, with the reading of the environment in the front being at significant variance with the prescribed response in the back. This demonstrates once again how much easier it is in an open, pluralistic process to gain consensus on what is being observed than to know how we should respond to that observed change. However, the process in 1989–90 did show the potential of the document to force assessments of events and developments that might otherwise have been avoided.

### The 1991 National Security Strategy Report

The quickening pace of world change—and a deepening crisis and, ultimately, war in the Middle East—also served to delay the 1991 report. Key decisionmakers focused on multiple, demanding developments. After August 2, at least, the foreground was taken by Iraq's invasion of Kuwait, coalition building, and military action. In the background, and occasionally intruding to the fore, were fundamental changes in the U.S.-Soviet relationship, major treaties on strategic and conventional weaponry, and the final dissolution of the Warsaw Pact. There was little room in anyone's focus, particularly within the NSC staff, to develop, coordinate, and publish a comprehensive and definitive presidential statement of strategy. Although its major elements had been drafted by February, the 1991 report was not published until August.

Events forced the focus of the 1991 report to the U.S.-Soviet relationship as the departure point for any discussion of U.S. strategy. More than preceding reports, however, this one attempted to broaden the definition of national security. In purely military terms, it proclaimed regional conflict as the organizing principle for U.S. military forces and suggested that new terms of reference for nuclear deterrence would shortly be needed. Politically it attempted to turn the compass on arms control from east-west to north-south for a much expanded discussion of policy to retard proliferation. Even more than the previous reports, the document attempted to communicate the idea that American economic well-being was included in the definition of national security, even though discussions of specific programs to improve competitiveness or to combat trade and budget deficits were generally lacking.

## CONCLUSIONS

Several conclusions can be drawn from these experiences. They are conclusions of process and substance that may have been generated from the unique NSC perspective.

The first conclusion is obvious from the earlier discussions but so deeply pervades all else that I want to state it explicitly: There is no real consensus today as to the appropriate grand strategy for the United States. More important, this lack of consensus is due far less to any type of constraint on strategic thinking than it is to the fundamental value differences in our electorate and the resulting legacy of federal government divided institutionally between the political parties. It is easy to agree with the academics who are concerned that the current dysfunctions of "divided government" increasingly preclude coherent strategic behavior on the part of our nation.[6]

After all, grand strategy is the idea of allocating resources to create in both the short and long term various instruments of power, instruments with which the nation provides for its defense and the furtherance of its aims in the world. True, there have been extraordinary changes in the external environment, and we have won the Cold War. But to many, including those working to formulate security strategy through this period of intense change, the erosion of consensus was apparent far earlier. One need look no farther than the foreign and economic assistance allocations from 1984 onward, or the endless clashes on strategic modernization or defenses, or the constant tug-of-war on war powers and treaty obligations, or the Reagan Administration's attempts to buttress aggressive unilateralism. And, as Iran-Contra showed to all during this period, without a modicum of consensus there can be no effective security strategy or policy.

This conclusion is stated first because it conditions those that follow, and because it conditions one's expectations for the specific mode of formulating national security strategy that is discussed in this chapter. A presidential strategy report can never be more than what it really is, a statement of preference from the executive branch as to current, and perhaps future, grand strategy. Given our divided government, it remains for a constructively adversarial process with the Congress to refine that preferential strategy into one that has any chance of being effective—one around which there can be created domestic political consensus, and thus an allocation of resources effective in creating instruments of national power.

The second conclusion focuses on the function of long-range planning, or strategic planning. This is the base from which security strategy formulation must be built. Simply stated, in my experience the executive branch of government does not do long-range planning in a substantive or systematic manner. (I make a sharp distinction between planning and programming.) To be sure, there are pockets of planning activity within the "permanent" government of many departments and agencies, particularly Defense and State. Some of this is good, comprehensive planning from the perspective of that particular agency. But it is devoid of the political dynamic that can be provided only by the participation of those who have won elections, which under our system of government provides the authority to set future directions and pace in security policy and strategy. In total, then, particularly given the number of departments and agencies within which there is little planning activity, I am comfortable stating this conclusion in stark form.

The phenomenon of a paucity of strategic planning is well documented in academic writings, particularly in the memoirs of former officials. And the causes are well known to political scientists.[7] In my own experience, two causes stand out. The first is the limit of what is physically possible for elected officials to do in any given amount of time. Long-range planning and strategy formulation always run a poor second to the pressing combination of crisis and management and near-term policy planning and implementation. There is seldom a week that the NSC staff and the planning staffs of the principal Cabinet officers are not *fully* involved in either preparation for or clean-up after a trip, or summit, or focused negotiation. This is as it should be; the maxim is true in diplomatic and political activity at this level that if today is not cared for, tomorrow will not arrive in a manageable form. Second, the pernicious effects of divided government, which are manifest in micromanaging and punitive legislation on the one hand and intractable stonewalling and relentless drives for efficiency on the other, preclude resources for permanent, long-range planning staffs.

In place of a systematic approach to long-range or strategic planning, what the executive branch does do (and in some cases does rather well) is episodic planning for particular events. One can describe the creation of each of the strategy reports as a focused, comprehensive effort of some two to three months' duration involving political leadership and permanent bureaucracies in the development of common vision and purpose for the near-term future. The often-cited NSC–68 and Presidential Review Memorandum–10 (PRM–10) reviews are historical examples of other successful, but episodic, strategic planning events.[8] A more recent example is the Ikle-Wohlstetter Commission of 1988.[9] To be sure, in most cases these were incremental responses to a rather consistent external security environment, made by administrations (often new) that were stewards of a consensus U.S. grand strategy. But the fact remains that these episodic events did produce in-depth reviews across the range of interests and instruments of national power, and they resulted in much more than rhetorical change to the overall strategy.

The relevant question now, it seems to me, given the inherent constraints to systematic, long-range planning, is whether it is wise in the future to attempt anything more than broad, but episodic, planning exercises for the formulation of grand strategy. More specifically, should the executive branch attempt a new statement of grand strategy every year? My own experience, reinforced by the historical examples given here, leads me to conclude that comprehensive strategy reviews should be executed only twice during an administration's tenure: during the first and third years, and presented early to each session of the Congress. Further, if the pace of change in external events subsides, a valid case could be made to conduct such a review only once, during the first year of a new administration.

Adoption of comprehensive strategy reviews at set intervals would address one problem with the coherent formulation of strategy, but a much more formidable constraint is apparent. Thus, as a third conclusion, I must note that the executive branch is not well organized to accommodate the changing metrics of national power,[10] particularly the reascendancy of economic power in the formulation and execution of future U.S. grand strategy.[11]

This problem does not stem from a failure to recognize and treat the economic element of power for what it is, the long-term strength underpinning the other elements of power.[12] Rather, it stems from a failure to agree on the appropriate policies at the federal level to preserve that essential power. Toward the end of the Cold War, this failure was manifest in several forms, notably the political inability to deal effectively with the twin deficits of the 1980s. They still have not been addressed in a seriously compelling manner early in the 1990s. Volumes have been written pinning the blame on both the chief executive and the Congress; but it appears there is quite enough for both, as neither has led the electorate to understand the severity of the issues or otherwise to forge consensus for resolution.

A second major contributor to the failure is the complexity of recent arrangements for making economic policy. At least four Cabinet officials have a significant role (Treasury, State, Defense, Commerce), and integrating responsibilities rest with three agencies within the Executive Office of the President (Economic Policy Council, National Security Council, Domestic Policy Council). Advice comes from two more bodies (Office of Management and Budget, Council of Economic Advisors). The integrated, coordinated use of economic instruments of power, particularly in the context of regional security strategies, are understandably difficult to achieve in this organizational environment.

Beyond the problems of finding time to work on strategy and finding someone to be in charge of economic policy, I conclude that there is another shortcoming of a different nature in the current process. The art of formulating strategy is that of combining the various elements of power and relating them to the desired end; the key is integration. This belief is derived as much from experience in crisis management as in strategy formulation. Too often, after a crisis was ongoing it was clear that there had been little prior coordination or integration of policy instruments focused on a particular region or country beforehand. Too often, the only effective instruments for immediate leverage were military. In retrospect it was clear that if we had been pursuing a well-documented and integrated strategic approach toward the region or country in question, one in which the current policy instruments drew from all elements of power, the possibility for more effective response would have been greatly enhanced.

Increasingly in this post–Cold War era, those ends toward which we are developing a strategic approach are being defined at the regional and subregional level. Even strategies for such transnational issues as terrorism and narcotics trafficking focus at the subregional level for implementation, as do many strategies for the use of economic power. But planning for the effective integration of policy instruments for the various regions and subregions remains problematic.

Last, contrary to some of what is contained in this chapter, I conclude that we should not concentrate exclusively on institutions and processes when discussing the development of national security strategy. As I have seen so often, it is people who really define the character of the institutions and who make the processes what they are. Almost uniformly I have observed people of intelligence and goodwill respond to the need to place national interests above those of organization or person. This is not to conclude, however, that all is well and that we can count on such people to consistently overcome the real constraints on strategic thinking and behavior in our government. But it is to conclude that it is much too early for a cynical approach to the strategic reformulation the nation is now experiencing.

## NOTES

1. 50 U.S.C. 402 (Title I of the National Security Act of 1947).

2. The author gratefully acknowledges the assistance of Colonel Michael Hayden, USAF, in providing insights on the preparation of the 1990 and 1991 reports. All judgments in this chapter remain, of course, solely the responsibility of the author.

3. Even though much of the reform literature, such as the 1985 Report of the Senate Armed Services Committee, "Organization of the Department of Defense—

The Need for Change," discusses needed reforms in both the executive and congressional branches, Congress chose only to pursue reform within DoD. Since Congress was not reforming itself, it was not in a position to lean directly on the Executive Office of the President for reforms.

4. *Report of the President's Special Review Board* (Washington, DC: U.S. Government Printing Office, 1987), also available as *The Tower Commission Report* by several publishers. Of particular interest to the context of this chapter are Part II, "Organizing for National Security," and Part V, "Recommendations."

5. *National Security Strategy of the United States* (Washington, DC: White House, January 1987), p. 40.

6. For example, see Aaron Friedberg, "Is the United States Capable of Acting Strategically?" *The Washington Quarterly* 14, No. 1 (Winter 1991), pp. 15–20.

7. David C. Kozak, "The Bureaucratic Politics Approach: The Evolution of the Paradigm," in *Bureaucratic Politics and National Security*, eds. David Kozak and James Keagle (Boulder, CO: Rienner Publishers, 1988), pp. 3–15.

8. John Lewis Gaddis, *Strategies of Containment* (New York: Oxford University Press, 1982), pp. 89–127; and Zbigniew Brzezinski, *Power and Principle* (New York: McGraw Hill, 1983), pp. 51–52.

9. Commission on Integrated Long-Term Strategy, *Discriminate Deterrence* (Washington, DC: U.S. Government Printing Office, 1989).

10. Joseph S. Nye, Jr., *Bound to Lead: The Changing Nature of American Power* (New York: Basic Books, 1990), pp. 200, 227; and Catherine McArdle Kelleher, "U.S. Foreign Policy and Europe, 1990–2000," *Brookings Review* 8, No. 4 (Fall 1990), pp. 8–10.

11. Samuel Huntington, "America's Changing Strategic Interests," *Survival* 33, No. 1 (January/February 1991), pp. 8–16; and Robert Hormats, "The Roots of American Power," *Foreign Affairs* 70, No. 3 (Summer 1991), pp. 130–135.

12. Hormats, "Roots," p. 130.

# 3

# The National Military Strategy

*Harry E. Rothmann*

This chapter concerns the role of process and people in the making of the U.S. national military strategy in the immediate aftermath of the Cold War. Although the title suggests that the perspective is from the Joint Staff, the view is really that of a Joint Staff Officer who has observed and participated in the forging of that strategy. Hence this is a personal account, with all of the biases and prejudices familiar to such endeavors.

The chapter consists of two parts. The first examines the new military strategy as a major departure from previous Cold War military strategies in the calculations of ways and means. The second compares and contrasts the way in which military strategy was supposed to be made, and the manner in which the major participants really developed it. In this latter part, I conclude that people, not process, have been more important in the forging of the new strategy. I further propose that strategic formulation is more art than science, more judgment than fact. I also make some observations on the impact of the Goldwater-Nichols Act on strategic formulation, and I stress the importance of the Chairman, Joint Chiefs of Staff (CJCS), in the process. The main theme is that strategic vision is vital to formulating strategies.

## THE NATIONAL MILITARY STRATEGY AND ITS ENDS

*The National Military Strategy 1992* was released in January 1992. The roots of that strategy can be found in a number of sources ranging from the President's speech at Aspen on August 2, 1990, and General Powell's speeches on the "Base Force," to the Joint Military Net Assessment (JMNA) of March 1991 and the *National Security Strategy* report to the Congress

**Figure 3.1**
**National Military Objectives**

- **DETER OR DEFEAT AGGRESSION, SINGLY, OR IN CONCERT WITH ALLIES**
  - DETER MILITARY ATTACK BY ANY NATION AGAINST THE UNITED STATES, ITS ALLIES, AND OTHER COUNTRIES WHOSE SOVEREIGNTY IS VITAL TO OUR OWN, AND DEFEAT SUCH ATTACK, SINGLY, OR IN CONCERT WITH OTHERS, SHOULD DETERRENCE FAIL.
- **ENSURE GLOBAL ACCESS AND INFLUENCE**
  - PROTECT FREE COMMERCE: ENHANCE THE SPREAD OF DEMOCRACY; GUARANTEE U.S. ACCESS TO WORLD MARKETS, ASSOCIATED CRITICAL RESOURCES, AIR AND SEA LOCS, AND SPACE; AND CONTRIBUTE TO U.S. INFLUENCE AROUND THE WORLD.
- **PROMOTE REGIONAL STABILITY AND COOPERATION**
  - CONTRIBUTE TO REGIONAL STABILITY THROUGH MILITARY PRESENCE, MUTUAL SECURITY ARRANGEMENTS, AND SECURITY ASSISTANCE, AND DISCOURAGE THEREBY, IN CONCERT WITH OTHER INSTRUMENTS OF NATIONAL POWER, POLICIES AND OBJECTIVES INIMICAL TO U.S. SECURITY INTERESTS.
- **STEM THE FLOW OF ILLEGAL DRUGS**
  - STEM THE PRODUCTION AND TRANSIT OF ILLEGAL DRUGS AND THEIR ENTRY INTO THE UNITED STATES
- **COMBAT TERRORISM**
  - PARTICIPATE IN THE NATIONAL PROGRAM TO THWART AND RESPOND TO THE ACTIONS OF TERRORIST ORGANIZATIONS

in August 1991.[1] The strategy's military objectives are summarized in Figure 3.1. They are derived from and support the national interests and security objectives detailed in the *National Security Strategy*. In many ways U.S. interests and security objectives—the ends of the strategy equation—have not changed.[2] Indeed, they reflect what our nation's leaders unanimously have observed: that despite the dramatic changes of the last several years, the United States has enduring global interests and must continue to remain involved in the world.

On the other hand, major changes in the security environment demand changes in the way we view the pursuit of those ends. Thus, with the demise of communism and the breakup of the Soviet Union into a Commonwealth of Independent States (CIS), the Administration has argued that U.S. security policy has significantly shifted from one of containment to one of "engagement."[3] As the President has noted on several occasions, continued U.S. leadership is indispensable to ensure orderly transition to a new world order—an environment based upon global community values and international consensus and action.[4] This significant shift in policy, reflecting not only dramatic changes but also enduring realities, is fundamental to the new military strategy. Indeed, this new policy and its associated geopolitical changes necessitate changing the focus from a threat-based strategy to one that is interest- and capabilities-based. In addition, the end of the Cold War has shifted the U.S. strategic purpose from one of waging a global war against the Soviets to one of managing regional matters of vital interest. Much more will be said about these transformations later.

## THE NATIONAL MILITARY STRATEGY AND ITS WAYS

The new military strategy consists of a dozen interrelated military strategic concepts, which are shown in Figure 3.2. Collectively, these concepts (referred to as strategic foundations and principles) express the way in which we intend to use or ensure the use of military force to achieve the objectives. Many of these concepts are familiar. Yet several represent a significant departure from previous military strategies. For instance, the combination of forward presence with crisis responses represents a change from a Cold War strategy of forward defense with significant forward stationed forces backed up by rapid reinforcement. The new concepts focus on retaining enough forward deployed or stationed and continental U.S.—based forces to provide certain functions and capabilities and to create certain effects. The intended effects of forward presence are to show commitment, to lend credibility to our alliances, and to enhance stability. The functions and capabilities that both concepts afford are the ability to respond to regional crises through readiness and the capability to deploy rapidly, prepositioning sympathetic infrastructure, combined military organizations, and exercises. The two concepts also take into account the realities of anticipated changes to resources available for the strategy.

A second set of concepts that together represent a significant change in our military strategy includes strategic deterrence, strategic defense, and reconstitution. Although strategic deterrence has been a military concept since the 1950s and strategic defense since the mid–1980s, the new concepts differ significantly in their scope. They now concentrate on the rising threat posed by global ballistic missile proliferation and the increasing possibility of an accidental or unauthorized launch resulting from political turmoil. Therefore, the focus is on primarily ground-based defense systems that can provide protection against limited strikes upon the United States, forward deployed or stationed forces, and our allies. Reconstitution also centers on the possibility of reemerging or emerging global conventional threats. Here the objective is to preserve a credible capability to either forestall any potential adversary from competing militarily with us, or to deter a potential threat from remilitarizing, or, if deterrence fails, to rebuild military power to wage a global conflict. The *National Military Strategy* document further clarifies that reconstitution involves forming, training, and fielding new fighting units. This includes initially drawing on cadre-type units and laid-up military assets; mobilizing previously trained or new manpower; and activating the industrial base on a large scale.[5] This set of concepts was, in the formative stages of development, heavily focused on the former Soviet Union. Since the disintegration of the old union and the recent far-reaching

**Figure 3.2**
**Military Strategy Concepts**

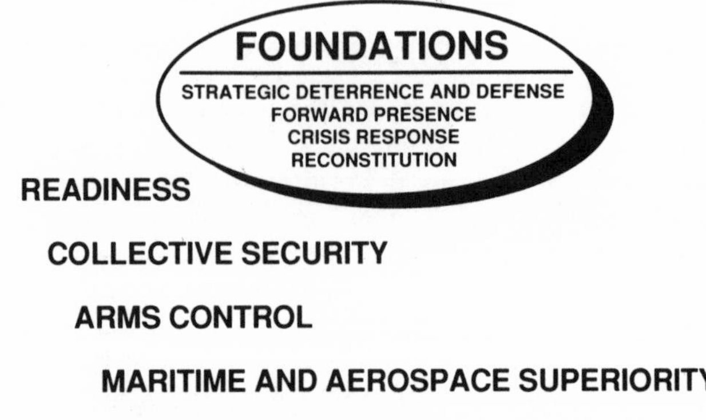


STRATEGIC AGILITY

POWER PROJECTION

TECHNOLOGICAL SUPERIORITY

DECISIVE FORCE

nuclear initiatives, the concepts have looked to more generic adversaries. Moreover, the resource that the strategy now anticipates for these concepts are considerably smaller.

There are two other strategic concepts that represent a significant departure from previous strategies: strategic agility and decisive force. Before the sweeping changes of the last three years and before Desert Storm, U.S. strategy and its supporting plans assumed that there would only be a certain number of days of strategic warning, that the likelihood of Soviet intervention in regional crises was high, that any regional conflict with the Soviets could develop into global war, and that the main theater of war would be Central Europe. As a consequence, strategic plans for both global and regional conflicts prioritized force deployments to Europe. For example, the Korean contingency plans had some Reserve forces in lieu of active because planners assumed that the latter would be needed in Europe. In addition, ground forces deployed in Allied Command Europe were not to be in plans for other theaters, nor even in contingency plans in European Command's other area of responsibility.

The geopolitical changes in Europe and in the former Soviet Union have offered an opportunity to alter these planning assumptions and concepts. Changes are incorporated in the phrase strategic agility. Most simply stated, "The force needed to win is assembled by the rapid movement of forces from wherever they are to wherever they are needed. US forces stationed in CONUS and overseas will be fully capable of worldwide employment on short notice."[6] The deployment and employment of forces from Europe to Southwest Asia in Desert Shield and Desert Storm demonstrated this concept. The Joint Strategic Capabilities Plan (JSCP) now apportions forces for planning based on this concept.

The concept of decisive force also reflects considerable change from previous strategic planning. As the new strategy notes:

> Once a decision for military action has been made, half-measures and confused objectives extract a severe price in the form of a protracted conflict which can cause needless waste of human lives and material resources, a divided nation at home, and defeat. Therefore, one of the essential elements of our national military strategy is the ability to rapidly assemble the forces needed to win—the concept of applying decisive force to overwhelm our adversaries and thereby terminate conflicts swiftly with a minimum loss of life.[7]

This concept highlights three important ingredients for U.S. military strategic planning and employment. First, military force should only be used with the commitment of the nation to the task at hand. Second, that commitment would have clear and obtainable objectives. Third, the force should be applied in such a manner as to ensure success quickly and decisively. As with strategic agility, Desert Storm also demonstrated the validity of this concept.

Before turning to the "means," or resource component, of the strategy, we must examine one other element of the new strategy. This element is called adaptive planning. As we have already noted, global conflict with the Soviets was the cornerpiece of U.S. strategic planning in the 1980s. Those plans, as well as many regional plans, were based upon a set of assumptions about warning, and they generally encompassed a single, rigid plan for war. The new strategy's adaptive planning construct, on the other hand, calls for the development of a diverse spectrum of military options—a menu from which the National Command Authority can choose in a crisis. These options are keyed to several different crisis conditions and assumptions about mobilization and transportation capabilities. The strategic plans recognize what Admiral J. C. Wylie so astutely has argued, "We cannot predict with certainty the pattern of the war or [crisis] for which we prepare ourselves. . . . [And] planning for certitude is the greatest of all mistakes."[8]

## THE NATIONAL MILITARY STRATEGY AND ITS MEANS

The Chairman's "Base Force," portrayed in Figure 3.3, is the means to carry out the new military strategy. By now the nature of this force is fairly well known. What may not be well known is what has determined its size. The Chairman and some members of the Joint Staff began a dialogue on

Figure 3.3
Force Composition

| | | FY 91 | BASE FORCE |
|---|---|---|---|
| STRATEGIC | Bombers | B-52 + B-1 | B-52H + B-1 + B-2 |
| | Missiles | 1000 | 550 |
| | SSBNs | 34 | 18 |
| ARMY | Active | 16 Divisions | 12 Divisions |
| | Reserve | 10 Divisions | 6 Divisions |
| | Cadre | | 2 Divisions |
| NAVY | Ships | 530 (15 CVBGs) | 450 (12 CVBGs) |
| | Active | 13 Air Wings | 11 Air Wings |
| | Reserve | 2 Air Wings | 2 Air Wings |
| USMC | Active | 3 MEFs | 3 MEFs |
| | Reserve | 1 Division/Wing | 1 Division/Wing |
| AIR FORCE | Active | 22 FWE | 15 FWE |
| | Reserve | 12 FWE | 11 FWE |

geopolitical and fiscal trends soon after General Powell took office in 1989.[9] This examination, driven heavily by the Chairman's personal views, culminated in a series of papers and briefs entitled "A View to the Nineties." This view represented a best educated guess on the future changing world order and anticipated domestic fiscal constraints. The needs of the new military strategy were then derived by (1) choosing contingencies that could be anticipated as likely, or (2) studying scenarios that the group felt were prudent missions for desired future military capabilities.[10] Among these were two major force-sizing scenarios and contingencies. One was a return by the Soviet Union to an aggressive military strategy and to force levels predating the conventional force agreements. The second was the need to be able to defend, almost simultaneously, our vital interests in several regions. The changes resulting in the breakup of the Soviet Union subsequently required adjustments to the Base Force as originally envisioned. These changes entailed reductions in strategic forces and adjustments to modernization and procurement programs. The National Command Authority, CJCS, the Joint Chiefs, and the Unified and Specified Commanders consider the remaining force structure shown in Figure 3.3 as the level necessary to execute the new strategy in the 1990s.

Several observations on the Base Force are worth emphasizing. First, it is a planned or programmed force—one that is designed for the 1995–96 time frame. It is the minimum force deemed necessary to deal with global threats as successfully as its designers can see them evolving in this decade. Moving to these levels sooner, or falling below them, would in the opinion

**Figure 3.4**
**Base Force Packages and Supporting Capabilities**

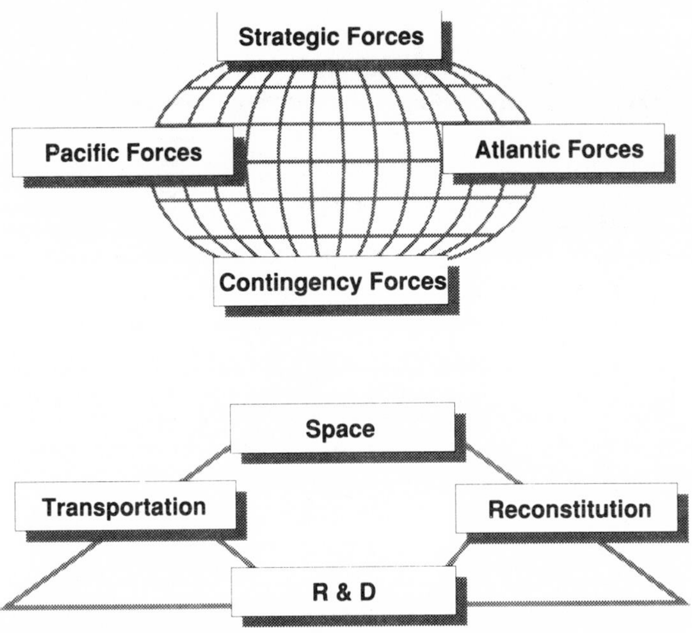


of the nation's military leadership risk the hollow force of the 1970s and could seriously erode the cohesion of the U.S. military. Of course, if other geopolitical changes occur that warrant further changes, then they could be made. But additional changes must be done prudently, keeping the right balance between Active and Reserve forces, and retaining a joint, coherent, effective warfighting capability. Thus, the new national military strategy refers to the Base Force as a "dynamic" force. Second, the Base Force is usually addressed in terms of conceptual force packages and supporting capabilities (see Figure 3.4). This is not meant to be a blueprint for a new command structure, but rather a way in which the Chairman has conceptualized and judged force sizes and capabilities to support strategic agility and adaptive planning.

## THE NATIONAL MILITARY STRATEGY: SOME OVERALL OBSERVATIONS

Before the process of developing the new military strategy is discussed, it is important to make three additional observations on the strategy as a whole. First, this is not a maritime, aerospace, or continental strategy. Rather, it is a comprehensive strategy that seeks to integrate jointly all military capabilities and apply them to protect or promote strategic centers of gravity. The new military strategy also accounts for all forms of national power, considers the U.S. strategic culture of decisive action and national commitment, and recognizes the unique U.S. geopolitical situation as a continental, maritime nation that has aerospace capabilities and the potential to exploit time and distance factors.[11] Second, some early critics of the strategy have argued that it does not "represent a new conceptual approach for a new security era but is essentially 'less of the same,' that is, a downsized force largely shaped by cold war priorities."[12] As the preceding discussion has indicated, the strategy and its forces have accounted not only for the changes in Europe brought about by the unification of Germany and dissolution of the Warsaw Pact, but also the disintegration of the former Soviet Union. The unenviable task now is to convince the congressional critics.

A third major observation of the new strategy is that it is not a threat-based strategy in the traditional sense. Although some specific threats can plausibly be identified, the real threat is the unknown, the uncertain. The strategy seeks to remain vigilant and prepared to handle a crisis that no one can predict. It does this by calling for a ready pool of tailorable, general purpose forces that can respond quickly and effectively to crises. This pool can also serve as the core for rebuilding or reconstituting forces should some unforeseen adversary attempt to create a global warfighting capability. Thus, the strategy recognizes a historical fact: For the most part, we have dealt with crises or fought wars with forces that were not specifically purchased for those particular contingencies. The key, then, is to have enough flexible forces to be able to adjust to the unknown. We can do this if we recognize the kinds of military capabilities that are currently fielded in the world, if we can anticipate technological changes, and if we can keep or develop capabilities to deal with those kinds of forces in areas of vital interest. In sum, the military strategy is capabilities- and interests-based for an uncertain world.

## FORGING THE NEW NATIONAL MILITARY STRATEGY

The remainder of this chapter discusses the process of developing the new military strategy. The Joint Strategic Planning System (JSPS) is the formal process by which the Chairman, the Joint Chiefs of Staff (JCS), and the Unified and Specified Commands formulate the strategy and interface with and advise the National Command Authority and Department of Defense on plans, programs, and requirements. The Joint Community revised that system in the beginning of 1990. The purpose was to incorporate the statutory responsibilities of the Chairman as delineated in the Goldwater-Nichols Act, and to streamline and simplify strategy formulation, operational planning, and force planning. The previous system was cumbersome, dependent on a myriad of planning documents, and characterized by a step-by-step process of JCS, Joint Staff, and Service planners meeting to reach agreement on usually contentious issues. The revamping of the system did not, in itself, eliminate all contention, rivalry and parochialism. But together with congressional pressure, changes in emphasis from Service duty to Joint duty, and greater participation of the Unified and Specified Commands, the joint planning system became a more effective process. It also became more reflective of the views of the CJCS and Commanders-in-Chief, and less reflective of service bickering. Hence, the focus of initiative, resolution, and advice has shifted in various degrees from the Services to the Joint Community.[13]

The participants who revised the system envisioned a process driven by a top-down systematic review of threats, capabilities, evolving global changes, and so forth. This review was to produce a series of written documents and culminate in a written Chairman's Guidance. This guidance was to feed the development of the *National Military Strategy* document (NMSD), which outlines the military strategy for presidential approval and presents programmatic advice for the Secretary of Defense's consideration. Upon completion of the NMSD, the Joint Staff, in coordination with the Unified and Specified Commands and the Services, would then develop the Joint Strategic Capabilities Plan (JSCP). The JSCP implements the military strategy through CJCS-approved planning guidance and apportioning forces for the development of contingency plans. An interesting aspect of this new system was the changed methodology for force planning. The previous system and its documents had created an elaborate series of force levels to compare and evaluate fiscally unconstrained and unreasonable military requirements. The objectives of these various force levels were to measure risks associated with budget realities and to make a case to support increased force structure. The new system takes a more reasonable approach by recognizing from the start that there will be fiscal constraints and by providing one risk evaluation force structure that could achieve national military objectives with a reasonable assurance of success.[14]

Since its inception, however, the new JSPS has not been executed as designed. Rather than working top-down, both policy and strategy formulation have been running concurrently. For example, the *National Military Strategy* document was not published until January 1992. The JSCP was already published in October 1991, thus propelling the planning community down the road to implement the strategy before it was finalized. The Joint Staff also had been drafting the *National Military Strategy* concurrent with the development of the *National Security Strategy* document until the latter was published in August 1991. In addition, there has been little formal production of written products from the Joint Strategic Review. For example, there has been no written Chairman's Guidance or formal establishment of a risk evaluation force. The reason for this apparent breakdown in the formal process is readily understandable. Simply, world events have been moving faster than any strategic formulation system, even one intentionally streamlined, can operate. Also, the bureaucracies and organizations just cannot keep up the pace of the changes that are forcing strategic alterations.

That is the bad news. The good news is that there has been strategic formulation and, as this chapter argues, it has been surprisingly effective. There are two major reasons. The first is that the Chairman has brought to his statutorily improved position a true strategic vision—the "View to the Nineties" and the Base Force. The second is that the nation's security and defense leadership have been able to work closely together to forge new strategies. Thus, vision and personal relationships have been the key to strategic formulation over the last several years.

Strategic vision is especially critical in overcoming bottlenecks in the formal planning process. The word *vision* has been much overused and is a somewhat unclear term. It appears to mean many things to many different people. Perry Smith equates strategic vision with long-range planning. In this sense he says that strategic planning (vision)

> is a way of thinking about the future, thinking about what we want (that is, defining our objectives and interests), thinking about the conditions which are likely to surround us in pursuing our objectives (projecting alternative environments), and thinking about ways to achieve our objectives either within the constraints of these environments or by influencing events to achieve a preferred environment.[15]

Some of the management literature seems to indicate that a vision can be anything from a broad statement of direction or "image" of a "possible and desirable future state of the organization" to a comprehensive codification of the "world you want to live in."[16]

I have done some historical research on strategic vision—what it may be, what makes some visions more effective than others, and what role it may have played in strategic formulation before World War I and between the two world wars. Insights from this research provide some interesting perspectives. The historical analysis indicates that an effective strategic vision appears to have several characteristics and elements. First, its purpose should be to guide strategic formulation and force planning. Second, it needs to focus on defining national interests and ensuring that plans and forces do not exceed or fall short of protecting those interests. In general, interests endure because they are primarily a product of geographical realities. Changes in the threat to those interests can be frequent. Changes in the threat, moreover, can distract one from vital interests toward lesser ones. Third, strategic vision should encompass all levels of warfare—strategic, operational, and tactical. Concepts valid at only one or two levels may be seriously flawed. Fourth, it should be specific and realistic enough to allow force planners to design, structure, and posture forces. Without that specificity and reality, the vision may be nothing more than a sloganeering campaign that encourages complacency and espouses traditional but invalid truths or myths. Finally, a strategic vision should recognize the uncertainty of the future and of war. It should attempt to anticipate but not predict. The Chairman's strategic vision, as described earlier, incorporates these characteristics and elements.[17]

As for the role that strategic vision can play, the research, not surprisingly, indicates that it is extremely important not only in guiding military strategy but in influencing grand strategies and developing military capabilities as well. Most important, in the absence of such vision there is no direction, no effective long- or mid-range planning, no focus on protecting vital strategic interests. Military leaders and organizations, without this vision, have failed to provide well thought-out and coherent advice to their civilian leaders. As the research study notes:

> A brief discussion of strategic leadership and vision . . . demonstrates several (strategic) successes and failures. For example, General Henry Wilson successfully argued the importance of a continental strategy to Britain, and he was specific, realistic, and clear in describing that strategy. The General also led the way toward civilian adoption of that strategy and explained its relevance to the national interests. During the interwar years, British strategists and force planners, for the most part, either did not have the foresight and imagination to recognize the importance of the Continent, or were not determined enough to lead the way in arguing its relevance to the national interest. . . . As a result, instead of providing a strategic vision, the military leaders allowed one to be imposed upon them primarily based on financial and domestic concerns. In addition, without a forward looking, specific strategic concept, bureaucratic politics and inertia dominated strategic formulation and force planning. This led to the incessant study of and delay in making the difficult choices. Thus, leaders and planners preferred incremental, evolutionary, and ineffective conservative approaches. When Hitler's actions finally revealed his intentions, the race to rearm and prepare for war was hectic and too late.[18]

Ironically, the situation the British military faced in the 1920s and early 1930s—the lack of a precise threat and the need to concentrate resources on solving domestic issues—is strikingly similar to that which we face today. Fortunately, we have a vision that provides a coherent strategic view of where to go, for what purpose, and with the right military capabilities.

There is ample evidence that the Chairman's strategic vision has already provided coherent, convincing advice to the National Command Authority. This counsel is a major reason, despite the concurrency difficulties discussed earlier, that the security strategy, defense policy, and military strategy are connected and complement one another. The other reason is that there has been a close working relationship between the CJCS, the Service Chiefs, the CINCs, and the civilian leadership. This relationship has allowed the new national military strategy to be a coordinated expression of the nation's needs in a dramatically and quickly changing strategic environment. But much of this dialogue and coordination has been informal. Thus, although there was no formal written Chairman's Guidance and many of the other documents of the Joint Strategic Review process were not produced, there were fora such as the annual CINCs' conferences at which the nation's military leaders discussed important strategic issues. Moreover, the Chairman used these gatherings to provide his verbal guidance and to discuss his vision. Following these conferences the staffs worked on significant unresolved issues. This resolution, for the most part, found its way into the appropriate documents. In addition, in lieu of lengthy formal meetings usually referred to as "tank" briefings, the CJCS, Service Chiefs, and key civilian defense leaders worked the phones, corridors, and offices in Washington to discuss and formulate strategy. The national military strategy is the result of that informal process in which personal relationships played such an essential part.

## CONCLUSION

In sharing his thoughts on military planning in peacetime with the Royal United Services Institute, Michael Howard observed that it is probably not possible to develop military strategies, forces, and doctrines that will be entirely right for the next conflict. Nevertheless, he emphasized the importance of peacetime planning for war, and he added that "it is the task of military science in an age of peace to prevent the doctrines from being too badly wrong."[19] From my view the new U.S. national military strategy is more than just not "being too badly wrong." It is an effective blueprint for protecting and promoting our security objectives in an uncertain world against unknown threats. It is a result of the best calculations of ends and means that the nation's military leaders can make. This strategy, however, was not born or forged through scientific, mathematical, or cut-and-dried calculations. Rather, the making of the new strategy has been more akin to Paul Kennedy's observations that "strategy can never be exact or foreordained. It relies, rather, upon the constant and intelligent reassessment of the policy's ends and means: it relies upon wisdom and judgment, those two intangibles which Clausewitz and Liddell Hart—despite their many differences—esteemed the most."[20] The real effectiveness of the new military strategy has yet to meet its true measure—whether it will survive the budget deliberations ahead, and whether it will serve the country's needs in the next crisis.

Finally, this chapter has argued that the making of the strategy depends more heavily upon informal, personal relationships than upon any formal process. Therefore, from the viewpoint of a political or social model, decision making is more like the bureaucratic politic model than the rational actor or organization models.[21] Consequently, persuasion and personal vision were key elements in effective decision making. Accordingly, this chapter has portrayed the Chairman's strategic vision and informal power of persuasion as being the two basic ingredients in forging the new strategy. Those two ingredients will also be critical in future budget hearings—hearings that will determine the ultimate outcome of the concepts described here.

## NOTES

1. A good compilation of these sources can be found in James J. Tritten, *America Promises to Come Back: Our New National Security Strategy* (Monterey, CA: Naval Post Graduate School, October 1991).

2. This chapter adopts Arthur F. Lykke's conceptual approach to understanding strategy as an equation in which "strategy equals Ends plus Ways plus Means" in his anthology *Military Strategy: Theory and Application* (Carlisle Barracks, PA: U.S. Army War College, June 1989), pp. 3–8.

3. Although as yet there has been no labeling of U.S. security policy in the post–Cold War period, sources describing that policy continuously refer to some sort of "engagement."

4. The White House, *National Security Strategy of the United States* (Washington, DC: U.S. Government Printing Office, August 1991), p. v.

5. Chairman, Joint Chiefs of Staff, *The National Military Strategy 1992* (Washington, DC: The Joint Staff, undated but published January 29, 1992), pp. 8–9.

6. Ibid., p. 9.

7. Ibid., p. 10.

8. Admiral J. C. Wylie, "Assumptions Underlying a General Theory," reprinted in Lykke, *Military Strategy*, pp. 26–27.

9. The author derived this account from unclassified portions of office files. It is an interpretation of these papers and is in no way authoritative.

10. These scenarios are outlined in the 1991 *Joint Military Net Assessment*, dated March 1991 and signed by the Secretary of Defense.

11. JSCP adaptive planning guidance, which implements the new strategy, calls for consideration of how economic, political, and diplomatic action in concert with military action may produce deterrent effects in regional crises. As for U.S. strategic culture, see Colin Gray, *The Geopolitics of Super Power* (Lexington: The University Press of Kentucky, 1988). It is interesting to note that when the CJCS has talked about the Base Force he refers to "enduring realities to the Pacific and to the Atlantic." In assessing the strategy in scenarios, the Joint Staff refers to major regional contingencies to the "East" and "West." We no longer view the Western Hemisphere and the United States on the left side of a world map looking east to Europe. Rather, the new strategy views the United States in a central global position enjoying interior lines between Pacific and Asia.

12. Representative Les Aspin, "National Security in the 1990s: Defining a New Basis for U.S. Military Forces," a speech delivered to the Atlantic Council of the United States, January 6, 1992, p. 1.

13. This judgment is based on the author's experience as a staff officer on the Army Staff in 1982–85 and on the Joint Staff from 1990 to 93.

14. The new JSPS is promulgated in Chairman, Joint Chiefs of Staff, Memorandum of Policy No. 7, January 30, 1990.

15. Perry Smith, et al., *Creating Strategic Vision: Long-Range Planning for National Security* (Washington, DC: National Defense University Press, 1987), p. 93.

16. For example, see Warren Bennis and Burt Nanus, *Leaders: The Strategies for Taking Charge* (New York: Harper and Row, 1985); and Rosabeth Kanter, *The Change Master: Innovation and Entrepreneurship in the American Corporation* (New York: Simon and Schuster, Touchtone Books), 1984.

17. Harry Rothmann, *The U.S. Army, Strategic Formulation and Force Planning: Past, Present, and Future* (Newport, RI: Naval War College, July 1990), unpublished monograph.

18. Ibid., pp. 123–124.

19. Michael Howard, "Military Science in an Age of Peace," *Journal of Royal United Services Institute*, No. 119 (March 1979), p. 4.

20. Paul Kennedy, ed., *Grand Strategies in War and Peace* (New Haven, CT: Yale University, 1991), p. 6.

21. Graham T. Allison, *Essence of Decision: Explaining the Cuban Missile Crisis* (Boston: Little, Brown, 1971). The Naval War College uses these and other models to examine decision-making case studies in its "Policy Making and Implementation" course.

# 4

# Strategy and Management in the Post–Cold War Pentagon

*Robert J. Art*

In response to the breathtaking developments in international politics since late 1989, the Bush Administration significantly revised the defense posture of the United States.[1] Four specific factors drove the revisions: the end of the Cold War, the breakup of the Soviet Union, the desire to retain both a superpower military force and an overseas U.S. military presence, and the American public's demands for cuts in defense spending. The basic elements of the U.S. post–Cold War defense strategy are now clear, even if the ultimate size, cost, and exact composition of the military forces to support it have not been settled.

There are two fundamental questions to ask about these changes in U.S. military strategy. First, do they make sense? Second, does the top political and military leadership of the Pentagon have sufficient control over the defense bureaucracy to make its decisions stick? An answer to the first question requires an analysis of how well suited the Bush strategy is to the needs of the post–Cold War world. An answer to the second requires an assessment of the effectiveness of the changes in defense management that have been made since the mid–1980s, especially those brought about by the 1986 Goldwater-Nichols Defense Reorganization Act. It will do the United States little good if it proclaims a military strategy that is ill adapted to U.S. interests in the post–Cold War world, or if it adopts a well-suited one but is unable to translate its general strategy into the detailed decisions that actually constitute policy.

This chapter attempts to answer both questions. First, there is much to

The author thanks the U.S. Institute for Peace and The Twentieth Century Fund for their generous support of this project.

commend in the Administration's "new military strategy," but crucial correctives need to be taken if the strategy is to be fully effective. Second, with the 1986 Defense Reorganization Act, the two top managers of the Pentagon—the Secretary of Defense and the Chairman of the Joint Chiefs of Staff—now possess the requisite management tools to get what they want from the bureaucracies they oversee. A few critical tests demonstrate that the 1986 reforms are working as intended. In assessing strategy and management, therefore, the latter appears to be in relatively better shape than the former.

The first section of this chapter lays out an alternative military strategy, compares it to the Bush Administration approach, and suggests two correctives: scrapping plans for a global-war reconstitution capability and altering the focus of the Strategic Defense Initiative (SDI) from a space- to a ground-based system. The second section sets forth three Pentagon budgetary and bureaucratic outcomes that traditionally occurred before the enactment of Goldwater-Nichols, compares them with the outcomes that have occurred since the 1986 Act, and explains why matters are getting better. The third section presents the case for "creeping jointness"—the view that defense management, especially on the military side, has significantly improved because the Goldwater-Nichols integrated approach to military planning is becoming institutionalized within the Defense Department. In the management area, then, what is called for is not sweeping new legislation but further refinement of the tools now available. Together with the Goldwater-Nichols reforms, such refinement makes it possible to preserve an effective U.S. military instrument even though significantly fewer resources will be devoted to it.

## THE NEW MILITARY STRATEGY

The United States has four vital foreign policy goals to pursue in the post–Cold War world: first, to protect the U.S. homeland from attack and destruction; second, to preserve an open international economic order; third, to maintain assured access to Persian Gulf oil; and fourth, to prevent great power wars on the Eurasian continent. It has three additional goals that are not vital but are highly desirable: fifth, to promote democratic institutions and human rights; sixth, to prevent, retard, or reverse the spread of weapons of mass destruction, including ballistic missiles and chemical and nuclear weapons; and seventh, to prevent the extensive slaughter of a nation's citizenry, either by a ruthless dictator or by the breakdown of governmental order that then results in ethnic slaughter, such as what recently happened in what was formerly Yugoslavia.

All seven goals, but especially the second, third, and fourth, can be served, though in varying ways and in differing degrees, by the peacetime deployment of U.S. military forces overseas. The primary functions of the overseas deployment are: to provide insurance and reassurance to key regional allies during the post–Cold War transition; to deter aggressive actions by states either toward other states or toward their own citizens; to make states feel secure enough against their neighbors such that they can keep their armaments limited and can avoid acquiring weapons of mass destruction; and to prevent power vacuums from materializing, should the United States precipitously withdraw; and, in general, to preserve regional stability. The fifth goal is best achieved through economic growth and the development of a middle class in a nation, though there may be rare instances in which a U.S. military intervention could tip the balance toward democracy. The sixth and seventh could well require the United States to intervene militarily in the affairs of other states in preemptive, preventive, peacemaking, and peacekeeping roles. Such interventions must be done sparingly and only in concert with selected regional allies. Only the first goal can be achieved through unilateral action by the United States, and for at least the next decade (and more likely well beyond that), it will be easily accomplished. The other six goals require the cooperation of other states.

### Four Elements of a Post–Cost War Strategy

From these seven foreign policy objectives we can construct the four elements of the post–Cold War U.S. military strategy. They are (1) severely reduced offensive nuclear forces, with a significant slowdown in qualitative modernization; 92) research and development on a continental defense against a limited ballistic missile attack, and a vigorous research and development effort and deployment, when successfully achieved, of effective theater ballistic missile defenses for U.S. overseas forces and key allies; (3) a continuing though much reduced overseas military presence in Europe, East Asia, and the Middle East; and (4) a ready, mobile reserve of conventional forces in the United States that can rapidly reinforce the forward deployed forces.

*Nuclear Deterrence.* First, in the post–Cold War era, there is no reason for the United States to abandon nuclear deterrence because it provides such a high degree of security at such a low cost. But with the Cold War's demise, the offensive nuclear force can be severely reduced in size and modernized much less rapidly than before. Most of the impetus for America's huge nuclear force and its frequent modernization came from the political competition between the United States and the Soviet Union. It was not the arms race that produced the political competition but the political competition that produced the arms race. With the breakup of the Soviet Union and the emergence of a significantly weakened and seemingly benign Russia, the United States can now size its strategic nuclear force closer to the dictates of homeland deterrence than to those of extended deterrence and damage limitation.[2] For homeland deterrence, what counts is the number of warheads that the nation can threaten to launch against an adversary's main cities in order to deter attack, not the number of warheads required to destroy the adversary's nuclear forces. Because the number of such cities is small, so, too, can be the forces required to target them. A homeland deterrent force could easily be under 1,000 warheads, and perhaps as few as 100 to 200, as long as there are a sufficient number of survivable platforms from which to launch them.[3]

Should the United States, then, reduce its strategic nuclear force to somewhere between 100 and 1,000 warheads? Cutting the force all the way down to a bare minimum deterrent makes sense only if the United States completely ignores the needs of extended deterrence. A strong argument can be made that the United States should maintain a nuclear force large enough to give other non-nuclear states over whom it continues to extend its nuclear umbrella confidence about its robustness. During the Cold War, this type of thinking had a powerful effect: Considerations of extended deterrence substantially drove up the size of America's nuclear force.[4] America's key allies did not view a U.S. minimum deterrent force as providing them with a credible nuclear umbrella against large Soviet nuclear forces; rather, such a force smacked of isolationist overtones. A large strategic nuclear force, together with the overseas deployment of U.S. tactical nuclear weapons, was equated with a robust and hence a credible U.S. nuclear umbrella. Even though there is at present no clear nuclear adversary threatening key U.S. allies that do not have their own nuclear weapons, such as Germany, Japan, and South Korea, there is still a rationale for extending the U.S. nuclear umbrella over them. It discourages them from acquiring their own nuclear weapons. And as long as they retain a residue of the belief that a larger nuclear force is a more credible umbrella than a smaller one, the United States will need nuclear forces larger than those it would require were it to take account only of its own defense, if it wishes—that is, to keep those states that could easily go nuclear, non-nuclear.

Were matters to rest here, the case for a larger nuclear force, precisely in order to prevent nuclear spread, has strong merit. There is, however, a second political force at work—nuclear delegitimization—whose purpose, just like extended deterrence, is to discourage nuclear proliferation. This force pushes the United States in the direction of a minimum, not a maximum, force. If the United States, in concert with Russia and the other nuclear great powers, wishes to delegitimize, or at least significantly diminish, the perceived political utility of nuclear arsenals in international politics, then it, together with the other nuclear powers, should scrap its nuclear force entirely, or at least reduce it to a minimum deterrent while relying more on maintaining a conventional deterrent force.[5] The United States cannot call upon other states to forego acquiring nuclear weapons when it shows by its own example, with large forces, how much political leverage they give.

Thus, there are two political forces that work at cross purposes, even though the goal of each is, paradoxically, to retard the further spread of nuclear weapons. The requirements of extended deterrence tug the United States away from a minimum force; those of nuclear delegitimization, toward it. The issue cannot be resolved by theoretical analysis because theory yields an indeterminate result. Instead, the exact size of the U.S. nuclear force will be determined ultimately by a political judgment as to how these two opposing political forces—extended deterrence versus nuclear delegitimization—balance out. That judgment, in turn, will depend mostly upon the attitudes about the credibility of the U.S. nuclear umbrella by states that do not have nuclear weapons but easily could. What should be clear from this discussion, however, is that the United States can do with an offensive nuclear force much smaller than it has had for nearly forty years, even if it does not go for the minimum one.

*Ballistic Missile Defense.* Second, the United States should continue with a vigorous research and development program on homeland ballistic missile defense, but it should avoid deployment at this time. The research program should be focused on ground-based defenses and space-based sensors. This is the program mandated by Congress through its passage in November 1991 of the Missile Defense Act. It requires the Secretary of Defense to "develop for deployment" the requisite technology, with the goal of a target deployment of a "cost-effective, operationally effective, and ABM Treaty compliant" Strategic Defense Initiative (SDI) system of 100 interceptors at one site by fiscal year 1996.[6] In this act the Congress explicitly stated that it had not given final approval for deployment of a homeland defense system, but it did want to be in a position to make a judgment in several years, based in part on an assessment of what the technology will then look like. Congress had an additional goal: to reorient the Bush Administration away from space-based defenses by causing it to accelerate development of ground-based defenses. The 1991 act therefore instructs the Defense Department to reorient its research away from space-based to ground-based interceptors, although the latter would make use of space-based sensors, which do not violate the terms of the 1972 Anti-Ballistic Missile Treaty. In addition, the 1991 act stressed the importance of developing an effective theater missile defense (TMD) to protect U.S. allies and U.S. forces stationed abroad.

The 1991 Missile Act is sensible. If the United States keeps forces stationed overseas, then it must take the steps necessary to defend them. Because the spread of ballistic missile technology has put at risk U.S. forces stationed abroad, the United States cannot leave its overseas troops vulnerable to them.[7] Moreover, U.S. allies that come under range of hostile ballistic missiles deserve protection; and theater defenses may aid U.S. efforts, even if only marginally, to retard the spread of massively destructive weapons. For these three reasons, there is a strong case for developing and deploying theater missile defenses. Deployment of a limited homeland defense, however, is not now warranted. The only Third World nation that can attack the United States at present and for the next ten years is China. The United States has lived under China's ballistic missile threat for quite some time, just as China has lived under ours. All other Third World ballistic missile forces are only regional in their range, not intercontinental.[8] Development of a hedge for the future emergence of crazy or ruthless Third World leaders and terrorists is a reasonable step at this time, but the hedge requires only an active research and development program that is compatible with the ABM treaty, not deployment.

*An Overseas Military Presence.* Third, the United States should retain overseas somewhere between 175,000 and 250,000 troops, roughly one-third to one-half the 510,000 troops that it had stationed abroad at the tail end of the Cold War. These forces should remain deployed primarily in Western Europe and East Asia, with a small residual presence, primarily offshore, in the Persian Gulf area. There are several reasons why the United States should continue to keep some combat forces overseas.

One reason why U.S. troops should remain abroad is that there is as yet no reliable collective substitute for the potential peacemaking role that U.S. forces can play in Europe, East Asia, and the Middle East. Peacemaking means either deterring aggression (the deterrence aspect of peacemaking) or punishing it should it occur (the punishment aspect). In contrast, peacekeeping generally means the insertion of forces between combatants, after they have ceased fighting and with their agreement, to help preserve the peace to which they have agreed. In both its deterrent and punishment aspects, peacemaking is a more demanding task than peacekeeping. U.S. overseas forces can strengthen the deterrent aspect of peacemaking in these three regions simply by their presence. Ultimately, however, if deterrence is to remain credible, these forces may have to be used, in concert with the forces of other regional powers and under the aegis of either the United Nations or other regional organizations, to punish aggression should it take place. There will be those infrequent instances when vital U.S. and allied interests are so directly and forcibly challenged that not to react in kind would be to weaken deterrence fatally. Only in these rare instances should U.S. force actually be used, and they must remain infrequent because the United States cannot allow itself to become the world's policeman. Neither the American public nor other nations will tolerate that. Under what circumstances U.S. forces should be used to defend vital interests by punishing aggression is *the* central question about U.S. military power for the future.

The point remains that there is as yet no viable substitute for U.S. forces. The European Community, for one, has proven militarily impotent in dealing with the breakup of Yugoslavia.[9] The United Nations, for another, has not yet demonstrated that it can become an effective global collective security force, though its record in peacekeeping actions and in voting sanctions since 1989 has been impressive. The UN was effective in its forceful peacemaking role against Saddam Hussein in 1990–91 primarily because the United States wanted it to be and because the United States did the hard work necessary to get the UN to act. U.S. forces, moreover, provided the bulk of the air and armored forces used in this peacemaking action. Since then, the UN has imposed economic sanctions twice, once against Libya on April 15, 1992, and then against Serbia on May 30, 1992.

No one can know for certain whether the United Nations will evolve into a truly effective world collective security organization. The rich industrialized nations have signaled their political intention to work to make it so.[10] But until that day arrives, if ever, U.S. troops in Europe, East Asia, and the Middle East continue to provide a useful peacemaking (deterrent) role. Even if that day arrives, U.S. forces will need to be involved in UN peacemaking operations of any size. Whether a UN military force is organized along an ad hoc or a permanent standing basis, large-scale punishment actions will be facilitated by the overseas presence of U.S. forces.[11]

A second reason for U.S. troops to remain in Western Europe, East Asia, and the Middle East is that many of the governments in those regions, whether allies of the United States or not, want U.S. troops to stay. They see U.S. military power as a stabilizing force.[12] For example, the Japanese government views the presence of U.S. troops as reassuring its East Asia neighbors that there will not be a revival of Japanese militarism. The Chinese government, although it holds to the principle that no nation should station troops outside of its territory, admits that there are "certain historical conditions" that justify the presence of U.S. troops in East Asia for the time being. South Korea's views about the deterrent effect of U.S. troops against North Korea are well known. In Western Europe, no government, not even the French, wants U.S. troops to leave Europe. They are seen as insurance against a sudden adverse turn of events in Russia or against the "renationalization" of defense in Western Europe; as reassurance against the reemergence of a militarily powerful, united Germany; and as a stabilizing influence that helps keep the path smooth for European political union. The nations of Eastern Europe, especially Poland, Czechoslovakia, and Hungary, want to join NATO because they view it as the only reliable security organization functioning in Europe today.[13] Their initial enthusiasm for the Conference on Security and Cooperation in Europe (CSCE) has waned, especially because the CSCE proved impotent in dealing with the ethnic slaughter that accompanied the breakup of Yugoslavia. Similarly, the desire of the Persian Gulf sheikdoms to retain some U.S. military presence, although as invisible as possible, is clear. In these three regions, the U.S. military presence can help the United States to serve as a stabilizer, a mediator, and an "honest broker" among regional rivals.

The third reason for U.S. troops to remain abroad is that it serves U.S. interests, not simply those of others. A U.S. presence in Europe and East Asia helps to discourage Germany and Japan from acquiring their own nuclear forces and thereby strengthens the global regime against the spread of nuclear weapons. The U.S. presence helps to preserve stability and thereby provides the political framework conducive to international trade and the economic growth that creates the middle classes central to the emergence of democratic institutions.The U.S. presence keeps the likelihood of a great power war on the Eurasian continent, which is quite low as it is, lower still. The U.S. presence increases the security that states experience and thereby lessens the pressures for them to acquire large military forces, including weapons of mass destruction. Finally, a U.S. residual presence in the Persian Gulf serves as a warning to any future would-be regional hegemon that the United States will do what is necessary to preserve access to Middle Eastern oil.

*Reinforcement Capability.* The fourth and final element of America's new military strategy is a credible reinforcement capability: highly ready forces in reserve in the continental United States that can be sent abroad quickly should that prove necessary. A residual U.S. overseas presence means little in and of itself. What the overseas forces represent is the tangible commitment of American might. Unless backed up by sufficient power within the United States, the forces abroad will come to be seen simply as tokens. An overseas residual presence can carry with it a credible U.S. guarantee only if others are convinced that the presence can be quickly expanded to a credible warfighting force. Again, this is not a license for the United States to intervene in each and every dispute abroad. Rather, the capability for rapid reinforcement is a strategy primarily for dampening the likelihood that the conflicts that would seriously threaten U.S. interests would happen in the first place and, secondarily, for dealing with them should they occur. If U.S. forces overseas are to serve a stabilizing function, then they require the same two elements that all deterrent forces have always required: the will and the capability to use them.

## Two Criticisms of the Pentagon's Strategy

How does the Pentagon's strategy fit with this recommended post–Cold War strategy? The four elements of the Cheney-Powell strategy are strategic deterrence and defense, a forward presence, crisis response, and a reconstitution capability. The second and third elements are sensible because they are equivalent to the overseas presence and the reinforcement capability just described. The two major flaws in the Pentagon's proposed strategy are its first and fourth elements: its ambitious plans for strategic defense, and its desire to develop and retain a reconstitution capability for global war.

*Space-Based Defense.* In contrast to congressional mandates, the Bush Administration wanted to deploy a space-based defense system for global protection against limited strikes (GPALS) of up to 200 nuclear warheads on the homeland of the United States and that of its allies. Space-based interceptors are expensive to deploy, and the technology is by no means proven.[14] Space-based systems will not be effective against missile attacks by regional rivals that threaten U.S. allies because these missiles will have depressed trajectories well below the range of U.S. space-based interceptors. The United States can better project its allies from such regional threats by deploying theater-based defensive systems. For the next decade, moreover, there is no Third World ballistic missile threat against the U.S. homeland and hence no need for a homeland defense, space- or land-based.

Finally, a space-based defense is a violation of the 1972 Anti-Ballistic Missile (ABM) Treaty. It makes little sense at this stage in the political evolution of Russia for the United States to take a hard line on security matters by violating the 1972 ABM Treaty. At a time when the United States is trying to deal with the consequences for nuclear spread of the breakup of the Soviet Union, it is counterproductive to pursue policies that will only embolden conservative opponents of the democratic reformers and anger the democratic reformers themselves. The United States needs the passive acquiescence of the former and the active cooperation of the latter. Deploying a system that the United States does not currently require for its security is foolhardy when such an action could threaten the nuclear reductions already agreed to, as well as those proposed by, the United States and Russia.[15] Thus, GPALS is expensive, not yet technologically feasible, not necessary at present, not effective for all the missions assigned to it, and politically counterproductive. GPALS' time has not yet come.

*Reconstitution Capability*. Similarly, the Pentagon's strategy for a global reconstitution capability is not well founded. The Pentagon intends reconstitution "to deter any potential adversary from attempting to build forces capable of posing a global challenge to the United States and, if deterrence fails, to provide a global warfighting capability."[16] As defined by the Pentagon, reconstitution is the ability to quickly rebuild U.S. forces to wage global war by preserving those elements of military power that take the longest to acquire, such as highly trained and specialized personnel, weapons with long lead times to produce, and an industrial base that can rapidly gear up for mass production. Providing for some reconstitution capability is sensible, if by that one means the ability to quickly accelerate the output of existing production lines and to mobilize the reserves of trained manpower in a crisis. But this is a surge capability for a limited regional crisis, not a reconstitution capability for all-out global war.[17] This is precisely the capability that the United States will require because the wars that will confront it in the future will be regional, not global, in nature. They are likely to be no larger than the size of the Desert Storm operation, which the Base Force can handle, and probably much smaller. And the United States will deal with them as it has done in the past, one at a time. What is required for crisis response, therefore, is a limited surge, not an all-out reconstitution, capability.

Moreover, were such a would-be hegemon to appear on the horizon, the United States would have ample warning time to rebuild its forces without reinvesting in a reconstitution capability now. There is no country today that can hide from U.S. intelligence assets the military buildup that would be required to wage global war against the United States. If such a threat materialized, the United States would know about it well in advance of when military action would have to be taken so that it could build up the necessary forces. As the Pentagon envisions it, the ability to reconstitute forces is, fundamentally, the ability to transform one's industrial capability from peacetime to an all-out wartime effort. The United States would have the time to do this. Whether it did would depend not on advanced warning, but on the will to do it.

The United States does not now need to get a leg up on such a potential adversary. Moreover, taking visible actions to do so will only make such an event more rather than less likely. In the post–Cold War era, the United States must use its power carefully and avoid actions that smack of arrogant unilaterialism. During the Cold War the United States needed its key allies, but they needed the United States more than it needed them. Their need for U.S. protection against the Soviet Union dampened their understandable reactions to frequent U.S. unilateralist actions. In the post–Cold War era, the cement of the anti-Soviet alliance is no longer there to counter the political strains produced by U.S. unilateralism. Without this dampening effect, the arrogant exercise of U.S. power will produce counterreactions, as balance of power theory predicts.[18] Thus, plans taken now to gear up U.S. forces against potential global hegemons partake of the arrogant, overweening actions that the United States should avoid.[19] It must walk the fine line: use its considerable power to assume the leadership role where its vital interests and those of its key allies are at stake, but in doing so, avoid running roughshod over them, thereby provoking them to build up their own power or to construct a coalition against the United States. Walking the fine line between leadership and dominance is what Secretary of State Baker meant by "collective engagement": The United States must be the leader of coalitions that take into account the interests of all the members, not act unilaterally as the lone superpower.[20]

Finally, however, the whole scenario of a large scale, sustained, conventional global war in the nuclear age is a flight of fancy. It is absurd to think of spending many resources to develop the capability to wage such a war against an unidentifiable adversary. It made no sense for the United States to spend dollars for such a war against the Soviet Union, which the Reagan Administration made some attempts to do. It makes no more sense now. There is little that the United States could do short of using its military power preemptively against it, to prevent the emergence of a global military competitor, because such a global competitor would generate its resources through its own internal efforts. This is exactly how the Soviet Union challenged the United States. A preemptive use of U.S. military power in such a case is something it never did against the Soviet Union, something the American people would probably never tolerate, and something that would be equivalent to national suicide, because such a would-be global challenger would have first acquired a nuclear force precisely to deter such a preemptive U.S. attack. Moreover, a global conventional war did not occur during the Cold War era because of nuclear deterrence. As long as there is nuclear deterrence, why would it occur in the future? Were such a global adversary to emerge, it would be nuclear-armed. Were it and the United States somehow to blunder into a conventional war, that war would not last long. Either it would quickly become nuclear because one side would escalate to the use of nuclear weapons to end it, or, more likely, either or both nations would employ nuclear escalatory threats to bring it to a prompt end. On practically every count, therefore, reconstitution for global war smacks of a poorly designed rationale for an inflated defense budget.

Instead of planning to gear up for global conventional wars, the United States should concern itself with the readiness and sustainability of the active and reserve forces that it will have on hand at the time. Wars of the future are likely to be intense, short, and limited. The U.S. forces will have to go on short notice, rely on existing stocks of materials, mobilize the reserve forces and the critical personnel they contain, and surge existing production lines for ammunition and weapons. What the United States needs to plan for is a well-equipped, ready, sustainable, and mobile force. It will not have the leisure to take several years to double the size of its military forces and produce exotic new weapons. Defense policy should not focus on global war reconstitution issues but on the maintenance of critical skills, the requisite lines of production tailored to smaller forces, and the preservation of U.S. high technology. In part, this is what the Defense Department means, or should mean, by reconstitution. The emphasis should be on keeping the forces that will be available, both active and reserve, well equipped and well lead, not on increasing their size by some significant factor for a fantasy scenario.

## THE NEW MANAGEMENT TOOLS

If the four elements just described constitute a sound post–Cold War military strategy, does the Defense Department have the management tools to implement it? The question is important to address because a sound strategy means little if it cannot be the governing element in constructing the programs and budgets that yield the nation's military forces. A sound defense strategy can quickly unravel unless the Pentagon's top leadership is able to make certain that the thousands of detailed programmatic and budgetary decisions that the defense bureaucracy subsequently makes are consistent with it. A coherent strategy, together with the requisite program elements and budgets that give it meaning, has the best chance of surviving the political gauntlet of congressional review. The Pentagon has done well with the Congress when its decisions have been integrated; it has fared poorly when its decisions have been disjointed.

In the past, Pentagon leaders have experienced considerable difficulty in getting from the military services what they have wanted. Are they doing better now? The simplest way to assess the current relationship between strategy and management is to compare the Pentagon's programmatic and budgetary outcomes before passage of the 1986 Goldwater-Nichols legislation with those that have come after it. Such a comparison demonstrates that the legislation is having many of the effects its authors intended, though matters are by no means perfect.

## Cold War Outcomes

The traditional decision-making outcomes that prevailed from 1947, when the Defense Department was first created, until 1986, when it was last reorganized, were a product in part of the Defense Department's organizational structure. The Cold War Pentagon had four characteristics. First, it began as a system of halfway measures, representing a compromise between a highly centralized, tightly integrated Army plan, on the one hand, and a loosely coordinated, committee-like Navy plan, on the other. The separate services were housed in one governmental department, but they remained distinct and autonomous organizations. As it evolved over the years, the Pentagon moved gradually from the Navy's and toward the Army's conception. Second, the statutory changes in organizational structure that were made until 1986 were far-reaching on the civilian side but modest on the military side. Several acts of the Congress significantly increased the power of the Secretary of Defense, but until the 1986 Act, when the power of the Chairman of the Joint Chiefs of Staff was increased, the Chairman's ability to get things done depended mostly on his persuasiveness with his fellow chiefs and his relationship with the Secretary of Defense. His person was so important precisely because his statutory powers were so weak. For forty years after its creation, a fundamental statutory imbalance therefore persisted between a powerful Secretary of Defense and a weak Chairman of the Joint Chiefs of Staff. Third, throughout all the reorganizations until the one in 1986, the military services retained considerable autonomy to develop war plans, to train and equip the forces, and to allocate resources in ways each judged best for their own interests. As a consequence, until 1986, the only agent in the Pentagon that could effectively countervail against service insularity was the Secretary of Defense.

This organizational structure produced three perverse bureaucratic outcomes. First, spending by the services tended to be unbalanced. Because the services retained a large degree of control over how they spent the funds allocated to them, they typically gave too much to modernizing their preferred weapons, bought too few of them because they goldplated them, and allocated too little to the more mundane tasks involved in enhancing the readiness of the forces for combat. The users of the forces that the services trained and equipped—the Commanders-in-Chief (CINCs) of the warfighting commands—had little say over how the resources were spent in peacetime, but they had all the responsibility for fighting with them in wartime. The CINCs want many things, but the readiness of their forces is always high on their list. There was thus a significant disconnection between the ultimate users of defense recourses (the CINCs) and the providers of them (the services). No central military figure stood above the users and providers, effectively able to adjudicate between them.

Second, too much emphasis throughout the entire Pentagon was put on annual budgeteering at the expense of other important activities. Because there was no integrative force on the military side of the Pentagon, the Office of the Secretary of Defense (OSD) spent too much of its time fighting the annual budget wars with the services and the Congress and too little on planning and oversight. As a consequence, OSD became overburdened, overextended into detailed daily management, and overly involved in matters that the military should have initially handled. Rather than oversee and react to military initiatives on those matters that the military properly should have dealt with first, OSD was forced to do the work that the military did not do.

Third, there was too much of what Samuel Huntington called "servicism"—too much of a focus on separate service interests. The services experienced roles and missions conflicts with one another that absorbed too much of their energies. The Army and the Air Force fought over close air support; the Air Force and the Navy, over power projection; the Army and the Marines, over intervention forces. Servicism also led to a less than optimal integration of differing military functions across the services. This lack of integration was often manifested in the interoperability of equipment among the services, especially in communications. In the Grenada operation, for example, the Army on land could not easily communicate with the Navy at sea. Reportedly, because he could not directly speak to the Navy offshore, an Army officer had to use his credit card at a pay phone to call the military command in the United States and be patched through to the naval officers on board ship off the Grenada coast.[21] Servicism also led to service slighting, or downright neglect, of those functions that they did not favor but that were vital to the other services and to the nation's overall military effectiveness. The Air Force and the Navy, for example, traditionally spent fewer funds on air and sea lift than were required to take the Army to where it had to fight. The Air Force traditionally preferred to have dogfights with enemy aircraft in the sky rather than support the Army's troops on the battlefield by bombing enemy positions. Thus, focused mainly on their own interests, the services cooperated less fully with one another than they should have in allocating resources, developing contingency plans for war, and waging war.

## POST–COLD WAR OUTCOMES

How do the current outcomes compare with the traditional ones? Is Pentagon spending unbalanced? Is there too much budgeteering and too little planning? Is there still rampant servicism? A preliminary assessment of Pentagon decision making since 1987 demonstrates that in the first two areas—in the balance struck among modernization, the size of the forces, and their readiness, and in comprehensive, integrated planning—real progress has been made. In the third area—servicism—more moderate but still measurable progress is occurring.[22]

These are exactly the outcomes to be expected given the nature of the Goldwater-Nichols reforms. The 1986 legislation brought about four significant changes in the military side of the Pentagon. First, the legislation strengthened the powers of the Chairman of the Joint Chiefs of Staff. He was made the principal military advisor to the President and the Secretary of Defense and was charged with the responsibility of giving military advice that looked across the services rather than merely reflecting the corporate, compromised view of the Joint Chiefs. He was given control over the Joint Staff, which now works for him. And he was charged with the responsibility for developing strategic and contingency plans and for giving the President and the Secretary advice on matters of resource allocation. Second, the legislation enhanced the voice of the CINCs in the resource allocation process by encouraging them to express their preferences on resource allocation throughout the Pentagon's Planning, Programming and Budgeting System (PPBS) and by requiring the Chairman to provide advice to the Secretary of Defense on the priorities of the CINCs. In essence, the Chair was made the spokesman for the CINCs. Third, the legislation took steps to make the CINCs' command authority commensurate with their responsibilities. They could, for example, now fire their component commanders and could issue orders directly to the forces under their control rather than through the component commanders, as had been the case. Fourth, the legislation created a joint officer specialty and required that all officers who make it to flag rank must first have served in designated joint billets. The Act altered officer career incentives by making joint duty mandatory for promotion. The effect of the 1986 reforms has been to produce more integrated military planning and to create a counterweight on the military side of the Pentagon against servicism. In the post–Cold War Pentagon, there is no longer simply one institutional countervailer against service parochialism, but two: the Secretary and the Chairman.

By themselves, however, the 1986 reforms could not have produced such measurable progress without two additional ingredients: an aggressive Chairman determined to exploit his newfound authority, and a Defense Secretary determined to control the Pentagon and to manage in as planned and balanced a fashion as possible the downsizing of the military establishment. The Cheney-Powell management team has made an effort to increase the effectiveness of Pentagon planning by spending more time on it, by continuing to use biennial budgeting for Pentagon purposes, and by aggressively using the Defense Planning Guidance (DPG) mechanism to give better direction to Pentagon planning.

## FOUR TESTS OF GOLDWATER-NICHOLS

We can derive an approximate assessment of the effectiveness of both the Goldwater-Nichols reforms and the Cheney-Powell management style by looking at four examples of Pentagon action since 1989: (1) the development of the Base Force and the new military strategy; (2) the balance that has been planned over the next five years among modernization, readiness, and force size; (3) the military conduct of the Persian Gulf War; and (4) the current status of the roles and missions disputes among the services. The first example bears upon the nature of current planning in the Pentagon; the second, on the degree of balance in resource allocation; and the third and fourth, on the state of servicism. The first two examples show that real progress has been made in planning and resource balance, though much work still needs to be done; the third, that significant progress in the joint conduct of military operations has been brought about; the fourth, that the improvement in coping with roles and missions disputes is more mixed.

### The Base Force and the New Military Strategy

The development of the base force and the new military strategy were top-down exercises. Both were developed more or less in tandem and, in the case of the Base Force, in some secrecy by the Joint Staff. Both came at the instigation of Cheney and Powell. Both avoided the cumbersome, oftentimes convoluted, and nearly always stylized process of strategic planning that had characterized previous exercises. Both were then presented to the service chiefs for their approval.[23] As Sharon Weiner notes:

> It was only after the concept [of Base Force] was fully developed and reviewed that it was presented to the services [by Powell himself] by way of an audience with the service chiefs. By this time, the base force concept was a fait accompli; the service chiefs voiced little disagreement in public.... The key is to remember that the base force was developed by the Chairman and sold to the defense establishment from the top down.[24]

In the case of the Base Force, it was the budget that drove force planning. The Base Force was designed around the resources that the Joint Staff estimated would be available by fiscal year 1996. Preliminary planning for the Base Force began in the Joint Staff at the end of Admiral Crowe's tenure as Chairman and was based on an informed estimate that a 25 percent reduction in the defense budget was in the offing.[25] This early preliminary estimate proved remarkably accurate because the 1990 Budget Enforcement Act mandated an 11.3 percent decline in real budget authority for defense in fiscal year 1991 and a 3 percent per annum decrease after that for the next four years, or about 25 percent for the five-year period.[26] Powell wanted to avert budgetary warfare and open bloodletting among the services and have the military itself guide the cuts. He therefore had the Joint Staff further refine the work done under Crowe and then presented it to the service chiefs on May 22, 1989, nearly five months before the passage of the 1990 Budget Enforcement Act, and he gained their acquiescence to it.[27] In developing and selling the Base Force, General Powell clearly exploited the authority given to him by the Goldwater-Nichols Act to present his views on resource allocation. It was a prime example of an aggressive Chairman taking full advantage of the powers that had been granted him.

The development of the new military strategy followed a similar course. It came out of the Office of the Undersecretary of Defense for Policy, with heavy input from the Chairman and the Joint Staff. After assuming his position, Secretary Cheney revamped the strategic planning system of the Pentagon in order to strengthen the planning component of the PPBS system. The Defense Guidance was renamed the Defense Planning Guidance (DPG) and was now to be more of a top-down, not a bottom-up exercise. In addition, beginning with the drafting of Cheney's first DPG in the fall of 1989, detailed program guidance would no longer be given; instead, there would be a broader focus on policy and strategy. The intent was to make the DPG more of a planning than a programming document.[28] In conjunction with the drafting of the first DPG in the fall of 1989, the Office of the Undersecretary of Defense conducted a study of the emerging security environment. What resulted from this study were the conceptual fundamentals of the Base Force—strategic deterrence, forward presence, crisis response, and reconstitution.

Similarly, the Joint Staff revamped the military side of the strategic planning process, known as the Joint Strategic Planning System (JSPS), both in order to incorporate the new statutory responsibilities that the Goldwater-Nichols Act had given to the Chairman and to simplify a process that had become cumbersome. However, much of Powell's input into the new military strategy, which culminated in the January 1992 document *The National Military Strategy 1992*, came not in the guise of formal written guidance from the Chairman that had ground its way through the revised process, but in the form of oral communications to the Joint Staff and the services. Harry Rothmann argues that oral rather than written instructions from Powell were issued because of the rapid changes in the international environment. There simply was not the time to send the Chairman's guidance through the JSPS, no matter how streamlined it may have become, because events were continually outpacing the planning system.

This explanation may be plausible, although the Base Force and the new strategy were at a general enough level, and forward looking enough, that they did not have to be overtaken by daily events. For whatever reason it was done, the fact that Powell made his required input into the JSPS and set the bounds of overall strategy through oral utterances shows how strong he had become. Again, Powell, in conjunction with the OSD, made aggressive use of his new statutory authority to give advice to the Secretary and the President on strategic planning.

## Degree of Balanced Spending

The second example of Pentagon action since 1989—the planned allocation of resources among the modernization, force size, and readiness accounts—shows some progress, though there is still substantial room for improvement. Any given defense budget can be broken up into three areas: investment (research-development and procurement), or how much is spent to modernize weapons; force size, or how many and what type of standing combat forces to have; and readiness, or how well trained the standing forces are for war, how quickly they can be sent to where they are needed, and how sustainable they are once in combat.[29] Too often in the past, the readiness of the forces, the number of major weapons with which they were equipped, the air and sea lift to transport them abroad, and their sustainability were all less than they should have been because they were partially sacrificed for modernization. Previously, new weapons were valued above all else.

In planning for the Base Force, Cheney and Powell attempted to strike a better balance among these three components. They made a deliberate decision to have a smaller, but well-trained, ready, transportable, and sustainable standing force.[30] The tradeoff made was to decrease procurement by significantly slowing down the pace of weapons modernization. In analyzing the Defense Department's fiscal years 1992–96 defense program, William Kaufmann and John Steinbruner noted that Cheney had cut procurement by 27 percent, personnel by 22 percent, research and development by 21.3 percent, and operation and maintenance by 20.4 percent. They stated that "the biggest loser is Pentagon procurement" and that "he [Cheney] has reduced operation and maintenance less than military personnel, which suggests that he is giving combat readiness more than lip service."[31] Even though Kaufmann and Steinbruner are tough critics of Cheney's 1992–96 budgets, believing the request to be too large and arguing that the same missions could be done with a smaller and less costly force, they still found a more reasoned balance in the force that Cheney was requesting.

Cheney and Powell, however, have not been completely successful in the effort to strike a better balance. Their own projections show an increase in the defense budget beginning in 1997.[32] In analyzing the five-year program, Robert Hale, Assistant Director of the National Security Division of the Congressional Budget Office, argued that "the level of real defense budget authority the Administration has proposed for 1995 will not be enough to support the smaller forces in the long run."[33] The reason is that the next generation of weapons systems that the Pentagon hopes to procure in the later 1990s will be more expensive than the Pentagon has planned for. Hale estimated that the annual procurement costs to maintain the 1995 forces over the long term, figured in 1991 dollars, is $67 billion with current equipment and $109 billion with the planned-for modernized equipment, or $40 billion more than the amount budgeted for procurement in fiscal year 1995.[34] Thus, while a better balance has been struck for the next five years, the problem has not been solved beyond 1997.

Still, by the Pentagon's past performance, this is measurable, even if not overwhelming, progress. The fact that some real improvement in spending balance has been made is due to Cheney's and Powell's determination to have a ready and sustainable military instrument and to advice on the allocation resources that a strengthened and determined Chairman can now offer.[35]

## Conduct of the Persian Gulf War

The actual military conduct of the Persian Gulf War is a third benchmark by which to measure the effectiveness of the 1986 changes in Pentagon management. The Desert Storm campaign was not without its blemishes, and it revealed some important shortcomings in the forces. But compared to past combat action, it was outstanding in one crucial respect: Because of the greater authority the 1986 legislation gave to the theater commanders (the CINCs), General Schwarzkopf was able to command his forces without undue interference from the services and from Washington. Goldwater-Nichols simplified the chain of command between Washington and the theater and gave the CINCs more authority over their component commands. The difference this made for the operation of the forces in the field is easily measured by comparing the Defense Department's post mortem on the 1983 Beirut operation with its interim report on Desert Storm.

The U.S. forces sent to Beirut by President Reagan in 1983 for a "presence" mission were attacked by a suicidal terrorist driving a truck loaded with explosives and suffered over 200 casualties. The Long Commission concluded:

that the "presence" mission was not interpreted the same by all levels of the chain of command and that perceptual differences regarding that mission, including the responsibility of the USMNF [United States Multinational Forces] for the security of Beirut International Airport, should have been recognized and corrected by the chain of command.[36]

The Long Commission found that security at the U.S. base was lax because the forces in the field were not alerted to intelligence reports circulating in Washington that an attack might occur. Washington was aware of these reports, as was the U.S. Commander in Chief, Europe (USCINCEUR), under whose responsibility the Beirut operation ultimately fell. The Long Commission found that there was "a lack of effective command supervision of the United States Multinational Force security posture." Because of the great distance of CINCEUR from Beirut and because of the undue length in the chain of command, this information from Washington never got to the field commander of the forces in Beirut. Washington had been alerted to a possible terrorist attack, but the forces at the airport were not. As a consequence, they had not taken simple precautions that could have foiled it. The subsequent withdrawal of U.S. forces from Lebanon heavily damaged U.S. credibility among its Middle Eastern Allies.

In its interim report on Desert Storm, the Defense Department concluded: "The success of these operations can be partially attributed to the impact GNA [the Goldwater-Nichols Act] has had on the Defense Department."[37] The House Armed Services analysis was more explicit in its assessment:

Goldwater-Nichols gave the CINCs authorities commensurate with their long-held responsibility for the conduct of war. Most of the added authorities, such as command, employment of forces, and hiring and firing of subordinates were exercised by General Schwarzkopf in the Persian Gulf war. It also gave the CINC significant authority over logistics and support.

The most identifiable feature was the streamlined chain of command from Washington to the field commander. General Schwarzkopf, not the Joint Chiefs of Staff, controlled operations in the theater. The theater commander also was in complete control over combat forces.

Because of the single chain of command, there was little opportunity to revisit decisions endlessly, as is the usual Pentagon practice. *Goldwater-Nichols did not terminate interservice disagreements—it made their resolution possible.*[38]

Desert Storm was a success for many reasons, but one of them was because the warfighter could fight without one hand tied behind his back.

### Roles and Missions Disputes

The final example by which to assess the effectiveness of current Pentagon management is the status of the roles and missions disputes among the services. Here the record is less impressive, and the progress in resolving long-standing issues hardly noticeable. At first glance, this assessment may appear strange. How can an argument be made that more integrated military planning and better resource allocation is taking place when little or no progress is being made in resolving roles and missions disputes? Does not the persistence of the latter prevent the existence of the former? Are the two not mutually exclusive?

The apparent paradox is easily explained, and the key lies in the last quotation from the House Armed Services Committee's report on Desert Storm. Goldwater-Nichols did not abolish service disputes over roles and missions because it did not abolish the services. What it did try to do was to make the services primarily trainers, equippers, and weapons developers for the warfighters and to make the Chairman of the JCS, the Joint Staff, and the CINCs the transservice integrators and warfighters. As long as the services exist, however, as long as they have a role in training, equipping, and developing the forces, they will inject their preferences into the military establishment. That is not all bad. After all, the services do have tremendous expertise about different modes of warfare. They engender a sense of loyalty, tradition, and comradeship that is essential to successful combat. They do train and equip the forces. Much of what they offer is crucial to an effective U.S. military establishment. What Goldwater-Nichols did, then, was not to end interservice disputes, but rather to create an institutionalized force on the military side to wage constant war against it.

Disputes will rise to the fore from time to time as long as the services exist. In one respect, they are healthy because competition produces better results than monopoly. In another respect, they are unhealthy because they often produce too much redundancy. The trick is to manage interservice disputes in such a way as to maximize the benefits of competition and minimize the costs of duplication. Interservice rivalries should be viewed as one of the costs of doing business, but, as with all business costs, they should be kept low.[39]

## CONCLUSION: THE CASE FOR "CREEPING JOINTNESS"

The Goldwater-Nichols reforms were the fourth major legislative reorganization of the U.S. military establishment since the end of World War II. The 1947 National Security Act created a national military establishment and set the precedent for a single defense department. The 1949 Amendments to that act established the Department of Defense and significantly enhanced the authority of the Secretary of Defense. The 1958 Reorganization Act created a powerful Secretary of Defense. The 1986 Act created a powerful Chairman of the Joint Chiefs of Staff. Are more such reorganizations required?

The answer offered here is "no." Rather, a strong case can be made that, barring the abolishment of the military services, such reorganizations for the time being have run their course. Instead, what is required is time for the 1986 reforms to fully work their will. This is a matter more of what I call "creeping jointness" than it is of additional legislative reorganizations. The evidence presented here suggests that the 1986 reforms are working and that Pentagon management has improved significantly. Other studies have confirmed the conclusions reached here.[40] What appeared to many at the time as marginal changes have begun to produce big results. An early, but perceptive, observer of the post-1986 Pentagon wrote:

> Although on the surface changes in the roles and structure of joint organizations may appear relatively minor, a major cultural change is under way. The predominance of the services in planning, programming, and budgeting is gradually being modified to give a significant role to the joint military structure, particularly to the chairman, the CINCs, and the Joint Staff. The services, of necessity, must continue to play key roles as they fund, administer, support, train, and provide forces for the CINCs, but the joint voice is being heard and listened to far more than before. As one CINC told the author, "When we knock they have to open the door."[41]

The issue now is for future Defense Secretaries and Chairmen of the JCS to fully utilize the statutory authority they currently have. Secretary of Defense Weinberger initially opposed the Goldwater-Nichols legislation and did little during his tenure to make it work. Cheney has been committed to it. Chairman Crowe went slowly with the Goldwater-Nichols reforms. He chose his issues carefully so as not to antagonize the services and went cautiously in implementing the legislation so as to preserve their spirit of hesitant cooperation. But he had an agenda and favored the 1986 Act. Powell accelerated the pace of implementing Goldwater-Nichols. In retrospect, he had little choice. With two military operations and severe budget cuts, all during his first two years, he had to exploit the powers the 1986 Act gave him if he wanted to run a successful military operation. The Gulf War was especially critical in pushing Powell to take full advantage of the powers Goldwater-Nichols had granted him. As Powell was reputed to have said during the warplanning phase of Desert Storm: "We go, we win."[42] The reputation of the U.S. military establishment was on the line. No more Vietnams could be tolerated. The crucible of war forced the pace of reform.

The ultimate test of the effectiveness of the Goldwater-Nichols reforms is what the military officers who have to live with them think. The evidence is clear about the impact of the reforms on career tracks. In the past, the fast track to flag rank was a service command billet and then a posting on the service staff in the Pentagon. Today, the fast track is a command billet and then a posting on the Joint Staff. Before, the service staffs got the best of their officers; the Joint Staff, whatever was left. Now, the Joint Staff gets the best the services have, and the service staffs get whatever is left. What inside participants disagree about is whether the officers who seek out joint duty become less parochial in their outlook, less service focused, and evolve to a truly joint outlook; or whether they are merely punching their tickets, donning the cloak of jointness when required, and then casting it off when returning to their service. The system does work with only joint ticket punchers. It will work best with truly joint thinkers who place the coherence of the national military strategy above service parochialism.

## NOTES

1. President Bush first spelled out the new strategy in his speech to the Aspen Institute Symposium, Aspen, Colorado, on August 2, 1990. Secretary of Defense Cheney elaborated on it in his testimony before the House and Senate Armed Services Committees in connection with the Department of Defense fiscal year 1992–93 budget on February 7 and 21, 1991, respectively. The most recent complete statements of the new military strategy are found in Colin L. Powell, *The National Military Strategy 1992* (Washington, DC: U.S. Government Printing Office, 1992); and Richard Cheney, *Annual Report of the Secretary of Defense to the President and the Congress* (Washington, DC: U.S. Government Printing Office, 1992), pp. 1–19.

2. During the Cold War, four criteria were used to size the U.S. nuclear force: (1) finite or minimum deterrence—the forces needed to destroy a significant percentage of the Soviet Union's most populated cities; (2) equality in the size of forces—the forces needed to match the size of the Soviet forces, on the grounds that forces equal in size were equal in political effect; (3) extended deterrence—the forces needed to convince the Western Europeans and the Japanese over whom the U.S. nuclear umbrella was extended that they were well protected; and (4) damage limitation—the forces needed to minimize damage to the U.S. homeland should it have to wage a nuclear war against the Soviets. Only the first criterion invariably calls for a small deterrent; the next three criteria were used by U.S. Administrations during the Cold War to justify forces much larger than the minimum deterrent. With the United States and Russia already on the path toward nuclear reduction, the second and fourth factors will no longer drive up the size of the U.S. nuclear force. This leaves the first and third factors as the ones that will primarily determine the size of the U.S. nuclear force in the post–Cold War world.

3. Before the United States and the Soviet Union signed the Strategic Arms Reductions Treaty (START) on July 31, 1991, the United States and the Soviet Union had, respectively, about 11,600 and 10,200 strategic nuclear warheads. Under the terms of the START Treaty, each nation is required to reduce its warhead arsenals by about 30 percent, giving the United States 8,600 to 9,000 warheads and the Soviet Union 6,500 to 7,000. The START Treaty limits both powers to 6,000 accountable warheads on 1,600 deployed strategic nuclear delivery vehicles. (The discrepancy between the higher figures and accountable warheads results from the fact that gravity bombs on planes are counted only as one warhead, even though bombers carry more than one bomb). Unilateral initiatives and the Bush-Yeltsin Summit in June 1992 produced additional agreements to reduce strategic arsenals on both sides to a range of 3,000 to 3,500 warheads by the year 2003. The flexible

ceiling reflects agreement to deploy asymmetrical force levels. More important, the Russians agreed to destroy all multiple, independent target reentry vehicles (MIRVed) for land-based intercontinental ballistic missiles (ICBMs), the core of their strategic force structure, and the most long-standing goal in U.S. arms negotiating strategy. The United States also agreed to reduce its deployed submarine-launched ballistic missile (SLBM) forces by 50 percent. See R. Jeffrey Smith, "Arms Talks Devoid of Usual Anxieties," *The Washington Post*, June 18, 1992, p. A38; and Thomas L. Friedman, "Reducing the Russian Arms Threat," *The New York Times*, June 17, 1992, p. A11.

4. Concerns about the credibility of the U.S. nuclear umbrella to the Western Europeans, for example, drove up the size of the ballistic missile force constructed by the Kennedy Administration, probably by a factor of three or more. See Robert J. Art, "The United States: Nuclear Weapons and Grand Strategy," in *Security with Nuclear Weapons?*, ed. Regina Cowen Karp, (Oxford: Oxford University Press, 1991), pp. 77–86.

5. The Nuclear Non-Proliferation Treaty (NPT), which is up for review in 1995, requires the nuclear powers to take steps to reduce their arsenals in return for the NPT signatories' agreement to remain non-nuclear.

6. The Missile Defense Act as quoted in *Missing the Target: SDI in the 1990s*, A Report by the Union of Concerned Scientists (Cambridge, MA: 1992), p. 10. See also Lewis A. Dunn, *Containing Nuclear Proliferation*, Adelphi Paper No. 263 (London: International Institute of Strategic Studies, Winter 1991), pp. 63–65; and mimeo from the office of Congressman Les Aspin, "From Deterrence to Denuking: Dealing with Proliferation in the 1990s," February 18, 1992.

7. If they can be made effective and not easily offset by countermeasures, TMD could offer some protection to overseas U.S. forces against ballistic missiles armed with high-explosive conventional or chemical warheads. Because TMD will never be leakproof, they could offer little hope against a ballistic missile nuclear attack. But U.S. nuclear forces should be able to deter such an attack. For a skeptical view of the military value of theater defenses, see Theodore A. Postal, "Lessons of the Gulf War Experience with Patriot," *International Security* 16, No. 3 (Winter 1991–92), pp. 119–172.

8. Matthew Bunn, "Star Wars Redux: Limited Defenses, Unlimited Dilemmas," *Arms Control Today* 21, No. 4 (May 1991), pp. 13, 14; and Harold Brown, "Yes on Patriot, No on SDI," *The Washington Post*, March 27, 1991. For an argument in favor of limited homeland deployment, see Michael Krepon, "Limited ABM Defense: A Prudent Step," *Arms Control Today* 21, No. 8 (October 1991), pp. 15, 19, 20.

9. The United Nations has proved reasonably effective in peacekeeping between Croatia and Serbia, but as with most peacekeeping operations, only after a lot of slaughter had first taken place and only after exhaustion in both warring camps had set in. It has proved unable to engage in successful peacekeeping between Bosnia-Hersgovina and Serbia.

10. The G–7 political leaders (the United States, the United Kingdom, France, Germany, Italy, Japan, and Canada) declared at their July 1991 summit meeting: "We believe the conditions now exist for the United Nations to fulfill completely the promise and the vision of its founders.... We commit ourselves to making the U.N. stronger, more efficient and more effective in order to protect human rights,

to maintain peace and security for all and to deter aggression." "Text of the G–7 Political Declaration," *Asahi Evening News*, July 17, 1991, p. 3. See also Paul Lewis, "World Leaders at the U.N. Pledge to Broaden Its Role to Achieve a Lasting Peace," *The New York Times*, February 1, 1992, p. A1.

11. A standing U.N. military force is likely to be more of a deterrent to aggression than one organized on an ad hoc basis after aggression has occurred, as was the case in the Gulf War. The problem is that the first type of force is more difficult to bring into existence than the second. Thus, the type of force best suited for deterrent purposes is the one hardest to create.

12. The information about the attitudes of government leaders in East Asia and Western Europe toward a U.S. military presence is based on 17 interviews conducted with governmental officials and with scholars in research institutes close to official thinking in Tokyo in July 1991; 20 interviews with scholars in research institutes close to official thinking in Beijing in July 1991; and 40 interviews conducted with NATO officials in Brussels and with officials of defense and foreign affairs ministries in London, Brussels, Paris, and Bonn in January 1992.

13. This statement is based on interviews conducted in Washington, DC, in May and December 1991 with U.S. government officials who carefully monitor East European matters. NATO has not yet agreed to membership for these three nations, but it has devised an arrangement called the North Atlantic Cooperation Council (NACC), which is an expansion of the North Atlantic Council, to provide a more formal NATO link to the former Warsaw Pact nations and the republics of the former Soviet Union. Through this mechanism, all these nations are members of a NATO organization even though they are not members of NATO itself. For a concise description of the NACC, see Stephen J. Flanagan, "NATO and Central Europe," *The Washington Quarterly* 15, No. 2 (Spring 1992), pp. 141–153.

14. For three alternatives to GPALS, each of which would cost less than the Bush proposal, see Congressional Budget Office, *Costs of Alternative Approaches to SDI*, CBO Papers, May 1992.

15. The same logic of averting deployment at this time of a space-based defense also applies to a land-based defense. From one standpoint, the issue of deployment of a land-based defense is moot because the Pentagon has slipped the date from 1997 to 1998. From another standpoint, the issue is crucial because plans made now to deploy systems later might adversely affect the current internal political evolution of Russia. Congress has made clear that the 1991 Missile Act is not a decision to deploy, but one to develop a system for deployment. This distinction should be maintained. The political evolution of Russia should be a critical factor in any deployment decision, which means that it should not be made on technical grounds alone.

16. Cheney, *Annual Report of the Secretary of Defense*, p. 9.

17. I am indebted to Samuel P. Huntington for this insight from his speech delivered at the Conference on Reconstitution, Force Structure, and Industrial Strategy held by the John M. Olin Institute for Strategic Studies, Center for International Affairs, Harvard University, Cambridge, MA, May 7–8, 1992.

18. Because I believe in the predictions of balance of power theory, I am skeptical that the United States can indefinitely retain its preeminent position. The use of power is never benign to all actors, and it begets counters and checks to it. What I prescribe is therefore more in the way of a delaying than a preventive tactic. For a

short, perceptive statement about the potential effects of unbalanced power, see Kenneth N. Waltz, "America as a Model for the World?" *PS: Political Science and Politics*, December 1991, pp. 667–670.

19. The Pentagon's Draft Planning Guidance (DPG) for the fiscal years 1994–99 time frame smacked of such arrogant unilaterialism. As described in an excerpt: "Our first objective is to prevent the reemergence of a new rival, either on the territory of the former Soviet Union or elsewhere, that poses a threat on the order of that posed formerly by the Soviet Union. After much political opposition within the United States and from abroad, particularly on the grounds that such planning could provoke the very thing it was designed to avoid, the DPG was revised to put more emphasis on regional threats: "The third goal is to preclude any hostile power from dominating a region critical to our interests, and also thereby to strengthen the barriers against the re-emergence of a global threat to the interests of the U.S. and our allies." The language appears somewhat softened, though the ultimate goal to me looks the same. It appears that the State Department's preferences for "collective engagement" prevailed over those of the Defense Department for U.S. unilateralism. For the first quote, see *The New York Times*, March 8, 1992, p. 8; for the second, *The New York Times*, May 24, 1992, p. 14.

20. For more details on Secretary of State Baker's views on collective engagement, see Thomas L. Friedman, "Baker Spells Out U.S. Approach: Alliances and 'Democratic Peace,' " *The New York Times*, April 22, 1992, p. A6.

21. This rumor was investigated by the Senate Armed Services Committee and was found to be correct in its fundamentals. I am indebted to John Hamre, who works on the Senate committee, for verification of this newspaper report.

22. It is important to stress that this assessment of the effectiveness of the Goldwater-Nichols reforms must be preliminary. The Goldwater-Nichols reforms made four important changes, three of which have produced clear results. The fourth will take more time because it tackles the hardest area of all—changing the mental attitudes of officers and their emotional attachments to their service roles and missions. Thinking jointly, not simply acting jointly, will take time through the educational and socialization reforms prescribed by Goldwater-Nichols.

23. For information about the development of the Base Force and the new military strategy, I have relied on Harry E. Rothmann, "The National Military Strategy," Chapter 3 of this text; and Sharon K. Weiner, "Adapting to Change: U.S. Defense Policy Confronts the New World Order," unpublished paper, MIT Department of Political Science, August 1991. Colonel Rothmann, as chief of the Strategy Applications Branch, Strategy Division, J–5, Joint Staff, was a participant in the development of both the Base Force and the new military strategy. Sharon K. Weiner conducted a series of interviews with participants in the Base Force deliberations.

24. Weiner, "Adapting to Change," pp. 27–28.

25. Ibid., p. 25.

26. Patrick J. Garrity and Sharon K. Weiner, "U.S. Defense Strategy after the Cold War," *The Washington Quarterly* 15, No. 2 (Spring 1992), p. 58.

27. Weiner, "Adapting to Change," p. 28.

28. From a telephone interview with a civilian in the Pentagon who works in the Office of the Undersecretary of Defense and is involved in the resource allocation process, February 4, 1992.

29. These three accounts correspond, respectively, to the research and develop-

ment and procurement titles, the personnel title, and the operation and maintenance title in the congressional authorizing and appropriations legislation.

30. Cheney first laid out his approach in his testimony before the House Armed Services Committee on February 7, 1991. See pp. 6–12 of that testimony (Department of Defense mimeo).

31. William Kaufmann and John Steinbruner, *Decisions for Defense: Prospects for a New Order* (Washington, DC: The Brookings Institution, 1991), p. 38. I must add that although they note these trends in the fiscal years 1992–96 budget proposal, Kaufmann and Steinbruner are critical of the size of the budget request and believe that the same missions can be accomplished for less cost. See Chapters 7 and 8 of *Decisions for Defense*.

32. "DOD Budget Briefing with Secretary of Defense Dick Cheney," January 29, 1992, appended tables.

33. Robert F. Hale, Statement before the House Armed Services Committee, March 19, 1991, Congressional Budget Office (mimeo), p. 23.

34. Ibid., pp. 23–24.

35. Part of this improvement must be attributed to the greater role that the CINCs play in the Pentagon PPBS system. This role began in the early 1980s but was immeasurably strengthened by the Goldwater-Nichols reforms. For an analysis of how the CINCs have operated in the PPBS system since 1986, see U.S. General Accounting Office, *Roles of Joint Military Organizations in Resource Allocations*, NSIAD–90–76, June 1990.

36. *Report of the DOD Commission on Beirut International Airport Terrorist Act, October 23, 1983* (The Long Commission), Washington, DC: The Commission, December 20, 1983, p. 122.

37. Department of Defense, *Conduct of the Persian Gulf Conflict: An Interim Report to Congress* (Washington, DC: U.S. Government Printing Office, July 1991), p. 26–31.

38. *Defense for a New Era: Lessons of the Persian Gulf War* (Washington, DC: U.S. Government Printing Office, 1992), pp. 41–42. Emphasis added.

39. I do not want to be misunderstood on this point. The Secretary and the Chairman can do more to mitigate interservice rivalry. The four tactical air forces that the Pentagon currently has—the Army's, the Air Force's, the Navy's, and the Marines'—are an excellent place to begin. My only point is that short of abolishing the services, there will always be a degree of rivalry among them for missions because it is impossible to draw hard and fast lines around modern warfare.

40. See Barry Blechman and James Blackwell, eds., *Making Defense Reforms Work* (Washington, DC: Pergamon-Brassy's, 1990), Chapters 6 and 7; U.S. General Accounting Office, *Compliance with Legislative Mandate for Contingency Planning*, NSIAD–91–312, September 1991; U.S. General Accounting Office, *Roles of Joint Military Organizations in Resource Allocations*, NSIAD–90–76, June 1990; U.S. General Accounting Office, *Implementation Status of Joint Officer Personnel Policies*, NSIAD–89–113, April 1989; U.S. General Accounting Office, *Progress and Concerns at JCS and Combatant Commands*, NSIAD–89–83, March 1989; *1992 Annual Report of the Secretary of Defense to the President and the Congress*, pp. 141–153; House Committee on Armed Services, Investigations Subcommittee, *Hearings on Implementation of the Goldwater-Nichols DoD Reorganization Act of 1986*, 100th Congress, 2nd Session, 1988; House Committee on Armed Services,

Investigations Subcommittee, *Hearing on DoD Reorganization Implementation*, 101st Congress, 1st Session, 1989.

41. Admiral Robert P. Hilton, "The Role of Joint Military Institutions in Defense Resource Planning," in Blechman and Blackwell, *Making Defense Reforms Work*, p. 163.

42. Quoted in Bob Woodward, *The Commanders* (New York: Simon and Schuster, 1991), p. 314.

# 5

# The New Politics of the Defense Budget

## *Gordon Adams*

The United States is at a major turning point in its defense plans and budgets. These changes suggest that the politics of defense budgets and spending are dramatically more complex than are sometimes argued. For much of the Cold War period, defense budgets in peacetime remained relatively stable and successive generations of military hardware proceeded largely uninterrupted. Few bases were closed, and overall employment in the defense industry remained relatively stable.

The stability of policy and the apparent imperviousness of the defense structure to major changes encouraged the development of a school of thought that saw that structure as a "military-industrial complex" or "national security state." According to this analytical construct, defense decisions were made within relatively closed boundaries, among a constituency that linked the Department of Defense (DoD) and the military services to the defense industry and both to constituencies and elected representatives who benefited from defense spending decisions.[1] This system was well defended against major change or systematic reform; hardware programs advanced almost inexorably into production, and bases were carefully protected by the services, local supporters, and elected representatives in Washington, D.C.

The unraveling of the Cold War military architecture and the budgets that sustained it indicate that this theory of the politics of defense was, at best, inadequate and, at worst, inaccurate. The power of the military-industrial complex, if it was real, ought to have been sufficient to prevent severe budget decline, hardware cancellation, and base closings, the very events that took place in the 1990s.

This chapter argues that the politics of defense have always been more complex than simple theory suggests. Defense decisions and budgetary allocations have always been influenced by international forces and events, fiscal and economic requirements, bureaucratic behavior, and domestic politics. These factors tend to be discussed as if each were, by itself, a sufficient explanation of defense plans, programs, and budgets. In fact, each of these elements interacts with the others. Those who would separate politics and finance from policy in the defense policy arena cannot fully understand how and why defense decisions are made.[2]

International forces and events clearly set a critical context for defense plans and budgets. U.S. national security documents are written in response to the international situation, laying out a national strategy that is sometimes asserted as the sole explanation for defense plans and budgets. By contrast, the international arena is said by some to play a secondary or even inconsequential role in shaping the programs and details in the annual DoD budgetary presentation.

Fiscal and economic considerations also play a role in defense plans. The defense budget began to decline in fiscal year 1986, well before the international upheavals of the late 1980s had begun. Even during the height of the Cold War, overall federal fiscal policy and the state of the economy played a role in the volume of resources available for defense and the rate at which those resources were obligated.[3]

Global events and fiscal constraints are still insufficient to explain a wide number of defense decisions, including the persistence of duplicate roles and missions among the military services and the acquisition of some hardware programs whose relationship to overall national strategy is questionable or whose actual military value is doubtful. The logic of bureaucratic behavior is the third factor in the politics of defense. There is demonstrable evidence that the push and pull of bureaucratic lobbying and conflict have an impact on defense outcomes.[4]

Finally, defense planning, decision making, and budgeting are an integral part of the U.S. political system, involving Congress, communities, industry, and the national electorate. Debates over the survival or demise of key weapons programs, over decisions to go to war, over base closings and contract awards, and even over the size of the defense budget itself are played out in a domestic political context. It is hard to doubt, for example, that the strong national defense stand taken by candidate Ronald Reagan in 1980 had an impact on his electoral fortunes, which in turn made possible the defense budget and program expansion of the early 1980s.[5]

The interplay among these different factors is nothing new. Arguably, however, that interplay was somewhat less visible during much of the 1950s to the 1980s, since peacetime defense budgets remained relatively stable, as did the specific, major military threat to the United States. Periods of great change, however, tend to expose these complexities of the policy process.

As the United States enters the post–Cold War world, the defense policy process faces a difficult set of fundamental choices: a dramatically changed world with a smaller immediate threat; severe fiscal constraints; a need to redefine military roles and missions, and the forces, hardware, and budgets that go with them; all in the context of a congressional and public debate over the pace of defense reductions and the uses of savings from a smaller military budget. The defense plans, programs, and budgets of the twenty-first century will be shaped by the interaction of these forces.

Moreover, each of the factors that has an impact on defense is changing. The first observable change was fiscal, as the debate over defense budgets shifted from the turf of the threat to the turf of the deficit, with the passage of the Gramm-Rudman-Hollings Deficit Reduction Act in October 1985.[6] The second major change was global as the Soviet threat declined, and first the Warsaw Pact and then the Soviet Union itself disintegrated. The bureaucratic politics inside DoD also moved from an ethos of relative agreement to one of competition for scarce resources and a simultaneous necessity for greater joint cooperation in planning and operations. Congressional views of defense shifted from a policy to a fiscal perspective, while the congressional process underwent an explosion of staff, committees, subcommittees, and nondefense-related members and committee involvement in defense issues. Finally, the politics of the country shifted from a concern with global threats and competition to an inner-directed focus on domestic problems. Combined, these changes are putting the defense budget and planning system under the greatest stress it has faced since the buildup prior to World War II.

## GLOBAL CHANGE AND NATIONAL STRATEGY

Since the Korean War, it has been relatively easy to argue the case for some significant level of U.S. defense spending. The large strategic and conventional military capabilities of the Soviet Union, combined with an apparently aggressive Soviet strategy of involvement in conflicts in other regions of the world, set a baseline against which most U.S. defense budgets were justified by a succession of administrations.

The Soviet threat provided an understandable explanation for the size and distribution of technologies in U.S. strategic nuclear forces, especially with the clear Soviet attempt to "catch up" to U.S. strategic capabilities after the Cuban missile crisis in 1962. The United States, seeking to maintain some rough parity with Soviet strategic forces, needed (1) a triad of capabilities, some part of which would remain invulnerable to Soviet attack; (2) bombers that could penetrate sophisticated and extensive Soviet air defenses; and (3) in the mid–1980s, plans to develop the kind of strategic defenses that could protect against a limited Soviet attack and complicate nuclear battle planning for the Soviet military.

So, too, Soviet and Warsaw Pact conventional military capabilities justified U.S. (and NATO) conventional forces and hardware, as well as tactical nuclear capabilities. As long as a massive Soviet military force was forward positioned in the heart of Europe, along with Soviet-armed client states, a firm Western alliance was needed to defend its member countries and to provide the framework for a significant, forward deployed U.S. military presence in Europe. The U.S. conventional military hardware programs could be justified as necessary to compete technologically with a massive Soviet military investment, from helicopters to tanks to aircraft to air defenses.

U.S. forward deployed tactical nuclear weapons could be justified by the need to confront overwhelming Warsaw Pact nuclear superiority with the risk that an attack would be met with a nuclear response. The need to rebuff a Warsaw Pact attack justified a sizeable U.S.-based conventional force, as well as significant airlift and mobilization planning. A growing Soviet naval capability clearly provided one important justification for a sizeable U.S. Navy, with up to fifteen carrier battle groups. By and large, moreover, the Soviet nuclear and conventional capabilities based in eastern Russia and Siberia, as well as the risk of a Soviet proxy attack from North Korea, provided a justification for forces deployed in Japan, South Korea, and the Pacific.

There were debates among U.S. military planners over the wider framework within which U.S. force structure could be explained,[7] but even forces designed for and used between 1950 and 1990 in regions other than Europe and the Northern Pacific were derivative of the forces developed for those theaters. Moreover, U.S. uses of force, whether in Latin America or Southeast Asia, were justified in terms of the global threat posed by Soviet military power and intervention. The Eurasian focus of a global conflict drove force planning and most acquisition choices, even if the forces never actually engaged in combat against the Soviet Union and its allies.

If one had to imagine a change that would significantly undermine Cold War force structure justifications, hardware choices, and strategic planning, it would be hard to find one more fundamental than the dissolution of the Warsaw Pact, the disintegration of the Soviet Union, and the withering away of the Soviet military and its research and production complex. Yet all this took place between 1989 and 1992. The weltanschauung of the Cold War simply evaporated. Although one could continue to argue that the military forces that remain in the successor states to the Soviet Union are sizeable, having large nuclear capabilities and a significant number of personnel and equipment, their capabilities have declined rapidly and it is virtually impossible to argue that these forces pose a direct and immediate threat to the United States. As CIA Director Robert Gates testified in January 1992:

> The threat to the United States of deliberate attack from [the former Soviet Union] has all but disappeared for the foreseeable future. . . . [T]he capabilities of the strategic

forces are being significantly reduced. Modernization programs are likely to be delayed or abandoned and training will be cut back. The readiness of conventional forces is at the lowest level in many years. Naval deployments continue to decline from already reduced levels and inadequate training is degrading the combat capability of the general-purpose forces.[8]

Smaller nuclear forces, with a divided command, could pose security problems for the United States, but these are clearly of a different nature than the problem of strategic deterrence in the face of a Soviet nuclear superpower. Strategic forces that are scarcely being modernized require dramatically different planning assumptions for U.S. strategic force acquisition. A dissolved conventional military structure and military alliance eliminates much of the justification for large, forward deployed forces in Europe. Significantly longer warning times lead to basic changes in the planning assumptions for land and air forces, both active and reserve, based in the United States. The complete disappearance of significant Soviet activity in other regions, from Asia to Africa to Latin America, requires entirely different assumptions about the role of the U.S. military in those theaters.

In the 1990s, U.S. strategic policy and defense planners find themselves at a juncture much like the one they faced in the late 1940s, when previous assumptions about the U.S. role in the world and the place of military force were fundamentally outdated. A new strategic rationale for forces and budgets had yet to emerge. The size, composition, roles, and missions of the military had to be shaped and redefined. The 1990s constitute another basic starting point.

The military situation of the United States in the 1990s is different, however, from that of the 1940s. In 1990, the nation had a 2 million–person military corps in place, with another 1.5 million in reserve; 28 Army divisions, 14 carrier battle groups, more than 500 ships in the Navy, and 36 Air Force wing equivalents. What justifies this size and structure? How will the debate over its downsizing and restructuring proceed? In which directions should it be reshaped?

A national debate has begun on these issues as part of a broader discussion of national strategy in the post–Cold War world. The DoD has offered its plan for downsizing the forces to a Base Force, which by 1995 would consist of 1.6 million people, 900,000 reservists, 18 Army divisions (plus two cadre divisions), 12 carriers and 450 ships in the Navy, 3 slightly thinned Marine divisions, and 26 Air Force wing equivalents. In 1992, the DoD provided a strategic rationale for this force based largely on regional contingencies, the need for crisis response and the potential need to reconstitute larger forces.[9]

The DoD's global view has not gone uncontested, given the dramatic changes on the international scene. A wide range of views have been put forward, proposing forces ranging from somewhat similar to considerably smaller than those projected by the Defense Department.[10] Perhaps most significant, the Chairman of the House Armed Services has undertaken the unprecedented exercise of laying out a rather detailed set of alternative force structures, all smaller than that presented by DoD, which are intended to guide program and policy decisions made by that committee.[11]

Although many of the alternative proposals cannot be fully separated from the desire to appropriate defense resources for other purposes such as deficit reduction, tax cuts, or domestic programs, each is laid out in the context of a view of the post–Cold War world. Each analyst lays out the likely sources of conflict and threat to the United States and a vision of the role the United States and its military forces should play in the world. Such world views range from proposals that the United States withdraw from much of its involvement in the world to assertions that the post–Cold War world makes international cooperative security possible, hence reducing the need for U.S. military forces.[12]

What is striking about this debate over the future directions of U.S. national strategy is its fundamental nature and the seriousness with which alternative proposals are being treated. The definition of U.S. national security, the content of policy and strategy, and the size and structure of military forces are all at stake. It is also evident that this policy debate is providing only partial guidance, at best, for the reshaping of defense budgets and military forces.

In fact, the debate reflects similar disagreements that prevailed before the Cold War, when the rationale for U.S. national strategy and its forces was equally unclear. One could argue that the United States lacked an integrated strategy, while strong strains of neutrality and anti-militarism existed in the domestic political arena, until the early 1950s.[13] Due to the strength of isolationism in U.S. politics prior to World War II, the scope of U.S. foreign policy was limited. The nation shunned entangling alliances and concentrated most of its efforts on hemispheric affairs. The restricted parameters of U.S. foreign policy made a large standing army unnecessary and the need for close integration between diplomacy and the armed forces unnecessary.[14] It has been suggested that the U.S. victory in World War II was accomplished in large part without the guidance of an integrated national strategy.[15]

Only in 1950, after a difficult process of national reassessment, was a coherent plan created to direct America's external relations and establish objectives that could form the basis of an integrated military force posture.[16] The disappearance of the principal threat to the United States and its interests has thrown that apparently coherent plan into disarray. The weakness of the link between national strategy and specific defense decisions, in the environment of the 1990s, reveals more starkly the interplay of other factors in defense decision making.

## RESOURCE PRESSURES

Defense planning, programs, and budgets have never been free from considerations of resource constraints, though policymakers have consistently argued that they should be.[17] As already noted, defense budgets began to decline well before the disintegration of the Warsaw Pact and the Soviet Union, largely in response to resource constraints. Although the early years of the Reagan Administration saw a rapid growth in defense funding, by mid-decade the rapid increase in the federal deficit had led to a congressional reaction. Defense budget reductions began in fiscal year 1986, as the result of a broader domestic fiscal decision: the passage of Gramm-Rudman-Hollings in October 1985. Given the broad political resistance to revenue increases and further reductions in discretionary domestic spending, the deficit reduction targets could only be met through reductions in the defense budget.

The pressures initiated with the Deficit Reduction Act of 1985 have only increased with time. Although federal deficits briefly shrank to 3.0 percent of U.S. gross national product (GNP) in fiscal year 1989 (from a high of 6.3 percent in fiscal year 1983), they had risen again to 4.7 percent of GNP by fiscal year 1991. Deficits of $352 billion were projected, as of January 1992, for fiscal year 1993. During the 1992 consideration of the defense budget, the Congressional Budget Office (CBO) pointed out that the first priority for any savings from lower-than-projected defense budgets should be devoted first to deficit reduction, since this use was likely to have the most positive effect on long-term U.S. economic growth.[18]

Deficit pressures were joined in the late 1980s by a growing demand for a "peace dividend" to be applied to domestic programs. The White House–Congress budget summit agreement of September 1990 made it difficult to realize such a dividend, since it erected barriers between defense and non-defense spending that prevented the transfer of defense savings to other spending programs. In their early discussions over the fiscal year 1993 defense budget, members of Congress suggested that a strong effort would be made to bring down those walls, permitting such a transfer, potentially in large amounts.[19] The inability of Congress to gather a veto-proof majority for this effort, combined with political considerations discussed later in this chapter, meant its failure. The desire for some such savings, however, clearly continued downward pressure on defense resources.

Resource pressures on defense planning are not new, though they take on a stark relief in the 1990s in the absence of a clear national strategy. Since the ability to raise armies depends on the federal government's capacity to raise revenues, on the state of the economy, and on the public's perception of its ability to support military spending, resource availability has to be considered in the debate over the defense budget.[20] Even in the era of clear statements of national strategy, resource considerations had an impact on defense spending. For example, the *Gaither Report* of 1960 stated:

> However, even large increases in defense spending would not have drastic consequences for our way of life. We could manage moderate increases in defense without any reduction of our present levels of consumption and investment. Even large increases might be possible without any reduction in the private sector of the economy.[21]

President Eisenhower refused to adopt the recommendations of the *Gaither Report*, however, almost entirely for economic reasons. This decision at the end of his term was consistent with the tone of defense policy throughout his administration. The "new look" was a means to escape the heavy expenditures that the strategy of containment required, and it rejected the premise of NSC–68, the 1950 strategic policy statement, that the United States could afford to devote 20 percent of its GNP to defense.

The early history of the Reagan Administration is the exception that proves the resource constraint rule. One of the first defense decisions of the new administration was to request a $32.6 billion increase in the defense budget, the largest and fastest increase in peacetime history.[22] That fiscal buildup continued through fiscal year 1985, but throughout the subsequent years fiscal restraint has largely dominated the defense debate.

## INTERSERVICE RIVALRIES AND JOINTNESS

With the end of the Cold War and the struggle to define defense budgets in a context of shrinking resources, the relationship among the military services has also begun to emerge as a major factor influencing defense policies, programs, and funding. It became clear during and after the Gulf War that each service was determined to ensure for itself a major role in that conflict, driven in part by the desire to demonstrate its utility for military missions beyond those considered part of the Cold War confrontation with the Soviet Union. Six Navy carrier battle groups were mobilized in the region; their contribution to the military effort has been a subject of debate. Marine forces were used in a ground combat mode, while amphibious forces remained offshore. The Air Force has drawn attention to the important role played by combat air power in softening Iraqi defenses, while the Army has demonstrated its capability to deploy in force outside the European region.[23]

Given the resource constraints of the 1990s, the services have also been struggling over the size of the wedges in the budgetary pie. The Navy and the Air Force, for example, have argued over the power projection mission, with an undertone that carriers and strategic bombers provide competing capabilities for that mission. Both the Army and the Marine Corps argue for an important role in providing early deployment of significant ground forces to combat zones. Vice Admiral Roger F. Bacon, Assistant Chief of Naval Operations for Undersea Warfare, noted in April 1992 that attack submarines could provide a wide range of important military capabilities, including missile land attack and covert insertion of special forces, missions not typically assigned to the submarine force.[24]

At the same time that shrinking budgetary resources have exacerbated interservice tensions, they have also increased the pressures for "jointness," ranging from increased cooperative procurement to joint training and exercising. The Air Force and the Army have signed an agreement on joint doctrine; the Navy and the Air Force continue to explore possible cross-service applications of the Navy AX attack bomber technology. One crucial lesson of the Gulf War was clearly the growing need for joint exercises and training to enhance interservice combat operations.[25]

The history of interservice tension in the U.S. military is a long one; it will be only briefly discussed here. Military bureaucracies, like other bureaucracies, develop their own internal values and operating procedures and regularly promote their claim for fiscal resources against each other. Given the size of the U.S. military and the existence of one semi-independent and three independent services, it is hardly surprising that such tensions occur and that each service asserts its independent mission.

The Navy has generally tended to equate U.S. security with command of the sea; the Air Force has defended the importance of air superiority and strategic bombing; and the Army and Marine Corps have argued strongly for the importance of early and consistent domination of the ground. In the 1990s, manifestation of this military "bureaucratic politics" is not new.[26]

The DoD Reorganization Act of 1986, commonly referred to as Goldwater-Nichols (after its major congressional sponsors), has begun to alter the pattern of bureaucratic politics among the services by giving greater decision-making authority to the Chairman of the Joint Chiefs of Staff and the joint service commanders, the ten Commanders-in-Chief (CINCs). As Harry Rothmann describes in Chapter 3, the system for formulating military strategy and for advising the Secretary of Defense has been streamlined to make operational planning and the broad outlines of the military force structure more reflective of the Chairman's views and less captive of service parochialism.

Reforms have not eliminated service rivalries or bureaucratic politics, but combined with a powerful Chairman, the purging of redundant planning documents that were little more than platforms for bureaucratic haggling, and an enforced emphasis on joint duty, they have ameliorated the political playing field where services sought to dominate the planning process. There are, for example, fewer opportunities for what former JCS Chairman David C. Jones describes as "negotiated treaties," which can lead to gaps and unwarranted duplications in our defense capabilities, because individual service chiefs settle disagreements by agreeing to each other's requests even if there is not always a clear strategic justification.[27]

Without the Soviet threat to justify duplications and inefficiencies, the politics of interservice rivalry and negotiation are likely to become significantly more transparent as a source of force and budgetary planning for DoD. The absence of a clear threat or strategic design, combined with rapidly declining resources, is likely to exacerbate both inter- and intra-service tensions. At the same time, the need for a strategic design and for greater efficiency in the use of existing resources is also likely to intensify pressure for interservice agreement, jointness, and the elimination of inefficiencies in the administrative structures of the services. This paradox of conflicting pressures will require future Chairmen to combine strategic vision with the authority granted by Goldwater-Nichols to forge a united military voice in the decision-making process. Not to do so risks opening an irreconcilable gap between resources and missions, and strains the already fragile credibility the Pentagon carries to Capitol Hill when defending its force structure proposals and cost predictions. The failure of reforms to produce a genuine joint approach to planning and force structure issues could pose a major setback to restructuring U.S. military power.

## THE DOMESTIC POLITICS OF DEFENSE

Strategy, resource constraints, and bureaucratic behavior among the armed services provide a partial but still incomplete explanation for defense plans, programs, and resources. The U.S. defense debates take place in a political context that has its own impact on the policy and hardware outcomes. There can be no doubt, in the atmosphere of the early 1990s, that domestic politics has played and will continue to play a forceful role in the evolution of U.S. military forces and budgets. Debates over long-term strategy and force structure pit prominent spokespersons from Congress against the Secretary of Defense, the Chairman of the Joint Chiefs of Staff, and the heads of the military services. Debates over the future of such hardware programs as the Marine Corps' V–22 Osprey, the Navy's F–14 fighter, the Air Force's strategic bomber, and the Navy Seawolf submarine further reflect the impact of the wider domestic political context on defense.

More broadly, as already noted, the compelling political demand for some kind of peace dividend, whether for deficit reduction or domestic needs, is putting inexorable downward pressure on defense resources. More, perhaps, than at any point in time in the post–Cold War era, domestic politics and political needs have intruded into the defense debate. As the Cold War rationale for defense budgets and program choices disappears, the domestic politics of defense becomes a more apparent and (at least in the short term) a more decisive factor in defense policy and budgeting.

Although some analysts are inclined to argue that domestic politics dominate defense decisions, political impact on the behavior of the services and other policymakers is actually relatively subtle. To some extent, the depth of information and resources needed for a detailed scrutiny of national strategy, force structure, and the defense budget, as well as the complex structure of the defense acquisition system, insulate a large number of defense decisions from outside political pressures. Nevertheless, congressional and electoral politics historically have intruded in significant ways into the defense policy process.

The defense budget clearly provides the principal context for the domestic politics of defense, while Congress and national elections provide the arena. The budget is the mechanism through which the executive branch sets defense priorities and reflects its policies. Hardware choices are only possible with funding; troops are trained and exercised, bases built and sustained, and ships sailed with budget resources. Moreover, the defense budget is the communications link between the executive branch and Congress. Through it, elected legislators fashion their own role in military policy and oversee the activities of the services and the Pentagon.

Congress is deeply involved in the process of defense decision making and funding through its scrutiny of the budget. In contrast with many other countries, Congress starts with a significant database on defense choices, policies, and programs, including the Office of Management and Budget's budget document, the Secretary of Defense's annual report, detailed descriptions and cost data on major weapons systems, research and development, military construction, operations and maintenance programs, an itemization of military construction projects, detailed data on the composition of the military forces, volumes of financial data on DoD spending, historical data on DoD spending covering more than forty years, as well as a variety of specialized briefing sheets and publications.

Moreover, Congress and its defense committees receive even more detailed classified data justifying DoD's budget requests, as well as unclassified and classified briefings and testimony from a stream of witnesses from DoD and the military services. From the start, Congress faces less of a problem ferreting out secrets from the Pentagon than it does sifting through the volume of data to separate the important from the insignificant.[28]

The congressional process for reviewing these data is complex. Congressional committees play the key role in this process. The Appropriations committees of the House and Senate have primary responsibility for approving expenditures. Since the 1960s the Armed Services committees of the two chambers, whose membership does not usually overlap with the appropriators, have also become major participants in the defense budget process, authorizing funding for specific programs.[29] After 1974, a third layer of congressional review was created, the Budget committees. The Budget Committee in each chamber considers the entire executive branch budget request and approves overall funding levels for thirteen functions of the federal budget, including national defense.[30]

The Budget Committee receives the defense budget first, along with the entire federal budget, and votes a resolution, which is subsequently debated and passed on the floor of the House and Senate, setting the overall level of defense budget authority. Although the Budget committees do not approve any specific personnel or weapons programs line-items, by virtue of their authority to set overall levels, committee actions can constrain the choices the Armed Services and Appropriations committees can make.

The Armed Services and Appropriations committees hold open and closed hearings involving a stream of executive branch witnesses. Working within the budget ceilings, these committees approve bills covering funding decisions on specific programs, as well as a wide variety of legislative provisions requesting specific items of action by DoD or reports to Congress within the following year. After passage of the authorization and appropriations acts in each house, the differences between the two versions are reconciled through a conference of representatives of the two committees.

To support its complex process for defense decision making, moreover, Congress has considerable resources at its disposal. In and around the formal interactions between congressional committees and the services stand a number of less formal institutions that fill critical information needs for Congress or ensure constant interaction between Congress and DoD over the defense budget. Perhaps most important, Congress has developed an ample supply of staff expertise on defense matters, both for individual members and for the defense committees, as well as a variety of research institutions reporting to Congress on defense matters.[31] Individual members each have at least one staff person with sole or partial responsibility for defense. Each of the committees reviewing the defense budget has staff—minimal for the Budget Committee, but numerous for the Armed Services and Defense Appropriations committees. These committee staff are often people with military or defense policy experience who sometimes move back and forth between the Pentagon and Congress. The possession of a skilled, experienced staff ensures that members of Congress, especially on the key committees, have their own capability to assess defense budgets independently of the Pentagon.

This independent capability has been substantially reinforced by the existence of a number of governmental research and auditing institutions that report to Congress on defense matters, including the budget. For years the General Accounting Office, an auditing arm of Congress, has conducted close scrutiny of defense budgets and spending through its National Security and International Affairs Division. The Congressional Research Service also maintains a staff capability to research defense budget issues for Congress.[32] The 1974 Budget and Impoundment Act created still another organization, the CBO. It includes a significant National Security Division, which researches budget proposals and options in the defense arena for Congress. Most recently, the congressional Office of Technology Assessment (OTA) has begun to analyze defense policy issues for Congress. These different, even overlapping, research capabilities significantly strengthen the ability of Congress to analyze and understand defense budget issues independently of DoD.

Still another important network, which intrudes into the political debate over defense, is the vast array of private and nonprofit think tanks, research and policy groups, trade associations, and contracting firms that focus on the defense budget, defense policy, and defense acquisition, among other concerns.[33] Although not all focus exclusively on the budget, many of them scrutinize the DoD budget request closely and provide Congress (and the Pentagon) with their views.

The military services themselves also maintain constant communication with legislators through (1) congressional liaison offices within the Pentagon that respond to congressional inquiries, and (2) extensions of those offices on Capitol Hill, where the military can brief Congress on budget and policy issues and make themselves available to respond to congressional needs.

Finally, the media provide another important element in the domestic debate over defense, including a substantial "trade press" devoted to specialized coverage of defense matters. Well-informed, consistent coverage of the significant flow of defense information and of congressional debate informs that debate, translates arcane data into accessible language for policymakers, and serves as an informational beltway among Congress, the executive branch, and the defense analytical community.[34]

Thus, there are multiple channels through which defense choices encounter domestic politics. That the debate becomes political is made all the more possible by the fact that *the budget is not delivered to Congress in the framework of a national strategy*. The titles in the budget are devoid of any strategic meaning or measure of military output: Military Personnel, Operations and Maintenance, Procurement, Research and Development, Family Housing, and so forth. This structural characteristic tends to decouple resource allocation decisions from the strategic goals of national security policy.

As a consequence, the political debate over the defense budget tends to be dominated by line-items.[35] The incentives for elected representatives, moreover, have not favored debate over strategy, since their primary concern is reelection.[36] When it comes to defense matters, the priorities of constituents are typically focused on the level and location of spending, not its strategic rationale. Even with the end of the Cold War, members of Congress have little to gain by reducing or eliminating defense bases or projects, while the electoral rewards for promoting defense spending in the district are great.

Although the retention of military bases is the common example of congressional promotion of district interests, there are also frequent congressional wrangles over hardware programs, motivated in part by pressures from constituents.[37] In 1986, for example, the Air Force decided to terminate the T–46 trainer program due to cost overruns and delays. The Senate concurred with the Air Force's decision and voted no funds for the plane in its 1987 defense budget. The maker of the plane, Fairchild Republic Company, is headquartered in New York. After intense lobbying by the New York congressional delegation, the House voted to approve an earlier House Armed Services Committee provision that delayed cancellation and required the Air Force to complete additional testing before reducing or eliminating the T–46 program.[38]

Even strong critics of the Pentagon are not immune from constituent pressures to protect programs and spending levels. Senator Alan Cranston of California campaigned for President in 1984 on a platform that called for deep cutbacks in defense spending and cancellation of several strategic weapons programs. His enthusiasm for reducing defense spending did not include the B–1B bomber, however, a strategic weapon produced in California.[39] In the early 1990s, Senator Christopher Dodd of Connecticut, who was generally critical of defense budget requests, became a strong supporter of the Navy's Seawolf submarine, a program that DoD sought to cancel after one boat with its fiscal year 1993 defense budget request.[40]

Defense contractors are often well aware of the importance of such political support. They work closely with committees and members of Congress to encourage support and, to some degree, activate the local networks of subcontractors and suppliers involved in such programs to provide grass roots encouragement for their programs.

The highly visible political interaction between the contractors and Congress, often with the active involvement of DoD, is what has given rise to the "military industrial complex" school of analysis. One major problem with this school, however, is the reality that not all efforts to maintain a base or a hardware program succeed. In fact, DoD, acting under congressionally sponsored legislation, announced two successive rounds of base-closing in 1988 and 1991.[41] Moreover, with declining defense budgets in the late 1980s, DoD has been able to cancel a large number of weapons programs involving significant employment in many congressional districts.[42]

A close scrutiny of the politics of defense budgets and weapons systems contracting suggests that this "complex" has not been able to prevent such changes. There appears to have been little correlation between the location of a contract and the votes in Congress for or against that contract or between contractor campaign contributions to members of Congress and their votes on particular contractors' programs. Moreover, there is very little evidence that Congress has had a significant impact on the source selection process inside the military services or DoD.

In the post–Cold War world, the congressional politics of defense is likely to become more prominent. Combined with the absence of a perceived threat, bureaucratic infighting, and resource limitations, the struggle for survival in defense will be played out visibly in this political arena. Tensions between DoD and Congress had already begun to grow after 1989, focusing increasingly on disagreements over specific hardware decisions. Congressional decisions in 1990, 1991, and 1992 regularly returned to the budget funding the Pentagon had eliminated for such programs as the M–1 tank, the F–14 fighter, and the V–22 Osprey, while funding for other programs, such as the F–15 fighter, disappeared despite congressional opposition to the Pentagon's decision. The arguments over these programs tend to mix issues of politics, fiscal constraint, and policy.

With respect to the Marine Corps' V–22 Osprey, for example, the Secretary of Defense canceled the program in 1989, arguing that although it was an attractive technology for future Marine Corps lift requirements, it was not affordable in declining budgets. Members of Congress have supported the program with a wide variety of arguments, including the importance of modernizing Marine Corps lift for missions it would undertake in the post–Cold War era, the significant improvement the V–22 represented over current helicopter lift, the cost effectiveness of the V–22 option, and the potential of the technology for commercial applications, as well as the harmful consequences of termination for economic activity and employment in such states as Texas and Pennsylvania.[43] Although the latter argument has been cited as a case of politics prevailing over policy choices, it is far from clear that the other defenses of the V–22 are irrelevant. In reality, as with many such arguments, the politics are difficult to separate from the policy issues involved.[44]

Moreover, as the budget decline has continued, tension has increased in Congress between the rate of that decline overall and the pressures a rapid budget reduction would have on eliminating bases and hardware programs, leading to increased layoffs in congressional districts. This broader budget priorities issue constitutes the link between the specifics of the defense debate and broader issues in national politics. National electoral politics and spending priorities have often had an influence over defense choices.

Since defense spending has been a vehicle for a display of presidential "toughness," the defense budget has been manipulated symbolically as a presidential campaign issue. At various times, national campaign promises have influenced changes in defense decisions.[45] In 1980, for example, presidential candidate Ronald Reagan made defense budget and the B–1 bomber major symbols of his commitment to restoring strong defenses. Once elected, he increased defense budgets dramatically and reversed the Carter Administration's 1977 decision terminating production of the bomber. In 1988, commentators characterized President Reagan's veto of the 1989 Defense Authorization bill, which had broad bipartisan support, as an effort to make the Democratic Party appear weak on defense and to boost the campaign of then Vice President Bush.

Defense plans and decisions clearly take place in a political context, which has an influence on the outcomes of those decisions. The interplay is complex, however, combining strategy with bureaucratic and resource issues. In an era of declining major threats to U.S. security and rising demands for alternative uses of budget resources, political demands are likely to have a large and visible impact on defense decisions.

## CONCLUSION

Like most areas of federal policy, the politics of defense decisions are not reducible to just one factor. Some would prefer to argue that national interests and national strategy guide defense planning and budgeting. Although this has clearly been the case since the late 1940s, it constitutes an incomplete explanation for defense outcomes. Moreover, with the dramatic change in global events since 1989, the lines that connect defense plans and budgets to specific international threats have become significantly blurred.

The absence of a clear link between interests, strategies, forces, and budgets has brought into sharper relief the other factors that influence the defense debate. Resource limitations, which have always had some effect on defense decisions, loom large in the 1990s as a factor driving military forces and budgets downward. To a large extent, the defense budgets from fiscal year 1986 through fiscal year 1993 could be said to have been driven as much, if not more, by fiscal limitations than by a clearly defined threat and strategy.

Bureaucratic behavior as a factor in defense decision making has also become clearer in the post–Cold War era. Without a clear justification for specific forces, infrastructure, or hardware, the services have been pressured into strategies that defend their size, program, and budget as much by the intrinsic need to slow the downsizing process itself as by a clear definition of military requirement. Contrarily, the services are also gradually being forced into greater jointness by the inexorable logic of constrained resources and the increasing inability of any one service to provide a full menu of military capabilities.

Finally, issues of strategy, resources, and bureaucratic behavior are being played out in increasingly visible ways in the political arena. The future of national goals and interests and global defense strategy are being debated at the presidential and even the congressional level. Parochialism and electoral self-protection combine with policy disagreements, leading members of Congress to walk a fine line between the desire for defense budgetary savings, the wish to define a different defense policy for the 1990s, and the need to protect district interests.

The defense political game is indeed complex and has become even more so. It will provide ample material for case studies in the political process throughout the decade of the 1990s. For those who are responsible for formulating the nation's defense strategy, the game will require broad expertise and political skill.

## NOTES

1. For perspectives on this concept, see Richard F. Kaufman, *The War Profiteers* (New York: Doubleday, 1972); Paul A. C. Koistinen, *The Military-Industrial Complex: A Historical Perspective* (New York: Praeger, 1980); and Seymour Melman, *The Permanent War Economy* (New York: Simon and Schuster, 1964), among others. For the "national security state" perspective, see Marcus Raskin, *The Politics of National Security* (New Brunswick, NJ: Transaction Books, 1979). Another view of this relationship describes it as a "subgovernment" or an "iron triangle," similar to other close relationships between the private sector, congressional actors, and executive branch agencies. See Gordon Adams, *The Politics of Defense Contracting: The Iron Triangle* (New Brunswick, NJ: Transaction Books, 1981), especially Chapter 1, note 18. For a more critical view of this concept, see Kenneth R. Mayer, *The Political Economy of Defense Contracting* (New Haven, CT: Yale University Press, 1991).

2. As William T. R. Fox stated,

> The myth that questions of national security are above or at any rate somehow apart from politics has died hard. A more rational choice of defense policies and levels of defense expenditures requires that we recognize and come to understand the political process as it operates to define national security policy rather than that we ignore or deny that process.

"Introduction," in *Strategy, Politics, and Defense Budgets*, eds. Warner R. Schilling, Paul E. Hammond, and Glen Snyder (New York: Columbia University Press, 1962), p. viii.

3. The annual reports of the Secretaries of Defense and the annual posture statements of the Joint Chiefs of Staff are written solely in this context. At the other extreme, some of the military-industrial complex literature tends to dismiss international events as a significant component of defense planning and budgeting. Other analysts suggest that the fit between programs, budgets, and national strategy is relatively accidental. In the words of the Senate Armed Services Committee staff,

> The concern [with acquisition] is that there is not an assured connection between the national military strategy and the formulation of military requirements. The reason that the term "assured connection" is used is because it would be an overstatement to say that there is no connection. In many cases, weapon systems that are developed fit well with the national strategy. Such a fit may exist more through chance than as a result of a careful planning process that assures such a fit.

U.S. Senate, Staff Report to the Committee on Armed Services, *Defense Organization: The Need for Change*, 99th Congress, 1st session (Washington, DC: U.S. Government Printing Office, 1985), p. 538.

4. There is a wealth of literature on the bureaucratic behavior of the Defense Department and the military services, including a number of significant case studies. See, among others, Robert Art, *The TFX Decision: McNamara and the Military* (Boston: Little, Brown, 1968); Harvey M. Sapolsky, *The Polaris System Development: Bureaucratic and Programmatic Success in Government* (Cambridge, MA: Harvard University Press, 1972); Ted Greenwood, *Making the MIRV: A Study of Defense Decision Making* (Cambridge, MA: Ballinger, 1975); J. Ronald Fox, *Arming America: How the U.S. Buys Weapons* (Boston: Division of Research, Graduate School of Business Administration, Harvard University, 1974); and Merton J. Peck and Frederic M. Scherer, *The Weapons Acquisition Process* (Boston: Division of Research, Graduate School of Business Administration, Harvard University, 1962).

5. David Stockman describes the rather casual planning session that led to the early Reagan Administration decision to increase defense spending over five years at twice the rate promised by Ronald Reagan during the campaign. Such a decision was clearly possible because of the political mandate Reagan had received. David Stockman, *The Triumph of Politics* (New York: Harper and Row, 1986), pp. 277–278.

6. The Gramm-Rudman-Hollings (GRH) Act set specific legal targets, procedures, and a time line for federal deficit reduction. Although the GRH process has not resulted in the elimination of the deficit, it has put severe constraints on all areas of federal spending. See Glenn Gotz, "Notes on the Gramm-Rudman-Hollings Deficit Reduction Plan" (Santa Monica, CA: RAND Corporation, March 1986).

7. Linda P. Brady, "The Economic Dimension of Defence: the United States," in *Strategic Power USA/USSR*, ed. Carl G. Jacobsen (London: MacMillan Press, 1990), p. 261; Amos Jordan, William Taylor, Jr., and Lawrence Korb, *American National Security Policy and Process*, 3d ed. (Baltimore: The Johns Hopkins University, 1989), p. 75; Melvin Laird, Gale McGee, Robert Griffin, and Thomas Schelling, *The Nixon Doctrine: Town Hall Meeting* (Washington, DC: American Enterprise Institute for Public Research, 1972); and Lawrence J. Korb, "The Budget Process in the Department of Defense, 1947–77: The Strengths and Weaknesses of Three Systems," *Public Administration Review*, July/August 1977, p. 341.

8. Federal News Service transcript, Robert Gates, CIA director, "Testimony before Senate Armed Services Committee," January 22, 1992, p. V–3–3. Secretary Cheney noted the same day to the West Point Society of the District of Columbia that "we no longer need to be concerned with the threat of a massive, quick-thrust Warsaw Pact invasion into Western Europe that could quickly go global and perhaps even involve the use of nuclear weapons." Federal News Service transcript, Secretary of Defense Dick Cheney, speech to West Point Society, Washington, DC, January 22, 1992, p. DC–3–1.

9. Joint Chiefs of Staff, *The National Military Strategy 1992* (Washington, DC: Joint Chiefs of Staff, February 1992), pp. 6–7.

10. See, among others, Defense Budget Project, *Responding to Changing Threats: A Report of the DBP's Task Force on the FY 1992–FY 1997 Defense Plan* (Washington, DC: Defense Budget Project, June 1991); John D. Steinbruner, The Brookings Institution, "Statement to the House Budget Committee," February 13, 1992; "Testimony of Lawrence J. Korb, The Brookings Institution, before the House Budget Committee," February 13, 1992; Cato Institute, *America's Peace Dividend: Income*

*Tax Reductions from the New Strategic Realities* (Washington, DC: Cato Institute, August 7, 1990); Angelo Codevilla, Murray Weidenbaum, and Dov Zakheim, "How to Cut the Defense Budget by $100 Billion," *Heritage Foundation Policy Review*, No. 60, Spring 1992.

11. Representative Les Aspin, "An Approach to Sizing American Conventional Forces for the Post-Soviet Era: Four Illustrative Options" (Washington, DC: House Armed Services Committee, February 25, 1992).

12. The Cato report could be characterized as the former and the Brookings report as the latter.

13. Barbara Tuchman has noted that "Americans have shown their dislike of organized war by a desperate attachment to three principles: unpreparedness until the eleventh hour; the quickest feasible strategy for victory regardless of political aims; and instant demobilization, no matter how inadvisable, the moment hostilities are over." Barbara Tuchman, "The American People and Military Power in an Historical Perspective," in *America's Security in the 1980s*, Adelphi Paper No. 173 (London: International Institute of Strategic Studies, 1982), p. 5.

14. According to Warner Schilling, "In the first half of the century, except just before and during time of war itself, civilian statesmen demonstrated very little interest in how the plans and preparations of the armed forces were related to the nation's foreign policy. Military planners were left to guess at the course of the nation's foreign policy as best they could." Warner R. Schilling, "The Politics of National Defense: Fiscal 1950, Introduction," in *Strategy, Politics, and Defense Budgets*, p. 11.

15. Samuel Huntington, *The Soldier and the State: The Theory and Politics of Civil-Military Relations* (Cambridge, MA: Belknap Press of Harvard University Press, 1985).

16. Robert W. Komer, "Strategymaking in the Pentagon," in *Reorganizing America's Defense*, eds. Robert J. Art, Vincent Davis, and Samuel P. Huntington (New York: Pergamon-Brassey's, 1985), p. 208; John Lewis Gaddis, *Strategies of Containment* (New York: Oxford University Press, 1982), p. 90.

17. Secretary Weinberger regularly argued during the 1980s that defenses needed to be planned in relationship to the threat, regardless of their costs. Richard A. Stubbing, *The Defense Game* (New York: Harper and Row, 1986), pp. 376–379. In the 1960s, Secretary of Defense Robert McNamara argued, "Two points seem to me axiomatic. The first is that the United States is well able to spend whatever it needs to spend on national security. The second point is that this ability does not excuse us from applying strict standards of effectiveness and efficiency to the way we spend our defense dollars." Robert McNamara, *The Essence of Security* (New York: Harper and Row, 1968), p. 88.

18. CBO, "The Economic Effects of Reduced Defense Spending" (Washington, DC: U.S. Government Printing Office, February 1992).

19. Defense Budget Project, "Various Congressional Budget Proposals to Cut Defense Spending" (Washington, DC: Defense Budget Project, January 24, 1992); "Democrats Falter in Drive to Claim Peace Dividend," *Congressional Quarterly*, March 28, 1992, pp. 789–791.

20. Lawrence Korb makes a strong argument that budgets and military needs should be examined together: "When needs and costs are separated, there will inevitably be an imbalance between objectives and forces and ultimately an imbal-

ance between planned forces and the actual budgets and programs provided to support them." See Korb, "The Budget Process," p. 340.

21. The *Gaither Report*, released by Henry Rowen and his committee, portrayed a grim view of the future of U.S. security based on comparisons between the U.S. and Soviet economies and military capacities and on the rising security threat from China. The report recommended significant increases in defense spending for civilian defense, and nuclear and conventional forces. Stephen Ambrose, *Rise to Globalism*, 3d ed. (New York: Penguin Books, 1985), pp. 167–168.

22. According to Richard Stubbing, former Office of Management and Budget official,

> The Reagan defense buildup formally began ten days after the inauguration, when Defense Secretary Casper Weinberger and Budget Director David Stockman acceded to the demands of powerful senators in the new Republican majority and added $32 billion to the outgoing Carter defense budgets for 1981–1982 (which had already provided $20 billion in real growth over the two years). There were no justifying analyses or supporting programs; these were to be developed later.

Richard Stubbing, "The Defense Program: Buildup or Binge?" *Foreign Affairs* 63, No. 4 (Spring 1985), p. 849.

23. Representatives Les Aspin and William Dickinson, House Armed Services Committee, *Defense for a New Era: Lessons of the Persian Gulf War* (Washington, DC: U.S. Government Printing Office, 1992), pp. 7, 19.

24. Barton Gellman, "The 'Silent Service' Breaks the Ice: Submariners Test Waters for New Role as Soviet Threat Dries Up," *The Washington Post*, April 19, 1992, pp. A1, A4–A5.

25. "Navy–Air Force Agreement on AX," *Inside the Navy*, March 16, 1992, p. 11; "USAF Involvement in Navy A–X Programs Said to Be Informal Arrangement Only," *Inside the Air Force*, May 31, 1991, p. 11. Both positive and negative lessons about jointness were drawn from the Gulf experience.

26. See Morton Halperin, "The Limited Influence of the Military-Industrial Complex," in *The Political Economy of the Military-Industrial Complex*, eds. Morton Halperin, Jacob Stockfisch, and Murray Weidenbaum (Berkeley: University of California Institute of Business and Economic Research, 1973), pp. 13–14.

27. Cited in U.S. Senate Staff Report to the Committee on Armed Services, *Defense Organization: The Need for Change* (Washington, DC: U.S. Government Printing Office, 1985), p. 619.

28. The Defense Department notes that DoD officials, on average, provide six witness and fourteen hours of testimony for each day Congress is in session. Department of Defense, Office of the Secretary of Defense, *Defense Management Report to the President* (Washington, DC: Office of the Secretary of Defense, July 1989), p. 27. Senior DoD officials spend approximately 3,000 hours each year preparing and giving testimony to Congress. The Department also presents over 1,000 briefings to members and their staffs in addition to responding to telephone and written inquiries. Report to the President by the Secretary of Defense, *White Paper on the Department of Defense and the Congress* (Washington, DC: Office of the Secretary of Defense, January 1990).

29. Until the 1960s, the Armed Services committees authorized programs for

DoD but did not pass on funding levels for those programs. The Air Force would be authorized to purchase a particular number of aircraft, but approval of funds for those aircraft was the task of the Appropriations Committee. In the 1960s, the Armed Services committees gradually extended their consideration of funding, making it necessary for Armed Services to "authorize an appropriation," which would subsequently be "appropriated" by the Appropriations committees.

30. For defense, this function is known as "national defense" and includes not only the DoD budget but nuclear weapons activities in the Department of Energy (DoE). DoE, which succeeded an earlier Atomic Energy Commission in the federal bureaucracy, conducts all research and production activity on nuclear warheads for the military.

31. Congressional staff in general, and for defense committees in particular, has grown substantially over the past twenty years. Overall, congressional committee staffs increased by 237 percent from 1960 to 1985; the increase from 1964 to 1989 in defense committee staffers was 268 percent. During that period the defense subcommittees on Appropriations and the Armed Services committees went from 37 staff members to 99. An additional 66 staff members work on defense issues for committee members or congressional support agencies. See Wilbur D. Jones, Jr., "Congressional Involvement and Relations" (Ft. Belvoir, VA: Defense Systems Management College, July 1989).

32. See, for example, OTA, *After the Cold War: Living with Lower Defense Spending*, OTA-ITE–524 (Washington, DC: U.S. Congress, Office of Technology Assessment, February 1992). See also U.S. Congress, OTA, *The Defense Technology Base: Introduction and Overview*, OTA-ITE–443 (Washington, DC: U.S. Government Printing Office, March 1988).

33. Such groups include a wide number of institutes at the center of the political and policy spectrum: American Enterprise Institute, Brookings Institution, Carnegie Endowment, Center for Strategic and International Studies, Council on Foreign Relations and Defense Budget Project, among many others. There are also more advocacy-oriented defense policy groups.

34. See, inter alia, *Aviation Week & Space Technology, Aerospace Daily, Defense News, Defense Week*, and *Inside the Pentagon*, as well as detailed coverage of defense budget and policy and industry issues by specialized reporters in *The New York Times, The Washington Post, Wall Street Journal, Time, Newsweek, Business Week*, and many regional newspapers.

35. Former Chairman of the Senate Armed Services Committee Barry Goldwater has stated that "the budget process distorts the nature of congressional oversight by focusing primarily on the question of how much before we answer the key questions of what for, why, and how well." The Packard Commission, *A Quest for Excellence: Final Report to the President* (Washington, DC: U.S. Government Printing Office, 1986), p. xviii. See also Representative Les Aspin, "Games the Pentagon Plays," *Foreign Policy*, No. 51, Summer 1983, pp. 80–92.

36. Representative Aspin, Chairman of the House Committee on Armed Services, describes this preoccupation well:

> When a congressman first gets elected, one of the things he immediately starts thinking about is how to get reelected. That is, after all, what politics is all about. To get reelected, especially for a junior member with no chance to pass

> important national legislation, constituent service is important. What this means is that if the congressman comes from an area in which a big defense contractor is a major employer, it helps to be on the Armed Services Committee. So junior congressmen with defense constituents aim for the Armed Services Committee.

Aspin, "Games," p. 89. See also David Mayhew, *Congress: The Electoral Connection* (New Haven, CT: Yale University Press, 1974), and Gordon Adams, "Disarming the Military Subgovernment," *Harvard Journal on Legislation* 14, No. 3 (April 1977), pp. 459–504.

37. A recent study concluded, "the general principle is established: that members will think about constituency level economic consequences when they decide whether to support funding for a weapon system," and "reelection prospects are heavily influenced by local economic conditions, and perceptions of whether or not members are providing sufficient benefits to their districts. Therefore, a major concern in congressional procurement decision-making is the place of production. Congressmen often think less about a weapon's military value than how many local jobs the ensuing defense contracts will provide." Mayer, *Political Economy of Defense Contracting*, p. 31.

38. Ibid., pp. 232–233.

39. Representative Thomas Downey (D-NY) is frank about his motivations for voting for the A–6 Intruder aircraft: "When the A–6 Intruder [Grumman] was going to be killed, I'm the congressman from that district and I'm on the Armed Services Committee. It's my job, whether I think the A–6 is good or not, to support it." Noted in Stubbing, "The Defense Program," p. 91.

40. "Democrats Set Sights on Bush Plan That Stresses R&D over Procurement," *Inside the Navy* 5, No. 5 (February 3, 1992), pp. 1, 5, 14; Miranda Spivack, "Old Seawolf Allies in Congress Growing Skeptical," *Hartford Courant*, February 25, 1992, p. A1.

41. The bill that led to the base closing commission process was introduced by Representative Richard Armey in 1987. Susan F. Rasky, "House Votes Bill That Could Bring Shutdown of 20 U.S. Bases in '89," *The New York Times*, July 13, 1988, p. A1. See also the reports of the two base closings commissions: Defense Secretary's Commission on Base Realignment and Closure, *Base Realignments and Closures* (Washington, DC: Office of the Secretary of Defense, December 1988); and Defense Base Closure and Realignment Commission, *Report to the President* (Washington, DC: Defense Base Closure and Realignment Commission, July 1, 1991).

42. U.S. Congress, GAO, *Report to the Chairman, Committee on Armed Services, House of Representatives: Navy A–12 Cost and Requirements* (Washington, DC: General Accounting Office, December 1990); David Morrison, "Changing Speed," *National Journal*, No. 10 (March 10, 1992), pp. 554–557; David Morrison, "End of the Line," *National Journal*, No. 23 (June 8, 1991), pp. 1326–1330.

43. Michael Towle, "The Osprey's Fate Is Still up in the Air," *Fort Worth Star-Telegram*, February 17, 1991; Eric Rosenberg, "Coalition Leads Fight to Save Endangered Osprey," *Defense Weekly*, February 26, 1990, p. 5.

44. The same can be said for the disagreement between Congress and the Pentagon over the future of the Army Reserve and National Guard. Congressional defenders

of the Reserve and Guard argue that a declining threat means that more of the combat forces can be put into the Guard and Reserve, which are significantly cheaper to operate. Moreover, supporters have argued that these forces have a powerful, district-based political constituency. On the other hand, DoD has argued that Guard and Reserve units that provide support to active-duty Army units have no function when those active units are disbanded and, thus, should not be maintained, since they constitute a budgetary burden in a time of shrinking resources. See Art Pine, "In Defense of 2nd Line Defenders," *Los Angeles Times*, March 13, 1992, pp. A1, A7; David Morrison, "Reservists' Grass-Roots Firepower," *National Journal*, April 11, 1992, pp. 879–80.

45. Lawrence Korb asserts that "the Joint Chiefs have consistently allowed themselves to be intimidated by political leaders into supporting policies to which they were or should have been opposed. At one time or another, the chiefs publicly supported Truman's very low defense budgets, Eisenhower's 'New Look,' McNamara's methods, Lyndon Johnson's war policies and Nixon's secret bombings." Lawrence J. Korb, *The Role of the Joint Chiefs of Staff in the Strategic Arms Limitation Process: Changing or Consistent?* (Washington, DC: American Enterprise Institute for Public Policy Research, 1981), p. 180.

# 6

# The Armed Forces in a New Political Environment

*Gary L. Guertner*

Clausewitz was the first to record the rise of the nation-state and its ability to mobilize popular passions into mass armies. This transformation of politics, he observed, transformed the art of war. This was discussed in the context of Clausewitz's "remarkable trinity"—the government, the army, and the people. Any theory of war or grand strategy that ignored any one of these, Clausewitz warned, was certain to fail.

The modern corollary for the United States is the sudden post–Cold War shift in public attention from foreign to domestic crises. This political transformation is having profound consequences for the armed forces. The political relationships among the people, the government, and the army, in the truest Clausewitzian sense, will determine the resources available to support the national military strategy. This chapter describes the nature of the new domestic environment, what motivates it, and what its duration is likely to be.

## THE DOMESTIC ENVIRONMENT

The nation won the Cold War and its armed forces won a brilliant air-land campaign in the desert of Iraq that established U.S. military credibility during the transition to a new world order. But playing the role of midwife to a new era does not mean that the United States will be willing to lead or nurture a world that it was largely responsible for shaping. Historically, victory in war has never ensured that the American people or Congress would be willing to support the military forces necessary to make the next conflict less likely—and there has *always* been a next conflict.

World War I ended with a strident return to isolationism. The ambiguity of victory and the "unsavory" diplomacy of our allies (realpolitik) made it virtually impossible for President Wilson to sell his strategic vision of U.S. participation in a collective security system that was intended to replace the classic, but precarious, European balance of power. The war to "end all wars" wasn't and didn't.

World War II ended on the decisive and psychologically pleasing terms of unconditional surrender. But the victory was hardly unconditional, as the Cold War began even before the hot war ended. Even so, the American people were eager to bring the boys home, and they would have easily picked up the banner of isolationism again had not Harry Truman, with the support of converted Republican isolationists, "scared the hell" out of the public. A new generation of American leaders learned that isolationism and appeasement could not contain threats to U.S. interests. The role of the United States as a global superpower was born. But policy declarations and strategies for containing Soviet expansionism preceded real military capabilities. It was war in Korea that gave saliency to the global threat and brought dollars to the defense budget to support the large, permanent military forces that gave credibility to U.S. global commitments.

Victory in the Cold War may have ended a 45-year aberration in the public's fundamental preference for domestic issues. From conservative Republicans like Patrick Buchanan to moderate Democrats like William Hyland (former editor of *Foreign Affairs*) come calls for disengagement abroad in order to save resources for domestic priorities. Public opinion polls support these expressions. Surveys completed on the eve of the 1992 presidential campaign showed that 55 percent of the respondents believe that economic problems (unemployment, recession, inflation, the deficit, the poor) are the most important issues. By contrast, major foreign policy issues like the former Soviet Union, arms control, foreign aid, or the Middle East crisis were mentioned only by 2 to 5 percent of those surveyed as the most pressing problems facing the nation.[1]

These public attitudes should not be surprising. Domestic priorities are the norm when a nation's security is not directly threatened. Former Speaker of the House Thomas (Tip) O'Neill captured these tendencies in his reflections on a lifetime in politics: "All politics is local."[2] For that reason, we can predict a high probability of an extended period of public introversion that will last well into the Clinton Administration.

Post–Cold War world domestic problems are dramatically reducing the resources available for defense. These pressures are the result of a historic convergence of four deficits: (1) the *budget deficit*, compounded by the costs of the savings and loan (S&L) crisis and the political imperative to reduce federal spending; (2) the *trade deficit* and an ever more obvious need to make U.S. industry more competitive on the world market; (3) the *social deficit* visible in every congressional district in the form of local demands for resources in education, law enforcement, housing, public works (roads and bridges), health care, environmental protection and restoration, and above all, jobs; and finally (4) the *threat deficit*, which coincides with the surge in domestic demands on resources: We won the Cold War, and the Soviet threat to Europe and the Third World has retreated in geopolitical and philosophical defeat.

"Threat deficit" accurately describes the changes in the Soviet-American bipolar relationship. Yet, as this threat recedes, the Third World and Eastern Europe grow more unstable and volatile, endangering U.S. interests with diffuse challenges at constantly shifting points on the map. The Soviet threat deficit may, in fact, represent a shift from a centralized threat of global war to a highly decentralized threat of diverse regional conflicts that in the aggregate will require more versatile and flexible military capabilities in support of national strategy.

Formulating a new national military strategy and maintaining a force structure to execute it are not, however, priority items in Congress or the new administration. The members of Congress (and the President) read and are affected by opinion polls. The polls quoted previously suggest that some combination of six major themes ("social deficit" issues) will dominate the national dialogue after the election just as they did during the Presidential campaign:

- Economy (that is, jobs)
- Education (global competitiveness for jobs)
- Environment (as long as it doesn't cost jobs)
- Equality (women and minorities in the job market)
- Expectations (for health, safety, homes, quality of life, all reinforced by the growth of a politically powerful senior community)
- Extraction (from foreign policy commitments associated with the Cold War; more burden sharing by economically powerful allies)

The historic convergence of these four deficits and the mood swing toward "America first" dominated the 1992 election. They also coincide with significant demographic changes in American politics that suggest these trends will endure. Demographic data reveal:

- More women are becoming active in politics;
- More minorities are active in politics and are increasing in numbers relative to "traditional" power centers;
- A record high retired cohort by the end of the century as baby-boomers begin to retire and collect their pensions.

When public opinion polls isolate these cohorts, the data reveal a strong preference for domestic over foreign policy issues and voting patterns supportive of congressmen identified with these issues.[3]

Growing public support for retrenchment from global commitments as a superpower is reinforced by a long, continuing cycle of congressional dominance of the policymaking process. In recent decades, the pendulum has swung from executive to congressional hegemony. The last cycle of executive supremacy lasted from Pearl Harbor to Tet. World War II and the Cold War responsibilities of a global superpower created new and powerful executive bureaucracies. But Vietnam and the post-Vietnam era pushed the pendulum once again in the direction of congressional dominance. Perceptions of an "imperial presidency" created a new wave of congressional oversight and bureaucratic competition. New committees were formed, new organizations to serve and inform Congress were created, committee staff were expanded, and a series of restrictive legislation (e.g., War Powers) was passed as a direct result of the Cold War's most significant failure. Strategic victory in the Cold War has not resulted in any perceivable diminution in congressional power. Institutionally, Congress holds the key to the future of our military forces.

## CONGRESS AND THE MILITARY

Congress, is not the enemy. Congress is the playing field. It represents and reflects with reasonable accuracy the desires of the American electorate. The institution is neutral in the sense that it can be more or less useful and responsive depending on the bureaucratic skills of the organizations that depend on its decisions. The most significant problem is structural in nature. The executive branch is primarily responsible for establishing a strategic vision that identifies our international objectives and the strategies for pursuing them. The Congress combines authorizing legislation and budgeting authority to give it primary control of the means. This division of power and authority makes Washington a city in which decisions are not routinely made on the basis of strategic vision or rationality. Rather, policymaking is more often a contentious political process in which powerful bureaucracies and interest groups engage in conflict, bargaining, and compromise. We do what we can agree on, and the winners are those with superior political skills who can identify and communicate interests that they have in common with members of Congress and their constituents. [The same is true within the Office of the Secretary of Defense (OSD) and the Office of the Joint Chiefs of Staff (OJCS).]

The question is, therefore, what are the nation's post–Cold War security requirements and how do the armed forces get their message before Congress? What strategy is most likely to succeed in an arena dominated by the domestic agenda and with decisions being increasingly formulated by committees and staffs with no direct military experience?

## PRESERVING MILITARY SUFFICIENCY

If it is true that scarcity is the midwife of innovative strategic thinking, we are entering a golden age for strategists. The greatest difficulty will be the competitive resource allocation process controlled by a Congress that is preoccupied by the extensive domestic agenda. Given the current domestic environment, how do the armed forces maintain a Base Force that satisfies military requirements for the future? A three-step process is required: (1) Maintain the credibility of senior military leaders throughout the debate over resources; (2) Develop clear themes, rationales, and priorities in force levels, R&D, and acquisition that identify the most cost-effective *mix* of technologies, integrated in a concept of operations that give smaller forces greater combat power—avoid piecemeal justifications of budget line-items; and (3) Communicate these themes with persistence and in ways that link military strength with economic vitality.[4]

The most fundamental question that the military leadership must pose to Congress is, What do you want military forces to do? Only then can clear military priorities and force structures be established. Shortfalls between required missions and capabilities constitute risks. Both Congress and the executive branch should be reminded that excessive risk is like a large deductible in an insurance policy. In a crisis, it may prove to be both bad economics and bad strategy. American history is filled with examples of deteriorating military readiness that led to heavy losses and temporary defeat in America's "first battles" of most of our major wars.[5] The current concern of military leadership is to avoid the traditional and disastrous hollow state that normally follows a builddown in the wake of victory. General Sherman understood "downsizing" in his sardonic observation that peace and politics are always more damaging to an army than war.

Credibility and institutional prestige are among the most important assets to preserve during periods of "peace and politics." These will outlast the current fiscal crisis, provided that the armed forces build on their post–Desert Storm reputation for excellence. This reputation would be put at risk if the senior leadership paints an overly stark view of the world or consistently presses Congress with worst-case assumptions. Some damage has already been done as the result of seven hypothetical threat scenarios developed by the Joint Staff and leaked to the press.[6] This controversial "enemies list" was intended to identify the general scale of future conflicts rather than specific foes. Nevertheless, it sparked a war of scenarios that has made consensus building on the defense budget even more difficult.[7]

Excessive risk is the traditional byproduct of a broken policy consensus. Without consensus, the national strategy will grow increasingly disconnected from its military strategy and force structure. The range of U.S. interests in the world are unlikely to change. But interests, absent adequate military power, have never gone unmolested. The new world order is only a hope. Multipolarity with rampant nationalism and the proliferation of modern weapons is just as likely to be a Hobbesian world. If the Gulf War is our introduction to that world, its major lesson is that deterrence will fail again in the future. When it does, a weakened military can only have an equally adverse effect on U.S. political and economic instruments of power.

Military power, when not competing in the costly arms competitions that characterized the Cold War, lends credibility to the political and economic instruments of power. These synergistic effects are often taken for granted. Part of the fault is an unfortunate tendency of military strategists to think in terms of threat-based strategy. Military strategy and force structure are *always* interest-based. Interests are *defended* when threatened and *promoted* in the absence of proximate threats. The best way to achieve stability in the defense budget is to relate it to the issues that the American public worries about.

These interests remain largely unchanged. They include our own economic vitality, which is in turn linked to the stability of the industrial centers of Europe and northeast Asia, and free access to vital resources. Promoting these interests in peacetime does not require the United States to be the world's policeman. It does assume, however, that if we are given a clear choice, the national pride of the American people will support its status as a superpower, capable of promoting or defending these interests, albeit with more of the burdens of power shared by our allies.

Promoting interests nearly always involves friends and allies who are more inclined to develop long-term, mutually beneficial economic and political relations if they are confident that the United States can promote those interests in peace and defend them in war. The leverage of U.S. military power remains a vital component of national strategy.

In an era of growing uncertainty, the armed forces have a credible case to make. But that case needs to be repeated and refined for the duration of a long political process that has only just begun. In Congress and the White House, military requirements will be balanced against domestic ones. Opinion polls and the themes that dominated the 1992 presidential campaign show that the balance has shifted decidedly to domestic issues.

The military's role is to inform the debate over national priorities, emphasizing the resources that link military strength to economic well-being at home and abroad. In the end, success will be measured by our ability to retain our core military strength as we regain our solvency and confidence in the wake of a Cold War that cost us more than we might have imagined.

## NOTES

1. Michael R. Kagay, "As Candidates Hunt the Big Issues, Polls Can Give Them a Few Clues," *The New York Times*, October 20, 1991, p. E3. See also R. W. Apple,

"White House Race Is Recast: No Kremlin to Run Against," *The New York Times*, February 6, 1992, p. A1.

2. Tip O'Neill, *Man of the House* (New York: Random House, 1987), Chapter 1.

3. RAND Arroyo Center, "Modernizing under Uncertainty: A Framework for Thinking about the Army of the Future," RAND briefing dated May 1989, p. 6.

4. Studies by the Congressional Budget Office and the Office of Technology Assessment conclude that it is false to assume that reduced defense spending will solve the economic crisis. *Defense News*, February 24, 1992, p. 54.

5. The example of "No More Task Force Smiths" has found its way into Army strategic briefings. For a longer historical perspective, see Charles E. Heller and William A. Stofft, eds., *America's First Battles, 1776–1965* (Lawrence: University of Kansas Press, 1986).

6. See Patrick E. Tyler, "Hypothetical Conflicts Foreseen by the Pentagon," *The New York Times*, February 17, 1992, p. A8; "War Games, Money Games," editorial in *The Washington Post*, February 19, 1992, p. A20; and Barton Gellman, "Pentagon War Scenario Spotlights Russia," *The Washington Post*, February 20, 1992, p. A1. Reported assertions in one scenario that the defense of Lithuania against Russian attack is a vital U.S. interest is not the way to get a budget-conscious Congress to take defense requests seriously. See Barton Gellmann, "Pentagon Says War Scenario Doesn't Reflect or Predict U.S. Policy," *The Washington Post*, February 21, 1992, p. A12.

7. The most detailed "counter-scenario" came from Congressman Les Aspin, Chairman of the House Armed Services Committee. Aspin calculated four options against seven potential regional aggressors. He is attempting to build a consensus around a smaller Base Force. For example, 9 active Army divisions compared to 12 in the Administration's plan, 10 air wings instead of 15, and 360 ships instead of 450. See Patrick E. Tyler, "Top Congressman Proposes Deeper Cuts for the Military," *The New York Times*, February 23, 1992, p. A1; and Barton Gellman, "Debate over Military's Future Escalates into a War of Scenarios," *The Washington Post*, February 26, 1992, p. A20.

# PART II

---

# STRATEGY AS CREATIVE CONCEPTS AND APPLICATION: THE FUTURE OF DETERRENCE

# 7

# Deterrence before Hiroshima: The Past as Prologue

*George H. Quester*

As the United States and its allies anticipate dramatic reductions in nuclear weapons, we must continue to face the question of "conventional deterrence." Is something an oxymoron here? Is it not true that we have seen the concept of deterrence emerge only in the wake of the enormous destructive power of *nuclear* weapons? Are there in fact any precedents and lessons to be extracted from the past, from the years before 1945?

One can indeed find some relevant lessons from the past by reviewing what deterrence has meant in the nuclear years and by taking a closer look at some of the history. The lessons to be derived may be mixed and debatable at points, but they are still fundamental as we confront a new world without the Warsaw Pact and the Soviet Union.

## SOME ELEMENTARY POINTS

Glenn Snyder published an analysis more than thirty years ago laying out the basic continuum of deterrence by denial and deterrence by punishment.[1] Wars have been "deterred" often enough in the past by the simple prospect of frustration and defeat for either side launching a war. Consider the situation of the Swiss Army and the Austrian Army facing off against each other, each quite capable of defending its own mountains where it knows the proper places for tactical defense, and each equally incapable of invading the other's mountains. What dissuades each side from attacking, even if political disagreements or greed and lust for power would otherwise cause them to attack, is the simple prospect that such an attack would fail and be fruitless (deterrence by denial) *and* lead to the loss of a fair number of young soldiers' lives (deterrence by punishment). (We will return to speculate about whether this last element, the pain and loss of life, has been crucial to *conventional* deterrence; if all the attacker had to fear was that he would be painlessly repulsed, might he not have a try at the conquest anyway, on the off chance that it might succeed?)

Snyder makes the critical point that nuclear deterrence has relied much more heavily on punishment than on denial—indeed, that it works even when an attack could *not* be repulsed. Even if my armies could conquer your territory, while my air force and navy were destroying your air force and navy, the entire attack will not be launched, will be deterred, if *in the meantime* your navy and air force can deliver nuclear destruction to my cities. The destruction of my cities would make me lament the "victory" I had just won, and the prospect of this deters me from launching the war in the first place.

As we search for historical analogies, the obvious question will be whether such capacities for intra-war retaliatory destruction appeared only with nuclear weapons or had some important equivalent earlier, from which we can extract relevant lessons and experience. There are two such plausible equivalents.

Moving backward in time, we come first to the presumptions made about the countervalue possibilities of aerial bombardment during World War II, between the world wars, and during World War I.[2] Although such predictions turned out to be substantially wrong, they are nonetheless important as the premises upon which national planners and strategic theorists were operating. Many such analysts assumed that they were already equipped with, and burdened by, destructive capabilities in effect comparable to the atomic bomb. Extrapolating from the way the inhabitants of London and other cities had seemed unable to bear the primitive bombing raids of 1914 to 1918, such analysts (of whom Giulio Douhet[3] is the most publicized, but not the most profound, example) definitely sensed the ingredients for deterrence by punishment.

The second example comes even before the advent of flight. It is derived from the global growth of commerce in the nineteenth century, which generated the prospect that the British Navy or any other major navy could inflict tremendous pain on an enemy by harassing such commerce, by bombarding the coastal cities that had grown in connection with such commerce. As they considered how to exploit their preponderance of sea power after Trafalgar, British naval planners were thus conscious of the countervalue aspects of warfare and of the possibility that it could be applied to dissuade an enemy from attacking British possessions.

We can illustrate this in one of the most basic British strategic problems of the nineteenth century, how to make certain that the United States would not invade to conquer (liberate) Canada.[4] Given the geopolitically central position of the United States in North America, the problem was strikingly parallel to the British problem with regard to Czarist Russia and Eurasia, which of course became a U.S. problem after 1945 with regard to the Soviet Union and the defense of NATO. Whoever is at the center of a continental mass can move troops more easily into its peninsulas, while the defending power will have trouble in moving similar forces around by sea.

The British government for decades urged Canada to maintain a more robust militia system, just as the United States for decades urged the NATO countries to develop more extensive conventional defenses. Despite Canadian promises to generate such forces, they never quite came into being. Until the turn of the century, therefore, the real British fallback for the security of Canada was not deterrence by denial (the U.S. Army potential demonstrated in the Civil War could not be stopped), but the prospect of punishment, as the British Navy would sail in to burn cities like Baltimore, Washington, New York, and Boston. This would not have slowed the U.S. advance into Ontario, but the prospect of it might work to cool U.S. interest in such an attack (just as the nuclear bombing of Soviet cities might not have kept the Red Army from getting to Paris, but by its mere prospect worked to deter such an advance).

Lest one conclude that we are merely projecting "pre–nuclear deterrence" mechanisms backward from our nuclear experience, it can be easily documented that more than these prerequisites of retaliatory destructive capability were in place; indeed, that some relatively sophisticated discussions of the deterrence mechanism were already developed at the time.

One of the clearest examples of the naval mechanism can be found in the strategic writings of Sir Julian Corbett.[5] He became concerned at the beginning of the twentieth century that Britain might have given in too much to the demands of the United States and other neutrals that the freedom of the seas now be respected, that is, that the British naval blockades of the future be limited to purely military goods.

Extrapolating from naval warfare back to ground warfare and indeed to all warfare, Corbett (quoting a Prussian general, Von der Goltz) notes that military power, to be politically effective, may in the end have to be *punishment*, that is, countervalue. Although the classic and morally acceptable approach to warfare consisted of *denial* (i.e., a counterforce disarming of the enemy's military force), Corbett noted that the government and civilian population of the other side might still ignore and laugh off whatever directives we issued, if we were not somehow able to worsen the quality of their lives, if we were not able to impose some pain.

> [B]attles are only the means to enabling you to do that which really brings wars to an end—that is, to exert pressure on the citizens and their collective life. "After shattering the hostile main army," says Von der Goltz, "we still have the forcing of a peace as a separate and, in certain circumstances, more difficult task . . . to make the enemy's country feel the burdens of war with such weight that the desire for peace will prevail."[6]

Corbett's basic point through the quotation from von der Goltz was that despite the laws of war and the Western tradition of moral philosophy, war cannot simply be counterforce, with all countervalue punishment being eliminated. If we disarm the enemy's air force and army and navy, and then the other side's civilian population still refuses to obey our orders, are we still forbidden to "attack civilians"? International law forbids attacks on civilians *until* the enemy has lost control over an area of territory and we have assumed that control. Once we have assumed a sovereignty over an area, however temporary, we are then free to "attack" civilians when they do not accept the edicts of our martial law.

One can project the same distinctions into our ordinary law in peacetime. Is the imprisonment of criminals meant to be counterforce or countervalue? A certain school of thought would argue that prisons should be made as humane as possible, that their sole legitimate function is to protect the rest of society against murderers and other violent people. Yet, if we need to imprison murderers for a counterforce purpose, to "disarm" them, what of embezzlers, who (once identified) will never be trusted again with a bank's money? Here the imprisonment is less to "deny" than to "punish," that is, to deter similar acts in the future.

This entire chain, from imprisonment in civilian law to the punishments directed at civilians under the martial law of a foreign army, to blockades, to aerial bombardment, merely serves to illustrate that pain-infliction and deterrence are old concepts in international military and political practice. We have a real body of experience to tap on conventional deterrence, offering lessons that alternate between encouraging and discouraging.

For example, the British in 1914 ignored whatever pledges they had made to the United States and to the rest of the world about a "painless" blockade, attempting to coerce Imperial Germany into surrender by stopping food and all other imports. The prospect of the pain that British naval power could impose may or may not have been crucial for keeping U.S. troops out of Canada. In the end, the pain and suffering imposed by the naval force was very important for driving German forces out of France.

The first German air attacks on British cities in World War I were in part rationalized as retaliation (escalation) for the countervalue naval blockade being imposed by the British Navy. As noted, Londoners bore badly under the attacks of the German Zeppelin airships and the primitive biplane bombers, far less well than in the World War II "Blitz." Projecting forward from the 1914–18 experience, all the major powers thus approached World War II dreading air attacks; even Hitler showed significant concerns. By mechanisms we will have to discuss, the prospects of air attacks were not sufficient to deter the outbreak of war; deterrence failed in 1939. For a time. however, the mechanism of aerial bombardment still seemed sufficiently awesome to deter its opposite equivalent, as one of the last messages dispatched between Germany and Britain via Birger Dahlerus, the Swedish intermediary striving to avoid a war, was that the Luftwaffe would not bomb British cities as long as the Royal Air Force did not bomb German cities.

"Limited war" is the logical other side of the coin from deterrence, as each side fights with only part of its potential, precisely because the other side is doing the same. From September 1939 to the late spring of 1940, such a very strange kind of war was indeed undertaken, as each side so much feared what the other could inflict by aerial bombardment that it withheld what it could do itself.

The entire logic of the possibilities had already been developed during World War I, as the British Imperial War Cabinet contemplated the uses it would make of aerial attacks. Should they be directed toward destroying the other side's air force, or toward destroying the other side's military capacity more generally, perhaps by attacks on population? Or, because such attacks on population were so painful, should they be withheld and considered a retaliation to be imposed only if the other side engaged in such attacks?[7] As such options were contemplated after 1918, a fair number of theorists came to lean in the direction of simple deterrence, whereby such aerial bombardment, typically expected to include poison gas attacks, would be used as a deterrent.

As an aside, one of the persisting issues of the Cold War years was whether the Soviets really understood "deterrence," whether the Russian language even had a word for this concept. Various hawkish or even dovish Americans professed the view that it was somehow ethnocentric to project the concept of deterrence onto others. Deterrence was allegedly an American concept made up by American strategists.[8] At the minimum, we have shown here that it was understood by the British and the Germans long before the wave of American strategic analysis of the subject in the 1950s, long before the atomic bomb.

It does have to be noted that the "limited air war" of 1939–40 did not remain limited. Just as deterrence failed by the mere fact that World War II broke out, it failed also in that escalations occurred to all-out air war (but it did not fail in the ban imposed on chemical warfare after 1919, which somehow was respected all through World War II). Whatever lessons we will extract here will indeed have to take such "failures" into account.

Yet to note that the deterrence mechanism failed in these cases (i.e., did not persist in its effectiveness) is a far cry from reverting to the commonsense perception that no such mechanisms existed in the prenuclear years. Pessimists about the future of deterrence have sometimes (at least before the breakup of the Warsaw Pact) come to the pessimistic conclusion that conventional deterrence tends to fail. The most important task will be to calibrate the validity of this generalization.

## EARLY "EXTENDED DETERRENCE"

There has been less doubt and difficulty about whether basic nuclear deterrence would succeed once both the superpowers acquired the ability to impose assured destruction. If the Soviet Union attacked and destroyed U.S. cities, the United States would retaliate by destroying Soviet cities; and vice versa.

The real anguish of all discussions of deterrence theory since 1949 has pertained to whether extended deterrence was credible and workable, that is, to whether the United States would be willing to escalate to all-out nuclear destruction if the Soviet Union did nothing more than attack the cities of Europe (leaving those of North America untouched), or did nothing more than send its tanks forward to occupy and communize the cities of Europe. Would any rational and sensible U.S. President expose the American population to nuclear attack when the Soviet plan of aggression offered such a clear exemption from this?

Will there be a need for such extended deterrence after the events of 1989 and 1991, or is the threat of Soviet tank attack now so much weakened that this is a remedy for which there is no longer a disease? Was there any equivalent to such extended deterrence before nuclear weapons were invented, in the earlier days of conventional deterrence?

As we review the various mechanisms by which Presidents from Truman to Bush renewed the U.S. commitment to escalate on behalf of the Western European NATO countries, we can look for analogies to this from the past. Sometimes the link was established by simple jawboning in public statements and treaty commitments by which Europe was to become dear enough to the United States that it would be seen as "the fifty-first state." Sometimes the key mechanism seemed to be the deployment of U.S. troops abroad, so that they would be involved in combat if Europe was attacked and so that U.S. anger and commitments would be engaged. Often the key seemed to be the deployment of U.S. "tactical" or "theater" nuclear weapons in the likely path of the Soviet advance, so that such weapons would have a fair probability of coming into use in the event of a Soviet attack, even if a "rational" U.S. President chose not to use them when American cities still had not been attacked.

The analog to the symbolic commitment of forward deployment of U.S. troops is easy to find in earlier history. Consider the well-known French response in 1939 to the question of how many British troops were needed on the French defensive line against Germany: "One, and we will make certain he is killed on the first day."

Similarly, there are many examples of commitments made by verbal statements. Consider the British guarantees to Poland in 1939. It did not "naturally" make sense for Britain to enter a war if Poland was attacked, imposing naval blockade and perhaps air attack on the Germans rather than directly contributing to Polish defenses; but the statement, once made, became a matter of national honor and would therefore change what was natural to do thereafter. One could hope that this mechanism of threat would work to deter the Germans from ever attacking Poland (even while it risked German attacks on British commerce and German air raids on Britain in counter-retaliation, if deterrence failed, and the British threats then had to be carried through).

Yet the most important linkage for extended nuclear deterrence over the past forty years may have been less the public statements of various Presidents, or even the presence of U.S. forces on the scene (there were 500,000 U.S. troops in Vietnam at the peak of that conflict, and we still allowed Vietnam to be conquered by communist forces), but rather the simple physical presence in West Germany and South Korea of weapons of mass destruction, albeit labeled tactical nuclear weapons. If the Soviet tanks rolled, they would sooner or later encounter some batteries of nuclear artillery; these batteries would then become a trip-wire making escalation almost automatic. The "threat that leaves something to chance"[9] in this case included a decided risk that such weapons would be fired, rather than being allowed to fall into the hands of the enemy; the follow-on risk was always that the destruction would be so great that uncontrollable escalation would follow, including the devastation of Moscow and other major Soviet cities, and indeed of all the world's cities. The mere prospect of this presumably kept Soviet tanks from ever being sent forward; that is, extended deterrence succeeded.

For the trip-wire mechanism of having the deadliest of weapons deployed forward, to eliminate doubts about whether they would be used, there is no ready historical equivalent. Not enough destructive power was at hand to be put together into such small packages. What any single officer near the front elected to do in the heat of battle might not make enough difference. Projecting forward into a world relying less on nuclear weapons in the future, it is similarly more difficult to see how extended deterrence can be made to work.

Britain, as an island and a maritime power, had long felt the problem of how to make its threats credible around the world. If anyone were to try to take over all of Europe, it was credible that the British would intervene on the side of the weaker party to prevent a continental hegemony and head off threats to Britain itself. But what if the British commitment was instead to the self-government of Poland, which was not yet directly linked to the immediate safety of the British Isles? What of the British commitment to the protection of India against Russian approaches, which so much worried the inventor of "geopolitics," Halford Mackinder,[10] or to the independence of Canada from the United States? These were the two problems that vexed London all throughout the nineteenth century.

Deploying troops to India, maintaining an Indian Army, and extending advance posts up to the Khyber Pass amounted to deterrence by denial, which, as we have noted, is not really very analogous to nuclear deterrence.

Somewhat more analogous was the British threat of naval power in the nineteenth century for shielding Canada against the United States (unlike Czarist Russia, the United States was more vulnerable to the countervalue applications of a major navy). The basic British strategy was to threaten that in the event of a U.S. attack on Canada, the response would be as in the War of 1812, with attacks on U.S. commercial ships and on U.S. cities along the coasts. Washington might be burned again as in 1814, and Baltimore attacked (and many other cities), even while the British would have to fear countervalue counterattacks on their own commerce from the numerically inferior U.S. Navy, in the tradition of John Paul Jones and the raiders of 1812.

What made this form of extended deterrence by punishment so credible? Was it that some British naval vessels were deployed at bases along the Atlantic and Pacific coasts of Canada, so that they would automatically come into use if a war with the United States broke out? The linkage is not strong enough to amount to a trip-wire, because no single naval vessel packaged the escalatory or destructive equivalent of a nuclear artillery battery of the 1970s. Moreover, a U.S. ground advance toward Toronto would not have to cross British naval bases in New Brunswick or on Vancouver Island.

The extended deterrence linkage was more like the situation in Europe from 1945 to 1949, when the Soviets had no nuclear weapons at all and when the question of whether the United States would use its nuclear arsenal in response to a Soviet attack on Western Europe was very easy to answer. The U.S. Navy in 1876 had no way of destroying a city on the coast of England, but the British Navy had a very plausible capability for imposing major destruction on Boston, New York, or San Francisco. Even if Independence Day speeches in the United States still called for the liberation of Canada from British imperial rule, extended deterrence was quite credible here.

Desert Storm demonstrated how effective the conventional weapons of the U.S. armed forces can be, in countervalue impact as well as counterforce. If the U.S. military, in purely conventional terms, remains as much superior to its opposite numbers throughout the 1990s as the British Navy was a century earlier, we may maintain some important possibilities of extended non-nuclear deterrence by punishment. Thus, in one way extended deterrence can still work: in classic problem areas where an adversary would have the advantage over our allies if a conventional war ever broke out, and where our allies would otherwise be intimidated by the advantage.

It has to be stressed that there was always a double problem for Western Europe. The Soviet tanks might have actually rolled in an attempt at conquest, as tanks had done in Korea in 1950; or the mere prospect of conventional aggression and conquest might have intimidated the West Europeans into steering their behavior in the direction Moscow desired (the latter being allegedly what transpired in Finland since 1945, in what came to be labeled Finlandization). In the past, as in the future, the concerns are for both aspects of the problem; the mere shadow of a small possibility of military invasion can have important political effects.

The years of nuclear deterrence were years of an unusually strong need for extended deterrence, as Russian power had advanced much farther westward than in Mackinder's day, sitting at the Fulda Gap. They were years of an unusually easy coupling for extended deterrence, as the tactical nuclear weapons deployed just west of the Fulda Gap might suffice to make such deterrence credible. As we have noted, the earlier episodes of deterring extensions of commitment (what we may now have to call conventional extended deterrence) may have involved a less urgent need for such deterring of the military and geopolitical advantage, and less ability to couple so resoundingly.

## THE PROLIFERATION ISSUE

The coupling of extended deterrence in the nuclear years has depended on a degree of decentralization of command and control or of proliferation (which may amount to the same thing, as either increases the total of separate actors capable of initiating a nuclear war). An individual captain of artillery, or the French Premier, could at one time have caused nuclear escalation and the ultimate destruction of Moscow if Soviet tanks rolled forward, and that kept them from rolling in the first place.

We have made the case that what the theorists of air warfare *assumed* they had between 1918 and 1939 amounted to the atomic bomb. One has only to read Douhet's description of what air raids would be like to sense how much the actual air raids of World War II undershot the levels predicted. This explains why the mutual deterrence of air raids "worked" for a time between Hitler and the British, and then "failed."

> What could happen to a single city in a single day could also happen to ten, twenty, fifty cities. And, since news travels fast, even without telegraph, telephone or radio, what, I ask you, would be the effect upon civilians of other cities, not yet stricken but equally subject to bombing attacks? What civil or military authority could keep order, public services functioning, and production going under such a threat? . . . In short, normal life would be impossible in this constant nightmare of imminent death and destruction.[11]

Douhet's description of air raids might at first seem to match what actually occurred in Hamburg in 1943 and in Dresden and Tokyo in 1945, before nuclear weapons were even tested. But the important discrepancy is that such attacks with ordinary incendiary bombs constituted maximum efforts for the entire air forces executing them, such that the same fate could not have befallen other cities around Germany or around Japan on the same night. With nuclear warheads, one could indeed expect the same holocaust in a great number of cities in a single evening.

A second and very important difference is a corollary to this, for the non-nuclear destruction of a city, however awful as envisaged by the planners of the interwar years, could never be packaged into one bomb and thus could never pose such horrendous command and control problems. These are the command and control problems that we may have exploited as the trip-wire to make nuclear escalation and extended nuclear deterrence credible. These are the command and control problems that more generally worry us continuously, as we impose special psychological tests on all the officers assigned to such weapons and install Permissive Action Links (PAL) to physically prevent unauthorized use.

A single bomber pilot could deliver enough destruction to begin World War III and to plunge the world into the worst of thermonuclear exchanges. The missiles on board a single Submarine-launched ballistic missile (SLBM) submarine may be enough to initiate nuclear winter.

The result of such stark calculations is that the entire world now must be very concerned about the breakup of the Soviet Union. A repetition of the August 1991 coup attempt would arouse concerns about whether the nuclear weapons are locked up, or whether civil war could emerge in which rival factions brandished their nuclear weapons at each other and at the outside world's cities as well. Any more orderly secession of separate Soviet republics, in which nuclear weapons were carried off to become separate forces in a division of the inheritance, would similarly be a major cause for concern, both inside and outside the former Soviet Union.

The general proliferation problem with nuclear weapons has no real equivalent at this time with conventional weapons and conventional deterrence. The conventional U.S. Air Force can inflict damage comparable to nuclear weapons, as has recently been demonstrated in Iraq (counterforce) and was earlier demonstrated at Dresden and Tokyo (countervalue). But the Iraqi Air Force or the Israeli or Indian Air Force will probably never be able to inflict damage by conventional means comparable to what they could deliver by nuclear.

Perhaps, by the word *conventional* we really mean weapons that are limited in terms of how much destructiveness can be packaged. The total destruction that can be inflicted, in fire raids and in food blockades, is still severe: Hundreds of thousands of people could die of influenza in the wake of malnutrition, for example. But only entire countries can muster this—

and only larger countries—so that matching capabilities do not proliferate, so that one deterring countervalue capability can not be broken up into a dozen equally lethal packages, so that command and control do not become such an urgent problem, so that weapons can not so easily be deployed as trip-wires.

## CHEMICAL WEAPONS AS DEADLY WEAPONS

Does *conventional* with regard to weapon simply mean anything and everything that is non-nuclear? Or does it mean anything that does not offer extensive destruction in very small packages? Perhaps it is anything that does not involve an esoteric technology—esoteric by the standards, say, of 1910. Or is *conventional* anything that has not been banned by international agreement? Where do chemical weapons fit in?

The planners of the 1920s and 1930s expected that air raids would be much more destructive than what London actually experienced during the Blitz. Indeed, they expected that what Dresden experienced would occur quite often and quite early in a war. A very important part of their calculations was based on the use of chemical weapons in air attacks, along with the explosive and incendiary bombs that were indeed dropped. One of the more remarkable examples of conventional deterrence, for the duration of World War II, was that chemical weapons were not used on either side.

If the bans on such weapons are renewed, even after the recent breakdowns between Iran and Iraq, these may go on the shelf along with nuclear weapons. Former Secretary of Defense Robert McNamara argues that the only appropriate role for nuclear weapons is to deter the use of nuclear weapons on the other side.[12] Many will feel that the only appropriate use of chemical weapons is, likewise, to deter the use of chemical weapons on the other side. Then when we speak of conventional deterrence (i.e., whether war overall can be deterred), we would be leaving chemical weapons out of the picture just as we omit the nuclear.

However, if our discussion of conventional deterrence originates mainly from the world's aversion to *nuclear* weaponry, then, in light of recent trends in international military practice, chemical weapons may become more legitimized. Will chemical weapons and/or biological weapons then amount to the "poor man's H-bomb"? Will enough destructive power be packaged together here so that new trip-wires can be erected to make extended deterrence real, and so that all the logically equivalent worries about proliferation and command and control will then have to emerge?

The decisions taken by President Bush and the U.S. government, in pushing ahead with Desert Shield and Desert Storm, amounted at least to a certain debunking and shrugging off of the countervalue, as well as counterforce, awesomeness of chemical and biological weapons (CBW). Saddam Hussein in the end elected not to use such weapons, even though extensive use had been made against Iran. Was this all because the United States was well equipped with protection against such weapons, or was it because the United States was so well equipped with other conventional weapons that it could blunt and work around the Iraqi chemical arsenal? Some might conclude that the Iraqi restraints should be credited to the U.S. arsenal of nuclear weapons, with which Bush could have retaliated for any Iraqi CBW escalation.

Further breakthroughs remain possible in enhancing the deadliness of CBW weapons or in enhancing their battlefield impact. Such chemical or biological weapons in the end will probably settle between nuclear and conventional weapons with reference to several of the key attributes that we have been discussing here. They will be able to pose the threat of major countervalue damage, but never in such small packages (entailing a single push of a button) as thermonuclear weapons. A single submarine may today impose nuclear winter on the world, with everyone's concern being to ensure that the commanders of the submarine do not go berserk, but there is not likely to be an equivalent in CBW. A single nuclear artillery battery near the Fulda Gap may have imposed enough damage to initiate a chain of escalation that led to nuclear war, but there may not be enough catalytic impact in what a single such artillery battery could now do with CBW munitions.

## TARGETING FOR SURGICAL STRIKES

There is one more major difference in how conventional deterrence would work. Conventional weapons can now be coupled to greatly enhanced accuracies to produce what we have long advertised as surgical strikes, destroying what we seek while avoiding the destruction of other targets.

Nuclear deterrence was burdened with the certainty of hefty doses of collateral damage, almost no matter how the attack would be carried out. At times, this collateral damage has actually been welcomed, labeled as bonus destruction, as a way of getting around the immorality of targeting the innocent to deter the guilty. Hiroshima was thus labeled a military target in 1945, and the Strategic Air Command found military targets in virtually every major city of the Soviet Union. If one had wished to hit *only* military targets or *only* the Communist Party leadership, it would have been difficult to achieve.

As now previewed in the massive conventional air attacks on Iraq, however, it has become possible to aim precisely for command posts and for national leaders with conventional weapons (or only for military personnel in uniform) with a fair chance of avoiding massive killing of the civilians and the innocent. If Saddam Hussein escaped this form of high-technology punishment or assassination in 1991, it was indeed a close call (as also for

Khaddafy earlier), and the trend is definitely to make such leaders marked men.

An elementary understanding of deterrence logic suggests that one would not always want to punish or kill the leadership on the other side, for sometimes these people will be indispensable to the negotiation process. Much will depend on our intelligence estimates of who is playing what role. In the case of Desert Storm, the expectation was that it would be easier to achieve peace with Iraq if Saddam Hussein were killed. In World War II, it might have been easier to produce a German surrender and capitulation if Hitler were removed from the scene, and the U.S. Air Force did attempt one such operation against Berchtesgaden. By contrast, it would have been a great disaster for our hopes of terminating the war with Japan if the Emperor had been killed, for he proved crucial to accomplishing the Japanese surrender after the bombings of Hiroshima and Nagasaki.

One must remember that the level of total destruction imposed on Tokyo in the "conventional" fire-bombing of March 1945 was comparable to the casualties imposed on Hiroshima or Nagasaki. Yet there was one tremendous difference. In the 334-bomber incendiary raid on Tokyo, it was extremely likely that the Emperor would not die in the attack, as Japanese civil defense procedures would see to it that he was gotten to safety. Had the first atomic bomb been dropped on Tokyo, the Emperor would have been just as likely to die as anyone else in the surprise single-airplane attack.

Even in World War II, therefore, conventional weapons allowed the inflictor of retaliatory punishment to destroy one target while preserving another, and this will be much more the pattern in the future. Cities can be attacked or spared. National leaders can be spared or attacked. Military forces can be attacked without anything like the maximum attack on other targets. Or, if the military could be enlisted to restore what the attackers need, it could be spared while things it valued (e.g., its home towns, electric power plants, or national parks) were attacked.

## CHEMICAL WEAPONS AS DISCRIMINATE WEAPONS

Chemical weapons may be the wild card in all our predictions, perhaps offering the poor man's H-bomb, perhaps not. If the world turns very much against nuclear weapons, and if, at the same time, the precedents set in the Iran-Iraq war have eroded the taboo against chemical warfare, we may yet see CBW deterrence becoming an important part of conventional deterrence and/or a replacement for nuclear deterrence.[13]

Yet there is a different aspect of chemical warfare that some of its advocates would now intervene to address, namely that such weapons do not have to be deadly and, indeed, may offer almost totally nonlethal ways of fighting wars. If conventional warheads mated with high-accuracy delivery systems are markedly more discriminate than nuclear weapons, then even more discrimination and avoidance of unwanted damage—perhaps an avoidance of all permanent countervalue impact—can be achieved in the fuller development of CBW, especially of chemical weapons.

Chemical warfare was banned by international covenant in the 1920s, but this was at least in part a propaganda effort to impute evil to Germany; chemical weapons had been a German strong suit (allegedly used by the Germans first in World War I) and thus had to be painted as an illegitimate weapon. Yet the advocates of such weapons could cite World War I statistics to argue that these were ultimately the most humane instrument, disabling enemy machine guns without killing the soldiers manning such guns. The elementary ratio of disablement (counterforce) to death or crippling injury (countervalue) was better for poison gas than for rifle fire or machine gun or artillery fire, or bayonets, hand grenades, and the like. So why were such weapons to be banned?

An even stronger case can be made seven decades later, when totally nonlethal and noninjuring gases can be used to incapacitate a force of enemy soldiers as police would incapacitate a crowd of rioters. The irony of international law is that chemical warfare today can be used legally *only on civilians*. Where civilians are supposed to be exempt from attack by both conventional and nuclear weapons, only *soldiers* are legally exempt from all chemical attack. A government can use tear gas on its own civilians (and on enemy civilians, once their territory has been occupied), and this is now the most approved weapon for use against civilians. The Chinese government would have drawn much less disapproval for its handling of the students in Tiananmen if it had been equipped for and disposed to use such nonlethal weapons, rather than gunfire. But a government cannot legally use such a nonlethal chemical weapon against the enemy's soldiers in uniform (except when they have already laid down their arms to become prisoners of war).

The argument for resisting such lifting of the taboo against chemical and biological warfare is a powerful one, for once they are tampered with, taboos cannot easily be realigned or replaced. Although some very nonlethal weapons might be introduced, the same entire category of weapons includes new possibilities of supremely deadly weapons, as new diseases are perfected and new epidemics are launched, as deadly instruments are developed that could be packaged as small as an A-bomb or H-bomb. The legitimation of new techniques of deadliness would aggravate all the corners on proliferation and command and control.

Yet, as noted, the strength of the taboo against chemical warfare is already in question, and the choice may not be entirely ours on whether such weapons continue to be beyond the pale. As we speculate about a world in which nuclear weapons are more and more under a taboo, it may be a world in which chemical weapons are, relatively or absolutely, less so.

If the extreme of nonlethal chemical warfare were that soldiers would suffer nothing in combat except being put to sleep for a night, to awaken the next morning in a prisoner-of-war camp, what would this mean for deterrence as we know it? War might become no more destructive than a football game and might thus become too attractive. But deterrence is about making things unattractive.

## CONCLUSIONS

We must return to the fundamental philosophical question posed by Sir Julian Corbett, on whether military power can even be politically meaningful if no pain or spoiling of people's lives is involved. The ultimate conclusion would have to be that *any* kind of deterrence will continue to entail the imposition of suffering, even while the rules of civilization as they are applied to warfare continually claim to outlaw unnecessary suffering. In the artillery exchanges across the Suez Canal in 1970, the Egyptians and Israelis were attacking only "military targets" as men in uniform on each side were killed or wounded. Yet the intent on each side was to impose *pain*—letters would have to be sent home to grieving parents, as each side was trying to force the other to make concessions by such pain. The same holds for the terrorist attack on the U.S. Marine barracks in Beirut, officially a counterforce military target but a target chosen in no sense because its loss would incapacitate U.S. military power. On an enormously larger scale, the same holds for Falkenhayn's World War I offensive at Verdun in 1916, designed to lure the French into a defensive position in which they would suffer very high casualties, thus reducing their national willingness to persist with the war.

Chemical weapons may offer the physical capacity for totally nonlethal and noncountervalue war, much as with the Argentine use of rubber bullets in the initial invasion of the Falkland Islands in 1981. But the capacity for countervalue will remain and will almost surely be applied—indeed, it will have to be applied if there is to be any determinacy to deterrence patterns and patterns of peace and war.

## NOTES

1. Glenn Snyder, *Deterrence and Defense* (Princeton, New Jersey: Princeton University Press, 1961).
2. My elaborated analysis of these periods can be found in George H. Quester, *Deterrence before Hiroshima* (New York: John Wiley, 1966).
3. Giulio Douhet, *The Command of the Air* (New York: Coward-McCann, 1942).
4. See Kenneth Bourne, *Britain and the Balance of Power in North America* (Berkeley: University of California Press, 1967).
5. Sir Julian Corbett, *Principles of Maritime Strategy* (London: Conway Maritime Press, 1911).
6. Ibid., p. 94.

7. See H. A. Jones, *The War in the Air*, vol. 5 (Oxford: Clarendon Press, 1935).

8. For an example of such an argument, see Richard B. Foster, "On Prolonged Nuclear War," *International Security Review* 6, No. 4 (Winter 1981–82), pp. 497–518.

9. Thomas C. Schelling, *The Strategy of Conflict* (Cambridge, MA: Harvard University Press, 1960), pp. 182–203.

10. The fully developed version of what he began presenting at the beginning of the twentieth century is to be found in Halford J. Mackinder, *Democratic Ideals and Reality* (New York: W. W. Norton, 1962).

11. Douhet, *Command of the Air*, p. 58.

12. Robert S. McNamara, "The Military Role of Nuclear Weapons," *Foreign Affairs* 52, No. 1 (Fall 1983), pp. 59–80.

13. On the prospects for chemical warfare in general, see Victor Utgoff, *The Challenge of Chemical Weapons* (London: MacMillan, 1990).

# 8

# The Future of Deterrence in a New World Order

## *Robert P. Haffa, Jr.*

The United States is currently embarked on a search for a post–Cold War military strategy; the military strategies developed in support of postwar containment of the former Soviet Union are quickly being set aside. In deliberating on the role of deterrence within that future military strategy, we immediately encounter some theoretical and definitional problems. If strategy is defined as a means of matching ends and means, then deterrence has often, during the Cold War years, been described as a *strategy* that linked the objective of national security with the means needed to deter any aggression threatening the interests of the United States. As a grand strategy, therefore, deterrence also became an objective, and the military strategies designed in its support led to the means—the forces planned to underwrite deterrence. Now, in a new era, U.S. security interests endure, but the perception of the threat has eroded and the relevance of deterrence as an objective, or as a guide to military strategy and force planning, is called into question. Does deterrence have a future?

The thesis of this chapter is that deterrence, particularly conventional deterrence,[1] does have a future, but one very different from the way in which it was conceptualized and applied during the Cold War. The United States now faces a multipolar international political system, considerably altered from its bipolar predecessor, that may be characterized by the proliferation of advanced weaponry and armed conflict. However, there has been little thought given to the transferability of the theories and strategies of Cold War conventional deterrence to this new world order. Examining the use of conventional military power to deter in the future requires us to separate conventional deterrence from its Cold War past, when conventional threats were subordinated to those of theater or strategic nuclear weapons use.

Therefore, this chapter briefly reviews the theoretical foundations of conventional deterrence, questions the application of that theory to military strategy in light of a changed international political system and revolutionary conventional military capabilities, and suggests the strategic and force planning implications of adapting conventional deterrence to meet the challenges of a new world order.

## THEORETICAL FOUNDATIONS OF CONVENTIONAL DETERRENCE

Can we apply the tenets of classical deterrence theory to the new world order? There are some initial issues that we must deal with in thinking about the future of conventional deterrence. The first goes to the fundamental changes that are occurring in the international political system and the future U.S. role in that system. Whatever the new world order may turn out to be, it is not likely to be orderly or conflict-free. Historical grievances, unconstrained ambition, militant ideology, armed coercion, and the continued anarchical nature of the international system will provide plenty of opportunity and motivation for armed conflict—while making threats and planning contingencies difficult to foresee. Although democracies may be unlikely to go to war against each other, democratic states will remain decidedly in the minority. And the results of experiments with democracy in some states, as recent events in Haiti, Algeria, and Georgia suggest, may promote neither domestic nor international tranquillity.

Within this new world order, the United States retains vital interests and, despite some isolationist sentiments being expressed in the polls, will surely remain fully engaged in that system in pursuit of its political, economic, and strategic interests.[2] The rise of an increasingly global economy, on which American well-being and quality of life depends, also argues that a return to pre–world war isolationism is not very likely.

As the United States perceives adversaries in pursuing its interests in the new world order, the theories of deterrence developed as a guide to policy during the Cold War years are likely to be applied. That is because, in addition to the perceived success of those policies, deterrence goes to the heart of the central questions of international politics: How is force manipulated to attain political ends? How can wars be avoided?[3] Although we have seen neither the end of history's dialectical struggles nor the end of war, it is realistic as well as idealistic to continue to work toward an international system in which armed conflict becomes less probable, less destructive, and less costly. Although some universal concept of deterrence to render war obsolete—that all parties might calculate a negative cost benefit to the use of military force—may appear utopian at the end of mankind's bloodiest century, deterrence will remain an attractive way to exert U.S.

influence in the world and to dissuade would-be aggressors from challenging U.S. interests.[4]

To think about applying concepts of deterrence in this new post–Cold War world, we need to define some terms and examine the formulation of classic deterrence theory as it has been applied to conventional deterrence. In its most general form, deterrence is simply the persuasion of one's opponent that the costs and risks of a given course of action he might take outweigh its benefits. The classic concentration of deterrence theory, and the focus of this chapter as well, has been on using *military* capability to deter unwanted *military* acts. Thus, deterrence, for our purpose here, can be defined as a "policy that seeks to persuade an adversary, through the threat of military retaliation, that the costs of using military force to resolve political conflict will outweigh the benefit."[5] In deterrence terms, the primary function of military force should be to prevent its reciprocal use by one's opponents.

Is this formulation of deterrence, fashioned in the nuclear age, still relevant? As George Quester describes in the previous chapter, there was deterrence before Hiroshima, but conventional deterrence theory, as we have most recently known it, has been strongly influenced by the bipolar, nuclear, strategic U.S.–USSR relationships of the Cold War era.[6] What can we learn from classic deterrence theory that applies to concepts of conventional deterrence in a very different world? To answer that question, we need to remind ourselves of some of the requirements, components, and critiques of deterrence theory.[7]

The components of deterrence normally include the following requirements:

- *Capability*: the acquisition and deployment of military forces able to carry out plausible military threats to retaliate.
- *Credibility*: the declared intent and believable resolve to protect a given interest.
- *Communication*: relaying to the potential aggressor, in an unmistakable manner, the capability and will to carry out the deterrent threat.

These requirements, formulated principally at the level of strategic nuclear deterrence, have also been applied to deterrent confrontations involving conventional forces. Moreover, in addition to these requirements, a considerable amount of theoretical work has been done in an attempt to define and differentiate among the ways in which that theory might be applied:[8]

• We realize there is a difference between *immediate* deterrence (a potential attacker is actively considering the use of force, and the deterrer, aware of that threat, issues a counterthreat to deter) and *general* deterrence (the possibility of armed conflict is present, but the potential attacker is not actively considering the use of force to threaten the interests of the deterrer).

• We understand the difference between *pure* or *fundamental* deterrence (we are eyeball-to-eyeball with the adversary and, hopefully, he blinks) and *extended* deterrence (in which the objective is to defend allies and friends from attack). In the Cold War years, the United States focused on the *global* deterrence of a single adversary on a *regional* basis, and now, in a new world order, is attempting to make a transition to the regional deterrence of multiple actors on a global basis.

• We know the difference between *strategic nuclear* deterrence (the level at which the majority of the theorizing has occurred, at which the use of intercontinental thermonuclear weapons has been threatened, and at which deterrence is usually thought to have held) and *conventional* deterrence (the level that has received considerably less attention, at which, by definition, threats to use unconventional weapons of mass destruction are excluded, and at which deterrence, arguably, has been prone to fail). An important distinction drawn during Cold War formulations of this dichotomy, but subject to considerable question in the present environment, is that in cases of strategic nuclear deterrence, the costs of deterrent failure are inherently unacceptable, whereas in conventional deterrent situations the costs are more bearable and can, therefore, be traded for political or other gain. Theoretical discussions of deterrence have made clear that the range of likely cost/benefit calculations shifts dramatically when the deterrent calculus of strategic nuclear warfare is compared with regional conventional conflict. In the case of conventional deterrence, the actual use of force is not so destructive as to be completely irrational in the sense of not serving any reasonable ends.[9]

Despite the richness of this body of theory, classic formulations of deterrence, even in the purest of strategic nuclear deterrent situations, have encountered considerable criticism.[10] The most significant include the following:

• Although it can be argued that nuclear deterrence worked during the Cold War, we do not know that for sure. (The Soviet Union may never have wished to invade Europe or to attack the United States with nuclear weapons.) It is very difficult to prove deterrent successes because that would require showing why an event did not occur. There is inherent uncertainty about the antecedent causes one cites in such cases—other plausible factors can always be suggested.

• The emphasis on the rational calculation of the cost of a retaliatory response has also been faulted in deterrence theory; policymakers who start wars may pay more attention to their own domestic needs or to other internal or external factors than to the military capabilities or options of their possible adversaries or to the potential severity of the outcome.

• Deterrence theory has also been criticized for contributing to a spiral of conflict. The threat of retaliation may be so great and so destabilizing that it becomes in the aggressor's interest to preempt or escalate—the classic "security dilemma" that acting to enhance one's own security may weaken that of one's potential adversary.

• Deterrence at conventional levels has tended to "fail." On one hand, it has been argued that the use of conventional military force has not always equated to a failure of deterrent doctrine. Unless the requirements for deterrence were put in place, the theory could not be expected to hold; deterrence theory, owing to its incompleteness, could not be held accountable for the misapplications of deterrent strategy in U.S. foreign policy. Therefore, deterrence failures were not inconsistent with deterrence theory, provided they could be attributed to the absence of a clear commitment or to insufficient capability or credibility.[11] On the other hand, it has been argued that because the risks of conventional conflict could be perceived as relatively modest, the costs of choosing to go to conventional war, even if the likelihood of attaining a military victory was granted little confidence, could easily be outweighed by perceived political benefits.[12]

The differences between the perceived costs and risks of nuclear versus conventional deterrence are very important for our discussion here. Bipolar nuclear deterrence has a number of special properties that make its costs and risks relatively easy to calculate: two principal actors, well-defined strike scenarios, a finite number of weapons planned against a well-known target set, calculable and prohibitive losses under any plausible exchange. However, past attempts to conduct similar simulations at a conventional level, particularly when conventional deterrent strategies were often underpinned by theater or strategic nuclear weapons, have tended to make analysts and policymakers see conventional deterrence as less rigorous, far more context-dependent, and ultimately far more unreliable as a guide to strategy. That situation has changed. It has changed in terms of the nature and capabilities of the actors the United States may be attempting to deter in the new world order, and it has changed owing to the revolution in conventional military capabilities (e.g., space reconnaissance, global command and control, precision weapons and stealth technology) that has occurred over the last decade. For example, the development and deployment of survivable conventional delivery platforms and very precise munitions recently displayed in the Gulf War—the F–117s, with a probability of target destruction of about .8, approximated the requirements of the strategic nuclear war fighting plan (the single integrated operation plan or SIOP)—suggest that conventional force has immediately become more punishing, more usable, and therefore more credible.

In spite of these changes, which we might, with apologies to Thomas Kuhn, characterize as the signs of a "paradigm shift," the theoretical model of a conventional deterrent situation remains essentially unchanged at this time. Consider the following scenario. A potentially hostile power displays an interest and a capability, if not an immediate intent, to encroach on or to directly attack nation-states, other international actors, or geographic/

resource interests in which the United States has a major or vital interest in preserving the status quo. Such attacks can be deterred if that power calculates the results from that prospective military action to be problematic and unattractive, that is, the United States will defend that state, region, or interest and force the attacker to pay high costs.

Therefore, many of those searching for a post–Cold War strategy believe that much of the deterrence theory developed in the past is still relevant; the requirements of capability, credibility, and communication will continue to apply in the future. Although the central focus of the deterrent relationship has become multipolar and less nuclear-intensive, these were not relationships left unconsidered in the original development of the theory. It seems clear, therefore, that reinforcing the logic of conventional deterrence on its would-be adversaries should be the main objective of U.S. defense policy over the next decade or so. The principle stumbling block, in attempting to apply that deterrence theory to a coherent military strategy, appears to be the tendency of conventional deterrence to "fail." If conventional rather than nuclear forces are about to assume a central role in deterring conflict, theoretical work now needs to be focused on the use or threatened use of conventional force. How, in a new world order, can a policy of conventional deterrence be communicated and a supporting military strategy and force structure be justified? One unconventional proposition is that a past "failure" of conventional deterrence may be essential to a future deterrent success: *In order to communicate a credible deterrent threat, capable conventional military force must first be used.*

## APPLYING DETERRENCE THEORY TO CONVENTIONAL MILITARY STRATEGY

In the post–Gulf War world, deterrent theory fashioned during the Cold War may still prove helpful, but the implementation of deterrent strategy is likely to be considerably different. In other words, while the *requirements* of deterrence may be little changed, past formulations of conventional deterrent *strategies, or goals*, focusing on large ground armies facing each other across a central front may become increasingly irrelevant (although such a confrontation may yet remain, as in Korea, and can be created elsewhere, as in Kuwait).

There have been some major studies of conventional deterrence strategies to this point,[13] but it is not clear that they are very transferable to the deterrent problems of the future. For example, in the nuclear-dominated deterrent studies of the Cold War past, conventional deterrence has been seen as:

• A "handmaiden" to containment of the Soviet Union—in a bipolar setting, not generally applicable to less simple and less polarized crises.

• Appropriate only in support of "symmetrical" approaches to containment in order to match the enemy's moves at the level of provocation, for example, NSC–68 and "Flexible Response." Asymmetrical responses (shifting the nature of one's reaction into avenues better suited to one's strengths against the adversary's weaknesses) relied ultimately on threats of nuclear escalation.

• Most valuable for its ability to buy time to resolve disagreements peaceably.

• A *defensive* application of deterrence strategy. Flexible response in NATO Europe implied deterrence at all levels, but it was much weaker (purposefully?) at the conventional level and was politically restricted from preemptive or offensive options.

• Deterrence principally by *denial*—blocking the enemy's military objectives through the attrition of his attacking forces. Deterrence by *punishment*, that is, reaching over the battlefield to target the aggressor's leadership and infrastructure was left for nuclear weapons.

• A method of influencing primarily an opponent's political calculus of the acceptable costs and risks of his potential initiative, rather than threatening overwhelming punishment and societal destruction. Conventional forces did not provide the means to deter by force alone and had to be supplemented by diplomatic, political, and economic instruments. Conventional deterrence, unable to be operationalized at solely a military level, became very messy, very political, very context-dependent.

• A means of *extending* deterrence to allies and friends, but ultimately dependent on the credibility of a U.S. nuclear commitment. Conventional deterrence in Europe, for example, could not rely solely on the stationing of U.S. troops there (although that presence was clearly important politically and militarily but became an integral part of a broader, multifaceted influence process that, in the end, relied on nuclear threats.

Because conventional deterrence during the Cold War relied to such an extent on its coupling with nuclear threats, past military strategies of conventional deterrence are much less relevant to the new world order than is the body of theory examined in the first section of this chapter. For example, as the theory reminded us, most "failures" of conventional deterrence have resulted from a lack of credibility in the deterrent threat. Although capability may be evident and an interest communicated, the resolve of the deterrer is arguably the most difficult element of the deterrent equation to structure and to assess. Can the credibility of a conventional deterrent be enhanced for more effective application in the future? The requirements and applications of deterrence theory developed in the previous section suggest three areas of emphasis: (1) the visibility of the military force; (2) a documented record of willingness to use force in the past; and (3) the rationality of the use of force once deterrence has failed.

### Visibility of Military Forces

One of the critical requirements for deterrence has been the substantial deployment of U.S. forces overseas, not merely as a symbol or a trip-wire but as a significant military force to be reckoned with. If deterrence is to be extended, it must be seen to exist. The presence of U.S. conventional forces probably acted as a restraint on the spread of nuclear weapons to our allies, unless they found our assurances incredible (France) or we lacked the in-place treaties and troops (Israel). A new military strategy based on conventional deterrence must pose a "virtual presence," even in a period of U.S. military retrenchment and overseas base closures. For future U.S. conventional forces to deter, they must maintain some form of visibility in order to be perceived as credible and capable.

### Willingness to Use Force

Conventional deterrence "failures" have not been seen as inconsistent with deterrence theory, provided that failing could be attributed to the absence of a clear commitment or to insufficient credibility. Therefore, it was postulated, actions could be taken to forestall deterrence failures: conveying an early commitment, demonstrating resolve in addition to declaring interest, pointing to past uses of force. In post–Cold War conventional deterrence, however, deterrence "failures" may be part of the solution as well as part of the problem. It may be implicit that owing in part to a past U.S. declaratory policy and practice of preferring diplomatic or economic instruments to the use of military force, potential aggressors may simply not be persuaded that the United States will readily respond with force when its interests are threatened. It may have to become explicit, therefore, that *the use of force may be necessary in some cases for deterrence to hold in other crises.* In the past, the question has been asked if leaders of democratic states needed to commit armed forces over relatively unimportant issues in an attempt to establish credibility in more vital, yet more risky, regions. Deterrence theory stressed that not being tough enough in a situation may bring peace only at the expense of one's image of resolve and, therefore, at the cost of long-term deterrence and stability.[14] The argument here is that the use of conventional force is necessary to enhance credibility in the new world order, and that it now can be used in support of the most vital interests without undue risk. Thus, a theoretical deterrence "failure," such as in Iraq's invasion of Kuwait, may have significant strategic implications for the future of conventional deterrence.

### Rationality of the Use of Force

Somewhat ironically, despite its "failures," conventional deterrence is theoretically more credible in terms of carrying out deterrent threats than is nuclear deterrence. Once nuclear deterrence fails, it may be irrational for the deterrer to respond to the challenge owing to the enormous destruction to his own society that may result. In the words of Paul Nitze, he may be self-deterred.[15] A conventional deterrent, however, can be made to appear more certain and, therefore, more credible: Rationality does not have to fail; the nation does not have to threaten to "stumble into war" in order to respond; doomsday forecasts do no have to be considered. In practice as well as in theory, there are more likely to be greater risks and uncertainties resulting from not carrying out a conventional deterrent threat than in acting to support declared policy. The operational implication of that theoretical principle is a strategy of conventional deterrence that allows for the likely use of military force.

A central point of these arguments—overlooked in past conventional deterrence theory—is that the use of conventional force (presumed in the past to be a "failure" of conventional deterrence) can in the future be a major contributor to the deterrence of conventional conflict. If that is so, the problem now is that much on which the United States previously constructed its conventional deterrent is going away: U.S. base structure overseas is being rapidly drawn down, and the United States is moving toward a smaller military force structure relying on forward presence rather than forward deployment, with diminished power projection assets. This brings into serious question the ability of U.S. strategy and forces to meet the requirements of capability, credibility, and communication. What military strategies are available to match an objective of conventional deterrence with fewer forces stationed abroad and fewer forces available at home?

When we consider the strategies of conventional deterrence that have dominated the Cold War years, we find them inadequate in meeting the challenges of the new world order. For example, John Mearsheimer argued that the essence of conventional deterrence was being able to halt an enemy breakthrough, which in turn led to a successful blitzkrieg. As military analysts focused on the European central front, however, there was considerable debate regarding which military strategy could best meet that deterrent requirement:[16]

- *A conventional trip-wire.* This would demonstrate commitment but would be designed to fail quickly and rely on vertical escalation to deter.
- *Horizontal escalation.* It was assumed that direct conventional defense was beyond America's reach but that deterrence could be strengthened by threatening the adversary's other interests.
- *Conventional direct defense.* Many defense analysts characterized variously as optimists or reformers argued that a direct conventional de-

fense (and, therefore, deterrence) was possible with modest reforms or improvements in troop deployment, employment, strategy, or doctrine.

For a number of reasons, none of these strategies appear particularly appropriate or attractive in a post–Cold War world. Trip-wire theories encourage nuclear use and, perhaps, nuclear proliferation, and they fall into the same credibility traps of the past. Strategies of horizontal escalation are subject to the "spiral of conflict" critiques of deterrence, as well as to the argument that other regions might not be nearly as valuable as the focus of primary conflict—particularly when the challenger is a regional rather than a global power. Moreover, the United States and the world community are more interested in containing any conventional conflict, not expanding it. Structuring a direct conventional defense, which in the past was considered the most reliable of deterrent strategies, is less plausible in the future owing to the decline and retrenchment of U.S. general purpose forces and the uncertain nature of the threat. Which, then, appear to be the components of a military strategy that will effectively support the requirements of conventional deterrence in the new world order?

Based on the theoretical requirements that continue to hold, a conventional deterrent strategy must be both capable and credible. If we delve more deeply into the requirements developed in the previous section and apply them to the problem of conducting regional deterrence on a global basis, a conventional strategy of deterrence can be seen to have the following essential characteristics:

• *General as opposed to immediate.* However, the capability to invoke an immediate deterrent threat against a specific adversary must remain.

• *Extended as opposed to pure or fundamental.* This property has three components. First, the United States is not in danger of conventional attack on its homeland but is seeking a way to extend deterrence and defense to vital regions, resources, and interests. Given the capability, extended conventional deterrence is far more credible than extended nuclear deterrence, because it obviates the "trading Boston for Bonn" question. Although the United States will wish to maintain both strategic nuclear forces and theater nuclear power projection capability to deter the fractionated former Soviet empire as well as other potential proliferators, it appears that limited strategic and theater defenses will gradually replace some of the assured destruction deterrent theories enshrined in the ABM treaty. Second, we need to differentiate a Cold War strategy deterring *global* threats from a post–Cold War strategy deterring *regional* threats on a global scale. In other words, we are seeking a conventional capability that is *strategic* rather than *theater*. The U.S. forces designed to deter will primarily be based in the continental United States and therefore must have immediate global reach and power projection capability. Third, the implication of global or strategic capability is one of a massive attack, although we may wish to eschew the term *massive conventional retaliation*. The point is, if we have read Schelling, that we don't want to admit it.[17] This formulation of deterrence strategy is the antithesis of the graduated escalatory response that characterized the Cold War strategy in which sudden and massive escalation (fearful of the next, nuclear step) was avoided at all costs. The purpose here is to terminate conflict rapidly.

• *Conventional as opposed to nuclear*. It is in the interest of the United States to deemphasize nuclear deterrence, weapons, and systems, particularly as the former Soviet nuclear threat diminishes (and, one hopes, with it the nuclear capabilities and intentions of the members of the Commonwealth of Independent States). Conventional deterrence can also be seen as more effective than nuclear deterrence, as its capability is enhanced by the certainty (therefore, credibility) of its response. One of the striking differences regarding the future of conventional deterrence, at least in the near term, is that the United States enjoys an enormous margin of global reach and power projection capability over any immediately emerging conventional rival. Thus, the United States should not be self-deterred in a crisis, and the threat of use of conventional force, to include preemption, becomes more credible.[18]

Conventional deterrence in the post–Cold War world, then, requires a new military strategy that can be extended credibly to distant regions, that can be quick in response and decisive in application. The military success enjoyed by the United States and its coalition allies in the Gulf War suggests that relatively small but very powerful, precise, intense, and survivable forces may be able to meet the theoretical requirements and strategic needs of extended conventional deterrence. If so, the properties that will characterize conventional deterrent strategy will be very different from those that defined it during the Cold War. A strategy of effective conventional deterrence must be decoupled from nuclear threats, asymmetrical in threat and application, intense and overwhelming in its threat, offensive with a capability for punishment as well as denial, and extended globally through new technologies and weapons systems.

Based on this analysis, the United States is faced with developing a military strategy of conventional use that can be extended to interests abroad and can be generally applied. The United States now requires the military strategy and forces to underwrite a theory of general extended conventional deterrence. Can it be done?

## GENERAL EXTENDED CONVENTIONAL DETERRENCE AND HOW TO GET THERE

The United States has a difficult post–Cold War dilemma. It must remain actively engaged in the new international order to ensure the stability that favors U.S. interests at home and abroad, while cutting U.S. defense expenditures in order to allow some "peace dividend" transfers to other budgetary accounts and, in general, contributing to U.S. global economic competitiveness. What do we want U.S. military forces to be able to accomplish in the new world order? Unfortunately, the list of U.S. national security goals has not been reduced:[19]

- Halt nuclear proliferation, reduce nuclear arms, lower the nuclear threat;
- Ensure favorable regional control and supply of oil at a reasonable price;
- Extend deterrence in contingencies known (Persian Gulf, Korea) and unknown;
- Maintain military capability to deter or fight major wars;
- Continue the Cold War inhibitions against violent patterns of great power behavior;
- Provide reassurance to our allies while holding a nuclear card.

These national security objectives are, for the most part, Cold War goals that continue to apply. But even greater restrictions have been placed on the use of military force (and, therefore, on the formulation of conventional deterrence) since the Gulf War. Military planners are now receiving planning guidance that approximates the following:

> • Plan to conduct an effective military campaign in a distant region to deter a sophisticated adversary. He may possess unconventional (nuclear, biological, chemical) weapons and the capability to deliver those weapons within the region.
>
> • Plan to use continental U.S. (CONUS) based forces on very short notice. Although U.S. forces may be present in the region, they will not be there in numbers sufficient to conduct a stalwart defense or successful counterattack without immediate CONUS reinforcement.
>
> • Plan on defeating the enemy with U.S. forces alone early in the campaign. Significant allied military contributions, with the exception of indigenous forces in some contingencies, will not be available until later in the war.
>
> • Plan to defeat the enemy quickly by denying his objectives and, as required, by punishing his war-making infrastructure. Do this with as few friendly casualties as possible, while minimizing collateral damage.
>
> • Plan to do all this as quickly as possible, before public support dissolves or allied resolve weakens. Hedge against the possibility of a second, simultaneous regional contingency and plan your forces assuming continuing declines in the U.S. defense budget in the near future.

These new defense planning factors might make a force planner pine for the good old days of the "two and one-half war" strategic concept; certainly they should alleviate the fears of anyone who was concerned that the U.S. military would have little to do in the new world order. Can a strategy of general extended conventional deterrence coupled with the military capabilities demonstrated during the Gulf War, meet such demanding guidance?

Some have suggested that the U.S. military is already well on its way to meeting these goals. Writing in *Foreign Affairs* after the Gulf War, William Perry pointed to a "new conventional military capability" that "adds a powerful dimension to the ability of the United States to deter war."[20] Key to this new capability were "a new generation of military support systems"—intelligence sensors, defense-suppression systems, precision-guided munitions, and stealth technologies—that gave true and dramatic meaning to the term *force multiplier*. In order to avoid similar foreign entanglements in the future, Perry argued, the United States needs to use this new-found strength to deter future wars, not to fight them.

Critics of deterrence theory might be quick to note that Perry wrote the piece *after* the force had been used, after deterrence can be said to have failed. Why should we presume that the military force used in the Gulf should be effective in deterring future conventional conflict? Answering that question requires a degree of speculation as to why conflict resulted with Iraq, and it reinforces our proposition that conventional deterrence, to be effective, must rely on the occasional, purposeful, and discriminate use of conventional force.

Given what we now know—what Saddam Hussein was prepared to suffer—the deterrent threat required in August 1990 may have been well beyond what could have been credibly fashioned. Absent the visible commitment of U.S. forces to the region, the effectiveness of conventional deterrence in the Gulf depended, almost totally, on an invitation from Arab states in the region to the United States to intervene—something they were very reluctant to offer until the invasion of Kuwait had become a fait accompli. It is difficult, therefore, to conclude that deterrence failed in the Gulf because there was so little in place, in terms of commitment or capability, to deter the Iraqi invasion. Supporters of deterrence doctrine might also argue that rapid military and diplomatic measures by the United States and the UN deterred Iraq from moving beyond Kuwait into Saudi Arabia. But, as ever, aggressive intentions are difficult to prove. However, both supporters and critics of deterrence theory and strategy, in explaining the events leading to the crisis, would probably agree that Saddam apparently believed, or wanted to believe, that:[21]

- The United States would not use force;
- The United States would not fight or risk heavy casualties;

- Regional Arab states would not accept U.S. troops on their soil;
- If Arab states did invite U.S. troops in, their governments would face severe internal disruption and, perhaps, be overthrown.

Of course, we know now that the United States did act, the Arab states did support U.S. troop presence (albeit somewhat fleetingly), and the capability of U.S. forces and the credibility of U.S. commitments were broadcast to the world in real and prime time. Such demonstrated resolve and capability, as Perry has argued and as is being presented here, suggests that *the use of conventional force should be judged, rather than as a failure of conventional deterrence in a singular case, as an important element of establishing the credibility of a general, extended conventional deterrent in future crises.* It is not, as some have suggested, that Saddam Hussein was "undeterrable"; rather, it was that notions of how Saddam might be deterred were caught in the Cold War mindset of conventional deterrence. This discrete yet overwhelming use of conventional force, narrowly seen as a deterrent failure if one focuses on the single case study of Iraqi aggression in the summer of 1990, can also be seen (if some Cold War theoretical baggage is jettisoned) as an important first step in the structuring of a new strategy of general extended conventional deterrence that may influence international relations for a decade or more.

While the United States currently attempts to exploit its military success in the Gulf with diplomatic and economic initiatives, there is plenty of work to be done if it is to retain the military capability of acting quickly and decisively in future contingencies. What kinds of capabilities and what sorts of forces are going to be required to underwrite a strategy of extended general conventional deterrence? Contemporary economic conditions demand prudent choices in planning forces to underwrite conventional deterrence. One approach to help us choose wisely is to think of the military tasks that U.S. forces are most likely to confront:

• *Show of force*—force without war. With fewer U.S. forces stationed abroad, the need to project forces quickly to demonstrate U.S. commitment and resolve will remain important. Depending on the contingency, that force should be more than just the shadow of power; it will need sufficient, sustainable firepower.

• *Punitive raid*—the Libyan model. In response to a terrorist attack or in a preemptive conventional strike against unconventional capabilities, the United States must be able to strike multiple aim points simultaneously (200 or so in order to attack weapons sites, suppress enemy defenses, and take out command and control capabilities) across great distances, without seeking overflight, basing rights or access to facilities from any foreign state and to conduct that raid with impunity.

• *Police action*—Grenada and Panama. The United States will wish to retain the capability to restore order and protect U.S. citizens and property during times of turmoil and political unrest or government overthrow. The need is for rapid deployment of light infantry forces with adequate air cover, and precursor air strikes as required.

- *Air superiority*—the war against Iraq. Air Force doctrine has long held that establishing air superiority is essential to allowing air-to-surface and surface warfare to be conducted successfully. During the first twenty-four hours of air strikes on Baghdad, for example, the emphasis was placed on targeting key military facilities and $C_3$ infrastructure to blind the enemy and disrupt his ability to use and control his forces.
- *Halting, delaying or disrupting a cross-border invasion*—what if Saddam Hussein had not halted at the Saudi border? In the earliest days of a conflict (such as one that might have occurred if Saddam had elected to continue his offensive along the Gulf littoral), it may be necessary to bring in heavy firepower—available primarily through survivable, long-range airpower—to slow the onrush of enemy ground forces and buy time for the arrival of ground and naval forces or for other diplomatic and military actions.
- *Parallel (or simultaneous) warfare*—conducting an intense, coordinated coherent campaign. Although a concentration of U.S. military forces on a single aspect of enemy capability may be necessary in the first days of a conflict (and may even be required if resources are at a premium), the execution of parallel warfare, that is, concurrently executing multiple operations at every level of an enemy's target set, would prove far more effective in bringing the conflict to a rapid and decisive close while minimizing friendly casualties. Parallel warfare implies the ability to employ the kind of overwhelming but precise use of military force needed to underwrite a strategy of general extended conventional deterrence.

## CONCLUSIONS

In summary, to make viable a theory of conventional deterrence that can be extended to general threats to U.S. global interests in the coming decade, there will be a need for the United States to construct a coherent military strategy to defend those interests, ensure stability, and challenge would-be aggressors to adjust to the new world order—or pay the price. It can be declared softly, as long as a big stick is nearby. Without the extensive forward deployment of U.S. military forces that characterized the Cold War years, however, there will be a need for increased exercises and displays of power projection capability to demonstrate U.S. global reach. Those can be multilateral, two-way, or humanitarian—even UN peacekeeping missions—so long as they are visible.

*Most important, and in the greatest departure from Cold War formulations of conventional deterrence theory, it will be necessary to use the force in order for it to deter.* The Gulf War has provided the United States some leverage for the near term, but unwillingness to use the force—or a reluctance to declare that force will be used in moving from a general deterrent threat to an immediate one—will quickly squander that opportunity to influence. Above all, we must stop setting impossible standards for conventional deterrence. It will inevitably break down on occasion, but such occasions provide the opportunity to demonstrate the price of failure and rejuvenate the credibility of conventional deterrence, thereby contributing to a new period of stability. In other words, conventional deterrence can produce long cycles of stability instead of constant, overlapping intervals of conflict that are far more likely in the absence of a carefully constructed U.S. and allied deterrence capability.

The purpose of formulating a revised theory and strategy of general extended conventional deterrence is not only offered as a guide to military strategy in the post–Cold War years but also as a guide to planning the general purpose forces and capabilities the United States and its allies will need to underwrite that theory and strategy. At the macro-level, the implications for force planning for extended conventional deterrence appear to be as follows:

• *For U.S. ground forces*: U.S. Army and Marine forces will need to retain the capabilities to serve both as a deterrent/defense force to protect vital U.S. interests abroad and as an intervention force to restore stability in Third World countries. In either case, a rapidly deployable, flexible contingency force with an emphasis on airborne, air assault and light infantry forces will be required. Heavy, mechanized forces must be maintained to hedge against larger contingencies, but they will be diminished in role and size owing to the time it takes to deploy them from the CONUS and the declining probability of their near-term use. Prepositioning, as available, can be used to lessen deployment time in key regions, and strategic airlift will remain important to get the troops to the war on time.

• *For U.S. naval and marine forces*: Power projection, rather than sea lane protection and control, will become the mainstay of U.S. naval forces, and the instruments of that task will remain the carrier battle groups and amphibious ready groups, augmented, owing to their projected smaller numbers and force composition, by attack submarines employed in power projection roles.

• *For U.S. air forces*: Just as strategic air forces were the centerpiece of the strategy of massive retaliation in the 1950s, so will they be in underwriting extended conventional deterrence in the 1990s and beyond. Long-range strategic bombers, particularly limited numbers of stealthy ones, will play an ever more important role in the new world order because they are nondestabilizing; can carry large, varied, precise payloads; can project heavy firepower on short notice from U.S. bases; and are both flexible and survivable.

The thesis of this chapter has been that the United States has a major role to play in ensuring stability and security in a new world order and possesses unique military capabilities to deter acts of aggression that would threaten that order. However, the conventional deterrence theories and strategies of the past that were subordinated to a bipolar strategic nuclear competition are neither relevant nor welcome. A coherent concept of general extended conventional deterrence can guide U.S. military strategy in pursuit of a more stable and secure future international order and can assist prudent force planning within the reduced defense budgets of the 1990s.

## NOTES

1. This chapter focuses only on the future of conventional deterrence and does not address nuclear issues except to note that much of the theorizing about deterrence during the Cold War was necessarily wrapped in bipolar and strategic nuclear thinking. For some recent (and divergent) work on the future of nuclear deterrence and forces, see "The Role of Nuclear Weapons in the New World Order," briefing by Thomas C. Reed, Chairman of the JSTPS/SAG Deterrence Study Group, October 19, 1991, and "National Security in the 1990s: Defining a New Basis for U.S. Military Forces," by Congressman Les Aspin, delivered to the Atlantic Council, January 6, 1992.

2. In August 1990, President Bush called for a defense policy of "peacetime engagement every bit as constant and committed to the defense of our interests in today's world as in the time of conflict and cold war." See "In Defense of Defense," President George Bush's speech to the Aspen Institute Symposium, August 2, 1990, in Richard Cheney, Secretary of Defense, *Annual Report to the President and the Congress*, Washington, D.C.: U.S. Government Printing Office, January 1991, p. 131.

3. See Robert Jervis, "Deterrence Theory Revisited," *World Politics* 31 (January 1979), pp. 289–294.

4. See Carl Kaysen, "Is War Obsolete?" *International Security* 14, No. 4 (Spring 1990), p. 48.

5. Michael Howard, "Deterrence and Reassurance," *Foreign Affairs* 61, No. 2 (Winter 1982–83), pp. 309–324. Howard argued that the problem was one not only of deterrence but of reassurance: of persuading one's own people, allies, and friends that the benefits of military action, or preparation for it, will outweigh the costs. Howard's prescription for reassurance, in a Cold War of nuclear parity, was conventional defense. The concept of conventional deterrence being advanced here for a post–Cold War era should also reassure.

6. See George Quester, *Deterrence before Hiroshima* (New Brunswick, NJ: Transaction, 1986).

7. Classical deterrence theory was developed in the 1950s and 1960s by a group of "first wave" deterrence theorists including Brodie, Kaufmann, Kahn, Schelling, and Snyder, who assumed that states could be treated as unitary rational actors. See "Deterrence in the Nuclear Age: The Search for Evidence," in *Perspectives on Deterrence*, eds. Paul Stern, Robert Axelrod, Robert Jervis, and Roy Radner (New York: Oxford University Press, 1989).

8. Patrick Morgan has called deterrence "the subject of one of the more elaborate

attempts at rigorous theory in the social sciences." See Patrick Morgan, *Deterrence: A Conceptual Analysis* (Beverly Hills: Sage, 1977), p. 26. The following discussion also relies on Paul K. Huth's definitions in *Extended Deterrence and the Prevention of War* (New Haven, CT: Yale University Press, 1988).

9. The concept of rationality is critical to thinking through the theory and application of deterrence. In the bipolar, strategic nuclear case, scholars and practitioners assumed that nations of conflicting ideologies and interests would behave rationally to avoid nuclear war. In a purely conventional case, the costs and risks of using force could also be compared, and a rational course of action selected. In a new world order, it is plausible that the concept of extended conventional deterrence being presented here could also deter nascent nuclear powers. It is certainly not clear that bipolar models of strategic nuclear deterrence will operate to restrain proliferators whose views of the possession and use of nuclear weapons may be considerably different from those formulated by the United States and Soviet Union during the Cold War.

10. Among the more prominent deterrence critics are Robert Jervis, Richard Ned Lebow, and Janice Gross Stein. See their work, *Psychology and Deterrence* (Baltimore: The Johns Hopkins University Press, 1985).

11. See Alexander George and Richard Smoke, *Deterrence in American Foreign Policy* (New York: Columbia University Press, 1974); and John Orme, "Deterrence Failures: A Second Look," *International Security* 11, No. 4 (Spring 1987), pp. 96–104.

12. See John Mearsheimer, *Conventional Deterrence* (Ithaca: Cornell University Press, 1989), p. 211.

13. Mearsheimer's *Conventional Deterrence* remains the best. The difficulty of separating conventional deterrence from its theater and strategic nuclear linkages is demonstrated in works such as those by Thomas Boyd-Carpenter, *Conventional Deterrence into the 1990s* (New York: St. Martin's Press, 1989), and Gary Guertner, *Deterrence and Defense in a Post-Nuclear World* (New York: St. Martin's Press, 1990).

14. See Jervis, "Deterrence Theory Revisited."

15. In "Deterring Our Deterrent," *Foreign Policy*, No. 25 (Winter 1976–77), Nitze argued that it would not be rational for the United States to respond with a countervalue nuclear strike after the Soviet Union had launched an effective counterforce first strike on the United States, because of an assumed countervalue retaliation by the Soviet Union.

16. See Mearsheimer, *Conventional Deterrence*; and Joshua Epstein, *Strategy and Force Planning* (Washington, D.C.: Brookings, 1987), pp. 6–7.

17. As pointed out by George Quester in "Some Thoughts on Deterrence Failures" in Stern, Axelrod, Jervis, and Radner, *Perspectives on Deterrence*, p. 62. Perhaps, instead, practitioners of the new deterrence should reread Kissinger: "In my view, what appears balanced and safe in a crisis is often the most risky. Gradual escalation tempts the opponent to match every move; what is intended as a show of moderation may be interpreted as irresolution.... A leader ... must be prepared to escalate rapidly and brutally." Henry Kissinger, *White House Years* (Boston: Little, Brown, 1979), p. 621, quoted in Huth, *Extended Deterrence*.

18. Robert Gates, Director of the Central Intelligence Agency, recently testified that the United States did not need to fear an attack on its homeland until the end

of the decade. See "CIA Chief Says Threat by Ex-Soviets Is Small," *The New York Times*, January 29, 1992, p. A5.

19. See Robert Art, "A Defensible Defense: America's Grand Strategy after the Cold War," *International Security* 15, No. 4 (Spring 1991), pp. 5–53.

20. William J. Perry, "Desert Storm and Deterrence," *Foreign Affairs* 70, No. 4 (Fall 1991), pp. 66–82.

21. See Richard K. Herrmann, "The Middle East and the New World Order," *International Security* 16, No. 2 (Fall 1991), pp. 42–75.

# 9

# A Conventional Force Dominant Deterrent

*Gary L. Guertner*

Conventional deterrence has a future, but one very different from its past, in which it was subordinated to nuclear threats and derived from classic strategic nuclear theory. The United States now faces a multipolar international political system that may be destabilized by a proliferation of armed conflict and advanced weaponry. To secure stability, security, and influence in the new world order, the United States can use the military prowess it demonstrated in the Gulf War to good advantage. However, using that force effectively, or threatening to use it, requires the formulation of a coherent theory of general extended conventional deterrence and the prudent planning of general purpose forces that are credible and capable of underwriting the new military strategy.

Critics of conventional deterrence argue that history has already demonstrated its importance. By contrast, nuclear deterrence of the Soviet threat bought forty-five years of peace in Europe. The response to this standard critique is threefold. First, conditions now exist (and were demonstrated in the Gulf War) in which the technological advantages of U.S. conventional weapons and doctrine are so superior to the capabilities of all conceivable adversaries that their deterrence value against direct threats to U.S. interests is higher than at any period in U.S. history.

Second, technological superiority and operational doctrine allow many capabilities previously monopolized by nuclear strategy to be readily transferred to conventional forces. For example, Robert Haffa's chapter describes how conventional forces now have a combination of range, accuracy, survivability, and lethality to execute strategic attacks, simultaneously or sequentially, across a wide spectrum of target sets to include counterforce, command and control (including leadership), and economic.

Third, critics of conventional deterrence have traditionally set impossible standards for success. Over time, any form of deterrence may fail. We will always confront some form of nondeterrable deterrence. We will always confront some form of nondeterrable threat. Moreover, deterrence is a renewable commodity. It wears out and must periodically be renewed. Deterrence failures provide the opportunity to demonstrate the price of aggression, rejuvenate the credibility of deterrence (collective or unilateral), and establish a new period of stability. In other words, conventional deterrence can produce long cycles of stability instead of the perennial or overlapping intervals of conflict that would be far more likely in the absence of a carefully constructed U.S. and allied conventional force capability.

How we respond to deterrence failure will determine both our credibility and the scope of international stability. Figure 9.1 summarizes what we believe are reasonable standards for judging conventional deterrence. Long periods of stability may or may not be attributable to the success of deterrence. In any case, no deterrence system or force mix can guarantee an "end to history." Paradoxically, stability is dynamic in the sense that forces are constantly at work to undermine the status quo. Those forces, also summarized in Figure 9.1, mean that deterrence failures are, over time, inevitable. The United States should therefore base its military strategy on weapons that can be used without the threat of self-deterrence or of breaking up coalition forces needed for their political legitimacy and military capability. If we are serious about deterring regional threats on a global scale, this strategic logic will push us into a post–Cold War deterrence regime dominated by conventional forces.

## THE REQUIREMENTS FOR CONVENTIONAL DETERRENCE

Previous chapters have looked at both history (George Quester) and the future (Robert Haffa) for lessons and concepts that are applicable to a new military strategy based on conventional deterrence. Neither proponents nor critics should judge these works in isolation. Conventional deterrence cannot succeed unless it is underwritten by supporting policies and concepts. The strategic concepts in the current national military strategy document that appear to have the greatest synergistic value in support of conventional deterrence are as follows:[1]

- technological superiority,
- collective security,
- forward presence,
- strategic agility, and
- theater defenses.

**Figure 9.1**
**Conventional Deterrence and International Stability**

| Period of Stability → | Deterrence Failure → | Stability Restored OR– | Instability Spreads |
|---|---|---|---|
| • Military technology advances | • Crisis or war | • Aggression is countered | • Aggression succeeds |
| • Weapons proliferate | –Collective security | • Conventional forces/ doctrine demonstrates capabilities | • Deterrence fails |
| • Political and economic conflicts flare | –Collective defense | • Conventional deterrence revitalized | • Utility of aggression demonstrated |
| • Incentives for war increase | –Unilateral action | • New period of stability begins | • Period of instability extended in scope and duration |
| • Risk of miscalculation increases | | • U.S. interests protected | • U.S. interests at risk |
| • Deterrence fails | | | |

## Technological Superiority

Expected reductions in the overall force structure will make the force-multiplying effects of technological superiority more important than ever. Space-based sensors, defense-suppression systems, "brilliant weapons," and stealth technologies give true meaning to the concept of force multipliers. This broad mix of technologies can make conventional forces decisive provided that they are planned and integrated into an effective doctrine and concept of operations.

The most likely conflicts involving the United States will be against less capable states that have trouble employing their forces and their technology in effective combined arms operations. As Anthony Cordesman has concluded in his assessment of the Gulf War,

> the U.S. can cut its force structure and still maintain a decisive military edge over most threats in the Third World. It can exploit the heritage of four decades of arming to fight a far more sophisticated and combat ready enemy so that it can fight under conditions where it is outnumbered or suffers from significant operational disadvantages.[2]

Exploiting technology to get economies of force will require investments where the payoff in battlefield lethality is greatest. Given the threats that our forces are most likely to confront in regional contingencies, these technologies will include:

- Battle management resources for real-time integration of sensors-command-control and weapons systems that make enemy forces transparent and easily targeted;

- Mobility of conventional forces to fully exploit technological superiority and battlefield transparency;
- Smart conventional weapons with range and lethality; and
- Component upgrades for existing delivery platforms to avoid costly generational replacements. This means limited procurement of new tactical fighters, tanks, bombers, submarines, or other platforms that were originally conceived to counter a modernized Soviet threat.

Technology that leads to unaffordable procurement threatens us with force multipliers of less than 1.0. Net decreases in combat-capable forces can best be avoided through combinations of selective upgrading and selective low-rate procurement.

Technological superiority will also depend on concurrent political strategies. Technology is a double-edged sword; it can act as a force multiplier, but the laws of science apply equally to our potential adversaries. Multilateral support for the nonproliferation of both nuclear and critical conventional military technologies can be an equally effective means for preempting threats to our interests and for underwriting conventional deterrence.

## Collective Security

Collective security has become explicitly incorporated in the national military strategy. It is broadly defined to include both collective security (UN-sanctioned activities) and collective defense (formal alliances such as NATO) arrangements. These are linked informally in what could, if promoted by the United States, form transregional security linkages—a seamless web of collective action.[3]

The potential value of collective security to conventional deterrence is difficult to quantify because it requires the United States to link its security to the capabilities and political will of others. Its potential must always be balanced against the risk that collective action may require significant limitations on unilateral action. Nevertheless, there are three compelling reasons for the United States to embrace collective security.

First, allies or coalition partners are essential for basing or staging the range of capabilities required to fully exploit technologically superior forces against a regional hegemon.

Second, the American public shows little enthusiasm for an active role as the single, global superpower. Collective deterrence is politically essential for sharing not only the military burden but also the increasingly salient political and fiscal responsibilities.

Third, patterns of collective action, as demonstrated in the Gulf War, give conventional deterrence credibility and capabilities that the United

States can no longer afford or achieve on its own. Even though collective action and shared capabilities may limit our freedom of action, these limits are reassuring to others and may contribute more to stability than attempts by the world's only superpower to unilaterally impose deterrence—nuclear or conventional.

## Forward Presence

The post–Cold War shift in U.S. military strategy from large-scale forward deployments of military forces to limited or intermittent forward presence is linked to the credibility of both conventional deterrence and collective security.[4]

U.S. forces abroad will continue to be viewed as the most visible symbols of American resolve and commitment to regional stability. They are vital components of both short- and long-range stability because they (1) demonstrate U.S. leadership, commitment, and capabilities for collective security, collective defense, and peacekeeping operations; (2) contribute to the preservation of regional power balances and provide disincentives for the nationalization of regional defense policies and arms competitions; (3) contribute to the containment of security obstacles that, absent a U.S. presence, could disrupt regional economic integration and political union, both vital components for long-term regional stability.

The forward presence of U.S. military forces as part of collective security or collective defense regimes has a deterrent value in excess of its immediate military capabilities, provided that these symbols of U.S. commitments are backed by the strategic agility to bring credible military force to bear at decisive points and at decisive times in a crisis.

## Strategic Agility

Strategic agility is a generic concept that reflects the dramatic changes in Cold War forward deployment patterns that fixed U.S. forces on the most threatened frontiers in Germany and Korea. Old planning assumptions have given way to new requirements to meet diffuse regional contingencies. Simply stated, U.S. forces will be assembled by their rapid movement from wherever they are to wherever they are needed. Strategic agility requires mobile forces and adaptive planning for a diverse range of options. Many of these options signal our commitment and demonstrate military capabilities short of war. Joint exercises, UN peacekeeping missions, and even humanitarian/disaster relief operations provide opportunities to display power projection capabilities and global reach despite reduced forward deployment of forces.

### Theater Ballistic Missile Defenses

Nuclear and chemical weapons proliferation make theater air and anti-tactical ballistic missile defenses important components of conventional deterrence. The next states that are likely to acquire nuclear arms are under radical regimes that are openly hostile to U.S. interests (North Korea, Libya, Iran, and Iraq, if UN intervention fails).[5] The success of such regional powers in creating even a small nuclear umbrella under which they could commit aggression would represent a serious challenge to U.S. global strategy.

Theater defenses in support of conventional deterrence need not be a part of the grander objectives of the Strategic Defense Initiative (SDI) or its most recent variant, Global Protection Against Limited Strikes (GPALS). The layered, space-based weapons architecture of these costly systems seems, at best, technologically remote and, at worst, a vestige of the Cold War.[6] What is needed in the near term is a global, space-based early warning, command and control network that is linked to modernized, mobile, land-based theater defense systems (Patriot follow-on or Theater High-Altitude Area Defense—THAAD—interceptors designed for greater defense of countervalue targets).

## THEATER STRATEGIC TARGETING WITH CONVENTIONAL FORCES

Uncertainties about nondeterrable nuclear threats make it all the more imperative that the United States also have credible warfighting options. Nuclear preemption prior to an attack is not plausible, and there are uncertainties as to whether any President or his coalition partners would authorize a response in kind, even after nuclear first-use by the enemy. More plausible are the range of conventional options afforded by modern, high-tech weapons that have a theater strategic capability for both denial and punishment missions. The broad outline of a conventional deterrence strategy would include:

- Conventional preemption of the nuclear/chemical infrastructure and key command and control nodes to deny or disrupt an attack (deterrence by denial).
- Threats of conventional escalation to countervalue targets (economic) if nuclear weapons are used (deterrence by punishment).
- Threats to seize enemy territory (deterrence by punishment).
- Countervalue retaliation by conventional forces if deterrence and preemption fail (deterrence by punishment).
- Theater antitactical missile and air defenses (deterrence by denial).

The air war against Iraq demonstrated the limitations of counterforce targeting against missiles and nuclear/chemical infrastructures. Nevertheless, the impact of the coalition's technological superiority was felt throughout Iraq, particularly at the nerve center and heart of the Iraqi government and its warmaking capability. The success of the stealth systems and precision bombing capabilities projected some of the same physical and psychological aspects as weapons of massed destruction without the liabilities of these type of weapons. Operations that could target Saddam and his warmaking potential without causing widespread, indiscriminate destruction of the Iraqi people provided a counter to Saddam's attempts at influencing world opinion. Such precision prevented Saddam from successfully painting coalition actions as war on the Iraqi people.[7]

The imperfect capability of deterrence by denial (even with nuclear weapons) and the unknowable responses to threats of retaliation and punishment leave theater antitactical ballistic missile defenses as the last line of defense for U.S. and coalition forces. On balance, conventional deterrence that combines attempts to dissuade, capabilities to neutralize or capture, credible threats to retaliate, and the ability to defend is more credible than nuclear threats against regional powers. Together, these capabilities dramatically reduce the coercive potential of Third World nuclear programs. This does not mean, however, that nuclear forces have no role to play in the future of deterrence.

## THE ROLE OF NUCLEAR WEAPONS IN A CONVENTIONAL FORCE DOMINANT DETERRENT

*The National Military Strategy 1992* states that the purpose of nuclear forces is "to deter the use of weapons of mass destruction and to serve as a hedge against the emergence of an overwhelming conventional threat."[8]

The dilemma confronting the United States is still the same classic problem that confronted strategists throughout the Cold War. Nuclear weapons fulfill their declared deterrence function only if they are never used. Yet, if everyone knows that they will never be used, they lack the credibility to deter. The most credible means to resolve this dilemma involves a combination of declaratory policies and military capability that emphasizes the warfighting capabilities of conventional forces with strategic reach.[9]

There is, however, a potential paradox of success if aggressive Third World leaders believe that only weapons of mass destruction can offset U.S. advantages in conventional military power. Under such circumstances, theater nuclear weapons can have important signaling functions that communicate new risks and introduce greater costs for nuclear aggression that inflicts high casualties on U.S. forces or on allied countervalue targets.

Nuclear signaling can take the form of presidential or DoD declarations that U.S. ships deploying to a hostile theater of operations have been refitted with nuclear weapons carried by dual-capable aircraft (DCA) and Tomahawk Land Attack Missiles (TLAM).[10] Deployment options alone can play a critical role in the strategic calculus of aggressors who possess uncommitted nuclear capabilities.

The role of strategic nuclear forces is also directly related to the problems of reorienting the national military strategy from a global to a regional focus. The first problem is determining the force structure after the combined reductions of the START Treaty, unilateral initiatives, and the Bush-Yeltsin summit. The combined results will be dramatic cuts in U.S. strategic forces from some 12,000 warheads to 3,500 or less.[11] These cuts are prudent responses to the collapse of the Soviet Union, and they give us a long-sought opportunity to pull back from the nuclear brink where we so often found ourselves during the Cold War. Moreover, these reductions are consistent with obligations under the Nonproliferation Treaty (NPT). They should be accompanied by strong U.S. endorsements of the treaty and support for the strengthening of the nonproliferation regime as we move toward a critical NPT review conference in 1995.

The credibility of U.S. support for nonproliferation will also be affected by the declaratory policies and targeting strategy for a smaller strategic nuclear force structure. The most comprehensive review of the problem to date suggests that we could be moving in the right direction provided that the strategic role of conventional forces dominates future planning. A report by the Joint Strategic Target Planning Staff Advisory Group, chaired by former Secretary of the Air Force Thomas C. Reed, recommends major changes in the Single Integrated Operational Plan (SIOP).

The Cold War SIOP contained carefully calibrated strike options against the former Soviet Union. In its place, the panel recommends an Integrated Strike Employment Plan (ISEP) with a "near real time" flexibility to cover a wider range of targets with a smaller force structure. The proposal identifies five categories of plans:[12]

- *Plan Alpha* is a conventional force option against selective strategic targets of "every reasonable adversary."
- *Plan Echo* is a nuclear option for theater contingencies or "nuclear expeditionary forces."
- *Plan Lima* is a set of limited SIOP-like nuclear options against Russian force projection assets.
- *Plan Mike* is a more robust version of *Plan Lima* with graduated attack options in the 10s, 100s, and 1000s.
- *Plan Romeo* is a strategic nuclear reserve force (SRF) to deter escalation, support war termination, and preclude other nuclear powers not directly involved in an ongoing crisis from coercing the United States.

In their current form, these recommendations are excessive and favor a nuclear force structure that is not well suited for credible deterrence in the new world order. If they were misinterpreted as official policy, the United States could be accused of following a double standard in declaring the value of nuclear weapons at the same time that it was asking others to foreswear them.

In the case of the former Soviet Union, U.S. targeting policy should be muted. Prudence dictates that advantage be taken of every opportunity for mutual reductions of force levels and confidence-building measures such as lower alert rates, improved command and control structures, and cooperative steps to improve the safety of nuclear storage, transportation, and destruction procedures.[13]

Russia will remain a nuclear power with a potential to threaten the United States and its allies. On the other hand, it is no longer the center of a hostile global movement or the leader of a powerful military alliance threatening Europe with overwhelming force deep in its own territory. Russian behavior is leveraged more by its need for Western aid and technology than by U.S. military capabilities. It is difficult to conceive credible scenarios in which even the most reactionary great Russian nationalist could find in nuclear weapons the tools that could be used against the West in preplanned ways to coerce concessions or that might tempt revisionist leaders to adopt reckless and inflexible positions. Along with its British and French allies, the United States will and should retain nuclear options, but it is premature in the extreme to plan robust nuclear attacks against the "force projection assets" of a state that is struggling for democracy and economic reforms.[14]

Even though the United States may be a benevolent superpower, the political impact of global nuclear targeting is more likely to stimulate rather than deter nuclear proliferation. An alternative set of declaratory policies that are consistent with nonproliferation include commitments to deep cuts in nuclear forces coupled with a *defensive* strategy of direct retaliation against nuclear attacks on U.S. territory. Direct retaliation is one of the few credible missions for strategic nuclear forces in the post–Cold War world. Extending deterrence should be a function of conventional forces (the option embodied in *Plan Alpha*).

Global retargeting by nuclear forces is an unfortunate concept that is more likely to put U.S. interests at risk in the long run. Marshal Shaposhnikov, Commander-in-Chief of the Russian Armed Forces, struck a more positive image in his correct observation that retargeting frightens people. It is better, he said, to discuss "nontargeting," which lowers the level of alert to "zero flight assignments of missiles."[15]

The Marshal's formulations are too vague to serve as the basis of national policy. Nevertheless, his point should not be dismissed. The objectives of national military strategy are more likely to be achieved through the *implicit* flexibility to respond to nuclear aggression from any source rather than *explicit* declarations of global nuclear targeting. Many regional crises may be precipitated by the proliferation of nuclear weapons and ballistic missiles. U.S. strategy will, therefore, require a delicate balance not to give incentives to that very threat. A reassuring posture, in the eyes of regional actors and global partners, will require reexamination and "denuclearization" of deterrence in a new multipolar world.

Above all, this study's primary purpose has been to recommend the option of using modern conventional forces for strategic purposes. A reliance on offensive nuclear weapons carries enormous risks that brought us to the brink of war during several Cold War crises. The American public has every right to expect that the Cold War's principal legacy of danger not be deliberately extended into the new world order.

A conventional dominant deterrent will require full emancipation from Cold War thinking. As Fred Ikle has wisely noted, strategic thought "remains locked into place... by dated nuclear arsenals," and these forces remain tied to imaginative scenarios that "persist, like a genetic defect."[16]

Freeing U.S. military strategy from its nuclear past will require deeper cuts in the existing strategic nuclear force structure and in strategic defense spending. The Bush-Yeltsin summit was a dramatic step, but one that when fully implemented will leave the United States with nearly as many strategic nuclear warheads as it deployed in 1970, the period when serious efforts were just beginning for negotiated limits on Soviet and American nuclear forces.[17]

Deeper cuts will be required to win Congressional support for a conventional force structure that is capable of meeting the regional contingencies in the new national military strategy. Failure to clearly address how and why our force structure must change will result in an impotent mix of nuclear and conventional forces that will neither deter nor be capable of meeting threats to U.S. interests.

## NOTES

1. These strategic concepts are drawn from *The National Military Strategy 1992*, released by the Chairman of the Joint Chiefs of Staff in January 1992. Some have been narrowed in scope for ease of analysis. For example, the document lists strategic deterrence and defense as one of the four foundations on which our strategy is built. This study narrows the strategic concept to conventional deterrence and theater defense.

2. Anthony H. Cordesman, "Compensating for Smaller Forces: Adjusting Ways and Means through Technology," paper presented at the Third Annual Strategy Conference, U.S. Army War College, February 14, 1992, p. 2.

3. For a detailed assessment of collective security and U.S. strategy, see Inis Claude, Jr., Sheldon Simon, and Douglas Stuart, *Collective Security in Asia and Europe* (Carlisle, PA: U.S. Army War College, Strategic Studies Institute, March 2, 1992). Ironically, the Administration's pledge to support growing UN peacekeeping

activities is under attack by members of Congress because of a long-standing agreement that makes the United States responsible for 30 percent of the cost of every operation. Japan and Western Europe could conceivably relieve part of the perceived inequity, but Congress should also examine these costs in the larger context of collective security and global stability. See Don Oberdorfer, "Lawmakers Balk at Peacekeeping's Cost," *The Washington Post*, March 4, 1992, p. A17.

4. *The National Military Strategy 1992* describes forward presence operations to include forward stationed troops, forces afloat, periodic rotational deployments, access and storage agreements, military exercises, security and humanitarian assistance, port visits, and military-to-military contacts.

5. Leonard S. Spector, "Deterring Regional Threats from Nuclear Proliferation," paper presented at the Third Annual Strategy Conference, U.S. Army War College, Strategic Studies Institute, February 14, 1992, p. 31 and Appendix A.

6. In his testimony before the House Armed Services Committee on December 10, 1991, CIA Director Robert Gates stated that only Russian and Chinese missiles could threaten the territory of the United States. He did not expect direct risks from other countries for at least another decade. See "CIA Chief Says Threat by Ex-Soviets Is Small," *The New York Times*, January 29, 1992, p. A5.

7. Colonel Douglas Craft, *An Operational Analysis of the Persian Gulf War* (Carlisle, PA: Strategic Studies Institute, U.S. Army War College, August 1992).

8. *The National Military Strategy 1992*, p. 13.

9. A major thesis of this study is that conventional deterrence must occasionally give way to conflicts that demonstrate capabilities, thereby strengthening deterrence for a new phase of stability. The bombing of Hiroshima and Nagasaki had much the same effect on nuclear deterrence.

10. President Bush's unilateral initiatives in September 1991 eliminated ground-launched tactical nuclear weapons and withdrew them from surface ships and submarines. Some sea-based weapons are scheduled for destruction. Others are in storage; from there they can be redeployed for the "signaling" purposes advocated here.

11. President Bush's January 1992 initiative pledged cuts in strategic nuclear warheads up to 50 percent below START-permitted ceilings of approximately 8,000 warheads. At the Bush-Yeltsin summit on June 17, 1992, dramatic breakthroughs were announced that included the agreement to reduce strategic nuclear warheads to a range of 3,000 to 3,500 by 2003, the lowest levels since 1969. The flexible ceiling reflects agreement to deploy asymmetrical force levels. More important, the Russians agreed to destroy all MIRVed land-based ICBMs, the core of their strategic force structure, and the most long-standing goal in U.S. arms negotiating strategy. The United States also agreed to reduce its deployed SLBM forces by 50 percent. See R. Jeffrey Smith, "Arms Talks Devoid of Usual Anxieties," *The Washington Post*, June 18, 1992, p. A38; and Thomas L. Friedman, "Reducing the Russian Arms Threat," *The New York Times*, June 17, 1992, p. A11.

12. Thomas C. Reed and Michael O. Wheeler, "The Role of Nuclear Weapons in the New World Order," JSTPS/SAG Deterrence Study Group, October 19, 1991, pp. 33–34. See also R. Jeffrey Smith, "U.S. Urged to Cut 50% of A-Arms," *The Washington Post*, January 6, 1992, p. A1.

13. These latter steps are well under way. Congress allocated $400 million to assist Russian efforts to transport, store, and destroy nuclear weapons, and on March 26, 1992, the State Department announced the appointment of Retired Major Gen-

eral William F. Burns, former Director of the U.S. Arms Control and Disarmament Agency, to head the U.S. delegation on Safety, Security, and Dismantlement of Nuclear Weapons (SSD Talks). Moscow has agreed on U.S. assistance in the production of containers for fissile materials from dismantled nuclear weapons, conversion of rail cars for secure transport, construction of storage facilities, training in nuclear accident response, accounting procedures, and ultimate disposition of enriched uranium and plutonium. See Department of State Press Release, March 26, 1992.

14. Open discussions of nuclear targeting in the press were followed by equally controversial reporting of threat scenarios that were developed in the Office of the Chairman of the Joint Chiefs of Staff. These scenarios included a hypothetical NATO counterattack if Russia invaded Lithuania. There is virtually no support in NATO or in the U.S. Congress for such a course of action. However, the scenario does raise the question of what the United States should do in the event of a Russian-initiated civil war to reunite the former Soviet Union. Russian nationalists could indeed threaten nuclear retaliation against Western intervention. History suggests, however, that Western response would be political and economic, but not military, thus making nuclear threats irrelevant. "Threat" scenarios are discussed by Barton Gellman, "Pentagon War Scenario Spotlights Russia," *The Washington Post*, February 20, 1992, p. A1.

15. Marshal Ye. I. Shaposhnikov, interview in *Red Star*, February 22, 1992, pp. 1–3. Quoted in *FBIS-SOV–92–036*, February 24, 1992, p. 8.

16. Quoted in Michael Mazarr, "Nuclear Weapons after the Cold War," *Washington Quarterly*, Summer 1992, p. 198.

17. As noted in note 11, the Bush-Yeltsin summit agreement would reduce U.S. strategic nuclear warheads to 3,000–3,500 by 2003. In 1970, a period when the Soviets achieved strategic nuclear parity with the United States, strategic nuclear warheads numbered 3,780. Data compiled from *The Military Balance*, 1969–1972 editions (London: International Institute for Strategic Studies). Ironically, the Strategic Arms Limitations Talks (SALT I) initiated by President Nixon in 1969 resulted, over time, in a fourfold increase in U.S. strategic nuclear warheads.

# PART III

# STRATEGY AS CREATIVE CONCEPTS AND APPLICATION: TECHNOLOGICAL SUPERIORITY

# 10

# Compensating for Smaller Forces through Technology

*Anthony H. Cordesman*

There is no question that technology can have a critical impact on the need for force size and the outcome of war. Advances in weaponry have reshaped the balance of power since the beginning of history, and anyone who watched television coverage of the Gulf War is aware that technology had a massive impact on this conflict.

Superior technology gave UN coalition forces superior firepower, maneuverability, and sustainability. It destroyed the cohesion of the Iraqi air defense system in a matter of hours and made the Iraqi Air Force and land-based air defenses ineffective in a matter of days. It broke up much of the Iraqi command and control system. It permitted all-weather and night operations, as well as a major increase in the tempo and intensity of military operations. It provided a decisive superiority in intelligence, targeting, damage assessment, and battle management. It provided superior range at virtually every level of land and air engagement, and a level of lethality for many types of weapons that was far superior to that of Iraqi forces.

With the breakup of the Warsaw Pact and the Soviet Union, the United States may be able to enjoy similar advantages in many future conflicts. Rather than fight against developed states with a high degree of technological parity, it is likely to fight against far less sophisticated forces that have trouble using the level of technology they do possess, and even more problems in integrating it into effective combined arms and combined operations.

Under the right conditions, this means that the United States can cut its force structure and still maintain a decisive military edge over most threats in the Third World. It can exploit the heritage of four decades of arming to fight a far more sophisticated and combat-ready enemy so that it can fight under conditions where it is outnumbered or suffers from significant operational disadvantages.

Technology is not, however, a panacea, and it is experiencing at least as many resource problems as the U.S. force structure. Under the Base Force concept first announced in August 1990, the United States will cut its active division strength by at least 33 percent and its active Air Force fighter wings by 38 percent. The United States will also make major cuts in its military manpower, all aspects of its force structure, its basing and logistic capabilities, and many aspects of readiness and sustainability.

These force cuts will probably be sharply accelerated once the Congress finishes debating President Bush's fiscal years 1993–97 budget requests. Force cuts, however, are only part of the story. During fiscal years 1993–97, deployed technology will be cut much more rapidly than forces.

The Bush budget requests beginning in January 1992 call for major cuts in defense investment—research, development, procurement, and spares. They try to preserve the same force structure and readiness as the fiscal year 1992 budget but cut $63.8 billion out of the fiscal years 1993–97 program, virtually all of it from procurement.

The impact these cuts in defense investment will have in reducing the amount of technology deployed in the force structure is hard to estimate, but it is scarcely the beginning of a downward trend. A recent estimate by the Congressional Budget Office shows that defense investment has already dropped from a peak of over $170 billion in fiscal year 1985, in constant fiscal year 1992 dollars, to below $110 billion. It will drop to around $100 billion by fiscal year 1997, under the Bush Administration budget request for fiscal year 1992. It could well drop to $70–$80 billion under the plans now being advocated in the U.S. Congress.[1]

Military capabilities, however, are not measured by investment in Research, Development, Testing, and Evaluation (RDT&E), but rather by investment in procurement—the equipment and munitions actually deployed with U.S. forces. The Bush Administration has recently put a heavy emphasis on developing systems only to the point at which they are production ready, but not funding procurement pending some major change in the threat. As a result, procurement will drop drastically even if the Congress fully funds the Bush fiscal year 1993 budget request. While research and development will increase during 1990–93, from $36.5 billion to $38.8 billion in current dollars, procurement will drop from $81.4 billion to $54.4 billion. The supporting text of the Bush request indicates these trends will continue at least through fiscal year 1995, which would bring procurement down to half of its fiscal year 1990 level in current dollars. Its value in constant dollars would be roughly one-third of the fiscal year 1990 level.[2]

Even $35–$45 billion for procurement in constant dollars is still a considerable sum, and total defense investment will still approach the level of defense investment in constant dollars that the United States made in 1980, at the start of the Reagan buildup. These cuts do, however, mean a cumulative cut in defense investment of $105–$198 billion during fiscal years 1993–97, when compared with the level spent in fiscal year 1992.[3]

Another way of looking at the issue is in terms of program terminations. During fiscal years 1991 and 1992, the United States terminated over 100 weapons programs, including major tactical programs like the Apache helicopter, M–1 tank, F–14D, F–15, F–15E, F–16, and A–12, tactical aircraft. As of the fiscal year 1993 budget, it will terminate Army programs like the ADATS air defense system and TOW sight improvement program. It will develop programs like the Comanche RAH–66 helicopter, and it will stretch out the Block III tank and LOSAT (line of sight antitank) missile beyond the 1990s. It will terminate Air Force programs like the HARM and AAAM missiles; and Navy programs like the LMAP H landing craft, SQY–1 ASW combat system, vertical launch ASROC, E–2C, and LSD–41 amphibious ship, and will probably develop the AX only to the producibility stage.[4]

These cuts in investment and procurement spending, and termination plans, also understate many aspects of the problem the United States faces. The U.S. force and procurement plans do not exist in a vacuum. They take years to shape and have massive momentum in terms of major procurement programs. Many current programs for defense technology have been shaped by decisions made under the Reagan Administration. The last Reagan budget in fiscal year 1989 called for an average real increase in defense spending of 1.2 percent per year through fiscal year 1994, and it would have produced a defense budget of over $330 billion in fiscal year 1994. The Bush budgets submitted for fiscal year 1991 called for average cuts in real defense spending of 2 percent per year, and total defense spending of about $280 billion in fiscal year 1994. The Bush budget submitted for fiscal year 1992 came after an 11.9 percent real cut in defense spending during fiscal year 1991 and called for average cuts of 3 percent per year. It would produce a fiscal year 1994 budget of about $260 billion.[5]

The United States conducted Operation Desert Storm under conditions whereby it was able to draw down on nearly forty years of investment in the capability to fight a very different war, and it still had the equipment and stocks purchased under the Reagan defense buildup. Now, however, it has expanded much of its "capital" in Desert Storm, it has already experienced seven straight years of cuts in real defense spending, and most of its large-scale procurement programs were shaped at a time when real defense investment was expected to be near 50 to 100 percent larger than it is likely to be under the coming Future Years Defense Plan (FYDP).

More than forces are being downsized. In fact, it is questionable whether the levels of investment currently being projected can actually be achieved. They depend, among other things, on the United States having no major combat operations during the next five years or a one-for-one increase in its defense budget for all changes to the program. They also depend on Congress smoothly executing major cuts in manpower and the reserves, although Congress refused to do this in shaping the fiscal year 1992 defense budget. These problems could easily cut defense investment by another $20 to $30 billion over the next five years.

More arguably, the competition among programs, branches, and services for diminished resources has mortgaged defense technology and procurement by institutionalizing a "liar's contest" syndrome into many programs. Survival in an era of defense cuts often depends on exaggerating performance, sharply underestimating costs, promising early delivery, and minimizing technical risk and growth. No one can adequately factor the liar's contest problem into a quantitative estimate of the additional problems in using defense technology to offset force reductions, but every aircraft program currently in development, or canceled during the last three years, has already illustrated the seriousness of the situation.

These difficulties have been further compounded by the tendency to fight for individual weapons or procurement programs, or branch or service R&D and procurement efforts, in isolation from any assessment of how overall resource problems affect overall requirements. The tendency to defend "my toy," "my magic bullet," and "my shopping list" is a natural one, and it is necessary if programs are to have strong managers and advocates. However, it often makes funding and program survival a matter of chance, rather than necessity.

## TECHNOLOGY AND PRIORITIZATION

The United States is operating in a climate in which any discussion of the role of technology in offsetting force cuts has to be based on a broad understanding of the trade-offs involved. Technology does not work miracles, and the wrong kind of effort to use technology to offset force cuts can weaken forces rather than strengthen them. Overcommitment to advanced projects, and overambitious development and deployment goals often make technology the natural enemy of military effectiveness—particularly in a development-dominated culture like that of the Department of Defense, where the checks and balances necessary to integrate technology into effective force planning are often lacking.

He who dies with the most toys simply dies, he does not win. Technology will be valuable only to the extent it is integrated into an effective overall force structure. This requires a constant reassessment of every dollar spent on R&D and procurement against dollars spent on the other aspects of military capability. Technology must be tied to a systematic appraisal of every aspect of force effectiveness, and to the understanding that every dollar spent on technology means the sacrifice of some other aspect of deterrent and warfighting capability.

## UNDERSTANDING THE TRUE MEANING OF *FORCE MULTIPLIER*

The iron laws of the effective use of technology are straightforward and unbreakable:

- An effective concept of operations for employing the technology on a force-wide basis and in effective combined arms and combined operations.
- Proper training in both operating the individual technology and integrating it into full-scale combat operations.
- Funding effective munitions for sustainability in combat, and the necessary $C^3$I/BM targeting and damage assessment assets.
- Suitable power projection, logistics, service support, and combat support capability.
- Suitable maintenance, repair, and recovery capability for the specific contingency where the technology is to be employed.
- Immunity to cost-effective countermeasures and unexpected obsolescence within the required service life of the technology.
- Adequate skilled manpower to use the technology from the operator to the high command level.
- Reorganization, retraining, and adjustment of the concept of operations, technology mix, and force mix to suit the specific contingency, threat, and allied forces.

There is no such thing as a "force multiplier" in the sense that a given technology or weapon has a real-world military value that is independent of these eight requirements. In a period of sharply declining resources, it is frighteningly easy to buy glamorous or high profile technologies and underfund the effort to make them effective.

This means that the United States must make difficult trade-offs as to which technologies to preserve or acquire that are founded on as comprehensive an analysis of force-wide capabilities in a wide range of contingencies as possible. In an era of declining resources, technologies must either be funded for the purpose of mothballing them for the emergence of undefined high intensity combat contingencies—an extraordinarily high risk approach—or be funded on the basis of clear plans to fully integrate them into forces the United States can actually afford.

The United States no longer has the resources to pursue technologies and weapons on an incremental basis and because they offer marginal improvements over existing systems with similar capabilities. It can only take advantage of the benefits of technology if it is far more ruthless in insisting that development and acquisition be coupled with effective force structure, deployment, and readiness plans to use that technology.

The problems involved become clearer the moment one examines the term *force multiplier* in terms of its real-world meaning. All investments and choices in force planning involve force multipliers. It is all too easy, however, to create force multipliers of less than 1.0. This can be done by funding programs that are overambitious, undermanaged, or undercosted. The B–1B, A–12, D1VAD, and Tacit Rainbow are all examples of real-world cases in which the search for incremental improvements in technology wasted badly needed resources on undeployable and unaffordable systems. No one can determine whether they should be awarded a force multiplier of 0.1 or 0.9, but it is all too clear that the proper multiplier was less than 1.0.

These examples may be only a warning of the shape of things to come. Partly because of the end of the Cold War and partly because of a procurement system that systematically undercosts major programs while exaggerating performance and delivery schedules, all four services are currently committed to a wide range of programs that are either undeployable or deployable only at the cost of cuts in force structure or readiness.

Possible examples include the B–2, AX, F–18F, the new family of Army armored vehicles and artillery, V–22, and many lower profile programs. While any such estimates are speculative, at least some experts in the Department of Defense feel that the current R&D and procurement budget is undercosted by 10 to 20 percent and is filled with programs that cannot be deployed at even 60 percent of their currently planned procurement numbers and within years of their planned deployment times.

The need to honestly appraise the opportunity cost of every technology, however, is only part of the story. One-on-one assessments of weapons or technology—particularly against an idealized enemy or target—grossly inflate the value of that technology. In the real world, even technologies with force multiplier values of more than 1.0 rarely approach the goal of radically changing the need for other forces and capabilities. Even when major new technologies like stealth, the multilaunch rocket system (MLRS), thermal sights, and joint surveillance target attack radar system (JSTARS) are successfully introduced into combat against forces that have no similar weapons or countermeasures, they tend to affect a relatively restricted spectrum of operations.

These problems will grow with time for two reasons. First, the United States will face more and more situations in which it will have to deploy limited numbers against mass. Second, with the end of the Cold War, many contingencies are likely to involve fundamental political asymmetries in the ability to wage war. The United States will only be able to fight and win in many low- and mid-intensity conflict contingencies if it can do so with very low casualties. Third World threats will often be able to absorb major losses.

The current climate of resource limitations also will allow such threat nations to improve their forces faster than the United States can improve its mix of deployed technologies. Over time, technologies inevitably breed countermeasures. For example, theater nuclear weapons, anti-tank guided weapons, and attack helicopters were once seen as force multipliers that favored the West. The West did enjoy such an advantage for a few years, but it was ultimately the Warsaw Pact that deployed far superior numbers of each weapon system.

Third World nations can be expected to fund countermeasures such as improved surface-to-air missiles, anti-ship missiles, air control and warning (AC&W) aircraft, unmanned aerial vehicles (UAVs), GPS, thermal sights, and a host of other relatively low-cost countermeasures. These are unlikely to achieve technical parity at any time in the foreseeable future, but they are likely to correct at least some of the technical weaknesses found in Iraqi forces, and few contingencies are likely to allow the United States to commit forces with a similar freedom of action in either political or military terms.

## Compensating for Smaller Forces: Selecting the Right Emphasis on Technology

These arguments are not arguments against technology per se. They are warnings that the United States may have to massively restructure its current plans and management systems to use technology to compensate for smaller forces. It is not easy to operate in a climate in which every dollar spent on any weapon comes at the direct expense of some other aspect of warfighting capability, and every dollar spent on R&D and future procurement comes at the direct expense of present warfighting capability.

If the United States is to be successful in compensating for smaller forces and declining defense spending, it must tailor its use of technology to accomplish the following goals:

- Deal with the most likely contingency requirements;
- Exploit the weaknesses of the most likely threat forces;
- Compensate for major and long-standing weaknesses in U.S. forces and power projection capabilities;
- Establish effective force-on-force priorities; and
- Institutionalize improved methods of integrating technology into force planning.

At the same time, the United States must meet these goals with the understanding that technologies generally have a far more positive force multiplier effect when they interact synergistically. While individual technologies rarely achieve real-world force multipliers, a broad mix of new technologies—integrated into an effective concept of operations—can achieve "force-on-force multipliers" that are far more decisive.

This force-on-force multiplier effect was demonstrated in World War II when a Germany with inferior numbers of aircraft, tanks, and artillery—and qualitative inferiority in tanks, artillery, army logistic vehicles, and bomber range-payload—used a combination of new technologies and a new concept of operations to overwhelm Belgium, Britain, France, and the Netherlands. It was demonstrated again in Desert Storm when a wide range of deep strike, air-land battle, and air defense suppression technologies were used in unison in an effective concept of operations against an enemy that failed to properly prepare or react.

## Technology and Future Contingency Requirements

The mix of contingencies for which the United States must design its forces is changing rapidly. The fiscal year 1992 Joint Military Net Assessment of the Joint Chiefs describes a wide spectrum of contingencies from low intensity to high intensity combat, and it notes that although low intensity conflicts are the most likely conflicts, high intensity conflicts involve the greatest risks.

The Joint Staff, however, was focusing on the problems of optimizing forces for power projection while dealing with the risk of having to fight a major conflict with the Soviet Union and Warsaw Pact. These problems have largely disappeared. The Warsaw Pact and the Soviet Union no longer exist, the risk of a prolonged conventional war in the central region of Europe is negligible, and the remaining military R&D and production effort of the various former Soviet republics is far less threatening.

As a result, the United States is faced with the following kinds of "force-sizing contingencies":

*Reemergence of a serious threat to Europe or the United States from the Russian Republic.* This contingency is so drastic, and would involve sufficient warning in the case of a nonstrategic confrontation, as to allow the United States and its allies to restructure their spending and reconstitute their forces.

*Intervention in an East European or Soviet national conflict, ethnic conflict, or civil war.* This is more likely to be a peace-creating mission than a warfighting mission and is more likely to be performed by European than U.S. forces. Depending on the East European country involved, any use of U.S. forces would probably be part of a coalition involving ethnic warfare, some degree of urban warfare, difficult power projection conditions, major efforts to tilt U.S. actions toward a given side, and carefully tailored rules of engagement and limits on civilian casualties and collateral damage.

*A mid- or high-intensity conflict in Korea.* In some ways, this is the most likely worst case. The United States would have to reinforce a battle dominated by South Korean land forces with some potential for escalation to chemical or nuclear warfare. It would, however, fight a North Korea lacking the latest conventional weapons and short of most advanced $C^3$I/BM targeting, electronic warfare, and other high technology assets. It would also deal with a mass and unconventional warfare–oriented force lacking in advanced night and all-weather combat assets, many aspects of combined arms and air-land operations, and a flexible command structure.

*A mid- or high-intensity conflict with Iraq or Iran.* Any such conflict would involve engagement of a large force equipped with large amounts of modern armor, aircraft, artillery, and air defense weaponry and with some ability to escalate to biological and chemical warfare. Both nations can be expected to learn from the Gulf War and to try to (1) develop countermeasures against the technologies and concept of operations the United States used during the Gulf War, and (2) improve their own ability to employ advanced technology. Both, however, have severe political, cultural, and acquisition problems in improving their ability to use advanced technology in maneuver warfare, beyond line of sight operations, air-land operations, and virtually all aspects of $C^3$I/BM.

*A mid- or high-intensity conflict with Cuba.* Such a conflict would involve engagement of a large force equipped with large amounts of modern armor, aircraft, artillery, and air defense weaponry. It would differ from Iran or Iraq, however, in that it would require forced entry. Depending on the nature of the conflict, it might also involve warfare against a regime with considerable popular support in urban or highly populated areas.

*Intervention in a civil war to rescue a friendly regime.* These highly political conflicts can vary sharply in virtually every dimension. They can involve situations in which hours are critical or there are weeks of warning. They can be politically popular or highly unpopular. They can involve urban, jungle, desert, and/or mountain warfare. They can involve forced entry or friendly facilities. Such military actions will be political wars fought under highly unstable conditions in which today's allies may be tomorrow's enemies, and ethnic and religious factors are likely to be critical. Sample test cases would be dealing with a Shi'ite uprising in Bahrain or restoring stability in Cambodia. There would be a major risk in some such conflicts of escalation to prolonged guerrilla or revolutionary warfare, and some risk of a need for evacuation or forced exit.

*Intervention in a major border conflict in the Third World.* It is difficult to foresee a specific contingency at this time, but possible cases could involve an Algerian conflict with Morocco, a Libyan conflict with Tunisia, a hostile Burma or Cambodia attacking Thailand, a radical Malaysia attacking Singapore, or a Syrian attack on Lebanon or Jordan. Such conflicts would involve regular military forces but could involve unconventional forces as well. They would almost certainly involve coalition warfare. In many cases, the United States would be contributing high technology or high capability forces, rather than mass. Rather than fight in a direct force-on-force sense, the United States might use soft strategic strikes to halt the aggressor by confronting him with a situation in which rear area losses exceed the benefit of continuing the war. Such conflicts could involve widely different mixes of terrain and climate, distance, and required reaction times. Most conflicts would involve significant political complications and limitations on the conduct of the fighting.

*Wars involving chemical, biological, nuclear weapons, and/or long range missiles and strategic air strikes.* Although it is tempting to think of weapons of mass destruction in terms of relatively orthodox mid- or high-intensity conflict contingencies, the threat of the use of such weapons—and actual use by extremist groups or leaders—will be an increasing possibility in even the most limited or political contingencies. The need to deter or defend against missile and air strikes will grow with time. So, however, will the risk of terrorist or unorthodox (covert) delivery. The risk of a chemical or biological "Marine Corps Barracks" attack will affect many aspects of operations.

The end of the Warsaw Pact and Soviet Union eases some aspects of U.S. force planning, but the list of contingencies just given shows that the United States still faces a challenging range of contingencies. They cover the entire globe and present major problems in terms of time and distance. They involve very different levels of warning, which means that the United States must often rely on fully combat ready forces and rapid deployment. They involve a wide range of different tactical conditions in terms of climate, terrain, and weather, which means that U.S. weapons and technology must be able to fight under a very wide range of conditions.

Above all, they involve the reality that the United States cannot only plan to fight popular wars, fight along purely military lines, or fight under "Weinberger rules." Most post–Cold War contingencies are likely to involve high political risks, complex political constraints, and severe limits on civilian and collateral damage. At the same time, the United States may only be able to credibly threaten the use of force, engage in the use of force, and/or sustain the use of force to a successful conclusion if it can do so with extremely low casualties to its own forces and/or terminate the conflict relatively quickly.

The United States will also face a constant risk that any perceived defeat would impose severe domestic or foreign unwillingness to support further U.S. military action. In this sense, the United States will be an extremely fragile "superpower" regardless of the size of the forces it employs, and it must tailor its forces accordingly. In sum, U.S. forces must be capable of fighting highly political conflicts.

## EXPLOITING U.S. STRENGTHS AND THE WEAKNESSES OF POTENTIAL ADVERSARIES

There is no clear road to dealing with the military requirements of the post–Cold War period, or to using technology to compensate for smaller forces. The United States must maintain a mix of forces and technologies with sufficient flexibility to deal with a wide range of different requirements and warning periods. It must have global strategic mobility and forward bases, seaborne assets, and prepositioning. It must be able to rapidly integrate different force elements from each service into task forces tailored to specific contingency needs.

At the same time, many of the previous contingencies do involve threatening forces that are likely to share several major weaknesses that the right mix of U.S. technologies can exploit:

*Training and readiness.* In virtually every case, order of battle or force strength intelligence will give a completely misleading picture of military capability. There will be critical weaknesses in training, particularly in terms of maneuver, large scale offensive operations, integration of high technology systems, and combined arms and combined operations. At the same time, there will be gaps in readiness in addition to gaps in training, imposed by a wide range of factors. These qualitative weaknesses will make a threat force far less capable than a U.S. force of similar size and will create windows of opportunity that U.S. technology can exploit.

*Intelligence, reconnaissance, and damage assessment capabilities.* Most threats will lack satellite and advanced intelligence/reconnaissance/damage assessment capabilities. In most cases, the assets they do have will be vulnerable to attacks, air defenses, or countermeasures. The United States will often be able to partly "blind" the enemy.

*Beyond visual range.* For similar reasons, most threat forces will have only limited ability to match the United States in beyond visual range air-to-air combat, counterbattery, and artillery targeting capability. Even in some areas where direct line of sight target acquisition is possible, the United States may be able to acquire targets at longer ranges, particularly at night.

*$C^3I$ battle management/targeting.* Most threats will lack high technology battle management, communications, intelligence, and targeting systems. In many cases, at least individual elements of potential threat forces will have critical shortfalls in $C^3I$ capabilities and/or critical vulnerabilities. This will restrict many aspects of maneuver, and the tempo and intensity of operations will be restricted.

*Air control and warning and air defense.* Threat forces may have an

AC&W /air defense "system," but it will almost certainly be sharply inferior to U.S. levels of technology. Key weaknesses will include electronic warfare, electronic and other countermeasures, layering of different defenses, survivable sensors and command centers, area coverage, independence of action by individual aircraft [raid assessment, beyond visual range (BVR), and multi-aspect radar/fire control/weaponry]. Counter-stealth, counter-UAV, and anti-missile defenses are likely to be particularly weak.

*All-weather/night warfare.* Threat forces are likely to have severe limitations in maneuverability, firepower, and sustainability in poor weather or night operations. These problems are likely to grow steadily more severe as the tempo and intensity of U.S. operations are increased, and as threat operations are required to make effective use of combined arms or combined operations. They will be even more severe if the United States has the intelligence and targeting assets to detect the key problems limiting enemy all-weather or night operations in near real time.

*In broad terms, most threat forces will have organization, tactical, and equipment driven rigidities that can be exploited by the United States.* This will be particularly true of forces that are under tight central authoritarian control and that are separated by religious, ideological, and ethnic rivalries.

*Precision kill/smart munitions/lethal area munitions.* Threat forces are likely to lag significantly behind the United States in virtually every aspect of munitions lethality. Even when they possess the actual weapons and munitions, they will generally lack the ability to integrate them into an overall force mix matching U.S. capabilities.

*Maneuverability.* For similar reasons, threat forces will lack speed of maneuver and the ability to match the intensity of U.S. operations, with the possible exception of built-up areas and jungle/forested terrain.

*Sustainability.* Threat forces will often lack the capability to maintain equipment, recover it, conduct field or depot combat repairs, or allocate ammunition and spares. Sortie and operational availability rates will often be low or will depend on a few vulnerable facilities.

*Hard target killing.* Threat forces are unlikely to have the technology mix necessary to kill defended hard targets and may often depend highly on hardened command and control facilities.

*Loiter sensors/UAV killers.* Threat forces are likely to improve their use of UAVs and long endurance sensors and kill platforms with time, but they should generally be far behind U.S. forces in these areas.

*Soft strategic attacks.* In most cases involving hostile countries or regular military forces, the United States will be able to attack a wide range of soft strategic targets with near impunity. These include power plants, water facilities, bridges and tunnels, phone and radio facilities, and the like.

*Countermeasures.* Threat forces are unlikely to match the United States in countermeasures at virtually any level, ranging from electronic warfare to infrared. Where threat forces have parity in individual areas, they are unlikely to have it on a broad spectrum basis.

*Strategic mobility*. Most threat countries will find it difficult to conduct major redeployments, as distinguished from maneuver. Most will be severely constrained in intra-theater lift and mobility. When they can move units, they often will lack the ability to move support and maintenance capability.

*Vulnerable rear areas/logistics*. Threat forces will also find it difficult to protect rear areas and key logistic facilities. Many will be overconcentrated or overspecialized in a few narrow areas.

*Armor/anti-armor*. Although threat forces may have parity with the United States in a few aspects of armor and anti-armor capability, they are unlikely to have broad parity relative to fully deployed U.S. mechanized and armored divisions. Many will lack a balanced mix of tanks and other armor; others will lack advanced armor or fire control/sensor systems.

Each of these vulnerabilities sets priorities for U.S. use of technology to compensate for smaller forces. At the same time, the United States must exploit them with the clear understanding that these threat vulnerabilities do not depend on a given U.S. magic bullet, weapon system, or technology. All depend on U.S. ability to exploit a wide mix of combat ready technologies that are employed with effective operational concepts and are integrated into superior U.S. force-on-force capabilities.

## COMPENSATING FOR THE LONG-STANDING WEAKNESSES IN U.S. FORCES AND POWER PROJECTION CAPABILITIES

At the same time, these threat vulnerabilities must be kept in careful perspective. The United States has vulnerabilities of its own, and any effort to improve U.S. technology must be coupled with an effort to correct major deficiencies in U.S. forces.

The U.S. success in Desert Storm can be dangerously misleading. Iraq allowed the United States to exploit similar vulnerabilities without forcing the United States to confront its limitations in terms of strategic lift, the readiness of its combat and service support units, or individual weaknesses like mine warfare capability. Iraq gave the United States nearly half a year in which to adapt its weapons to the specific problems of desert warfare in the Gulf, to restructure its maintenance and support systems, to bring in spare parts and munitions from all over the world, to retrain its forces, and reorganize its command and control and battle management concepts. If Saddam Hussein had immediately invaded Saudi Arabia, the limits to U.S. power projection capabilities might have produced a very different outcome.

The United States cannot count on similar advantages in the future. If it is to use technology to compensate for smaller forces, the United States must devote the resources to correct the following problems in its current forces and capabilities:

*Intelligence.* The effective exploitation of threat weaknesses requires highly sophisticated political intelligence, detailed intelligence on the prewar vulnerabilities and shortcomings of threat forces, and sufficient theater assets and analysis capability after the war begins to update the original assessments. The United States has never provided such analytic assets in the past and often relies on order of battle intelligence—a shortcoming revealed in Desert Storm. Unless the present intelligence community and user "culture" is changed, the United States will experience severe problems in using many of its potential technical advantages.

*Lack of strategic, tactical, and amphibious lift and prepositioning.* The United States can move light divisions quickly and can deploy air assets even more quickly. It does, however, have major shortfalls in strategic lift if it has to operate for long periods from unimproved airfields and move mechanized or armored divisions. The present Future Year Defense Plan also has major shortages of intra-theater lift and leads to block obsolescence of many key amphibious ships in the mid–1990s.

*Lack of combat ready armored and mechanized expeditionary forces.* The U.S. Army lacks mechanized and armored expeditionary forces that are tailored for power projection, fully combat ready, and self-sustainable. Overdependence on Reserve and National Guard combat support, service support, and logistic units is a critical problem in scenarios requiring immediate deployment. The U.S. Marine Corps is still tied to the concept of amphibious forced entry, too light in armor and artillery, and lacking sustainability. These deficiencies greatly increase the "time-distance" problem the United States faces in power projection for most scenarios.

*Inadequate combat damage and human threat assessment capability.* U.S. capabilities in $C^3$I/BM targeting are far superior to its capabilities to accurately assess damage. The United States also has done far less to improve its technology in assessing human movements, targeting, and losses than to improve equipment tracking and targeting. This reflects a previous orientation toward the Warsaw Pact threat, but it also reflects a reluctance to come to grips with the "body count" issue. Unfortunately, many probable contingencies will be dominated by political or revolutionary combat in which accurate data on human numbers, movements, activities, and losses will be far more critical than attacking equipment or hard targets.

*Mine warfare and naval fire support.* The United States still lacks effective mine warfare capability, and the phaseout of the battleship deprives it of effective ship-based fire support. Coupled to aging amphibious lift and a lack of modern Marine Corps theater airlift, the United States has significant force-wide limitations in amphibious and naval operations.

*Force-wide sustainability problems.* Seven years of real defense cuts have been accompanied by seven years of disproportionate drawdowns of munitions and major spares. The Gulf War exacerbated this situation, and current funding does not permit recovery of munitions, major spares, and a number of maintenance and support activities through the end of fiscal year 1997—even if further unprogrammed cuts do not take place in defense spending. This form of "hollow Army" is considerably harder to quantify than the problems of the 1970s, but it is becoming no less real.

*Armor, anti-armor, and artillery programs.* The United States leads the world in armor, anti-armor, and artillery programs. It is important to note, however, that virtually all aspects of U.S. Army and Marine Corps armor, anti-armor, and artillery programs are now in a state of disarray. All aspects of armor development will have to be restructured, and funding of anti-armor and artillery programs has been cut back to the point where the table of organization and equipment (TO&E) will need to be significantly readjusted to absorb the JSTARS and to decide on a future mix of tube artillery, antitactical missiles (ATACMs), and the multilaunch rocket system (MLRS).

*Lack of advanced and long-range attack aircraft.* For different reasons, both the Navy and Air Force have been forced to delay deployment of an AX through at least 2010, unless a radical change takes place in funding. The A–6, F–16, and F–18 all exhibited serious range-payload, high performance attack, and air defense evasion problems during the Gulf War. The F–15E has only been procured in limited numbers; the F–111 is aging. Air Force and Navy procurement of next generation multirole fighters is likely to be significantly delayed beyond current plans, and far fewer aircraft are likely to be procured. The two-seat version of the F–18F is likely to be canceled. At the same time, plans to upgrade the A–10, F–14, F–15, and F–16 are being progressively cut back, and the B–2 will not be procured in sufficient numbers to offset the lack of an advanced attack aircraft. Although the United States will still retain a global lead in attack aircraft capability, it will experience severe shortfalls in meeting any of the procurement goals of the 1990s.

*High risk helicopter and close air support programs.* The Comanche and AH-G4 Longbow programs are critical to upgrading the U.S. Army attack helicopter capability, and the Air Force now depends on two wings of A–10s for the close air support mission and eventual upgrading of the F–16. Sophisticated UAV programs to supplement part of the mission capabilities of these aircraft, or to support them, are long delayed and still in development. Significant force cuts are likely in these programs that are disproportionate to cuts in other forces.

*Crew-sized heavy weapons.* U.S. advances in many areas of technology have led to only limited advances in crew-sized heavy weapons. U.S. forces tend to be tied too heavily to small arms or armored vehicles.

*Urban and built-up warfare capabilities.* Only selected units have had tailored training and improved equipment for urban and built-up area warfare. The overall mix of equipment and weaponry has provided improved combat capabilities for urban warfare, but has led to only limited advances in deployed dedicated systems.

*Jungle, forest, and mountain warfare.* The United States has a number of targeting and killing systems capable of greatly improving the ability to find and kill equipment in covered and rough terrain. It has far less capability to deal with infantry or guerrilla forces. These aspects of technology have received significantly lower priority since Vietnam, although a number of advances have occurred in sensors, navigation and troop management, and area weapons suited for such combat.

*IFF/identification of friend or foe.* The United States has already begun to react to the friendly fire problems of the Gulf War. More is involved, however, than dealing with U.S. forces. The United States does not have land and air warfare technology that easily lends itself to working with non-NATO coalition partners. More broadly, significant countermeasure and IFF gaps exist in dealing with forces equipped with U.S. and NATO European weaponry.

*Integrated and open $C^3I$/BM architectures.* The Gulf War revealed significant problems in integrating the $C^3I$/BM activities of all four services. At the same time, many systems lacked the ability to adapt to close cooperation with Third World forces that are not standardized—as were the Saudis—on U.S. systems and operating procedures.

*Reliability and maintenance.* The high operational readiness rates reached for land and air equipment in the Gulf War were possible only through a massive series of work arounds, crash adaptations, increases in maintenance loads, cannibalization, and use of civilian contractors. Substantial modification and reengineering of U.S. equipment are needed to ensure that such readiness levels can be reached without long preparation times and increases in maintenance efforts and resources.

*Fusing and practical lethality.* Many bombs and submunitions did not function reliably during the Gulf War, often revealing a systemic failure to properly test and field quality bomb fuses, air ordnance, and submunitions that affected many of the same categories of munitions in Vietnam.

*Operational feedback and fixes.* One of the most disturbing lessons of Desert Storm was the need to bypass virtually all existing service procedures to get rapid turnarounds on technical problems and tailoring weapons and technology to operational needs. In some cases, emergency fixes were substituted for problems whose solutions had been well known for two to five years. Technical fixes and procedures also were often not shared with the Reserves or National Guard or were done so on a basis that had no way of measuring compliance.

*Air and missile defense.* The United States has good man-portable surface-to-air missiles, and the PAC 3 version of the Patriot should combine good anti-air and anti-tactical ballistic missile capabilities. The United States does not, however, have modern vehicle-mounted medium air defenses, and the long history of program failures in this area means that major new deployments are unlikely to occur before 2005, even if current programs are successful.

*Chemical and biological defenses.* The United States scraped together a reasonably adequate mix of chemical/biological weapons (CBW) defenses for Desert Storm but did so only on a crash basis, and with significant gaps in capability and poor overall ergonomics in much of the equipment deployed. The United States will need substantially improved equipment to deal with toxins, dusty Mustard, advanced biological agents, and "cocktails" of different CBW agents.

This list of limitations must be kept in careful perspective. None will act as "show stoppers" in most contingencies, and the United States will lead the world in many areas of deployed technology in spite of these problems. The Gulf War did, however, reveal that several of these limitations can be overcome only through significant changes in the U.S. force mix and mix of deployed technologies. Further, the last half-decade has led to a cumulative and accelerating set of imbalances in force structure and procurement plans that need to be reshaped into a balance suited to the previous contingencies.

More broadly, the United States will always face the limitation that technology cannot compensate for favorable political conditions where the issue is not the size or effectiveness of U.S. forces, but the limits placed on the use of force. The United States enjoyed military and technological advantages in Vietnam that allowed it to win virtually every battle or large scale engagement of forces, but it operated under political conditions that led to a decisive defeat. Similarly, the United States had every military advantage in Lebanon, but the political conditions shaping U.S. military action prevented it from using military force to achieve a decisive result.

## ESTABLISHING EFFECTIVE FORCE-ON-FORCE PRIORITIES

The challenge the United States faces is not one of establishing simple priorities for a few high technology fixes or developing new shopping lists of expensive equipment. The challenge is to restructure virtually every aspect of its force plans to make the most effective use of what it already has, or has under development, to both exploit key threat vulnerabilities and correct the major weaknesses in U.S. forces.

If the United States is to deal effectively with the complex mix of new contingency requirements, threat vulnerabilities, and weaknesses in U.S. forces, it must do so on a force-on-force basis whereby the resulting force mix is designed to fixed resource limitations, not to theoretical military requirements.

This will not be easy for a military organized around a requirements-driven approach, or for a civil-military bureaucracy that emphasizes individual "magic bullets" or high technology "shopping lists." It will not be easy for a system whose structure and biases are built around four decades of emphasis on the Warsaw Pact threat.

This is not a matter of organization as much as one of priorities and methods:

- Integrated planning and budgeting will be needed at a functional level that is far more responsive and easy to update than the current system.
- Service-dominated planning based on vaguely defined global requirements must be replaced by interservice planning based on examination of the force packages necessary to deal with a range of contingencies similar to that listed earlier.
- Clear priorities need to be set within each area of technology and procurement with clearly designed cost and resource constraints. The present project-oriented shopping lists need to be replaced with tight management of an affordable overall force mix.
- Once technologies enter the development stage they must be integrated into an overall force mix plan that clearly shows their intended deployment dates and numbers and how they will affect the overall force mix.
- Firm and well-defined gates need to be established for all projects delineating cost, time, and performance. Given past enforcement of such gates within the services, they will probably have to be legislated for major programs so that it is clear such gates must be met or the program will no longer be funded. This will also require Congress to cease its pork-barrel approach to technological procurement.
- The improvements made in individual areas of R&D and procurement management need to be matched by much tighter review of overall programming.
- The current emphasis on lead technology needs to be replaced by a more realistic examination of trade-offs in continuing existing production, multistage improvement programs, and growth versions of existing systems.
- Integrated readiness reporting and planning are needed to ensure that suitable operating and maintenance funding, sustainability, and training are included to ensure that the full costs of development and procurement are considered, and that they are affordable within projected resource limits.

- Far more careful control will be needed of requirements and changes to requirements to halt the past bias toward worst-case optimization and procurement of technology "because it's there."
- The gradual evolution of operational test and evaluation systems that integrate field and technical testing into a hierarchy of simulations needs to be sharply accelerated to permit adequate force mix and force-on-force analysis.

This is a deliberately ambitious agenda for changing the way in which the Department of Defense and the Congress approach the use of technology in compensating for smaller forces, and it is almost certainly an unrealistic one. The United States cannot, however, rest on the technological advantages it gained in planning to fight the Warsaw Pact, nor can it rely on the "edge" it had during Desert Storm. The last few years have led to a long series of program problems and terminations that provide a warning of what is likely to happen if these changes do not occur. Similarly, the United States has failed to correct long-standing weaknesses in many of its power projection capabilities and has slowly allowed many elements of its combat readiness to decline.

In many ways, the most serious threat the United States faces in an era of diminishing resources is itself. No major foreign threat exists that can defeat the United States if it organizes properly to downsize its forces and adapt its technology mix to meet its changing contingency requirements. Historically, however, victors tend to refight past wars and bureaucracies are slow to adapt to the need for change. If the United States is to avoid defeating itself, it must improve its methods of integrating technology into its force plans and force mix.

## NOTES

1. "Effects of Deeper Defense Budget Reductions," Congressional Budget Office, January 1922, pp. 6, 14.
2. Figures taken from DoD Press Release 26–92, January 29, 1992.
3. "Effects of Deeper Defense Budget Reductions," pp. 6, 14.
4. Figures taken from DoD Press Release 26–92.
5. "An Overview of the Changing Department of Defense Strategy, Budget, and Forces," Department of Defense, October 1991, p. 4.

# 11

# Prospects and Risks of Technological Dependency

*James Blackwell*

Creating and executing a coherent strategic vision for the United States in the post–Cold War world is only half of the task that confronts strategists today. It will be at least as important to have a strategy that is both politically achievable and systematically efficient. These are not "either-or" propositions, they are necessary elements of sound strategy. For the United States to define and protect its interests in the new world order, we must generate and effect a strategy that is at once expedient and methodological. The hard part of matching ends to means is in maintaining the optimum balance among these often competing requirements. In assessing the prospects and risks of technological dependence the right balance is especially troublesome to effect as the very process of technological advancement is so poorly understood. Our very economic life depends on continual improvement in technology, yet nowhere is there either a model to explain and predict it or a corpus of the art to guide its development. Yet, in spite of this intellectual mélange, strategists have ascribed to technology a preeminent position both as an end and a means. A proper assessment of the prospects and risks of technological dependence will therefore not only consider the impact of U.S. dependence on *foreign* technology, the issue currently in vogue, but it should also consider the very premise on which it lies, namely whether technology should be depended on as an element of, and goal for, our national security strategy.

This chapter develops a framework for the consideration of technological dependence, both foreign and domestic. It then examines the risks inherent in a strategy dependent on technology before moving on to a more thorough investigation of the opportunities and risks of foreign technology dependence. Finally, some implications will be drawn as guidelines for the approach to technology in our national security strategy.

## THE DEFENSE TECHNOLOGY AND INDUSTRY BASE

The U.S. defense technology and industrial base[1] is defined as the aggregate ability to provide the manufacturing, production, technology, research, development, and resources necessary to produce the material for the common defense of the United States. This definition captures the essence of the defense technology and industrial base as it is, rather than as one might wish it to be. The definition also presumes that there is a market mechanism at work that results from the interaction of government policy, defense budget demand, and corporate decision making. The market mechanism produces the U.S. defense technology and industrial base.

This definition of the defense technology and industrial base presumes that any firm that provides—or potentially could provide—goods for the national defense (whether it is commercially owned and operated, whether it is completely or partially owned and operated, or whether it is domestic or foreign based) is part of the U.S. defense base.

As a matter of policy choice, what is observed in the analysis of the defense technology and industrial base may not be what is desired in regard to government control over critical defense technologies and production capacity or the amount of foreign intrusion into critical sectors. The definition itself, however, does not presuppose any particular mix of type or source of ownership.

The defense technology and industrial base must contribute to strategy in three fundamental ways: peacetime efficiency, technological competitiveness, and crisis flexibility. These form the criteria for assessing the health of the defense technology and industrial base. These contributions are the basis upon which to judge the current performance of the defense technology and industrial base and for recommended policy solutions for the future.

First, U.S. strategy presumes that peace will be the normal state of U.S. relations and that peace will be sustained by demonstrated readiness and willingness to fight to protect national interests. The primary vehicle that demonstrates this intent is the set of programs administered by the Department of Defense that man, equip, maintain, train, and operate U.S. forces around the globe. The defense technology and industrial base must respond to the demands of these programs with cost-effective, reliable, and capable systems. These demands shift over time both in the magnitude of the demand, as expressed in the changing defense budget top line, and in emphases of programs, as expressed in the allocation of resources to such defense functions as force structure, manpower, readiness, procurement, and research and development (R&D). The defense technology and industrial base must provide the goods required by the defense budget in an efficient manner.

Second, the defense technology and industrial base must provide U.S. forces with technologically superior material. Maintaining a technological advantage over potential adversaries, particularly the former Soviet Union, has been an explicit part of U.S. national security strategy since the end of World War II. Because it would be prohibitive in cost and alien to the U.S. democratic culture, the United States could not match the number of Soviet deployed forces during the Cold War. Recognizing the danger to U.S. national security from the massive Soviet military machine, the United States opted to respond to quantity with quality. This required the United States to maintain a significant margin of superiority over the Soviet Union in its ability to develop high performance, high quality, and cost-effective products and processes so that the United States did not have to match the Soviets soldier-for-soldier or gun-for-gun. Unquestionably, it was in the U.S. defense technology and industrial base that this lead was developed and maintained.

Finally, because deterrence may not always preserve the peace and because there is the risk that low-level threats may bring the United States into conflict, the defense technology and industrial base must retain some flexibility to convert from peacetime R&D and production to expanded levels of production and development required for anticipated forms of future conflict. If post–World War II history is a guide, then the defense technology and industry base must be capable of short-term surge, long-term expansion, and postwar recovery. The surge requirement was demonstrated in the 1973 Arab-Israeli War when U.S. war reserve stocks in tanks and anti-tank guided missiles, for example, in a very short time were so severely depleted that weapons in the hands of U.S. active forces were taken and given to the Israelis to prevent the utter defeat of a valued U.S. ally. The Vietnam War required U.S. industry to gradually develop a production capacity for many combat items not stocked in sufficient quantity in peacetime, such as small arms and artillery ammunition.

Achieving these three criteria is problematic because efforts designed to achieve one goal may be counterproductive in preserving another. For example, if the United States spends large sums of defense budget dollars to build excess production capacity for anticipated surge requirements, it would be building an inherent economic inefficiency into the peacetime production of the military goods. Unit costs for peacetime requirements would carry an exorbitant premium to amortize the investment in the excess—but idle—capacity set aside for anticipated surge production. Indeed, the failure to recognize such fundamental trade-offs and to devote adequate resources and analysis to these issues have led to disarray in current defense technology and industrial base policy.

## DEPENDING ON TECHNOLOGY

In the context of the strategic framework for understanding the technology base, there may be an opportunity to maximize the payoff from investments in resources for security by an emphasis on technology. A resources strategy that can minimize the needs for efficiency and flexibility can afford to make its major investments in technological superiority. But a strategy that pursues technological advancement as a principal end must provide some kind of insurance against the future need for efficiency and flexibility, and that insurance will certainly not be free; it may not be cheap.

## Efficiency

If the defense technology and industry base is not efficient it will not generate political support for any investment. We need not review the literature of the 1980s on the inefficiencies in the U.S. defense acquisition system; it is replete with documentation on the phenomenon.[2] The American taxpayers paid about a 25 percent inefficiency premium on U.S. defense investment because of the way business was done and, as a result, research, development, and procurement programs became favorite targets of political opposition even when support for the defense spending top-line was widely favorable. The pursuit of military technology must be perceived to be at least not wasteful in order to elicit broad support in our political system.

Efficiency is of course valuable in its own right in support of technological advancement since it can be defined as the greatest value for the least cost. In the systems analysis world of the Cold War, efficiency took on a rather rigorous meaning. Ultimately, the justification for an investment in a particular technology for a weapons system was based on measures of effectiveness that related capability to unit cost. The key to the precision of the measurement was that capabilities could be defined in relation to a specific threat—the military capabilities of the Soviet Union, or a Soviet-equipped surrogate. Thus, a fleet of approximately 130 B–2 bombers, for example, was judged to be a cost-effective solution to the need to penetrate Soviet airspace and deliver nuclear bombs to a specific set of strategic targets in the Soviet Union.

In the new strategic era, however, the old measures of effectiveness evaporated with the dissolution of the Soviet Union. Although we know that there is inherent value in the investment of billions of dollars in the unique military technologies for stealthy, long-range, manned, heavy-payload, precision-bombing aircraft, we cannot be as precise as we once were as to how much capability we can expect from those kinds of investments. Unit cost will no longer suffice as the measure of effectiveness, neither politically, where the costs of few-of-a-kind systems will likely be above the famous Augustine Curve,[3] nor in systems analysis terms, where the need will be for measures of scientific advancement rather than battle effectiveness against a definable enemy force. A challenge presently facing the analytic community is to derive new measures of effectiveness with which to judge efficiency for the new strategic era in the absence of an overarching threat upon which to base such calculations. We must begin to learn how to measure capabilities purchased, rather than threats defeated.

Even with such scientific tools, however, there is no escape from the fundamental historical experience in military technology; it is not cheap. Alan S. Milward has observed:

> Even the most ardent economic critics of warfare frequently concede that in one respect war brings economic benefit in its tendency to promote technological and scientific innovation.... The tendency of modern fighting is to become increasingly capital intensive. One measurement of this is the amount of capital expended on killing one enemy; this has been estimated as roughly ten times as much in the Korean war as in the Second World War.[4]

The dilemma facing strategists in the new era is that while the requirements for investments in new technology will continue to grow, the pool of capital from which those investments can be made—the defense budget top-line—will decline for the foreseeable future. As a result, the public policy consensus supporting such investments will demand a demonstrated level of efficiency out of the technology base, multiplying the need for new analytical measures of efficiency.

### Flexibility

The other criterion of the strategic effectiveness of the base is the flexibility of the system to respond to changing strategic needs. As U.S. national security strategy comes to rely more on quasi-mobilization concepts such as reconstitution, the ability of the base to return to military development and production will be a new need in the system. Market forces will neither preserve defense technological capability for unique military applications, nor maintain production capabilities for rapid, or even deliberate, surge requirements.

Although some industrial specialists hope for greater integration of commercial and defense technology and production capacity,[5] a full measure of skepticism is in order here based on the post–World War II experiences of defense firms that have tried to achieve economies of scope by transferring their military expertise into commercial applications. Most such attempts were unsuccessful.

In the Cold War era the defense technology and industrial base maintained an inherent level of flexibility because of the size and scope of defense acquisition efforts. Separate investments in surge production capacity were not needed when, for example, the Army's tank fleet of over 7,000 vehicles was replaced on the order of once every twenty to twenty-five years. Even if production in a given year was below minimum economic levels, the unused capacity did not go away because there was the prospect of future production. On the technology side of the base, promising new applications could generally find a programmatic champion without having to identify a so-called bill-payer from which to take funding.

In the new strategic era, not only will maintaining flexibility require new investments to replace robust acquisition programs, but it will require new bureaucratic approaches. The entire defense program and budget process has become a negative-sum game. New program initiatives must not only provide justification on the merits of the military capability purchased, they must also convince decisionmakers that other programs already slated for cuts should be cut further or terminated. As new technologies are created, new military flexibilities can be gained, especially if the innovations are in process technology as well as product applications. But to the extent that technology competes for declining budget resources, flexibility may be sacrificed to technology development priorities. A lack of flexibility becomes a calculated risk in pursuing a technology-based strategy. That risk can be minimized by maximizing the response time available to apply new resources to technology development and production expansion, given necessary political decision making under conditions of sufficient warning. The record of the past in making such decisions and in obtaining such warning time illustrates the kinds of policy choices that face strategists today.

Prior to World War II, the manufacture of weapons systems was limited primarily by the structure of the machine tool industries among the combatants. The United States and Germany were the world's leaders in machine tools, but they followed opposite technology strategies. German industry had been manufacturing so-called universal machine tools during the reconstruction of Germany's heavy industry after World War I. Such tools were able to be switched rapidly from commercial production to military production because they had built-in adjustability features. During the war, Germany therefore had no need to surge production of new machine tools, as did the United States. Of course, such machines were more complicated and expensive than those made with the special-tools approach followed by the United States, the other machine tool giant of the 1930s and 1940s, which again illustrates the inherent trade-off between efficiency and flexibility.

During World War II, Germany did not increase its machine tool capacity utilization, it mostly switched from one type of production to another. But the United States—with Great Britain and Japan following suit—had to go through a period of innovation and expansion in the machine tool industries to develop new kinds of tooling to make new weapons and to create new capacity for manufacturing.[6]

The inherent size and potential strength of the underlying American heavy industries provided the flexibility to shift into wartime technology and production, while German industry had purchased that flexibility by investing in a more adaptable industrial structure.

Given the strategy adopted by the Roosevelt Administration of steady expansion of military industrial capabilities beginning as early as 1939, the U.S. industrial approach proved to be quite effective indeed. Acting on sufficient warning, the U.S. defense industrial and technology base became the "arsenal of democracy," producing 296,000 aircraft; 1,201 major naval vessels; 64,546 landing craft; 86,333 tanks; and 41.585 billion rounds of small arms ammunition between July 1, 1940, and July 31, 1945.[7] But this great feat was accomplished by government action initiated well before the outbreak of the war. The process began with the U.S. providing material to allies under various assistance programs and ultimately required direct government control over large segments of the economy. It included the outright construction of 1,600 new defense plants and direct financing for the expansion of many others.

It is highly unlikely that future regional contingencies of the types anticipated by strategists today would engender a public consensus for mobilization of the magnitude achieved for World War II. Thus, we will have to provide for industrial and technological flexibility as a hedge against the risks that the Base Force will not be able to handle the short-term situations we anticipate, or that we will have insufficient warning time to act on the emergence of greater threats, or that political leaders will equivocate or err in judging the nature of future threats. These risks will require investments in some near- and mid-term flexibility as an insurance policy beyond the need to invest in the flexibility needed to secure industrial and technological capability to reconstitute the base to meet the unforeseen global threat for which we expect to have five years or more to plan. Again, investments in flexibility will compete with investments in technology in the defense drawdown. So the first element of risk inherent in a strategy that depends on technology is that the application of resources guided by that strategy, an inherently imprecise process compared to the systems analysis approach of the Cold War era, may result in insufficient investment in the two other dimensions of industrial and technological capability, namely efficiency and flexibility. There is a second element of risk at work as well. The technological superiority approach may be wrong.

## Quantity versus Quality

For decades during the Cold War, U.S. national security strategy has explicitly relied on technological superiority to overcome acknowledged quantitative shortcomings. We have never intended to match our potential opponents man-for-man or gun-for-gun. We have instead opted to apply the creative genius of the American character to the design and development of better weapons, both for the defeat of the enemy and for the protection of American fighting men and women. This approach served us well during the Cold War and was vindicated by the low casualty rate of the Gulf War. But will it be the best way to apply limited resources for the future?

One hazard in continuing to pursue technological approaches is that if the total U.S. defense technological effort declines, we may lose our relative advantage over potential adversaries. Already, the diffusion of technology has brought a number of Third World states into advanced technology bases of their own in various fields including electronics, nuclear weapons, precision guided weapons, command and control systems, missiles, and others. The U.S. military technology policy and investments must be directed to ensure that we stay ahead of potential opponents (in terms of greater capabilities and countermeasures) and must also help dampen, or at least provide some control over, the proliferation of advanced military technologies.

A second consideration has to do with the evolution of the art of war. Having just come through a military technology revolution, have we reached the limits of the leverage we can get from technology for the present era? While it may be somewhat un-American to suggest that we might not be able to create new breakthroughs in military technology in our lifetime, history teaches us that such technological revolutions occur neither at a steady state nor at regular intervals. Preeminent military historian Trevor Dupuy has observed:

> The dates of the significant advances of the age of technological innovation are curiously bunched. The conoidal bullet, an effective breech-loading rifle, and breech-loading rifled field artillery appeared between 1841 and 1849. The modern machine-gun, the high-explosive shell, the Mauser bolt-operated magazine rifle, smokeless powder, and quick-firing modern artillery appeared between 1883 and the mid–1890s. The tank and fighter bomber appeared in a two-year period in World War I (1916–1917). Ballistic missiles and the atomic bomb were introduced within a year of each other in World War II.[8]

It is premature to eulogize the passing of the current military technological age, but a strategy that counts on the continuation of the current revolution must hedge against the historical probability that we are near the end of the current "bunching" period.

Finally, dependence on technological superiority might not work. Although it did work under the circumstances of the Gulf War, it did not work under the less favorable conditions of the Vietnam War. In many ways, World War II German military technology outclassed American systems. But America's superior ability to produce greater numbers of good weapons was instrumental in overcoming the limited numbers of advanced systems the Germans could bring to bear during the war. Even in the Gulf War it was not the technology alone that caused the defeat of the Iraqi forces in the field; "people" factors were more important. The combination of a highly motivated, well-trained force under superb leadership employing combined arms operations doctrine that exploited the technology was decisive.[9] Again, history teaches that superior technology does guarantee victory in battle.

### Technology Bust

The third task of pursuing a technology superiority strategy is that technology may fail to continue to progress. It has become an article of faith that the United States is the engine of technological advancement. We have become accustomed to an ever accelerating pace of improvements in our ability to apply science to improve productivity and to solve new problems. But we do not understand the process very clearly, and there is no guarantee that we will continue to reap the benefits of technological change.

Economist Frederick M. Scherer has argued from a Schumpeterian perspective that:

> It should not be concluded that there is a necessary correlation between the magnitude of research and development expenditures and the importance of inventions produced. Many major advances in science and technology have been brought into the world at relatively little expense.... On the other hand, the enormous outlays made to create many of our very complex new products and processes frequently contribute little in the way of basically new technology.[10]

Joseph Schumpeter held that technological change is indeed the engine of prosperity in capitalist economies, but that it was not competition that stimulated technological progress. Instead, he believed that the expectation of a monopoly position was the motivation behind invention, which in turn produced technological innovation and economic growth. Schumpeter wrote, "In this respect, perfect competition is not only impossible, but inferior, and has no title to being set up as a model of ideal efficiency."[11] Scherer takes the argument a step further to point out that in the creation of basic inventions it is the intangibles that dominate:

> Physical resources allocated to the support of basic research, or simply to bringing scientists and engineers into contact with the unsolved problems of technology, provide the institutional setting where these intangibles operate. But when, where, and how a basic invention will occur is difficult if not impossible to predict.[12]

The fact that it is the expectation of monopoly profits that stimulates innovation was confirmed in a more recent work by Eric von Hippel. Von Hippel surveyed innovations in a cross section of industries to determine if there was a relationship between the source of innovation and the type of industry. He found that the functional source of innovation varies widely and cannot be predicted:

In some fields, innovation users develop most innovations. In others, suppliers of innovation-related components and materials are the typical sources of innovation. In still other fields, conventional wisdom holds and product manufacturers are indeed the typical innovators.[13]

But he also concluded that those firms that did successfully innovate could "reasonably anticipate higher profits than non-innovating firms."[14] In the industrial sectors that are important to defense technology, the record of financial performance has not been favorable for meeting such expectations.[15]

American companies are becoming increasingly unwilling to do business with the Defense Department (DoD). There was in the 1980s a virtual stampede of producers out of the defense business. In 1982 there were more than 188,000 companies providing manufactured goods to DoD. In 1987 there were fewer than 40,000. Some that left went out of business altogether, including 20,000 small companies. But most companies have simply quit doing business with DoD and have opted for more reasonable customers. This is remarkable, because at the same time the defense procurement budget grew from $54.9 billion to $87 billion in constant fiscal 1989 dollars.

Defense business simply is not being pursued by profit-seekers. In fact, many companies that are highly dependent on defense business for survival are engaged in behavior (such as predatory pricing) that in other sectors would be illegal or suicidal. In the sometimes perverse world of defense contracting, such behavior is often the only way to survive.

The reason is that defense is, comparatively, not a profit-making business. Return on sales in defense has been about the same overall as in commercial manufacturing, falling from 4.9 percent in 1980 to 3.8 percent in 1986. But many defense sectors posted precipitous declines in this time; and, remember, those profits had to go to pay the 25 percent defense inefficiency premium. Return on fixed assets (ROA) was higher in defense manufacturing (44.7 percent) than in commercial manufacturing (11.3 percent) in 1986. But those apparently favorable ratings mask some troubling basic trends.

Defense is one business in which a company does not own all its production facilities. Many are owned by the government. Much of the capital equipment that defense companies do own is old and has been depreciated well beyond zero in present value. Thus, the book value of the assets held by defense contractors is artificially low. ROA is thus not a good measure of profitability in the defense business. At any rate, ROA in defense sectors declined by over 4 percentage points from 1980 to 1986, including huge drops in small arms, aircraft, and shipbuilding.

The drop in profitability in the defense industrial base is reflected in the investment climate surrounding the military manufacturing sector. In U.S. manufacturing as a whole, the ratio of capital spending to value of goods shipped was 3.8 percent in 1980 and 5.4 percent in 1985. The defense industrial base performed worse, actually falling from 3.9 percent in 1980 to 3.5 percent in 1985, while capacity and productivity in defense sectors were no better than in manufacturing overall.

One of the most important national security aspects of industrial performance is import penetration into the domestic industry. In total, the import penetration grew between 1980 and 1986 in 104 defense sectors out of 122 sectors for which data were available.

Who is to say that our explosive technological progress experienced since the end of World War II will continue? Even if it does, can we count on always being ahead of our potential military opponents in relative terms? Already, the Defense Department has identified a number of technologies critical to national security in which foreign countries either have a lead or could soon gain it.[16] Even if our potential adversaries cannot soon match all or most of our military technologies, they may be able to deny us the advantage of those technologies by developing countervailing technologies in other fields. The risk of reaching "technology bust" in pursuing our strategy of technological superiority is at once the least understood and potentially the most dangerous.

A strategy of depending on technological superiority served us well during the Cold War. It went a long way toward deterring conflict in the first place, and when properly employed by skilled military organizations operating within clear and achievable political mandates, it was instrumental in winning the wars that did occur. It served to compensate for the unbearable burdens that would have been necessary to accomplish the same ends with a large standing armed force capable of meeting our principal opponents in quantitative terms. It was, in fact, a force multiplier.

For the future, technology may well continue to deter potential threats to U.S. interests. Although it may be difficult to determine how long a shadow U.S. technological dominance casts,[17] there is some leverage to be obtained from maintaining our technology lead. In fact, there may be new strength for conventional deterrence from the dramatic demonstration of U.S. military technology during the Gulf War.[18]

But a continuation of the strategy of technological dependence should not go unquestioned as we move into the new strategic era. There are risks inherent in the strategy, and those risks are not well understood at present. Much more analysis must be put into efforts to assess the nature and magnitude of the risks and to develop affordable insurance policies to hedge against those risks.

## PROSPECTS AND RISKS OF DEPENDENCE ON FOREIGN TECHNOLOGY

A subset of the question of technology dependence is the question of foreign technology dependence. Depending on foreign sources for technological advantage in military systems compounds both the potential benefits from technology and the inherent jeopardy associated with such dependence.

Foreign technology dependence is an inevitability in the new strategic era, although in past times autarky seemed to be the most desirable strategy. The globalization of military technology has been well argued.[19] But the full extent of this global integration is not fully known.[20] It is very difficult to know with much certainty the exact national origin of all the various components and parts of a given weapon, although a number of systems have been documented.[21] To the extent that dependence maintains U.S. access to foreign sources of technology not otherwise available to the United States, such dependency need not be detrimental and indeed may be a net benefit.

But there are risks associated with foreign technology dependence. A good framework for understanding those risks was developed at the now-disestablished Mobilization Concepts Development Center (MCDC) at the National Defense University in 1987.[22] A foreign source is defined as a source of supply, manufacture, or technology outside the United States or Canada.[23] A foreign vulnerability is a dependency on a foreign country whose lack of reliability and substitutability jeopardizes national security by precluding the production, or significantly reducing the capability, of a critical weapons systems. The MCDC project examined case studies based on conflict scenarios embodied in then-current contingency plans and existing weapons systems priorities as detailed in the defense acquisition system.

In precision-guided munitions (PGMs) the study found that only 1 to 2 percent of the value of PGMs comes from overseas sources, but the foreign content was concentrated in a few vital components and a cutoff in a crisis would result in cessation of production. For petroleum and nonfuel minerals in an extended war, the project found that provable domestic reserves or alternatives would probably increase under the price pressures of wartime and that strategic stockpiles would serve to provide sufficient time to bring new or alternative sources on line. For integrated circuits, the project found that there was no recourse to the loss of technology for integrated circuits other than a peacetime industrial strategy to recapture that technology for national security purposes. It found similar situations potentially developing in a number of other critical technologies. That crisis situations could disrupt the availability of militarily relevant technology for U.S. armed forces was hinted at during the Gulf War when the Department of Commerce had to engage in jawboning procedures to get Japanese suppliers to provide certain computer electronic components on short notice.[24]

Although this framework is widely accepted for understanding the nature of the foreign dependency problem, there is little consensus on how to approach the problem. The MCDC study identified four policy approaches. The first was a continuation of the present haphazard market approach of attempting simultaneously to emphasize the preservation of the domestic base, cooperating with allies, and maximizing our competitive position globally. This seems to be the approach favored by the Department of Defense at the end of the Bush Administration.[25]

There are advocates of a "Buy American" approach that would provide maximum protection against disruption. But such an approach would be costly in terms of maintaining idle capacity in peacetime and duplicating the technology efforts of foreign partners. It would probably mean that we would not have access to the world's best technology, and it might risk a trade war. At another extreme, the United States could pursue a "Buy World" strategy in which we count on being able to participate as a buyer, if not as a seller, in any sector of the global technology market regardless of what those market forces do to the development of those sectors on U.S. soil. This would pose the greatest risk of foreign vulnerability as the twin processes of technology diffusion and industrial integration continue.

Rejecting all these approaches, the MCDC authors suggest a strategy of managed risk wherein some rational combination of market competition is pursued to a point, at which the worst risks of foreign vulnerability would be managed by optimal solutions of protection of domestic sources, enhanced access to foreign sources, and allied cooperative agreements. There would not appear to be a rational method of optimizing such politically loaded policy approaches.

Recognizing the inherently political nature of the managed approach, more recent academic study has concentrated on economic solutions to the problems of foreign technology dependence. Georgetown University Professor Theodore Moran has suggested an approach that assesses foreign dependence in terms of the global concentration of industries in the militarily relevant technologies.[26] He borrows from industrial organization economics[27] the notion of a concentration ratio, which is the share of the total output of an industry captured by the top few—usually four or eight—firms. Industrial organization economists hold that market concentration does not result in the opportunity for monopoly profits unless a few firms control a majority share of the market and can exert control over pricing behavior of all the other firms or potential entrants. An elaborate body of theory has been held up as legal basis for antitrust action based on market concentration measures developed under this branch of economic theory.

Moran argues that the threat of foreign control is similarly a function of the degree of external concentration in the industries upon which the defense effort depends, not solely the nationality of the firms. Moran suggests that the United States should follow a 4–4–50 rule in allowing foreign participation in the U.S. defense technology and industry base. If any combination of four firms in four countries has 50 percent or more control over the world market, then those firms or countries could place U.S. access to those industries or technologies at risk. If it takes more than four firms or more than four countries to reach the 50 percent control threshold, then it would be highly unlikely that any combination of opponents could deny U.S. access without a suitable alternative source, including a domestic U.S. source, being available.

For strategic policy purposes, Moran believes that diversification and multiplication of companies and locales from which the nation can draw is the most dependable method of providing insurance to minimize the threat of foreign control. If the 4–4–50 rule is violated, Moran suggests voluntary application of a domestic U.S. location requirement for production and technological development as a prerequisite for foreign firm entry. If such arrangements cannot be made voluntarily, Moran argues that the most effective enforcement mechanism would be a tariff or countervailing duty. He argues strongly against strategic trade policies that would attempt to combine protection with promotion of select high technology sectors. He also opposes propelling national champions into a commanding global lead, citing examples—such as the British Nimrod program—of achieving national champion status but at unacceptable cost.

More recently, a group at the RAND Corporation[28] has taken Moran's "insurance policy" notion a step further and has argued that the foreign vulnerability question is really a problem of the marginal cost of providing adequate insurance. The policy question, according to the RAND researchers, is not whether the insurance policy is complete or perfect, for it will never operate in a globally integrated economy. Rather, they believe the policy issue is one of adequacy, and it should be judged in terms of the marginal cost of obtaining it versus the marginal benefits thus obtained.

They point out several factors that lead private sector participants in the defense industry and technology base to have inadequate insurance including an expectaton of price controls, public sector monopsony, corporate income tax rates, regulatory policies, contracting policies, and poor information about conflict contingencies. On the government side, inadequate insurance is brought on by short time horizons, political pressure from concentrated interests, foreign government policy, and the potential for interdiction. The researchers found inadequate insurance in the Tritium (government) and High Definition Television (private) industries, while the Surface Acoustic Wave and Dynamic Random Access Memory chips sectors seemed to have adequate insurance. Such economic approaches as proposed by Moran and the RAND group, as sensible as they may seem to the analytic community, may not have the political appeal necessary to find their way into national security strategy and policy. But there is a window of opportunity opening for a time after the 1992 presidential election. We would serve the country well to attempt to explain these approaches in understandable fashion and to insert them into the public debate over the national security strategy for the new era.

## STRATEGY AND TECHNOLOGY IN THE NEW ERA

There is no question that technology will continue to be a major component of U.S. global security strategy for the future. The important questions are how great a role technology should play, how much the nation can afford to invest in technology, and how to organize the application of technology to protecting national interests. The basic requirements of efficiency, superiority, and flexibility still apply, but as the defense drawdown continues into the 1990s it will become increasingly difficult to optimize the balance of investments to achieve these goals.

The United States must begin to explore new approaches to strategic technologies. Finding new ways to evaluate both the risks and opportunities presented by foreign dependencies and foreign investments will be an increasingly important dimension of this policy area. At the same time, there will remain requirements for defense-specific investments in critical military technologies that will not be supported by commercial market forces.

It may also prove to be more cost-effective to abandon the Cold War approach of pursuing the most advanced technologies in all areas of military significance in favor of a more selective approach. In some cases it may be cheaper to pursue quantity over quality in military technologies in which strategic assessment would prove the approach to be prudent. In such cases, maintaining production capacity may be more important than pushing forward the envelope of technology. In some cases, our technological lead may be so far ahead of potential adversaries that we can afford to maintain large existing inventories, already paid for during the Cold War, while pursuing only a modest level of investment in the pursuit of new technologies. Where we do choose to invest, we would be wise to exploit our opportunities to have access to foreign developments rather than maintaining high walls of protection around our own laboratories and factories.

## NOTES

1. The following discussion is taken from the framework developed in: Center for Strategic and International Studies, *Deterrence in Decay: The Future of the U.S. Defense Industrial Base*, The Final Report of the CSIS Defense Industrial Base Project (Washington, DC: Center for Strategic and International Studies, May 1989).

2. See *A Quest for Excellence: Final Report of the President's Blue Ribbon Commission on Defense Management*, David Packard, chairman (Washington, DC: The Commission, June 1986); Center for Strategic and International Studies, *U.S. Defense Acquisition: A Process in Trouble* (Washington, DC: CSIS, 1987).

3. Norman R. Augustine, *Augustine's Laws* (New York: Viking, 1986).

4. Alan S. Milward, *War, Economy and Society, 1939–1945* (Berkeley: University of California Press, 1977), p. 169. Data from secondary source, see footnote 1.

5. See, especially, Center for Strategic and International Studies, *Integrating Technology for National Security* (Washington, DC: CSIS, May 1991).

6. The discussion of machine tool industries in the World War II period is taken from Milward, *War, Economy and Society*, pp. 181–185.

7. CSIS, *Deterrence in Decay*, p. 11. For a more detailed historical summary of industrial mobilization in the United States, see Roderick L. Vawter, *Industrial Mobilization: The Relevant History*, An Industrial College of the Armed Forces Study in Mobilization and Defense Management, rev. ed. (Washington, DC: National Defense University Press, 1983).

8. Colonel Trevor N. Dupuy, U.S. Army, Ret., *The Evolution of Weapons and Warfare* (New York: Bobbs-Merrill, 1980), p. 299.

9. The most credible of the "lessons learned" studies and after action reports make this point. See Department of Defense, *Conduct of the Persian Gulf Conflict: An Interim Report to the Congress* (Washington, DC: U.S. Department of Defense, June 1991), pp. 7–1 to 7–7; Center for Strategic and International Studies, *Military Lessons Learned from the Persian Gulf War* (Washington, DC: CSIS, p. 37; and James Blackwell, *Thunder in the Desert: The Strategy and Tactics of the Persian Gulf War* (New York: Bantam Books, 1991), pp. 213–230.

10. F. M. Scherer, *Innovation and Growth: Schumpeterian Perspectives* (Cambridge, MA: The MIT Press, 1984), p. 3.

11. Joseph A. Schumpeter, *Capitalism, Socialism, and Democracy* (New York: Harper, 1942), p. 106.

12. Scherer, *Innovation and Growth*, p. 6.

13. Eric von Hippel, *The Sources of Innovation* (New York: Oxford University Press, 1988), p. 3.

14. Ibid., p. 5.

15. The following data are taken from CSIS, *Detterence in Decay*, pp. 33–44.

16. *Department of Defense Critical Technologies Report* (Washington, D.C.: Department of Defense, 1990).

17. On the notion of an explicit strategy of conventional deterrence based on technological superiority, see Theodore S. Gold and Richard L. Wagner, Jr., "Long Shadows and Virtual Swords: Managing Defense Resources in the Changing Security Environment," unpublished paper provided to Undersecretary of Defense for Acquisition, U.S. Department of Defense, February 1, 1990.

18. For an early discussion of the relationship between technology and conventional deterrence, see chapters by Michael Gordon and Michael Brown in *Conventional Deterrence: Alternatives for European Defense*, eds. James R. Golden, Asa A. Clark, and Bruce E. Arlinghaus (Lexington, MA: Lexington Books, 1984).

19. See, especially, DoD Critical Technologies Report; OTA report ITA-ISC–449, *Arming Our Allies: Cooperation and Competition in Defense Technology*, May 1990; OTA report OTA-ISC–374, *The Defense Technology Base: Introduction and Overview*, March 1988; OTA report OTA-ISC–460, *Global Arms Trade*, June 1991; US GAO report NSIAD 91–93; "Industrial Base Significance of DoD's Foreign Dependence," 1991; OTA report, *Holding the Edge: Maintaining the Defense Technology Base*, 1990; OTA report, *Adjusting to a New Security Environment: The Defense Technology and Industrial Base Challenge*, February 1991; OTA report, *Redesigning Defense: Planning the Transition to the Future U.S. Defense Industrial*

*Base*, July 1991; and The Defense Science Board, *The Defense Industrial and Technology Base*, October 1988.

20. See various reports identifying this deficiency, especially, CSIS, *Deterrence in Decay*, pp. 53–54; and the GAO 1991 report.

21. A noteworthy example is the Joint Logistics Commanders 1987 Precision Guided Munitions Study.

22. Martin Libicki, Jack Nunn, and Bill Taylor, *U.S. Industrial Base Dependence/Vulnerability: Phase II—Analysis* (Washington, DC: National Defense University, November 1987).

23. The notion that Canada is not a foreign country when it comes to consideration of defense technology base analysis is in fact embodied in law and is supposed to be governed by a joint U.S.-Canadian watchdog agency called the North American Defense Industrial Base Organization (NADIBO).

24 Blackwell, *Thunder in the Desert*, p. 9.

25. See the November 1991 Defense Department Report, *The Defense Industrial Base*.

26. Theodore H. Moran, "The Globalization of America's Defense Industries: Managing the Threat of Foreign Dependence," *International Security* 15, No. 1 (Summer 1990), pp. 57–99.

27. The basic text is F. M. Scherer, *Industrial Market Structure and Economic Performance* (Boston: Houghton Mifflin Company, 1980).

28. Benjamin Zycher, Kenneth A. Solomon, and Loren Yager, *An "Adequate Insurance" Approach to Critical Dependencies of the Department of Defense* (Santa Monica, CA: RAND Corporation National Defense Research Institute, 1991).

# 12

# Deterring Regional Threats from Weapons Proliferation

*Leonard S. Spector*

The 1991 Gulf War and the more recent disintegration of the Soviet Union strongly suggest that the most serious challenges to U.S. security in the coming decade are likely to be posed by hostile regional powers. Such powers will be able to endanger American interests abroad, as well as American forces deployed overseas, neighboring American allies, and in some cases, even the continental United States. *The success of such regional actors in challenging American power will depend in large part on their ability to threaten the United States or its allies with injury so severe in comparison to the U.S. interests at issue that American decisionmakers shrink from employing economic or military coercion to achieve national foreign policy objectives.* A regional adversary's possession of even a small number of nuclear weapons could be sufficient to deter the United States from carrying out such actions.

If this analysis is correct, then protecting U.S. interests in the future may ultimately depend in large measure on preventing the spread of nuclear arms. Curbing the buildup of potent non-nuclear forces by hostile regional states may be a necessary corollary to this axiom, however, since such capabilities, if targeted against U.S. friends in the region, can provide a deterrent umbrella under which would-be nuclear-weapon states can pursue their ambitions. Uncertainties as to whether regional nuclear adversaries can be deterred from using nuclear arms, and questions as to whether defenses can be developed against such weapons if deterrence fails, make preventive steps all the more imperative. The use of military force to block the spread of nuclear-weapon capabilities to potential new adversaries will rarely be an attractive alternative, but diplomatic efforts may be able to achieve this goal, if they are pursued aggressively and backed with the threat of military force in appropriate cases.

## RECALIBRATING U.S. RISKS AND BENEFITS

Implicit in the foregoing hypotheses is the premise that with the end of the Cold War, a new risk/benefit calculus will infuse U.S. strategy. During the Cold War, the fear of domination by a militant superpower espousing an abhorrent political ideology gave rise to a credible U.S. deterrent posture based on a willingness to risk annihilation in the defense of the American way of life. Even during this period, however, questions were raised about the viability of U.S. nuclear deterrence in terms of the protection of Europe and other allies. Widespread doubts about the willingness of the United States to risk its own nuclear destruction in the defense of its NATO partners led to the deployment of U.S. intermediate-range nuclear missiles in Europe in the mid–1980s, whose purpose was to convince friend and foe alike that the United States was indeed prepared to escalate to strategic nuclear war in defense of its European allies.

As we look to the next decade, the stakes for the United States arising from new regional challenges, albeit important, are likely to be far less weighty than those that were at issue during the Cold War. U.S. economic interests and those of friendly industrialized states may be endangered. The principles of democracy, human rights, and international law may be jeopardized. Regional allies less closely tied to the United States than Europe, Japan, or South Korea may be imperiled. Although Iraq's invasion of Kuwait in August 1990 embodied all these challenges and led to war, future confrontations may implicate only some of these U.S. interests. Threats to the very existence of the United States and its principal allies—that is, threats comparable to those posed by the Soviet Union during the Cold War—appear increasingly implausible.

With the stakes thus likely to be reduced in comparison to those of recent decades, how much will the United States be prepared to risk in pursuit of lesser national objectives? Again, the case of the Gulf War is instructive. During the latter half of 1990, the United States was deeply divided on the question of using force to oust Iraq from Kuwait despite the multiple U.S. interests at issue, and in January 1991 the Congress endorsed military action by only the narrowest of margins. At the time, it was well understood that Saddam Hussein lacked the ability to attack the United States directly—although there were fears that he might launch a wave of terrorism against U.S. targets. The greatest concern was that war might result in thousands of U.S. military casualties, some caused by Iraq's expected use of chemical weapons. Even this moderate threat was nearly sufficient to deter U.S. intervention.

The victory over Iraq on the part of the United States and its allies, with its astonishingly low casualty rate, proved that at least in some regional settings the United States can use force without suffering a heavy toll in human lives. This may well increase the readiness of the U.S. polity to support military action the next time an American president seeks a mandate to employ it. At the same time, however, by creating the sense that victory can be had with little human cost, the experience of the Gulf War has undoubtedly reinforced U.S. aversion to conflicts where greater sacrifices may be demanded.

As the Gulf War began, the upper bounds of the potential threat that Iraq posed to the United States and to most U.S. allies in the region was directly related to the status of Iraq's programs to develop weapons of mass destruction and advanced delivery systems. The war implicitly established a ranking of the threat posed by weapons in these categories. Neither the United States, Israel, nor any other member of the U.S.-led coalition perceived Iraq's chemical weapons, for example, as having the ability to inflict damage so grave as to deter military intervention. The most important reason for this was undoubtedly that military and civilian defensive measures appeared sufficient to address chemical attacks, had they come. Moreover, it was thought that threats of massive conventional retaliation, hints of a U.S. or Israeli nuclear response, and the implicit U.S. threat to expand the aims of the war to include the occupation of Iraq and the toppling of Saddam Hussein provided a deterrent against Iraq's use of these arms.[1]

Before the war, Iraq was also thought to possess the ability to deploy biological weapons (both infectious agents and toxins)—a capability confirmed by postwar United Nations inspections. Again, however, this potential was insufficient to deter the United States and its coalition partners from military action. Defensive measures, in particular the inoculation of military personnel, and the implicit threats of escalation again provided confidence that the coalition could withstand Iraq's use of this capability and offered the hope that Saddam Hussein would be dissuaded from employing it.

Iraq's well-known ballistic missile capabilities did not pose a sufficiently serious threat to keep the coalition from going to war. The expectation that preventive air strikes against Iraqi missile launchers would quickly eliminate this capability and the deployment of anti-missile defenses reduced concerns over this component of the Iraqi arsenal, although in practice, blunting this threat proved more difficult than anticipated.

It is important to note that it was also widely understood before the war that Iraq did *not* possess the ability to manufacture nuclear weapons, although there were concerns that it might be able to fabricate one or two nuclear devices by mid–1991 by diverting a quantity of weapons-grade uranium fuel supplied during the 1980s by France and the Soviet Union. The basic assessment that Iraq was not nuclear-capable was correct; postwar inspections have revealed, however, that Iraq was pursuing a massive, clandestine nuclear weapons program, akin to the Manhattan Project, that would have given it the ability to produce a number of nuclear bombs by the mid–1990s.

If, prior to the war, Iraq had possessed even one or two nuclear devices, and if the whereabouts of these weapons had not been known, the possibility that they might have been smuggled into Israel, Saudi Arabia, Western Europe, or the United States would have greatly affected the risk/benefit calculations of going to war in Washington and other coalition capitals. Unlike the case with chemical weapons and ballistic missiles, no defenses would have been available to the coalition against Iraqi nuclear blackmail, and with the strong U.S. interest in upholding the taboo against using nuclear arms and its commitment to avoiding civilian casualties, there is some question as to whether Saddam Hussein would have perceived the threat of U.S. nuclear retaliation as credible. Given the major divisions that were seen in the United States over the use of force even in the absence of such a nuclear threat and the availability of a widely supported alternative course of action—namely, waiting to see whether economic sanctions would be sufficient to oust Iraq from Kuwait—it is highly likely that had Iraq possessed nuclear arms, U.S. military intervention would have been delayed, if not abandoned altogether.

In the Gulf War, substantial though not paramount U.S. interests were at issue, although the military threat that Iraq posed to the United States was only moderate. Accordingly, the potential benefits of going to war outweighed the disincentives against doing so. In future regional confrontations the magnitude of U.S. interests at stake is unlikely to be any greater, but the military threat posed by the regional adversary could be far more fearsome than that posed by Iraq if that adversary possesses even a handful of nuclear arms.[2] In this context, the risks to the United States of intervention could easily outweigh the potential benefits, and coercive U.S. action could well be deterred, even by a minimal nuclear force.

## THE CURRENT REGIONAL NUCLEAR POWERS AND THE NON-PROLIFERATION REGIME

Nuclear arms have spread slowly. The United States acquired its first nuclear weapons in 1945, the Soviet Union in 1949, Great Britain in 1952, France in 1960, and China in 1964. Since the arrival of these five declared nuclear-weapon states, only four additional nations that have sought to manufacture nuclear arms have acquired the ability to do so: Israel in 1968–1969, India in 1970–1971, South Africa in 1980–1981, and Pakistan in 1986. (A summary of the nuclear status of these and other regional states is provided in the Appendix to this chapter).

As the uncertainty surrounding these dates suggests, proliferation in the latter four states has followed a significantly different pattern from proliferation involving the five major powers. Each of the five unambiguously demonstrated its arrival as a nuclear-weapon state with an announced nuclear-weapon detonation. However, the states that subsequently crossed the nuclear-weapon threshold have kept their nuclear status ambiguous, averring that they are not building nuclear arms.[3] Moreover, except for a single nuclear detonation by India in 1974, none of the four de facto nuclear states is known to have conducted any nuclear-weapon tests,[4] although there has been widespread but unsubstantiated speculation that a signal observed in September 1979 by a U.S. monitoring satellite flying over the South Atlantic was that of an Israeli nuclear test conducted with the aid of South African facilities.[5]

Despite the lack of tests, however, few observers doubt that emerging nuclear states can develop reliable, early generation fission weapons—that is, "atomic" bombs that use the principles of the Hiroshima and Nagasaki devices—by using information available in the unclassified literature, along with computer simulations and assiduous testing of the non-nuclear components of such arms. Three of the four threshold states, moreover, are thought to have obtained nuclear-weapon design information from more advanced nuclear powers: Israel from France and possibly, by illicit means, the United States; South Africa from Israel; and Pakistan from China.

Since the most difficult and time-consuming step in developing nuclear weapons is producing the fissile material for the core—either highly enriched uranium (used for the core of the Hiroshima bomb) or plutonium (used for the core of the Nagasaki bomb)—the arrival of Israel, India, South Africa, and Pakistan as de facto nuclear powers is usually dated from the point at which they acquired the ability to produce such materials. This effort, which requires the construction and operation of a chain of complex facilities, has taken each of these countries at least ten years.

In broad terms, the reluctance of the four states to become declared nuclear powers or to broadcast their capabilities through extensive nuclear testing programs has stemmed from the judgment that ambiguity represented the optimal strategy. Because considerable information about their respective nuclear activities has leaked out over the years, these countries enjoyed most of the deterrent benefits of an overt nuclear posture but avoided the international opprobrium that such a posture would have incurred. In addition, ambiguity was less likely to stimulate neighboring states to develop countervailing nuclear capabilities.

Lack of nuclear testing is generally thought to have prevented emerging nuclear states from graduating to full-fledged thermonuclear "hydrogen" bombs and the enhanced radiation variant, the "neutron bomb."[6] Nonetheless, the de facto nuclear powers have not limited themselves to simple atomic weapons deliverable from aircraft. Data provided to the London *Sunday Times* in 1986 by former Israeli nuclear technician Mordechai Vanunu indicates that Israel has developed "boosted" nuclear weapons, that is, fission weapons that use the principle of thermonuclear fusion to enhance their efficiency.[7] This means it probably has weapons that are several times more powerful than the Nagasaki device. India and Pakistan are also known to be developing the technology needed for such armaments.

Similarly, Israel is believed to have deployed 400-mile-range, nuclear-armed ballistic missiles and, apparently in collaboration with South Africa, is developing systems with substantially greater reach. India will soon deploy a 150-mile-range, nuclear-capable missile and is developing an intermediate range system able to travel 1,500 miles. Pakistan also has a nuclear-capable surface-to-surface missile under development and has sought to purchase a 180-mile-range system from China.

As the programs of the four de facto nuclear-weapon states evolved, international efforts spearheaded by the United States and actively supported by the Soviet Union led to the creation of the nuclear nonproliferation regime, a series of interlocking treaties, inspection arrangements, and other international undertakings that has considerably constrained the spread of nuclear arms and has helped to establish a global norm against their acquisition. At the heart of the regime are the International Atomic Energy Agency (IAEA) and the Nuclear Non-Proliferation Treaty (NPT).

The IAEA is a Vienna-based multilateral organization with over 150 member countries that was established in 1957 to promote the peaceful uses of nuclear energy and to apply a system of accounting controls and on-site inspections, known collectively as safeguards, to verify that nuclear materials and facilities voluntarily submitted for such monitoring were not used for the development of nuclear arms. The NPT came into force in 1970. Under the treaty "non-nuclear-weapon state" parties—that is, parties that had not detonated a nuclear explosion prior to January 1, 1967—formally pledge not to manufacture nuclear explosives of any kind and agree to accept IAEA safeguards on all their nuclear activities (except for those that might relate to nuclear submarine propulsion), an arrangement known as full-scope safeguards. The weapon-state NPT parties are exempted from these restrictions but are prohibited from transferring nuclear explosives to non-nuclear-weapon states and from assisting them to manufacture such devices. Weapon-state parties also pledge to make good faith efforts to end the nuclear arms race and to work toward global disarmament. All countries accepting the treaty agree not to export nuclear equipment or material to non-nuclear-weapon states except under IAEA safeguards, a condition that has become the basis for a robust system of national and multilateral export control programs implemented by the industrialized, nuclear supplier countries.

The United States, Great Britain, and the Soviet Union were original nuclear-weapon-state parties to the treaty. In 1992 France and China, the two remaining nuclear-weapon states, joined the pact, a step that reinforced the normative value of the accord. Additionally, South Africa became the first de facto but undeclared nuclear state to renounce a nuclear-weapons option when it joined the NPT in 1991. More than 145 non-nuclear-weapon states have also joined the treaty, making it the most widely accepted arms control treaty today. However, Iraq's extensive violations of the accord have raised questions as to its effectiveness, particularly with respect to Libya, Iran, and North Korea. The commitment to the treaty by these non-nuclear-weapon states has been questioned because of their apparent interest in acquiring nuclear arms. Israel, India, and Pakistan all remain outside the treaty, operating nuclear facilities not subject to IAEA safeguards that provide the highly enriched uranium or plutonium needed for nuclear arms.

Active and sustained U.S. diplomatic efforts have been another major pillar of the nonproliferation regime. The U.S. initiative has been instrumental not only in the creation of the IAEA and the NPT but also in addressing proliferation threats posed by specific countries. For example, U.S. pressure is widely credited with dissuading South Korea and Taiwan from pursuing nascent nuclear-weapon programs in the mid–1970s and more recently has been central to efforts to constrain North Korean and Iranian interest in nuclear arms.

The norms established by the nonproliferation regime and the threat of U.S. and international pressure have been instrumental in discouraging the four de facto regional nuclear powers from adopting overt, open-ended nuclear-weapon programs. At the same time, the ambiguous postures of these states has been far less damaging to the nonproliferation regime than the emergence of newly declared nuclear-weapon states would have been and has sustained the dichotomy in the Non-Proliferation Treaty that legitimates only five nuclear powers.

Most important, ambiguity has helped keep alive the possibility that a de facto nuclear-weapon state might some day formally and convincingly renounce nuclear arms. Indeed, as mentioned previously, in a dramatic shift of position South Africa took this step in July 1991 by adhering to the NPT. In 1992 the International Atomic Energy Agency began the process of applying safeguards to all nuclear materials in that country and to the facilities processing them. A key first step is the establishment of an initial inventory of nuclear materials, including the weapons-grade materials that South Africa produced during the 1980s. The treaty permits non-nuclear-weapon states to possess weapons-grade nuclear materials under safeguards as part of peaceful nuclear programs. South Africa will probably be encouraged to dilute its weapons-grade uranium, however, to rule out the possibility that it might abrogate or withdraw from the NPT[8] at some future time and rapidly manufacture nuclear arms.

South Africa's abandonment of its undeclared nuclear-weapons program resulted from a series of circumstances that are not likely to be duplicated in the case of other regional nuclear powers for many years. Most important, the regional security threat that gave rise to the program, namely Soviet and Cuban involvement in southern Africa, evaporated with the end of the

Cold War, leading to a settlement in Angola and the independence of Namibia. In contrast, Israel's fears of its Arab neighbors, India's fears of China, and Pakistan's fears of India are likely to be enduring features of the international scene.[9]

Currently, the United States is attempting to promote a process of confidence building and negotiation in these various settings, aimed at resolving underlying disputes and reducing the risks of nuclear confrontation. In the Middle East, the centerpiece of the U.S. effort is furthering the Arab-Israeli peace process through direct talks among the parties. It is extremely unlikely, however, that Israel would consider any restrictions on its nuclear activities until there has been significant progress toward a regional peace settlement. Even then, Israel will undoubtedly want to retain its nuclear capability as an insurance policy against the possible resurgence of Arab militancy.

The United States has proposed a freeze on the production of weapons-grade nuclear materials in the region as part of a comprehensive Middle East arms control package, which would also include regional bans on chemical and biological weapons. Since Israel is the only Middle Eastern state that produces weapons-grade nuclear material today, the proposal in effect seeks to cap Israel's de facto nuclear arsenal but does not contemplate Israel's renunciation of its existing nuclear armory. However, even this partial step is unlikely to be attractive to Israel, which perceives it as a first step toward nuclear disarmament. The Arab states are equally likely to reject the proposal as one-sided, since it allows Israel to keep its most potent weapons while requiring the Arab states to renounce theirs.

In South Asia, Washington is encouraging the expansion of confidence-building measures between Pakistan and India. These now include an agreement for advance notification of military exercises, a hot line between the militaries of the two countries, understandings about accidental cross-border military overflights, and an agreement by each state not to attack the nuclear installations of the other. Washington is continuing its attempts to launch five-way talks on nuclear restraints involving India, Pakistan, the United States, Russia, and China.[10]

In addition, since the late 1970s Washington has sought to keep Pakistan from crossing the nuclear-weapon threshold by conditioning military and economic assistance on Pakistan's acceptance of a variety of nonproliferation controls. Washington waived a number of these restrictions during the 1980s to bolster Islamabad after the Soviet occupation of Afghanistan, but in 1985 Congress enacted a provision known as the Pressler Amendment, specifying that aid to Pakistan could be provided only after the President certified during the fiscal year in which the aid would be given that Pakistan did not "possess a nuclear explosive device."[11] Presidents Reagan and Bush made this certification for each fiscal year through the fall of 1989, even though Pakistan's nuclear advances continued. During the spring of 1990, however, when a crisis with India over Kashmir threatened to lead to hostilities, Pakistan apparently for the first time manufactured all the components needed for nuclear weapons, and in the fall of 1990, at the beginning of fiscal year 1991, President Bush declined to make the certification that the country did not possess a nuclear device. This lead to the termination of U.S. assistance.[12]

In early February 1992, Pakistan, in an apparent effort to obtain the restoration of U.S. assistance by accepting a new set of nonproliferation restrictions, departed from the traditional stance of the emerging nuclear powers and declared that it had indeed built the components for one or more nuclear weapons. It then pledged that it would not assemble any nuclear devices, conduct any nuclear tests, or transfer any weapons-related nuclear technology to others, and it announced that it had "permanently" frozen its nuclear-weapons program.[13] The Pakistani declaration—openly confirming the purport of President Bush's failure since late 1990 to certify that the country did not possess a nuclear device—led to immediate calls by hawkish Hindu elements in India for the state to declare itself a nuclear power.[14] Thus far, New Delhi has resisted such demands.

## THE NEXT WAVE: THE HOSTILE PROLIFERATORS

Historically Israel, India, South Africa, and Pakistan have either been friends of the United States or at least not been its enemies. Until recently, therefore, the principal danger posed to the United States by the emergence of these countries as de facto nuclear-weapon states was that their use or threatened use of nuclear arms in a regional conflict might have triggered a U.S.-Soviet nuclear confrontation with unpredictable consequences. With the end of the Cold War and the disintegration of the Soviet Union, however, this danger has largely passed. Accordingly, concerns over proliferation in Israel, India, and Pakistan (the remaining undeclared nuclear states of interest, now that South Africa has joined the NPT) are currently focused on the potential impacts of their future behavior on global nonproliferation objectives, such as preserving the 46-year-old taboo against the use of nuclear arms, reducing incentives for new states to develop such weapons, and limiting transfers of weapons-relevant nuclear technology.

Far more disturbing for U.S. policymakers than the activities of today's de facto nuclear powers, therefore, are the efforts of a second group of states to attain this status. This group includes Iraq, North Korea, Iran, Libya, and perhaps Algeria. The first four of these states, led by radical leaders opposed to the international status quo, have been profoundly hostile to the United States and/or its regional allies for many years. As was suggested earlier, their acquisition of even a small number of nuclear arms could have a grave impact on U.S. security, making prevention of this outcome an urgent priority.

The country-by-country summaries in the Appendix describe the status of the nuclear programs in each of these states and indicate that all are a number of years away from acquiring nuclear arms; North Korea is the closest to attaining this goal. The key element lacking in every instance is access to weapons-grade nuclear material.

A variety of military and diplomatic options are potentially available for slowing the progress of these states toward the nuclear-weapon threshold. The Gulf War has lent a certain legitimacy to the former. Indeed, twice during 1991 South Korean Defense Minister Lee Jong Koo indicated that his government might consider military action to destroy key nuclear installations in North Korea.[15] Nonetheless, such steps are rarely likely to be an attractive alternative, even assuming that the circumstances provide a legal basis and a modicum of international backing for the effort, and even assuming that the action involves acceptable risks to the personnel involved in the action.

First, in most instances, states that are seeking to develop nuclear arms already possess significant conventional military power that would allow them to strike back if their nuclear installations were attacked. Iraq was unable to respond during the Gulf War or in 1981, when Israel destroyed the Osiraq reactor outside Baghdad, but this is more likely the exception than the rule.

In the event of a U.S. and/or South Korean attack against key North Korean facilities at Yongbyon, for example, the North could easily retaliate by targeting Seoul with Scud missiles, which the North is thought to possess in far greater numbers than Iraq did in 1991. The North might also attempt to damage South Korean nuclear power plants either with such missiles, through air strikes, or by sabotage of the South's economic infrastructure. The risk of attacks by North Korean ground forces and the possible escalation to general war must also be recognized.

Similarly, if the United States attacked suspected clandestine nuclear facilities in Iran, the latter could easily retaliate against U.S. allies in the Persian Gulf, including Saudi Arabia and the Arab emirates. Libya, if its nuclear sites were attacked, might attempt to retaliate against Egypt or NATO forces in the Mediterranean.[16]

In such instances, the conventional military power of the target country can provide a deterrent umbrella under which it can pursue development of its nuclear weapon. To be sure, it might be possible for the United States or its regional partners to counter-deter the target state from retaliating through the threat of further escalation, but the effectiveness of such measures would be unpredictable and the very possibility of escalation could in some cases tip the risk/benefit balance against undertaking the attack in the first instance. This suggests an added reason for seeking to constrain the conventional military capabilities of potential nuclear states.

A second factor making military force less appealing as a means for checking the nuclear advances of the next wave of would-be nuclear-weapon powers is that it may simply be unable to achieve the desired objective. Prior to the Gulf War, Iraq dispersed its nuclear activities widely and disguised the facilities that housed them. As a result, a repeat of Israel's single-site bombing attack would have done little to arrest the Iraqi nuclear program, and even the extensive U.S. and coalition bombing raids during the conflict failed to destroy certain key Iraqi nuclear installations. Moreover, during the war Iraq was able to move nuclear materials and some essential equipment out of harm's way before installations that had housed them were destroyed. Thus, even if the coalition's intelligence had been perfect, its bombing campaign would have been only partially effective in halting Iraqi's nuclear advances.

A third shadow on the use of military force against nuclear installations is the danger of radiological consequences. Significant radioactive releases are likely principally from attacks on nuclear reactors; uranium-processing and enrichment plants and plutonium extraction facilities contain much smaller inventories of volatile radioactive elements. The U.S. bombing raids against Iraqi nuclear targets were the first in history to attack operating nuclear reactors. Fortunately, the two units at the Tuwaitha Nuclear Complex outside Baghdad had small power levels of five megawatts and less than one megawatt, and any radioactive releases would probably have been confined to the complex itself. In fact, the United States was able to avoid any releases by employing bombing tactics that caused the facilities to collapse inwardly and that did not damage fuel contained in the facilities' water-filled reactor vessels.[17] An attack against North Korea's thirty-megawatt reactor in Yongbyon, however, would be highly likely to have substantial off-site radiological consequences, exposing the attacking state to (1) accusations that it had engaged in unconventional warfare, and (2) substantial international criticism.

Despite these limitations, military force cannot be dropped from the list of options for preventing the advent of nuclear-armed radical states. Indeed, the *threat of force* can be a useful tool to back diplomatic efforts to enforce nonproliferation controls. It was invoked on a number of occasions during the summer and fall of 1991 to pressure Saddam Hussein to comply with the special UN-IAEA inspection regime implemented to seek out and destroy Iraq's unconventional weapons programs under Security Council Resolution 687.

Diplomatic initiatives to constrain the spread of nuclear arms, including the implementation of the nuclear nonproliferation regime, have had a number of important successes. Two examples are the arrested nuclear-weapons efforts of South Korea and Taiwan, and the fact that South Africa gave up its status as a de facto nuclear-weapons state.[18] It must be recognized, however, the circumstances surrounding each of these episodes were unique and that in less favorable situations the efforts of the United States and other interested parties were insufficient to dissuade Israel, India, and Pakistan from developing their respective nuclear capabilities.

One of the key elements underpinning diplomatic efforts to retard the spread of nuclear arms is the Nuclear Non-Proliferation Treaty, which, with its full-scope IAEA safeguards and considerable normative value, can have a significant impact on target states. Iraq, Iran, Libya, and North Korea are parties, and in December 1991, just prior to the electoral crisis that led to the ouster of Algerian President Chedli Benjedid, his government indicated that Algeria might be prepared to join the pact. Supplier state export controls can also significantly retard nuclear programs in developing countries, where indigenous technological and industrial capabilities are limited.

The case of North Korea provides a current example of the potential effectiveness of nonproliferation diplomacy. North Korea signed the Nuclear Non-Proliferation Treaty in December 1985. For the next six years, however, it refused to sign an agreement with the International Atomic Energy Agency to place all its nuclear materials (except uranium ore and natural uranium concentrate) and the facilities that process them under IAEA inspection. Although the North's obligation to sign and implement a full-scope safeguards agreement is absolute, in the late 1980s it began insisting upon a nuclear quid pro quo from the United States as a condition for signing the accord. Most often, it demanded the removal of U.S. nuclear weapons from South Korea.

Throughout 1990 and 1991, as U.S. concerns increased, the Bush Administration gradually intensified its efforts to slow the North Korean nuclear program, raising the issue persistently at the IAEA, at the 1990 NPT Review Conference, and at similar fora; pressing North Korea in bilateral discussions to sign its agreement with the IAEA; successfully encouraging Japan to condition recognition of the Democratic People's Republic of Korea (DPRK) and the provision of financial aid to the North on the latter's taking this step; coordinating closely with South Korea; and seeking the support of the Soviet Union and China in restraining Pyongyang.

The collapse of the Soviet Union and President Bush's September 27, 1992, decision to withdraw all U.S. tactical ground- and sea-launched nuclear weapons from deployment around the world broke the impasse. By the end of December, South Korean President Roh Tae Woo announced that all nuclear arms had been withdrawn from his country (including air-launched systems thought to have been deployed there); North and South Korea signed a historic non-aggression pact; and the two countries signed a comprehensive nuclear accord, establishing a nuclear-weapon-free zone on the Korean Peninsula, providing for bilateral nuclear inspections, and prohibiting either state from operating facilities (such as the one North Korea has been building) capable of producing weapons-grade nuclear materials. Finally, on January 29, 1992, the North signed its safeguards agreement with the IAEA. The IAEA has since conducted inspections of North Korea's nuclear materials; however, the bilateral inspections regime with South Korea has yet to be implemented.

Despite progress in the case of North Korea, much will depend on the effectiveness of continuing IAEA inspections under the NPT—inspections that failed to constrain Iraq, raising serious questions about the adequacy of the treaty and the IAEA system. Under the NPT, Iraq was required to declare all its nuclear installations and materials (except uranium ore and ore concentrate) and submit them to IAEA inspection to allow verification that they were not being used for the development of nuclear weapons. Iraq repeatedly violated this obligation, operating a number of undeclared facilities for processing raw uranium into feedstock for the uranium enrichment process and enriching the material on a trial basis. Moreover, even at the five-megawatt reactor and nearby laboratories at Tuwaitha, which were under IAEA monitoring, Iraq was able to circumvent the agency's controls and covertly produce a small quantity of plutonium.

Historically, the IAEA has relied on the inspected state to declare all its nuclear activities voluntarily and has then limited its inspections to the declared material and facilities. Although IAEA agreements with NPT parties authorize the agency to undertake "special inspections" of suspected undeclared nuclear sites with the consent of the inspected country, the agency had never attempted to exercise this authority. In the wake of its failures in Iraq, however, the agency's secretariat has declared that it will begin to employ this special inspection authority, and at its December 1991 meeting, the agency's board of governors quietly approved its reactivation.

An important test of the fortified inspection system is taking place in Iran. U.S. officials have been quoted as stating that the country is engaged in a secret nuclear-weapons development program. Although the location of weapons-related activities remains uncertain, several sites are under suspicion, including one northwest of Tehran and another near Qazvin.[19] In February 1992, the IAEA visited several such suspect sites at the invitation of the Rafsanjani government. Following the visit, the IAEA announced that it had found no evidence of a clandestine nuclear-weapons program at the locations it observed. The agency's credibility was marred, however, by accusations that it had been misled into visiting an alternate location with the same name as one of Iran's allegedly undeclared nuclear facilities. With continuing suspicions in the international community as to Iran's nuclear intentions, it remains to be seen whether the agency will request further special visits to validate its initial findings.

The availability of special inspections could play an important role in North Korea, providing an additional element of confidence in the web of verification that is being established on the Peninsula.[20]

In addition, the nuclear accord between North and South Korea embodies an important restraint that has been seen in a number of other settings recently and is emerging as an important adjunct to the traditional elements of the nonproliferation regime: restrictions on the acquisition of weapons-grade nuclear materials. Even before it joined the NPT, for example, South Africa closed the facility thought to be its sole source of weapons-grade enriched uranium, an important confidence-building measure that effectively capped its nuclear-weapons potential. As noted earlier, the U.S. Middle East arms control plan also calls for a freeze on the production of weapons-grade nuclear materials; and in parallel with their 1991 agreement for comprehensive mutual nuclear inspections under IAEA oversight, both Argentina and Brazil have pledged to limit the output of their uranium enrichment plants to non-weapons-grade material. In these instances, diplomatic initiatives and agreements are having an important impact on restraining the spread of nuclear arms.[21]

Finally, nuclear export controls, though far from completely effective, were able to slow the pace of Iraqi nuclear advances somewhat and are currently being strengthened in a number of respects. Nuclear-supplier-country control lists are being expanded to include dual-use items; China, by joining the NPT, is accepting binding legal commitments to require IAEA safeguards on all its nuclear exports—a policy it has voluntarily embraced in the past but implemented only intermittently; and efforts are under way to reduce the threat of leakage from the former Soviet Union of nuclear weapons or related expertise, technology, materials, or equipment.

This last issue, the impact on nuclear proliferation of the disintegration of the Soviet Union, is beyond the scope of this paper. It poses an enormous challenge, however; if a flood of nuclear materiel cascades from the republics of the Commonwealth of Independent States into the hands of would-be nuclear powers, it could all too easily overwhelm the treaties, inspections, and other elements of the nonproliferation regime.

## CONCLUSIONS

Today, the spread of nuclear arms to new states poses one of the most serious risks to U.S. security, in part because even a small number of nuclear weapons may be sufficient to deter forceful U.S. diplomatic or military intervention in instances where only its regional interests, rather than national survival, are at issue. The fact that the next states that are likely to acquire nuclear arms are under radical leaders who are openly hostile to U.S. interests provides particular cause for concern.

Because of the risk of retaliation by target countries against U.S. allies, questions of efficacy, and the danger of radiological releases, the use of military force to prevent further proliferation will rarely be an attractive alternative, even if the legal grounds for such action could be established in particular cases and a measure of international support for such measures obtained. Although the option of using military force to halt nuclear proliferation should be retained, usually as a last resort, diplomatic initiatives are clearly preferable and have proven effective in a number of instances, when aggressively pursued. Recent efforts to strengthen key elements of the nonproliferation regime should enhance the efficacy of this approach.

## APPENDIX

### ISRAEL De-facto N-Weapon State

- Probably has 75–100 undeclared N-weapons; possibly 300.
- Thought to have obtained first N-weapons in late 1960s.
- Beginning in 1982 apparently built "boosted" weapons that rely on H-bomb principles; may possess "neutron bombs" (low-blast, high radiation H-bombs).
- Thought to have deployed 400-mile-range nuclear capable Jericho missiles; testing intermediate-range missile (800 mi.? 2,000 mi.?) since 1987.
- May have conducted N-test in South Atlantic in 1979 (possibly three tests).
- Participating in Middle East Arms Control Talks; the United States has proposed regional freeze on production of weapons-grade nuclear materials as part of broader arms control package.
- Has recently threatened military action to destroy Iranian nuclear facilities if Iran's N-weapons program not halted.
- Not party to Nuclear Non-Proliferation Treaty (NPT).

### INDIA De-facto N-Weapon State

- Probably has essentials for 75–100 A-bombs that could be deployed quickly.
- Conducted single nuclear test in 1974; no further N-tests.
- Has greatly expanded N-weapons production capability in recent years; reportedly designing H-bomb.
- Tested N-capable short-range Prithvi missile five times since 1989. Tested Agni, an intermediate-range missile (1,500 mi.), in 1989 and conducted second test on May 29, 1992; claims system is a "technology demonstrator," not intended for deployment.
- Has declined to participate in five-power talks proposed by Pakistan that would include the United States, Russia, and P.R.C., but has agreed to continue dialogue with the United States on nuclear issues.
- Potential crisis looming over U.S.-supplied Tarapur reactors in 1993, when U.S. agreement covering reactors and French fuel-supply contract expire; India expected to claim right to suspend IAEA safeguards on reactors and plutonium-bearing spent fuel and right to extract plutonium without U.S. or French approval. U.S. (since 1980) and France (since 1991) prohibit major new N-exports to countries that operate facilities not under IAEA inspection: India has numerous uninspected facilities used to support N-weapons capability.

- Not party to NPT; unwilling to join even if Pakistan does so because of Chinese N-threat.

**PAKISTAN De-facto N-Weapon State**

- Probably has material, and possibly all components, for 15–20 undeclared A-bombs that could be deployed quickly.
- Apparently obtained material for first atomic weapon in 1986.
- U.S. aid and military sales terminated in 1990 when President Bush declined to certify that Pakistan did "not possess a nuclear explosive device," a condition for aid to Pakistan under U.S. law since 1985.
- On February 7, 1992, Foreign Secretary Shaharyar Khan declared that Pakistan possessed components for the core of at least one N-weapon but that Pakistan had "permanently frozen" its production of such components and of weapons-grade nuclear material. Subsequent official statements have reiterated Pakistan's traditional claim that its nuclear program is exclusively peaceful.
- No N-tests, but believed to have received N-weapon design from China.
- Attempting to develop "boosted" N-weapons.
- Tested N-capable short-range missile in 1989; sought similar "M–11" system from PRC in 1991, but no deliveries confirmed. China has agreed to abide by export control rules of the Missile Technology Control Regime, prohibiting transfers of missiles able to carry 1,100-pound payload to a distance of 190 miles or more and has agreed that M–11 is covered by this ban.
- Not party to NPT, but has stated it is willing to join if India does.

**S. AFRICA Abandoned De-facto N-Weapon Status by Joining NPT in July 1991**

- Assumed to have essentials for 15–25 N-weapons.
- Able to build N-weapons since 1980–81.
- May have assisted, and received data from, suspected 1979 Israeli N-test in South Atlantic.
- International Atomic Energy Agency (IAEA) conducting initial inventory pursuant to NPT in order to safeguard all existing N-materials and to ensure that none are used for weapons.
- Possibly in collaboration with Israel, developing intermediate-range (800 mi.? 2,000 mi.?) Arniston missile, suggesting some continuing interest in N-weapons.

**N. KOREA Presumed to Be Actively Seeking N-Weapons, but Currently Accepting New Nonproliferation Restraints**

- Late–1991 withdrawal of U.S. N-weapons from South Korea, long-demanded by North, paved way for December 31, 1991, agreement with South for the denuclearization of the Korean Peninsula, including bilateral inspections and mutual pledge not to build plutonium separation or uranium enrichment plants capable of producing weapons-grade nuclear materials. Mutual inspections were to have begun by mid-June 1992. The bilateral inspection talks have reached an impasse over the scope of inspections and the South's proposal for challenge inspections. They resumed June 30, 1992.

- Party to NPT (1985), but did not ratify IAEA safeguards agreement until April 9, 1992. First round of IAEA inspection of facilities completed June 8, 1992.
- IAEA confirmed existence of a partially completed plutonium separation (reprocessing) plant, a completed 5-megawatt (electric) reactor, and a partially completed 50-megawatt (electric) reactor at Nyongbyon and a partially completed 200-megawatt (electric) reactor at Taechon.
- North Korea claims 5-megawatt (electric) plant operated only intermittently since its completion in 1986 and produced no plutonium-bearing spent fuel; U.S. intelligence agencies believe reactor operated extensively (at unknown power level) and that North may be concealing stockpile of spent fuel. IAEA attempting to verify plant's operating history.
- North Korea plans to continue building reprocessing plant while under IAEA safeguards. South initially claimed plant to be in violation of North-South denuclearization agreement and demanded N. Korea halt construction. However, recent statements note that in its current state of construction, Seoul does not "consider the facilities to be a violation of the joint denuclearization declaration."
- North Korea has indicated willingness to stop its reprocessing program in exchange for light-water reactor technology and fuel supply guarantees, suggesting that it does not consider such activities prohibited by the North-South denuclearization accord.
- The United States, South Korea, and Japan are refusing to improve relations or, in the case of Japan, provide economic assistance until the North implements bilateral nuclear inspections with the South; in early June, the European Community adopted a similar stance.

**IRAQ Party to NPT; Found by IAEA in Mid–1991 to Have Repeatedly Violated Treaty by Producing Undeclared Nuclear Materials at Undeclared Facilities. N-Weapons Program Currently Being Dismantled Pursuant to U.N. Security Council Resolution 687**

- Earlier Iraqi N-weapons effort thwarted in 1981, when Israel destroyed Osiraq reactor.
- Post-Gulf War inspections revealed previously unknown multi-track program to enrich uranium to weapons grade and develop all other components of N-weapons; most facilities/equipment destroyed during or after 1991 Gulf War.
- U.S. Director of Central Intelligence, Robert Gates, has warned that once sanctions are removed, Iraq could rebuild its N-weapons program "within a few, but not many years."
- In April 1992, N-weapons experts from four N-weapons states concluded, after examining evidence compiled by the U.N. Special Commission on Iraq, that at the time of the Gulf War, Iraq was three years or more away from producing its first atomic weapon.

- Some aspects of Iraqi enrichment effort still unclear because of Iraqi refusal to supply procurement data to the U.N.; inspectors still searching for possible uranium enrichment centrifuges and possible underground plutonium production reactor.
- June 5, 1992, Iraq submitted its "full, final and complete" report on its weapons programs in compliance with U.N. Resolution 687. On June 17, 1992, however, U.N. Special Commission on Iraq determined that Iraq was "not in compliance" with U.N. resolutions. Concurrently, the IAEA recommended a tighter embargo and additional inspections to prevent Iraq from further developing nuclear weapons.

**IRAN Party to NPT, but Presumed to Be Seeking N-Weapons**

- Reactivating weapons program with some help from China and others; clandestinely seeking nuclear-weapons-relevant technology in Western Europe.
- No major N-weapon facilities apparently under construction, as yet, but related research believed to be taking place clandestinely at existing research sites.
- C.I.A. estimates of program have concluded that Iran not likely to produce N-weapons before the end of the decade.
- February 1992 special IAEA "visit" observed several locations not on list of declared nuclear sites; found no violations of NPT during visit.
- September 10, 1992, Teheran agrees to acquire 300 MW nuclear plant from China; U.S. officials have previously stated that Iran has purchased equipment for enriching uranium from China as well; signed agreement pledging that the cooperation between them is for totally peaceful purposes.
- Russian nuclear technicians are confirmed to be working at Georgian nuclear site near Caspian Sea where Russian reactors are to be installed.

**LIBYA Party to the NPT, but Presumed to Be Seeking N-Weapons**

- A number of years away from possibly building N-weapons indigenously.
- No major N-weapon facilities apparently under construction, as yet.
- Attempted to purchase atomic bomb in early 1970s and in 1981.
- During a visit by IAEA Director General Blix in spring 1992, Libya said it was ready to invite IAEA inspectors to any site they wished to see.

**ALGERIA Possibly Interested in N-Weapons, but Currently Lacks the Facilities to Produce N-Weapons Material**

- In 1986, secretly began construction with Chinese assistance of 15-megawatt (thermal) research reactor at Ain Oussera with potential to produce N-weapons material. Agreed to place unit under IAEA safeguards as result of U.S. pressure, after reactor's discovery in early 1991.
- Army and "High State Committee" seized power in December 1991 and ousted President Chedli Benjedid, fearing imminent elections would bring Muslim fundamentalists to power.

- Not party to NPT; IAEA visited Ain Oussera in January 1992 to review status of the reactor. Algiers signed safeguards agreement covering Ain Oussera facility with IAEA in February 1992.
- Prior to Benjedid's ouster, government indicated readiness to join NPT but has not subsequently reiterated this position.

**SYRIA Possibly Interested in N-Weapons; Party to NPT Since 1969; Signed Comprehensive IAEA Safeguards Agreement in February 1992**

- Taking first steps to develop nuclear infrastructure after years of inactivity by acquiring 30-kilowatt research reactor from China (subject to IAEA inspection); reactor incapable of producing significant amounts of weapons-usable plutonium.
- Despite Syrian claim that reactor intended for peaceful purposes, U.S. lists Syria among countries having "nuclear program with suspicious intentions."
- Has been seeking "strategic parity" with Israel through acquisition of ballistic missiles, chemical weapons, and advanced conventional armaments. Recently received Scud-C missiles from North Korea, with range of several hundred miles.

**BRAZIL Pursued N-Weapon Option During 1980s; Accepting New Nonproliferation Restraints**

- Military leaders launched N-weapons program in 1979; halted by current civilian government.
- Has built facilities necessary for N-weapons capability as part of nuclear energy and research program, but has not produced N-weapons material.
- Concluded agreement with Argentina in Nov. 1990 for comprehensive bilateral inspections under IAEA auspices; established the Argentine-Brazil Accounting and Control Commission (ABACC) in July 1991 to conduct bilateral inspections; signed agreement with IAEA, Argentina, and ABACC in Dec. 1991 formalizing IAEA participation, despite objections of the Brazilian military.
- Not party to NPT (but has accepted NPT-style inspections).
- Some work on short-range N-capable missiles; building space-launch vehicle with long-range missile potential.

**ARGENTINA Pursued N-Weapon Option During Early 1980s; Accepting New Nonproliferation Restraints**

- Has built facilities necessary for N-weapons capability as part of nuclear energy program, but has not produced N-weapons materials.
- Civilian government opposed to nuclear arming.
- Concluded agreement with Brazil in November 1990 for comprehensive bilateral inspections under IAEA auspices; established the Argentine-Brazil Accounting and Control Commission (ABACC) in July 1991 to conduct bilateral

inspections; signed agreement with IAEA, Brazil, and ABACC in Dec. 1991 formalizing IAEA participation.

- Not party to NPT (but has accepted NPT-style inspections).
- In 1980s, cooperated with Egypt and Iraq on N-capable, short-range Condor II missile; program halted in 1991.

**TAIWAN Party to NPT; Presumed to Have Abandoned Intermittent N-Weapons Effort**

- Has sizeable nuclear power program but lacks facilities to produce material for N-weapons.
- Built secret lab to extract plutonium in 1987 but dismantled unit under U.S. pressure before plutonium obtained. (Made similar attempt in mid–1970s, also thwarted by United States.)

## NOTES

1. Whether Iraq was deterred by these threats from using chemical weapons in the war or simply lacked the logistical and technical capabilities to employ them in the Kuwaiti theater remained uncertain after the conflict, but a growing body of evidence supported the latter hypothesis. In addition, Iraq apparently had not mastered the technology for mounting chemical warheads on its ballistic missiles; although such warheads were found by the UN inspectors after the war, they reportedly caused the missiles to behave erratically and were not deemed usable.

2. It is possible that biological weapons may some day also achieve this deterrent effect, if the prospect of their effective use against cities appears credible. This threshold was not reached in the Gulf War.

3. For decades, India, Pakistan, and South Africa consistently maintained that their nuclear programs were entirely peaceful, while Israel has long employed the ambiguous formula that it will not be the country to "introduce" nuclear weapons into the Middle East. Even in the months prior to the 1991 Gulf War, when Israel faced the possible threat of chemically armed Iraqi missiles, Israeli leaders only hinted at the country's nuclear potential, declaring that Israel would respond "a hundred times harder" if attacked with chemical weapons, without saying more. A recent change in Pakistan's declared policy is discussed in the text that follows.

4. Even India attempted to disguise its intentions by denominating its test a "peaceful nuclear explosion," of the type the United States and the Soviet Union were exploring at the time. India has not conducted further tests or deployed nuclear arms, although it has invested heavily in building the infrastructure to do so.

5. In a recent book on the Israeli nuclear program, investigative journalist Seymour Hersh stated that, in fact, Israel conducted three tests in September 1979, but only one was observed by the U.S. satellite. See Seymour M. Hersh, *The Samson Option* (New York: Random House, 1991), p. 271.

6. In *The Samson Option*, Seymour Hersh states that Israel possesses neutron bombs in considerable numbers. Hersh rests his conclusions on interviews with various U.S. and Israeli sources but does not provide any technical details. If Hersh

is correct that Israel conducted three nuclear tests in 1979, however, this might have provided Israel enough data to confirm the reliability of a neutron bomb design.

7. "Revealed: The Secrets of Israel's Nuclear Arsenal," *Sunday Times* (London), October 5, 1986.

8. Under Article X of the NPT, parties are permitted to withdraw from the pact on ninety days' notice if its "supreme interests related to the subject matter of this treaty" are jeopardized.

9. For many years it was also feared that Argentina and Brazil might emerge as de facto nuclear-weapon powers, particularly during the period when the two states were under military governments. Neither country reached the point of producing weapons-grade nuclear material, and as the two came under civilian control in the mid–1980s, they began a process of economic integration and confidence-building that led to a series of historic reciprocal visits to key nuclear installations. In 1991, the two began to implement a program of comprehensive bilateral nuclear inspections to be overseen by the International Atomic Energy Agency. Although both states continue to reject the NPT as discriminatory, the bilateral inspections are comparable to the full-scope IAEA safeguards required by that accord. Neither state has faced a significant external threat for many years, contributing to their readiness to renounce nuclear arms and accept comprehensive monitoring arrangements.

10. This initiative was first proposed by Pakistan. Pakistan for years has offered to enter into comprehensive bilateral nonproliferation agreements with India; but India has rejected these proposals, arguing that it cannot give up its nuclear weapons option as long as it faces a nuclear threat from China. Since Pakistan has been aware of India's stance, there has been some question as to whether Pakistan's offers have been sincere or more diplomatic gambits. The Pakistani proposal for five-way nuclear talks sought to address India's concerns about China by including Beijing in the discussions.

11. Amendment to the Foreign Assistance Act of 1961, section 620E (e).

12. India, which has received little in U.S. economic and military aid over the years, but which purchased a pair of U.S. nuclear power reactors in 1963, has been subject to somewhat different sanctions. Washington terminated all nuclear cooperation with respect to the facilities in 1982 because of India's refusal to place all of its nuclear installations under IAEA safeguards, including those that produce materials for India's de facto nuclear weapons program.

13. R. Jeffrey Smith, "Pakistan Official Affirms Capacity for Nuclear Device," *The Washington Post*, February 7, 1992; Paul Lewis, "Pakistan Tells of Its A-Bomb Capacity," *The New York Times*, February 8, 1992.

14. Steve Coll, "India Pressured on Bomb," *The Washington Post*, February 9, 1992.

15. David E. Sanger, "U.S. Officials Step Up Warnings to North Korea on Nuclear Arms," *The New York Times*, November 21, 1991.

16. On April 15, 1986, in retaliation for a U.S. air strike on several targets in Libya the previous day, Libya launched an attack with Scud-B missiles against the U.S. Coast Guard base on the Italian island of Lampedusa. However, the missile (or missiles) fell into the sea several hundred yards short of the U.S. base.

17. The U.S. attacks, though the first on operating reactors, were only the most recent of a substantial number of previous attacks on nuclear plants by a variety of

states. During World War II, for example, Allied warplanes attacked heavy water production sites in Norway. In September 1980, Iran unsuccessfully attacked Iraq's Osiraq reactor, also at the Tuwaitha site. The facility was subsequently destroyed by an Israeli air strike in June 1981.

Between March 1984 and July 1988, Iraqi warplanes struck Iran's nuclear power reactor construction site at Bushehr seven times, causing heavy damage and, according to Teheran radio, killing a total of thirteen individuals. The final Iraqi attack, on July 19, 1988, came one day after Iran had accepted a United Nations–sponsored ceasefire in the Iran-Iraq War.

18. See also the discussion of Argentina and Brazil in Note 9.

19. Charles Aldinger, "Iran Not Close to Developing Nuclear Arms," Associated Press, October 31, 1991; "The China-Iran Nuclear Cloud," *Mednews*, July 22, 1991 (giving the precise location of Iran's nuclear weapons research center as Moallem Kalayeh, in the Elburz Mountains, just north of Qazvin).

20. To be successful, the special inspection system—and, indeed, the entire nonproliferation regime and the diverse diplomatic efforts complementing it—must be backstopped by effective intelligence. The revelations about Iraq's clandestine nuclear activities have raised serious questions about the adequacy of nuclear intelligence–gathering by the United States and other concerned nations, inasmuch as these efforts failed to identify the portion of Iraq's nuclear programs that had advanced the farthest: its attempt to enrich uranium to weapons-grade using electromagnetic devices known as calutrons. The calutron program came to light only as the result of the postwar UN-IAEA inspection regime established under Security Council Resolution 687—and even then, the inspectors did not learn about the calutrons until an Iraqi electrical engineer who had worked on the program defected to U.S. forces.

21. With the end of the Cold War, the United States is substantially increasing the intelligence resources devoted to proliferation questions.

# 13

# Conventional Arms Transfers: Exporting Security or Arming Adversaries?

*Michael T. Klare*

For most of the Cold War era, U.S. policymakers generally viewed conventional arms transfers as a separate issue from that of nuclear, biological, and chemical (NBC) weapons proliferation. Thus, although the United States has signed or endorsed a number of international curbs on the spread of unconventional weapons, including the nuclear Non-Proliferation Treaty (NPT), the Biological Weapons Convention (BWC), and the proposed Chemical Weapons Convention (CWC), it has rarely supported such efforts in the conventional area. This dichotomy is also reflected in the organization of the U.S. government with respect to proliferation affairs: Whereas various laws and regulations prohibit the export of nuclear and chemical weapons, U.S. law (notably the Arms Export Control Act of 1976) provides for the lawful export of conventional weapons, and several government agencies, including the Defense Security Assistance Agency (DSAA) and the State Department's Office of Defense Trade, are directly or indirectly involved in the actual transfer of such munitions.

This dichotomy in the U.S. response to conventional and unconventional arms proliferation reflects the widespread belief that NBC proliferation is inherently destabilizing, no matter who the recipient might be, while transfers of conventional arms can enhance stability if provided to friendly powers. Specifically, U.S. policymakers have long maintained that arms transfers to key friends and allies in the Third World can enhance stability in vital areas (especially the Middle East) by deterring aggression by Soviet-backed regional powers. In articulating this point, Under Secretary of State James L. Buckley told an industry group in 1981 that the Reagan Administration "believes that arms transfers, judiciously applied, can complement and supplement our own defense efforts and serve as a vital and constructive instrument of our foreign policy."[1] On this basis, a succession of U.S. presidents have approved substantial deliveries of U.S. arms and military equipment to friendly nations in the Third World.[2]

With the end of the Cold War, however, the long-standing dichotomy in U.S. responses to conventional and unconventional proliferation has begun to disappear. Although the spread of NBC munitions continues to be seen as an especially significant peril, requiring stepped-up nonproliferation efforts, many policymakers now view conventional arms trafficking as a similar problem, with a comparable requirement for international controls. This new assessment of conventional arms is partly due to the greater sophistication of arms sold on the international market, and partly to a perception that arms transfers have fueled regional conflicts in areas of tension. An important case in point was the Iran-Iraq war of 1980–88, which killed an estimated one million people and jeopardized the strategic interests of the United States (namely, safe access to Persian Gulf petroleum supplies). The Iran-Iraq War also focused attention on the proliferation of ballistic missiles, which were used by both sides to attack cities and industrial zones. In the wake of the war, many world leaders called for fresh initiatives to curb the spread of sophisticated weapons to areas of conflict.

This new perception of the risks attendant upon the uncontrolled spread of advanced conventional weapons also began to appear in the security assessments of U.S. military leaders. Here, for instance, is former Army Chief of Staff General Carl E. Vuono, writing in the April 1990 issue of *Sea Power* magazine:

> The proliferation of military power in what is often called the "Third World" presents a troubling picture. Many Third World nations now possess mounting arsenals of tanks, heavy artillery, ballistic missiles, and chemical weapons. At least a dozen developing countries have more than 1,000 main battle tanks, and portable antiaircraft and antitank missiles are widespread as well.
>
> Regional rivalries supported by powerful armies have resulted in brutal and devastating conflicts in the Third World. We need look no further than the Iran-Iraq War to see the effects of weapons and technologies formerly reserved only for the superpowers. The proliferation of advanced military capabilities has given an increasing number of countries in the developing world the ability to wage sustained, mechanized land warfare. The United States cannot ignore the expanding military power of these countries, and the Army must retain the capability to defeat threats wherever they occur. This could mean confronting a well-equipped army in the Third World.[3]

When compared to similar statements by U.S. military officials during peak Cold War periods, Vuono's comments strike one as a sharp departure from prior practice. Rather than focusing specifically on Soviet arms transfers to particular Soviet clients in the Third World, as had been the standard practice in previous years, Vuono depicts weapons proliferation as a *generalized* problem, irrespective of the source of the weapons. In addition, Vuono suggests that such proliferation can fuel regional conflicts that are independent of the old U.S.-Soviet rivalry but that nevertheless threaten vital U.S. interests—thus sparking possible U.S. intervention. This represents a relatively new theme in U.S. security thinking, one that has gained increasing prominence during the past few years.

In recognition of the threat posed by the uncontrolled commerce in conventional arms, U.S. policymakers began to view such traffic as both a legitimate and an important concern for arms control. A significant milestone in this regard was the adoption of the Missile Technology Control Regime (MTCR) in 1987, the first multilateral measure of this sort to address the spread of non-NBC weapons. Although the focus on ballistic missiles was partly spurred by fears that they would be used for the delivery of NBC munitions, advocates of the MTCR also cited the dangers posed by their use in delivering conventional warheads. The United States also agreed in 1988 to participate in a UN-mandated study of the role of transparency in constraining conventional arms transfers.

So, even without the outbreak of the Persian Gulf crisis, it is likely that conventional arms transfers would come under increasing scrutiny by the United States and other countries in the post–Cold War era. Whether or not this would have led eventually to a fundamental change in U.S. arms export policy cannot, of course, be stated with any certainty. Once the crisis did break out, however, the arms trade issue received more attention than ever before and moved quickly to the top of the U.S. policy agenda.

The Persian Gulf crisis lent fresh importance to the arms trade issue for several reasons. First, the crisis itself can be attributed in part to uncontrolled arms transfers. In making the decision to occupy Kuwait, Saddam Hussein clearly believed that his powerful armies—equipped with large supplies of imported arms—would prove sufficiently menacing to deter any countermoves by unfriendly powers. Later, when it became evident that such countermoves were indeed possible, he refused to quit Kuwait in the apparent belief that his well-equipped forces would prevail in combat, or at least would inflict such heavy casualties on the coalition forces that they would agree to settle the conflict on terms favorable to Iraq. It can also be argued that the willingness of so many countries (including close allies of the United States) to supply Iraq with so many sophisticated arms—*despite* Baghdad's record of aggression and its use of chemical weapons against civilians—could have encouraged Hussein to believe that the major powers had no fundamental objection to his hegemonic aspirations.

Second, the Gulf War clearly demonstrated how the proliferation of sophisticated conventional arms has upped the risks for participation in regional conflicts of this sort. Although it is true that the United States suffered very few casualties during the course of the war, it must be also be recalled that U.S. strategists felt compelled to deploy the most powerful expeditionary force assembled since World War II to defeat Hussein's well-equipped armies. As it turned out, U.S. weaponry generally proved superior to the Soviet, French, and other European munitions in Iraqi hands; but the gap in technology was not all that great, and if Iraqi soldiers had been more adept in the use of their weapons they undoubtedly would have taken a much higher toll in allied lives. In future conflicts, where the technology on each side is roughly comparable and where the gap in skills, training, and doctrine is not as great as that experienced in the Gulf War, we are likely to witness much higher levels of death and destruction on all sides.

Finally, the Gulf conflict clearly demonstrated that the Iraq/Kuwait theater is but a part of the larger fabric of Middle Eastern conflicts and rivalries—all of which must be addressed if lasting peace and stability are to be established in the region. Both sides in the Gulf conflict sought to turn this reality to their advantage: Iraq by targeting Israel and Saudi Arabia with ballistic missiles, and by appealing to disaffected Arab masses; the United States by inviting Syria and Egypt to support the anti-Iraqi coalition. At the conclusion of the war, U.S. efforts to promote long-term stability in the Gulf area inevitably extended to the attempted resolution of other regional disputes. In addressing these disputes, moreover, U.S. policymakers have discovered how deeply proliferation issues are embedded in the regional security dilemma—for as long as the major actors believe that the acquisition of enhanced arms capabilities will invest them with a military advantage over any rivals, they will likely eschew a negotiated settlement of outstanding issues. Only by curbing arms deliveries to the region, it now appears, can the United States persuade these actors that they have nothing to gain by continued intransigence at the bargaining table.

For all these reasons, control of the conventional arms trade became a major U.S. and international priority in the wake of the Persian Gulf conflict. Thus, on February 6, 1991, Secretary of State James Baker told the House Foreign Affairs Committee that the establishment of such controls would be one of the primary U.S. foreign policy objectives in the post-conflict period. "The time has come," he affirmed, "to try to change the destructive pattern of military competition and proliferation in [the Middle East] and to reduce the arms flow into an area that is already over-militarized."[4] President Bush also spoke of the need for arms transfer restraints and returned to this point in his first formal press conference after the war's conclusion. "I will work very hard for peace, just as hard as I have in the prosecution of war," he declared on March 1, 1991. Curbing the spread of nuclear and chemical weapons would be the top priority, he noted, "but let's hope that out of all this there will be less proliferation of all different types of weapons, not just conventional weapons."[5]

In the weeks that followed, conventional arms transfer restraint became a major topic in Congress, with many lawmakers calling for the adoption of new legislative restrictions on foreign military sales. Characteristic of this outlook is a March 1991 speech by Senator Joseph Biden. "The window of opportunity for Middle East arms control is now open," he told colleagues in the Senate. "Before it begins to shut, we must apply the same diplomatic skill and ingenuity to arms control that we brought to reversing Saddam's aggression against Kuwait, lest some future dictator, armed with Western technology, again unleash the dogs of war in the cauldron we call the Middle East."[6] Along with other members of Congress, Biden called for a moratorium on U.S. arms transfers to the Middle East pending multilateral talks aimed at the adoption of international constraints on military exports to the region.[7]

In response to such efforts, and to similar calls from leaders of other friendly nations, President Bush on May 29, 1991, announced a Middle East Arms Control Initiative aimed at curbing the spread of nuclear arms, chemical munitions, ballistic missiles, and "destabilizing" conventional weapons. As part of this effort, Bush called for meetings with the five permanent members of the U.N. Security Council (the "Perm Five") to consider the adoption of mutual "guidelines" for the control of foreign military sales. As envisioned by Bush, the guidelines would oblige the major suppliers "to observe a general code of responsible arms transfers" and "to avoid destabilizing transfers."[8]

Bush's proposal for a meeting of major military suppliers was accepted by the other nations involved, and on July 8 and 9 representatives of the Perm Five met in Paris to discuss this and other measures for conventional arms transfer restraint. In a communiqué issued at the conclusion of the meeting, the participating officials declared that "They recognized that indiscriminate transfers of military weapons and technology contribute to regional instability." Moreover, "They are fully conscious of the special responsibilities that are incumbent upon them [as major military suppliers] to ensure that such risks be avoided, and of the special role they have to play in promoting greater responsibility, confidence, and transparency in this field."[9] In line with this view, the Perm Five called for further talks leading to the adoption of specific control measures.

Although it is phrased in polite diplomatic terms and requires little in the way of specific actions, this statement represents something of a sea-change in the attitude of the international community with respect to conventional arms transfers. Until very recently, conventional arms control had not been viewed as a legitimate function of global nonproliferation efforts, and individual suppliers generally contended that international law and practice allowed them to export such items free of international restrictions. Now, however, the major suppliers acknowledged that they bore "special responsibilities" to impose constraints on the conventional arms traffic.

In consonance with this outlook, representatives of the Perm Five continued to meet over the summer and early fall, and at a meeting in London on October 17–18, 1991, they adopted a set of formal guidelines for the control of conventional arms transfers. In signing the London document, the Perm Five promised to consult with one another regarding the flow of arms to particular regions and to "observe rules of restraint" when deciding on major arms export transactions. They further pledged to avoid arms transfers that would be likely to:

- prolong or aggravate an existing armed conflict;
- increase tension in a region or contribute to regional instability;
- introduce destabilizing military capabilities in a region;
- contravene embargoes or other relevant internationally agreed restraints to which they are parties;
- be used other than for the legitimate defense and security needs of the recipient state.

In addition, the Perm Five affirmed their support for the establishment, under UN supervision, of an annual "register" of conventional arms transfers.[10]

The adoption of these guidelines by the United States suggests a strong commitment to the principle of conventional arms transfer restraint. If they are followed up with other measures, including the UN register (approved by the United Nations on December 9, 1991), the London guidelines could provide the foundation for an international arms transfer control regime akin to the existing regimes for control of nuclear, chemical, and biological weapons and ballistic missile technology.[11]

Clearly, then, there is strong support in the United States and elsewhere for the adoption of multilateral controls on conventional arms transfers, reflecting the belief that uncontrolled transfers—irrespective of the supplier and recipients involved—pose a significant threat to international peace and stability. It is important to note, however, that many U.S. policymakers continue to adhere to the more traditional view that conventional arms transfers by the United States to friendly powers abroad greatly contribute to U.S. security and thus should be sheltered from international restraints.

This traditional view can be found in statements by a number of senior U.S. officials from the spring and summer of 1991, when the issue of arms transfer restraint was gaining such visibility in Washington. Thus, in response to queries from members of Congress regarding the value of such constraints, Secretary of Defense Richard Cheney remarked on March 19 that although he might be willing to consider some sort of arms transfer controls, "I think our first concern ought to be to work with our friends and allies to see to it that they're secure."[12] A similar outlook was expressed at the time by Richard N. Haass, the senior analyst for Near East affairs on the National Security Council, at a meeting of arms control specialists. "One should not get overly optimistic or idealistic about [conventional] arms control," he noted. "Conventional arms controls may tend to lock you in, and you may not want to be locked in, because the situation is fast evolving... and we are not neutral. There are some [Middle Eastern] countries we are closer to than others."[13]

This perspective continued to influence U.S. arms export policy even after the announcement of the President's Middle East Arms Control Initiative on May 29, 1991. Thus, on June 4, Cheney told reporters accompanying him on a trip to the Middle East that the United States would continue to satisfy requests from friends and allies in the region for access to advanced U.S. military equipment. "We simply can't fall into the trap of [saying] that arms control means we don't provide any arms to the Middle East," he noted. "That is not what we recommend... [and] it would be an unwise policy."[14] On this basis, the Bush Administration approved some $18 billion in arms transfers to Third World countries in 1991,[15] and in 1992 approved the sale of 150 F–16 fighters to Taiwan and 72 F–15 aircraft to Saudi Arabia.

In justifying these sales, U.S. officials argue that there is no contradiction between continuing transfers to friendly powers and the pursuit of multilateral arms restraint. "We do not believe that arms sales are necessarily destabilizing," Under Secretary of State Reginald Bartholomew told the Senate Foreign Relations Committee on June 6, 1991. Rather, such transfers can strengthen stability by enhancing the defensive capabilities of friendly nations. "That is why," he argued, "it is in no way a contradiction for the United States to be simultaneously seeking an arms transfer regime with the other major suppliers and continuing to supply arms needed by peaceful states to defend themselves against aggressors."[16]

This, in essence, represented the core of the Bush Administration's position on conventional arms transfers: Pursue moderate restraints at the international level while continuing to satisfy the military requirements of key allies and clients in the Third World. It is a position that appears to satisfy competing pressures and demands: on one hand, the pressure to follow through on pledges to establish international controls on arms trafficking; on the other, the pressure to preserve long-standing military relationships with friendly foreign governments. But although a compromise position of this sort is undoubtedly attractive to senior U.S. policymakers, it is not a stance that can be sustained indefinitely. Given the multiplicity of suppliers in the conventional arms marketplace and the strong economic pressures to sell that are now being experienced by many of these countries (in response to a decline in domestic military spending), any evidence of U.S. permissiveness regarding military sales to its clients and allies will inevitably be seen by other suppliers as justification for increased military sales to *their* clients and allies, thereby stimulating local arms races and undermining the incipient nonproliferation regime established in London. A rigorous nonproliferation stance, on the other hand, would require greater

U.S. resistance to appeals from friendly governments for access to sophisticated U.S. arms. It would also require others not to exploit U.S. restraint by rushing into new markets.

This dilemma is readily apparent to arms control experts and to many in Congress. Thus, in response to an earlier Bush Administration announcement regarding military sales to Egypt, Senator Biden observed in March 1991 that "our signals have become muddled. One day we promote the idea of Middle East arms control, the next day we step back; one day we promote a postwar order based on security with fewer weapons, and the next day the State Department notifies Congress of its intent to sell 46 F–16s to Egypt." Noting that other suppliers are ready and eager to increase their own sales to the region, Biden suggested that "the message [the F–16 sale] will send—both to other supplier nations and to nations in the region—will be this: the Middle East arms bazaar is once again open and ready for business."[17]

At this point, it appears that Biden's prediction is largely on the mark: Although it might be argued that the Middle East arms bazaar would be even more raucous in the absence of U.S. nonproliferation efforts, there is no doubt that the major states of the region (excluding Iraq) are enjoying a buyer's market in their pursuit of high technology weapons. A report conducted by the Congressional Research Service (CRS) at the request of Senator John McCain, on *Arms Sales to the Middle East since the Gulf War*, shows substantial deliveries of sophisticated arms to such states as Egypt, Iran, Israel, Kuwait, Oman, Saudi Arabia, Syria, and the United Arab Emirates (UAE); the principal suppliers named in the report include all five permanent members of the UN Security Council—the very countries that signed the London accords in October. "The key message [of the report]," Senator McCain concluded, "is that the threat to the Middle East is not over."[18]

It is evident, therefore, that despite the Bush Administration's efforts to balance competing demands, there will be a growing contradiction between selling arms to allies and pursuing multilateral constraints on arms transfers. The United States cannot pursue both objectives and expect to accomplish its stated policy goals. We must determine which approach best serves U.S. long-term security interests—and that means weighing the advantages and disadvantages of both.

The arguments in favor of the traditional approach are well known.[19] By strengthening the defensive capabilities of America's exposed friends and allies, we help to deter attacks on them by aspiring regional hegemons and to diminish the likelihood that U.S. forces will be required to repel such aggression in the event that deterrence fails. In justifying a 1986 arms shipment to Saudi Arabia, for instance, the State Department argued that "our willingness to support Saudi self-defense has served as a deterrent to Iran," then viewed as the major threat to stability in the Gulf. Moreover, "it will also reduce the chances that we would have to take emergency action later to protect our own interests."[20]

A new wrinkle has been added to this argument following the failure of the U.S.-supplied Kuwaiti Army to provide much resistance to invading Iraqi forces, and the subsequent failure of the U.S.-supplied Saudi Army to defend its territory on its own. Although it may not be possible to avert future U.S. interventions in the region, the argument now goes, arms transfers can help local states to defend themselves *long enough* to allow U.S. reinforcements to be flown in from afar, rather than from bases immediately in the region. "The policy which we're pursuing now [in the Gulf area] is one in which we want to minimize the U.S. military presence on the ground in the region," Secretary Cheney told the House Foreign Affairs Committee on March 19, 1991. "It's probably easier to do [this] if we help our friends like the Saudis and the Gulf states have sufficient capability to be able to defend themselves long enough for us to be able to get back."[21]

Should such action again prove necessary, a history of U.S. arms transfers to friends in the region will supposedly contribute to the smooth functioning of combined staffs and to the interoperability of equipment in U.S. and allied hands. "Much of our success in Desert Storm can be directly attributed to the close defense and military-to-military relationships we have developed with regional states over the last several decades," Deputy Assistant Secretary of Defense Arthur H. Hughes told a House Foreign Affairs subcommittee in March 1991. "These programs also provide the basis for the rapid integration of forces."[22]

These arguments have a certain amount of merit, and they were largely successful during the Cold War period in convincing Congress to support U.S. arms transfers to friendly nations in the Third World. But a policy that may have made sense in the bipolar world of the Cold War era does not necessarily make sense in the multipolar world of the post–Cold War era—a world in which long-standing loyalties and alliances are breaking down and in which every nation is scrambling to advance its own national interests. A sobering picture of this world was provided in the U.S. Army "Posture Statement" for fiscal year 1991:

> The United States faces as complex and varied a security environment as it enters the 1990s as at any time in its history. The world economy is becoming more integrated and new centers of influence are developing. The increased lethality of weaponry, and the proliferation of force in the developing world make regional conflicts more rather than less likely. Allies are becoming more assertive in pursuing their own interests and are less apt to follow the lead of a superpower. (p. I–1)

If this is an accurate picture of the post–Cold War world, and I believe that it is, we must ask whether it still makes sense to continue arming friendly Third World powers in the belief that U.S. interests will be well served thereby—or do we conclude instead that further U.S. arms transfers will simply add to the picture of instability sketched out in the Army report?

I believe that there *are* situations in which timely deliveries of purely defensive systems like the Patriot missile can contribute to regional stability. But these situations are rare. In most cases, U.S. deliveries to a given power in a region will only fuel the insecurities of neighboring powers—which may have sound historical reasons to question the intentions of the original recipient—thus provoking additional arms transfers into the region and placing the original country at greater rather than lesser risk. "The Bush Administration is correct in saying that the nations in the region have legitimate security concerns," former Director of the Arms Control and Disarmament Agency, Paul C. Warnke told the Permanent Senate Subcommittee on Investigations in June 1991; "however, their security interests are only made more precarious as the region becomes further laden with sophisticated conventional armaments."[23]

It is also risky, as repeatedly demonstrated by events in the Middle East, to assume that today's friendly regime will remain friendly in the future, or that it will successfully resist efforts by hostile political factions to replace it. The United States had no objection to French sales of sophisticated weapons to Saddam Hussein when he was viewed in Washington as a quasi-ally in the struggle against revolutionary Iran; now, only five years later, he is our sworn enemy. Similarly, the United States poured billions of dollars in sophisticated arms into Iran when we thought that the reign of the Shah would last forever; today, those same weapons (or at least those for which the Iranians have been able to obtain spare parts) are being used by the Shah's revolutionary successors to threaten stability in the Gulf area. "Plausible strategic justifications are of course offered for each sale to friendly recipients in the Third World," Edward Luttwak noted in November 1990, "but these are worthless when the recipients are fragile autocracies whose policies can change overnight."[24]

Nor can we have any confidence that substantial U.S. arms transfers to threatened allies will significantly reduce the need for U.S. intervention, should a key ally come under attack. "The Gulf War proved that, no matter how well [America's allies] are armed, the United States still is the ultimate guarantor of their security," Warnke testified in 1991. "We simply cannot arm Saudi Arabia or Israel or Egypt enough to ensure their physical safety, especially if we are arming their neighbors as well."[25]

Looking at the other side of the equation, it can be argued that rigorous international controls on the transfer of advanced conventional weapons would prove a real asset to U.S. security in the emerging post–Cold War era. Such controls, consisting of a system of reporting requirements ("transparency"), technology controls (on the model of the MTCR), and supplier restraints,[26] would enhance U.S. security in several ways:

*First, by preventing the rise of another heavily armed regional superpower like Saddam Hussein's Iraq.* A transparency system, based on the UN arms trade register (General Assembly Resolution A/47/342, passed on December 9, 1991) can provide early warning of major arms acquisitions efforts by aspiring regional powers; supplier restraints could then ensure that such efforts are curtailed before the recipient in question assembles a significant offensive capability. As suggested by the G–7 governments at the London Economic Summit of July 1991, "a register would alert the international community to an attempt by a state to build up holdings of conventional arms beyond a reasonable level." Once so alerted, the major suppliers could then "take steps to prevent the building up of disproportionate arsenals," notably by imposing mutual restraints on arms transfers "to countries and areas of particular concern."[27]

*Second, by moderating local arms races in areas of tension and prompting local states in these areas to pursue regional arms control and security pacts designed to minimize the risk of conflict.* As long as regional powers believe they can gain a military advantage over their neighbors through further acquisitions of advanced munitions, they will be disinclined to sit down with one another and adopt mutual restraints on regional arms levels; once the prospect of such acquisitions is foreclosed, however, they will have a much greater incentive to negotiate restraints. It is on this basis, indeed, that many members of Congress in 1991 supported a moratorium on arms sales to the Middle East. Such a moratorium, Representative Dante B. Fascell told President Bush in April 1991, "can be used effectively to bring supplier nations and regional states together to pursue a range of arms reduction and arms control proposals."[28]

*Third, by diminishing the risk that U.S. and friendly forces committed to future peacekeeping or contingency operations abroad will be attacked with large numbers of sophisticated conventional weapons.* This risk was particularly acute in the Persian Gulf conflict, and this, in turn, helps explain the upsurge in interest among the major powers in conventional arms control. "Although it should be obvious," Janne E. Nolan of the Brookings Institution wrote in 1991, "it perhaps needs to be reiterated that countries have abided by export restraints in the past [such as the MTCR] because of an interest in containing military developments in areas in which their own forces might be placed at risk."[29]

Given this assessment, it would appear that U.S. security interests—and those of our allies—can best be secured by constraining the flow of conventional arms to areas of conflict, and by persuading the nations of the area to join in regional peace talks aimed at reducing tensions and lowering the levels of regional arsenals. This assessment has, in fact, been written into U.S. law: As stated in the introduction (Section 401) to Title IV of the Foreign Relations Authorization Act for Fiscal Years 1992 and 1993, "future security and stability in the Middle East and Persian Gulf region would be enhanced by establishing a stable military balance among regional powers by restraining and reducing both conventional and unconventional weapons."[30] On this basis, the Act calls upon the executive branch to work with other arms suppliers to establish a multilateral arms transfer control regime similar to those now covering exports of nuclear, chemical, and missile technology (Section 402).

At this point, it is still too early to assess President Clinton's policy on conventional arms transfers. In a major foreign policy address at Georgetown University prior to the 1992 campaign, in December 1991, he indicated that arms transfer restraint would be a goal of his administration: "We need a broader policy toward the Middle East that limits the flow of arms into the region, as well as the materials needed to develop and deliver weapons of mass destruction."[31] However, Clinton subsequently endorsed the sale of F–16s to Taiwan and F–15s to Saudi Arabia. Hopefully, as Clinton comes to appreciate the link between unconstrained arms transfers and regional instability, he will adopt a more restrictive policy toward such exports in accordance with the guidelines laid out in Section 402 of the Foreign Relations Authorization Act for fiscal year 1992–1993.

I believe that a careful assessment of the validity of the two main approaches to conventional arms transfers will lead inescapably to the conclusion that in today's uncertain and chaotic world, it is safer to view most arms transfers as a potential proliferation risk rather than as an assured asset for U.S. national security. When it can unambiguously be shown that a particular delivery of defensive equipment will eliminate a clear and present danger from a potential aggressor, and when all political and diplomatic efforts have failed to eliminate the particular danger, then the transfer should be allowed to proceed. But our priority as a nation should be to pursue the establishment of an arms transfer control regime like that envisioned in Section 402 of the Foreign Relations Authorization Act, and to accelerate the efforts initiated by former Secretary Baker to promote a comprehensive peace settlement in the Middle East.

## NOTES

1. Address at Aerospace Industries Association, Williamsburg, VA, May 21, 1981 (Department of State transcript).

2. For an analysis of presidential policy on conventional arms exports from Kennedy to Reagan, see Michael Klare, *American Arms Supermarket* (Austin: University of Texas Press, 1984), pp. 39–53.

3. Carl E. Vuono, "Versatile, Deployable, and Lethal: The Strategic Army in the 1990s and Beyond," *Sea Power*, April 1990, pp. 59, 61.

4. Statement by James Baker before the House Foreign Affairs Committee, Washington, DC, February 6, 1991 (State Department text).

5. From the transcript of Bush's remarks in *The New York Times*, March 2, 1991.

6. Joseph Biden, "Window of Opportunity for Middle East Arms Control,"

*Congressional Record* 137, No. 43 (March 13, 1991), p. S3136–3137. For a similar view, see Lee H. Hamilton, "Middle East Arms Restraint: An Obligation to Act," *Arms Control Today*, June 1991, pp. 17–20.

7. For a summary of congressional initiatives in this area, see *Arms Control Today*, June 1991, pp. 18–19.

8. "Fact Sheet: Middle East Arms Control Initiative," *US Department of State Dispatch*, June 3, 1991, p. 393.

9. "Meeting of the Five on Arms Transfers and Non-Proliferation, Communiqué (Paris, 8th and 9th of July 1991)," reproduced in *World Military Expenditures and Arms Transfers 1990* (Washington, DC: U.S. Arms Control and Disarmament Agency, 1991), pp. 23–24.

10. Ibid., p. 24.

11. For discussion of such a conventional arms regime, see Michael Klare, "Gaining Control Towards a Comprehensive Arms Restraint System," *Arms Control Today*, June 1991, pp. 9–13.

12. Quoted in *The New York Times*, March 20, 1991.

13. Quoted in *Los Angeles Times*, March 18, 1991.

14. Quoted in *The Washington Post*, June 5, 1991.

15. *Arms Sales Monitor*, November-December 1991 (published by the Federation of American Scientists, Washington, DC).

16. Prepared statement, pp. 8–9.

17. Biden, "Window of Opportunity," p. S3137.

18. Senator John McCain, "Arms Sales to the Middle East since the Gulf War," mimeo from the senator's office, November 21, 1991.

19. For articulation of these arguments, see Paul Y. Hammond et al., *The Reluctant Supplier* (Cambridge, MA: Oelgeschlager, Gunn & Hain, 1983); and Roger P. Labrie et al., *U.S. Arms Sales Policy: Background and Issues* (Washington, DC: American Enterprise Institute, 1982).

20. "U.S. Proposes Arms Sales to Saudi Arabia," *Department of State Bulletin*, May 1986, p. 77.

21. Quoted in David C. Morrison, "Still Open for Business," *National Journal*, April 13, 1991, p. 851.

22. Statement of Arthur H. Hughes before the House Foreign Affairs Subcommittee on Europe and the Middle East, March 20, 1991 (Department of Defense text).

23. Written statement of Paul C. Warnke, June 12, 1991.

24. Edward N. Luttwak, "Stop Arming the Third World," *The New York Times*, November 4, 1990.

25. Warnke, written statement, p. 3.

26. For a discussion of such controls, see Klare, "Gaining Control."

27. London Economic Summit 1991, "Declaration on Conventional Arms Transfers and NBC Non-Proliferation," July 16, 1991.

28. Letter to President George Bush, April 4, 1991.

29. Janne E. Nolan, "The Global Arms Market after the Gulf War: Prospects for Control," *The Washington Quarterly*, Summer 1991, p. 132.

30. "Conference Report on H.R. 1415," *Congressional Record—House*, October 3, 1991, p. H7481.

31. "A New Covenant for American Security," *Harvard International Review*, Summer, 1992, p. 62.

# PART IV

---

# STRATEGY AS CREATIVE CONCEPTS AND APPLICATION: COLLECTIVE SECURITY AND COLLECTIVE DEFENSE

# 14

# Collective Security after the Cold War

*Inis L. Claude, Jr.*

## THE REVIVAL OF COLLECTIVE SECURITY

The ending of the Cold War has inspired a revival of serious discussion of prospects for a collective security system to maintain international order. There can be no doubt that the Cold War is over and that the threat of conquest or subversion formerly posed by the Soviet Union or by the international communist movement has evaporated. Equally, there can be no doubt that the end of history, in Francis Fukuyama's millennial sense,[1] has not arrived. Mankind faces the permanent necessity of dealing with a plethora of difficult problems, dangerous tendencies, and serious threats to order, stability, and decency in international relations. In short, national security and world order remain important and challenging problems. What is in doubt is the future of the collective security approach to the management of those problems. Is it possible, or probable, or desirable that collective security will finally become the operative method for upholding world order? If not, may some modified version of that approach come to prominence as statesmen search for appropriate and effective means to keep the peace in the international arena? Those are the questions that I address in this chapter.

It is necessary to begin by indicating the meaning that I attach to the term *collective security*. It first came into use after World War I, referring to the scheme developed during the war and championed by President Woodrow Wilson, for keeping the peace by setting up legal commitments and organizational arrangements designed to guarantee that aggression by any state against any other would be effectively resisted by the combined action of the other members of the multistate system. The prevention or defeat of aggression—that is, of the pursuit by any state of any objective by military means—would be regarded as the most fundamental interest of every state, and all states would therefore accept the solemn obligation to participate in diplomatic, economic, or military measures to suppress such behavior. Every potential aggressor should be intimidated by the threat of overwhelming collective resistance; every potential victim of aggression should be reassured by the promise of the community's protection. Champions of the League of Nations hoped and intended that it would serve as the agency of a collective security system; when events proved otherwise a considerable literature developed, deploring the League's delinquency and insisting that only the resolute acceptance and faithful carrying out of the responsibilities of a collective security system offered hope for order and stability in international relations.

Unfortunately, collective security is a term that easily lends itself to variant usages. It has sometimes been used so loosely that it appears as a synonym of peace or world order; in this usage, it refers not to a method for producing a result but to the presumed result itself, conflating means and ends. More often, collective security has been taken to refer to any and all multilateral efforts to deal with the problem of international peace and security, rather than specifically to the scheme that gained prominence after World War I. Most important, the label has frequently been attached to NATO and other alliances despite the fact that collective security was originally proposed as a substitute for the alliance system, a way of managing international relations that was deemed incompatible with, antithetical to, and infinitely more promising than the old system that featured competitive alliances. When one discusses collective security, it is obviously essential to indicate whether one refers to the old system that Wilsonians regarded as discredited, or to the new one that they proposed as its replacement.

I have always undertaken to use collective security in its original sense, distinguishing it from all other multilateral approaches to the issue of war and peace. Moreover, I should point out that much of the recent discussion of the potentialities of collective security conforms with that usage. When former Soviet President Mikhail Gorbachev endorsed collective security in 1987 and 1988, he clearly advocated making the United Nations the centerpiece of a general system for mobilizing collective resistance to disturbers of international peace.[2] Iraq's invasion of Kuwait in 1990 sparked President George Bush's public interest in collective security, and he repeatedly insisted that the United Nations stand against that act of aggression should be considered not an isolated case but the beginning of the organization's systematic and reliable functioning as "a center for international collective security," presiding over multilateral measures "to demonstrate that aggression will not be tolerated or rewarded."[3] Bush invoked the idea of a new world order resting upon a Wilsonian collective security system dedicated to the universal enforcement of the rule against aggression. The widespread expression of this hope or expectation justifies our taking a careful and critical look at the future possibilities of that kind of system.

## Is Collective Security Possible or Desirable?

I reached the conclusion some thirty years ago that the idea of creating a working collective security system had been definitively rejected and that at most the idea might occasionally receive lip service.[4] I have taken the view that the implementation of collective security theory is not a possibility to be taken seriously and that the United Nations should be turned to other, more promising because more acceptable, methods of contributing to world order. How then am I to explain the recent revival of interest in the concept of collective security?

The first element of that explanation is the ending of the Cold War, which means that the atmosphere of international politics is no longer poisoned by the mutual suspicions and animosities of the two superpowers and their blocs, that the United Nations Security Council is no longer likely to be paralyzed by clashes among the veto-wielding major powers, and that there is a good prospect for the kind of cooperation among the great powers that has always been regarded as the essential engine of a collective security system. Attention is frequently focused on the veto power; the United Nations was intended by its founders, so the argument runs, to function as a collective security system, but this has been impossible because the United States and the Soviet Union, preoccupied with Cold War concerns, used the veto to block each other and thereby disabled the Security Council. Now, relieved of this disability, the Security Council can at last operate normally and the United Nations can finally become what it was intended to be.

This line of analysis exaggerates the original commitment of the United Nations, as expressed in its Charter, to the collective security approach. There was rhetorical enthusiasm for collective security at the founding conference of 1945, but the completed Charter represented a very attenuated endorsement. The inclusion of the veto provision in arrangements for the Security Council indicated the conviction that collective security action must not be attempted—that it would be futile and dangerous to attempt it—against a major power or a state enjoying the support of a major power; this left severely limited scope for a United Nations enforcement system. The use of the veto during the Cold War has conformed with, rather than violated, the intentions and expectations of the founders, by preventing efforts at collective enforcement action that might have precipitated a showdown among major powers. If the United Nations should now become a full-fledged collective security system committed to frustrating every act of international aggression, this would represent not the realization but the expansion of the founders' ambitions and the abandonment of their caution.

The sweeping political changes of recent years have certainly increased the capacity of the Security Council to reach decisions with promptness and near unanimity. There may still be disagreements among the most powerful members of that body, but rather than being dedicated to frustrating each other, they are now disposed to cooperate and to support the United Nations. This is to say that the predictably blocked Security Council no longer exists as an impediment to collective security action. It would be wrong, however, to infer that such action will now reliably occur. The failure of the United Nations to serve as a collective security agency is attributable to the *rejection* of collective security obligations by its members, not to the frustration of their wish to act in fulfillment of those obligations. The United Nations has not consisted, and does not now consist, of states eager to take part in a collective security system and resolved to do so at the first opportunity. In removing the cause of the infeasibility of collective security, the favorable developments in the Security Council do not also remove the causes of its unacceptability to statesmen and peoples, some of which I consider in the subsequent discussion. An automobile does not climb the hill just because its brake has been released; rather, it requires a battery, fuel, and a driver intent on driving up the hill. So it is with collective security, which requires a motive force supplied by states convinced of the wisdom of, and willing to pay the price of participation in, the universal enforcement of the anti-aggression rule.

The notion that the removal of Cold War obstacles will initiate the implementation of the long-deferred Charter plan for the United Nations is fanciful enough to be dubbed the "Rip Van Winkle Theory" of the United Nations. I would argue that the United Nations has not been asleep for these forty-odd years, with its members waiting impatiently to develop the kind of organization contemplated in the Charter and ready to do so at the moment of its awakening. The organization has not been stalled and stymied; even the Security Council has suffered only partial paralysis, and the other organs, although significantly affected by the Cold War, have nonetheless been very active. Far from being dormant, the United Nations has changed in fundamental ways, becoming something quite different from the 1945 model. Its members have differed with each other, and with the framers of the Charter, about the purposes to which the United Nations should be directed, and the organization's political process has featured the redefining of its objectives as various blocs have succeeded in making it serve their interests and values. In particular, states of the Third World, having become a dominant majority in the General Assembly, have achieved substantial success in converting the United Nations into an instrument of their revolution against the status quo. Some states may wish to have the United Nations revert to the 1945 model, but members of the Third World are unlikely to join them; the ending of the Cold War poses no temptation to that group to relinquish control over the United Nations, give it back to its original owners, and allow it to become what its founding fathers had in mind.

For the United Nations to become a full-fledged collective security system would be especially distasteful to its present proprietors, because that would buttress the international status quo that they are intent upon subjecting to drastic modification. In rejecting forcible change, collective security limits change to that achievable by peaceful means, which often comes painfully close to meaning that one must accept the status quo. The pain in that proximity is especially acute for revolutionaries, but it is not confined to them, for prudent people of every ideological stripe have some degree of sympathetic understanding of the need for change and the disastrous consequences of rigidity. The United Nations has become, under the influence of the Third World, an agency for bestowing legitimacy upon, and lending some support to, demands for change in the name of justice, including in some instances violence in the expression of those demands. The ending of the Cold War cannot be expected to bring about such a political and moral transformation as to reverse that situation. To talk about the United Nations now becoming what its Charter envisaged is to contemplate turning the clock back, undoing the evolution of forty-odd years, rewinding its history—a dream as idle in this case as in most others. The United Nations will not move back to its Charter. It will move ahead. Whether it will move toward collective security depends not on the hopes of its founding fathers but on the attitudes and judgments of their operating sons and daughters.

Verbal support for collective security is never lacking as long as the focus is on the promise of peace. Many are quite properly skeptical of the expectation that a collective security system could reliably maintain a peaceful world in which all states enjoy security, but nobody confesses opposition to that outcome (at least for the long term; as I have noted, some would postpone that orderly situation until current objectives necessitating violent change are attained). Neither statesmen nor their peoples are likely to avow discomfort at being required to pledge abstention from aggression, if only because they will insist that any military measures that they undertake do not constitute aggression. But if states do not claim the right to commit aggression, they do claim and treasure the right to decide for themselves when, whether, and how to react to aggression committed by and against other states. Support for collective security is highly problematic when the focus is on the obligation to join in collective resistance to aggression.

I have argued elsewhere that collective security is the ideology of a coalition that is at or near the point of winning a major war, and that zeal for accepting the responsibilities of membership in a collective security system is ephemeral, "a product of the afterglow of successful war . . . that . . . seems to disappear after a few years, when the afterglow fades into mere aftermath, and a postwar period begins."[5] This phenomenon is easy to explain. States engaged in a successful joint venture against a common enemy are not impressed by the alleged difficulty of arriving at an agreed identification of an aggressor. They are acting on the conviction that it is less costly to defeat an aggressor than to give way to him, and they are proud of what they are doing. They readily accept the proposition that such resistance to aggression should become the rule of international life, and they harbor the notion that their sacrifice in the present case might have been rendered unnecessary if their resolve to defeat aggression had been clearly formulated and proclaimed in advance. Peacetime, however, brings increasing ambivalence about the merits of the claims of competing states, growing difficulty in creating and maintaining either domestic or international consensus on the handling of crises, and the steady advance of the view that confrontation is to be avoided at almost any cost in favor of concession and compromise. Negotiation becomes the magic word, and the collective security approach comes to be regarded as too rigid and bellicose, a hard-line approach that provides a recipe for exacerbating rather than easing international tensions, and for getting one's state into unnecessary trouble. As the successful collective action against the late aggressor fades into distant memory, acceptance and fulfillment of the duty to join in resistance to any and all aggressors begin to look less like principled and responsible statesmanship than like foolhardy overcommitment, imprudent attachment to the status quo, and dangerous sacrifice of sovereign discretion in responding to international developments.

The first surge of support for collective security came in the late stages of World War I, but members of the League of Nations progressively retreated from the obligation to enforce the peace during the next two decades. World War II inspired much brave talk about creating an international organization that would have teeth and the will to bite aggressors, but the resolution faded so quickly that the UN involvement in the American-led resistance to North Korea's aggression in 1950 seemed a surprising reversal of expectations and intentions. The Korean War sparked a fleeting enthusiasm for creating something resembling a collective security system, manifested in the Uniting for Peace Resolution of 1950, but that zeal did not survive the military difficulties and political anxieties caused by China's entry into the fray.

It may well be that the termination of the Cold War will produce a similar peak-and-valley pattern in the graph of support for the notion of collective security. Although in a certain sense that struggle was an alternative to war, an extraordinarily innovative relationship between antagonists that prevented the outbreak of the dreaded World War III, it may also be interpreted as a genuine war—as an extension of World War II, since there was no significant interval between that conflict and the Cold War, or perhaps as World War III itself, fought by other and generally less lethal means that the world had come to expect in global conflicts. At any rate, the Cold War was enough like a war for its termination to engender events and reactions characteristic of the final stages of major conflicts. These include the collapse of the defeated empire, the demise of the system that led it to disaster, and the recognition by the victors of their responsibility to give assistance so as to prevent total chaos and promote constructive rehabilitation. Postwar-like reactions to the end of the Cold War also include the initial exuberant expectation that this event would usher in an era of universal political and economic freedom and multilateral cooperation. New hopes for collective security are one aspect of this immediate post–Cold War exhilaration. There are already signs of the customary shift to the less positive mood of peacetime: Not only Americans but Westerners generally are increasingly looking inward, insisting on the primacy of domestic problems and questioning the necessity and justification for continuing to bear onerous international burdens. The next few years may well supply additional confirmation of the thesis that support for participation in a collective security system is a passing fancy, briefly entertained by victors in coalition wars.

## COLLECTIVE SECURITY AND U.S. LEADERSHIP

But what are we to make of the international response to Iraq's aggression in August 1990? In this instance, the United Nations Security Council acted promptly and almost unanimously to condemn the conquest of Kuwait, warn against further aggression, demand the withdrawal of Iraqi forces, order economic sanctions against Iraq, and authorize such military action as might prove necessary to bring the aggressor to heel. This official United Nations position enjoyed massive support and was in the end enforced by a brief but decisive military action, carried out by a coalition of some thirty states under U.S. leadership. This was a brilliantly successful case of collective enforcement. Did it mark the beginning of the development of a post–Cold War collective security system, or the beginning of the end of post–Cold War enthusiasm for collective security? Was it a precedent or a unique occasion?

I believe that the Gulf War was a special case; it may not prove to have been the last hurrah of collective security, but neither was it a resounding vote of confidence. What happened was substantially what would have occurred under the auspices of a collective security system, although there was more improvisation than should have been necessary if there had been a well-established system. It aroused a great deal of talk about creating such a system, but I think it did not in fact foreshadow or promote that project.

This was an ideal case for the application of collective security doctrine. Iraq was a flagrant aggressor led by a regime that attracted scant sympathy outside its borders. For most states, the perception of a vital national interest in forestalling Iraq's gaining control over a major portion of the oil that serves as their lifeblood provided a powerful supplement to, or an adequate substitute for, their adherence to the anti-aggression principle. The Soviet Union withdrew its long-standing support of Iraq, indicating that it would at least acquiesce in action against the aggressor, which thereby lost any prospect of significant external aid. The United States, with multiple interests in the Middle Eastern region, had a newly buttressed military capability and a new freedom from Cold War considerations that enabled it to serve as leader and protagonist. In the end, sharp and decisive action by coalition forces ousted Iraq from Kuwait at a surprisingly low cost. An aroused community overwhelmed an isolated offender. No champion of collective security could ask for a better advertisement for his cause.

Even this case, however, demonstrates the thinness and fragility of support for collective security. There were deep divisions in the United States, particularly about the decision to go beyond economic to military sanctions, and it is probable that only the speed and relative ease of the victory prevented the rise of virulent opposition. Although President Bush was extraordinarily effective in mobilizing the Security Council to enunciate the will to resist Iraq and in organizing the coalition that enforced that will, most members of the United Nations were more acquiescent than supportive. For many of them, the Gulf War was not a United Nations undertaking in which the United States served as the chief participant, but an American venture of dubious wisdom that the United Nations had been induced to endorse. The modesty and tentativeness of support for collective action in this case strongly suggest that the world is unlikely to unite in determination to act against aggression in all future cases. The validity of this judgment seems especially clear when one reflects on the fact that the more typical international conflict entails uncertainty and disagreement about the identity of aggressor and victim, divided sympathies and interests on the part of other states, and the possibility that collective involvement would trigger a long, costly, and indecisive struggle. Even this case, I think, vividly illustrates many of the difficulties about collective security that have contributed, and still contribute, to the general rejection of its prescription for the management of international relations.

The most basic of these difficulties lies in the fact that the ultimate reliance of a collective security system is on joint military operations to stop or repel aggressors; it requires that participating states be willing to fight for that purpose. Unfortunately for collective security, a fundamental precept of the foreign policy of modern democratic states is that war should be treated as an absolutely last resort, to be avoided as long as there is any remotely reasonable alternative. However, membership in a collective security system requires states, without themselves having been attacked, to choose to fight against the designated aggressor. From a nationally self-interested point of view, fulfillment of this obligation has the appearance of gratuitous involvement in potentially dangerous clashes. Moreover, the defensive character of that involvement is subject to challenge. Even though the state can claim that it is engaged in defense of a victim of aggression and of the principle essential to world order, the fact remains that it initiates battle against another state. Saddam Hussein wanted peace with the United States; George Bush decided to make war against Iraq.

The longer a military response to aggression is delayed—for whatever reasons, including the commendable urge to "give peace a chance" by exploring nonmilitary alternatives—the more vulnerable are the agents of collective security to the charge that they are themselves acting as aggressors, that is, that they are choosing rather than responding to war. The Gulf War illustrated this point; when the fight to oust Iraq from Kuwait began, after more than five months of futile effort to achieve that result peacefully, Coretta Scott King declared that she "strongly deplore[d] and was deeply saddened by the White House decision to launch a war against Iraq," and Pope John Paul II characterized the campaign as an outbreak of war that represented "a grave defeat for international law and the international community."[6] Such was the reception, by these and many other high-minded moralists, of an enterprise that had at least a substantial claim to being regarded as the liberation of a people from ruthless conquest and brutal occupation, the enforcement of the international prohibition of aggression, and the implementation of the proclaimed will and purpose of the United Nations.

Although the delay in the collective military response to Iraq's aggression was long enough to blur its defensive and reactive nature, it was not long enough to satisfy many critics in the United States and elsewhere who believed that nonmilitary measures, notably economic sanctions and diplomatic pressures, might in time have achieved the restoration of Kuwait's independence. Some of these critics, no doubt, were absolute or virtual pacifists who would never have been convinced that the time had come for military action. Many of them, however, simply adhered to the last-resort concept of war, recognized that Iraq was highly vulnerable to economic pressures, thought it important to test and demonstrate the potency of nonmilitary sanctions, and believed that within a reasonable time Iraq could be compelled to renounce its conquest without bloodshed and massive destruction. In retrospect, they appear to have been mistaken. The economic sanctions against Iraq were supplemented, not superseded, by military measures, which indeed vastly intensified their effect. Those sanctions, still in force, have at this writing operated for over three years without breaking the will or undermining the regime of Saddam; we have every reason to believe that without Desert Storm Iraq would still sit astride Kuwait. In that case, would the coalition still be available for military compulsion?

Nonetheless, the debate about whether and when to resort to collective force against Iraq was legitimate, and such collective force against Iraq was legitimate, and such uncertainties and disagreements are perennial features of collective security. At what point in an international crisis should efforts at settlement by pacific means such as negotiation or mediation give way to the collective security approach of identifying, condemning, and confronting the aggressor? How long should nonmilitary sanctions be given to do their work before military measures are added? How much delay is compatible with reasonable concern for the fate of the people victimized by aggression—who are, after all, the essential clients of a collective security system? How much delay is compatible with the retention of a military option, and with general recognition of that option's defensive character? We can be certain that these issues will always produce controversy, and that as peacetime lengthens, there will be increasing pressures for preferring compromise to confrontation and for postponing military responses to aggression.

Another significant difficulty about collective security lies in the uncertainty as to its actual and proper military objectives: When and where should it stop, what constitutes victory, and who should decide these issues? Theorists of collective security have offered little guidance beyond the simple formula that aggression should be deterred if possible and stopped or rolled back if necessary. Their emphasis on the promise of deterrence has discouraged close attention to the unpleasant details of what to do when deterrence fails, lest soft-line supporters be reminded that collective security is a hard-line approach to world order.

These issues were troublesome in the Korean War, in which military objectives were first expanded and then contracted, disagreement developed about the locus of authority to make such decisions, anxieties about the possibility of imprudent ends and means emerged, and ultimately the issue of whether the United Nations coalition won or lost the contest remained a matter of contention. In the Gulf War, there was initial agreement that the United Nations mandate called solely for the liberation of Kuwait. The United States was regarded by some, at home and abroad, as excessively belligerent, and concern was widely expressed as to whether President Bush would accept the limitations of that mandate or push on to destroy Iraq's forces and overthrow Saddam Hussein. His abrupt termination of Desert Storm when Iraq had been driven from Kuwait disarmed those who would have condemned him for going too far—but opened the way for subsequent criticism (perhaps by some of the same people) to the effect that he had not gone far enough, criticism inspired by the postwar behavior of Iraq's regime. This issue, as to whether a satisfactory conclusion of the UN-sponsored action would entail such additional achievements as a just solution of the Kurdish minority problem, the elimination of human rights abuses in Iraq, and the displacement of Saddam's dictatorship by a democratic and peace-minded government, calls to our attention the widespread discomfort with collective security's absolute and exclusive opposition to aggression.

Not only does the world reject the notion that every military effort to change the international status quo, without exception, should be condemned and collectively resisted, but it also denies that aggression is the only evil that requires and justifies concerted international response. Senator George J. Mitchell spoke for the Democratic Party when he responded to President Bush's discussion of the Gulf War in the 1991 State of the Union message by criticizing Bush's failure to react to events such as the massacre of students in China and the killing of priests in Central America as he had reacted to Iraq's invasion of Kuwait, saying: "We cannot oppose repression in one place and overlook it in another."[7] It is difficult to know whether such criticisms are really intended to expand the scope of collective enforcement action or to discourage its use even against aggression; most of the objectionable features of collective security would only be intensified if the targets of the system were broadened to include states guilty of malfeasance other than aggression. In any case, we are far from having reached a genuine international consensus on the objectives that should and should not trigger collective enforcement.

The question of the proper mission of collective forces leads us directly to issues of direction, control, and leadership. Collective security theory has largely ignored such matters; its theme is multilateralism, which emphasizes the mass of followers rather than the elite of leaders. Leadership smacks of unilateralism, with its unfortunate connotations. However, realism demands acknowledgement that the coalescence of many states into an anti-aggression force is not likely to be a spontaneous occurrence. Such an event requires contrivance, which depends upon leadership.

The dedicated multilateralist's favorite candidate for leadership of collective security is the Secretary-General of the United Nations, or, possibly, the Security Council. The former official has important responsibilities in this connection, but as I have argued elsewhere, he can be the effective leader only of activities carried out primarily by the Secretariat over which he presides.[8] Collective security is a job to be done by states, and it requires state leadership. Again, the Security Council has a crucial role to play in collective enforcement, but leadership is a function of individual states, not of a council of fifteen; the Security Council is an entity to be led, not to lead.

The only state that has thus far been found willing and able to lead collective enforcement actions on behalf of the United Nations is the United States. It did so in both the Korean War and the Gulf War, and it is clear that there would have been no multilateral response to aggression in either case without U.S. initiative and leadership. Early reactions to the ending of the Cold War included the expectation that the Soviet Union and the United States might henceforth serve as partners in leading the United Nations, but that hope has vanished as the former Soviet Union has come to appear more as a potential trouble spot than as a prospective codirector of the United Nations. By and large, the United Nations does not like U.S. leadership in anti-aggression ventures and complains about U.S. arrogance and inclination to run the show unilaterally, without adequate authorization, consultation, or control by the Security Council. When the United States cannot be charged with disregarding the United Nations, it is convicted by critics of exploiting the organization, twisting the UN's arm to secure endorsement of its own policy. This occurred in the case of the Gulf War, when unaccustomed deference to the United Nations brought the United States remarkably little credit. But timely and decisive action by multilateral bodies such as the United Nations is utterly dependent upon the determined leadership of a great power that has the resolution and audacity to move out front, to pull the majority along rather than to wait for it, to carry the lion's share of the burden while tolerating free riders, and to live with the inevitable criticism. Multilateralism is not the antithesis of unilateralism. It depends upon, and starts with, unilateralism. Multilateralism is unilateralism plus.

Although other leaders may emerge in the United Nations, for the foreseeable future the United States, the sole remaining superpower, is the only one available for ventures in collective enforcement. Thus, strictly speaking, there can be no full-scale collective security system, for the anti-aggression rule cannot be enforced against the United States. If the theory of mutual deterrence is to be taken seriously, the world now stands exposed to the danger of unbridled U.S. expansionism, given the demise of the opposing superpower. I suspect, however, that the world is, and ought to be, less concerned about a possible imperialist binge by the United States than about a probable isolationist tendency—a turning inward, a focus on pressing domestic issues, a diminishing interest in and capacity for active international leadership. On the one hand, the ending of the Cold War certainly increases the political feasibility of collective enforcement under U.S. leadership, and it may well increase the number of occasions requiring such action. On the other hand, the elimination of Cold War considerations sharply reduces the U.S. incentive for leadership in such matters.

In the absence of superpower competition, Americans may well doubt that the national interest requires or permits such costly and risky operations. Economic capacity as well as political will is involved in this potential lessening of U.S. international prominence; our triumph in the Cold War was in some respects a Pyrrhic victory, leaving us weakened, depleted, and dispirited. Despite its many assets, the United States is a society in crisis, struggling to muster the will and find the means for coping with fundamental problems. Is there, indeed, *one* surviving superpower? The world may yet have occasion to confess again that it is really most worried not about U.S. strength but U.S. weakness, not about its hyperactivity but its inability to act, not about its malfeasance but its nonfeasance.

I doubt that the members of the United Nations could be impelled, by any leader, to become active participants in a system designed to frustrate every military effort to alter the status quo. Most of them are, at the maximum, prepared to authorize the United States to act in certain instances;

for them, collective action is not a "do it yourself" but a "let the Americans do it" scheme. Moreover, I am aware of nothing in the current political climate or national mood of the United States that leads me to believe that either the American public or the new Clinton Administration are disposed to initiate or support such a system. The concurrent crises in Bosnia and Somalia are cases in point.

True, President Bush talked grandly of a new world order grounded on the principle that every act of aggression will be met by collective resistance. Such hyperbole is traditional in discussions of collective security; in such talk, "sometimes" becomes "always," and "perhaps" is inflated to "certainly." But statesmen do not adopt abstract principles such as the one just stated and derive from them policy for concrete situations; rather, they set policy in more pragmatic fashion and then defend it by asserting its conformity with principle. I suggest that Bush's actual position is well stated in a comment about the Gulf War made by Secretary of Defense Richard Cheney and not repudiated by the President:

> This happens to be one of those times when it is justified to . . . send American forces into combat to achieve important national objectives. But they are very rare. Just because we do it successfully this once, it doesn't mean we should therefore assume that it is something we ought to fall back on automatically as the easy answer to international problems in the future. We have to remember that we don't have a dog in every fight, that we don't want to get involved in every single conflict.[9]

The United States and most other members of the United Nations appear to be committed to a policy of *selective anti-aggression*, meaning that in some instances aggression will be condemned by the United Nations and countered with collective measures, blessed by the United Nations but mobilized largely by the United States. These measures will include military action only if other sanctions seem ineffective and if the United States is able to mobilize ad hoc coalitions that seem likely to replace the more formalized collective defense systems (e.g., NATO) of the Cold War. This policy, rather than the commitment to comprehensive anti-aggressive reaction entailed by collective security, seems to me to represent the wave of the future. The cases of Iraq and Bosnia are clear examples of selective anti-aggression.

## CONCLUSIONS

The choice of selectivity is not altogether reassuring. Discrimination among cases is always likely to appear arbitrary, inviting charges of double standards, hypocrisy, and invidious favoritism. There will be bitter disagreements about which aggressors to oppose and which victims to defend. The moral claim to principled behavior on behalf of world order will not ring true when some acts of aggression are ignored and the integrity of some states is sacrificed. Moreover, the selective approach fails the test of deterrence. It allows would-be aggressors to hope that they may be permitted to act with impunity and provides no sense of security to potential targets of aggression. Thomas Franck has suggested that the total abandonment of the principle that aggression must be defeated may be preferable to occasional adherence to it, on the grounds that "a principle with just enough life to rally defenders but not enough to deter violators is a particular danger to world stability, leading to unpredictability and potentially lethal miscalculations."[10] Selectivity clearly does not realize the collective security ideal of equalizing the security and neutralizing the aggressive ambitions of all states.

The real choice, however, is not between "sometimes" and "always," but between "sometimes" and "never." Is there value in the possibility of collective measures under United Nations auspices in some cases, even if not in all? I believe that there is, and that the selective approach has merits in addition to the obvious one of having the political acceptability that is denied to collective security.

One of those merits lies in the fact (which is understood and appreciated by most statesmen) that all acts of aggression are not equally threatening to world order. Some cases pose serious challenges to global stability, while others are relatively trivial or have only regional or local significance. Categorization depends upon the geographical setting of the conflict, the identities of the attacker and the state under attack, the scope of the attack, and a host of other circumstances. Statesmen have quite properly rejected the doctrine of collective security that requires every violation of the peace to be treated as if it were the beginning of World War III. Discrimination makes sense and is in fact a fundamental obligation of responsible statesmanship.

Selective enforcement of the anti-aggression principle has the merit of (1) respecting the mandate of national leaders to look after the interests of the societies they govern, and (2) pressing them to make sober and deliberate assessments of what that duty entails. Disregard of national interests by statesmen is neither probable nor proper; what is desirable is great care in identifying and ranking those interests and determining how best to serve them. Such sensible behavior is encouraged by the selective approach to peace enforcement, in favorable contrast to the demand by champions of collective security that statesmen simply and automatically assume that the national interest requires involvement in every case of international aggression.

A standard criticism of collective security is the charge that it risks turning every local encounter into a global conflict by drawing outsiders into the fray. Ideally, of course, a collective security system would prevent war altogether or convert the defeat of every aggressor into an easy police operation by overwhelming forces, but there is point in the argument that the world should prefer the insistent localization of clashes to a tactic that increases the risk of exacerbating and spreading conflict. It is a virtue of the principle of selectivity that it invites thoughtful consideration of the following question: Is the outbreak of a major international war likely to be prevented, or promoted, by the intrusion of the community at large into the present case?

Finally, the principle of selectivity encourages attention to the issue of the consequences likely to flow from victory by the aggressor in the case at hand. Will this case prove only prelude to further conquests by an emboldened and empowered aggressor, or is this a discrete instance, an effort at settlement of a specific grievance? Will the triumphant aggressor fasten a ruthless tyranny upon the conquered people for the indefinite future, or will it use its position to promote establishment of a more decent regime than existed before and then restore independence to the state? In identifying cases that justify or require general international reaction, the distinction between the probable aftermaths of an Iraqi conquest of Kuwait and a U.S. invasion of Panama is an important one. Selective anti-aggression, unlike collective security, conforms with today's United Nations consensus that the judgment of aggression should be affected by the cause that it is deemed likely to promote or damage.

All these merits that I impute to the selective approach to collective enforcement are dependent upon the exercise of sound and honest judgment. Abuses and mistakes are, of course, eminently possible—even probable, perhaps inevitable. We know from experience that world order is not as fragile and as susceptible to destruction by any and every act of aggression as the theory of collective security has insisted, but the identification of the cases that do (and those that do not) endanger the general stability will not be flawlessly performed. Statesmen will not invariably exhibit a correct understanding of the kind of international behavior required by the national interests of their peoples, and they will sometimes misjudge the consequences of their acting (or their deciding not to act) in response to aggression. To concede all this, however, is only to acknowledge that the conduct of international relations is an art rather than a science. The management of relationships in a multistate system requires prudence, a blend of courage and caution, a gift for creative improvisation, a sensitivity to circumstances, and—above all—good judgment and good luck. No formula can replace or guarantee wise statesmanship. This, I think, is the ultimate justification for the principle of selectivity.

In conclusion, let me emphasize that what states collectively do or decline to do about aggression by one state against another is not the only factor, and may not be the decisive one, in determining how peaceful and orderly the world will be or how secure individual states will feel. The world faces problems and prospective upheavals to which a scheme for dealing with international aggression, whether a collective security system or commitment to selective enforcement measures, is quite simply irrelevant. The anti-aggression motif concentrates on *policy* wars—wars begun by calculated decisions by states. But there are also *predicament* wars—conflicts into which states slip or drift; wars stemming from tensions, frictions, mutual fears, and misjudgments rather than from a predatory policy adopted by one side or the other; wars into which states are trapped by circumstances. The world has not seen the last of such conflicts, to which anti-aggression schemes do not apply. Moreover, such schemes have little bearing on situations of civil war, and it has already become evident that the ending of the Cold War and the associated dissolution of the Soviet Union have initiated a period of ethnic clashes and secessionist movements that are likely to trigger internal violence in numerous countries around the world. World order will be endangered by the domestic discontents produced by economic deprivation, social injustice, contempt for human rights, autocratic rule, and subordination of ethnic, religious, and other minorities. Coping with the problems of internal strife is a crucial aspect of the task of building an orderly world, an aspect essentially separate from, and no less important than, dealing with acts of aggression.

There is a case for optimism about the consequences of the liberation of the United Nations from the stultification imposed by the Cold War. That case does not lie, I think, in the hope that the organization will institute a collective security system, nor primarily in the possibility that it will promote collective enforcement measures in selective cases. Instead, it lies in the prospect that a revitalized United Nations may, by facilitating negotiation and cooperation and by developing its potential as a central service agency (Peacetime Engagement), contribute substantially to solution of problems distinct from (and in most instances not directly related to) external aggression (Somalia, for example). The major value of a resurgent world organization can be expected to derive not from increased power to coerce states but from expanded usefulness to states.

## NOTES

1. Francis Fukuyama, "The End of History?" *The National Interest*, Summer 1989, pp. 3–18.

2. Robert Legvold, "The Gulf Crisis and the Future of Gorbachev's Foreign Policy Revolution," (New York: Columbia University, The Harriman Institute Forum, October 1990).

3. U.S. Department of State, Current Policy No. 1303, George Bush, "The UN: World Parliament of Peace," Address to United Nations General Assembly, New York, October 1, 1990.

4. Inis L. Claude, Jr., *Power and International Relations* (New York: Random House, 1962), Chapter 5.

5. Inis L. Claude, Jr., *American Approaches to World Affairs* (Lanham, MD: University Press of America, 1986), p. 54.

6. Juan Williams, "Race and War in the Persian Gulf," *The Washington Post*, January 20, 1991, p. B2; and *Daily Progress* (Charlottesville, VA), January 19, 1991.

7. George J. Mitchell, "The Other Business of the Nation Won't Wait," *The Washington Post*, January 30, 1991, p. A15.

8. Inis L. Claude, Jr., "Reflections on the Role of the Secretary-General of the United Nations," Occasional Papers Series, No. 8 (New York: The Ralph Bunche Institute on the United Nations, 1991), pp. 5–6.

9. David S. Broder, "With Cheney in Charge," *The Washington Post*, February 27, 1991, p. A25.

10. Thomas M. Franck, "The Strategic Role of Legal Principles," in *The Falklands War*, eds. Alberto R. Coll and Anthony C. Arend (Boston: George Allen and Unwin, 1985), p. 32.

# 15

# Security Structures in Asia

*Sheldon W. Simon*

During the Cold War era, U.S. alliance goals in Asia were straightforward: to create a series of primarily bilateral security agreements that would serve as a *cordon sanitaire* around the Soviet Union and People's Republic of China as well as their allies in North Korea and Indochina. Hopefully, these alliances would deter any expansionist designs on the parts of Moscow, Beijing, Pyongyang, and Hanoi. When deterrence failed, the United States fought its only protracted wars since 1945, in Korea and Vietnam, with mixed results for Washington's future alliance commitments. The Nixon Doctrine (1969), formulated to cope with the disappointments and trauma of the Second Indochina War (1965–75), underlaid America's Asian strategy through the 1980s. Briefly, it promised military aid to friendly and allied states to assist in the creation of their own capacities to defend against potential communist aggressors; but it no longer guaranteed direct U.S. military involvement in the event of hostilities. Both the decision to go to war and its prosecution became the responsibility of Asian leaders, not American.

The singleminded focus on anti-communism from the 1950s well into the 1980s created other problems for U.S. foreign policy. In order to construct the largest possible coalition against the Soviet Union and its clients, Washington frequently subordinated and sometimes ignored other policy values such as human rights and democratic development. Repressive and habitually corrupt regimes were supported from Korea through Southeast Asia as long as they professed anti-communism. Additionally, the United States subsidized the early industrialization of its Asian allies' economies by providing preferential access for their products in the U.S. market and permitting protectionism against U.S. goods and services in Asian markets. These policies encouraged U.S., Japanese, and European multinational corporations to establish export industries throughout East Asia whose primary consumers were in the United States. Indeed, during the 1980s, exports to the United States generated by these corporations contributed substantially to the current U.S. balance of payments deficit. In short, America's Asian allies have also become important economic competitors, complicating the security relationships that have been established over the past thirty to forty years. In addition to military capabilities and intentions, then, security arrangements for the 1990s must take economic linkages into account. The key issue for U.S. strategic planners dealing with Asia will be whether alliances and economic rivalry can coexist. In other words, can U.S. political leaders continue to underwrite the defense of states for whom that subsidation enhances commercial competitiveness?

Throughout the twentieth century, U.S. interests in East Asia have been remarkably consistent through two world wars as well as the Cold War. As a trading nation, the United States has sought stability, opposition to hegemony by any regional power, and political and economic access for all to the region's goods and services. Since the end of the Second Indochina War, the United States has pursued these goals through a balance-of-power policy, endorsing the China-ASEAN Cambodian resistance coalition against a Soviet Vietnam–backed rival; bolstering South Korea against North Korea; urging increased military spending and more regional defense responsibilities upon Tokyo; fostering continued development of ASEAN (the Association of Southeast Asian Nations); and offsetting Soviet naval activities by maintaining forward deployed U.S. forces along the western Pacific littoral.[1]

By the 1990s, however, the underlying rationale for this strategy was unraveling. The Soviet Union had disintegrated. China was focusing inward on its own economic development and political stability. The ASEAN states and Vietnam were moving toward a new rapprochement as the latter abandoned its plan for Indochina hegemony and agreed to a United Nations Perm Five plan for resolution of the protracted Cambodian imbroglio; and the two Koreas finally seemed to agree on a program of peaceful coexistence, possibly leading to some form of confederation by the end of the century. In effect, the Cold War has ended with what appears to be a major Western triumph.

However, the dismantling of one international political structure does not mean the cessation of international politics. On the contrary, the transition through which the world now moves is potentially more unstable than its Cold War predecessor. Clear lines between old allies and enemies fade as the former become commercial competitors and the latter become new trade, aid, and investment partners.

The reduced East Asian military threat environment has been acknowledged by the Defense Department's April 1990 East Asian Security Initiative (EASI). While claiming to sustain all previous alliance commitments to

Japan, the Republic of Korea (ROK), Thailand, the Philippines, and Australia, DoD announced a 10 percent personnel cut of the 143,000 forward deployed U.S. forces in East Asia by 1993. Two subsequent phased reductions would draw down U.S. forces in the western Pacific to less than 100,000.

EASI logically follows the end of the Cold War and U.S. budgetary constraints. However, it also introduces new uncertainties into East Asian security considerations. First and foremost is the possible dissolution of the U.S.-Japan alliance, no longer buttressed by a common Soviet threat. This prospect is particularly unnerving to other Asian states, who fear that Japan will increase its own air and naval deployments to compensate for the loss of U.S. protection for its trade routes. The addition of a dominant Japanese military presence to its imposing regional economic position as major aid and investment partner could recreate the old "Greater East Asia Coprosperity Sphere" so prized by Japanese planners during the Pacific War (1937–45).

To assuage these concerns, former Assistant Secretary of State Richard Solomon insisted that the United States will maintain alliance commitments and that even reduced U.S. forces are sufficient to help sustain stability in a less threatening international environment. Moreover, since the number of U.S. military personnel in East Asia constitutes such a small portion of the total U.S. defense budget, they will not be further reduced.[2]

Tokyo is particularly concerned that its bilateral security ties with the United States remain a prominent regional security emblem despite (or perhaps partly because of) severe economic frictions. Japan remains virtually the only noncommunist Asian state that still sees Russia as a security threat. Although the formidable former Soviet Pacific fleet and air force are stationed in the Sea of Okhotskh and northern Sea of Japan, these forces no longer present an imminent threat of invasion. Indeed, they apparently lack resources for even normal exercises. Rather, Japan's emphasis on a continued threat from the north may best be understood as a means of sustaining the U.S. alliance. That alliance still serves as the linchpin in Japan's foreign policy. It reassures the rest of Asia that Japan's commercial dominance will not also expand into political and military hegemony. The U.S. alliance legitimates Japan's foreign economic policy for it insures that Japan will remain an incomplete superpower.[3]

The end of superpower confrontation has removed a layer of antagonism from other Asian regional disputes that has facilitated their resolution—this time with major power cooperation. The Perm Five plan for Cambodia's future and prospects for detente between the two Koreas could not have transpired without the concurrence of the United States, the former Soviet Union, and China. Vietnam's desire for rapprochement with the People's Republic of China (PRC) and its plans for some kind of association with ASEAN also emerged after Soviet abandonment. China, meanwhile, had completed its new relationship with the ASEAN states in 1990–91 when diplomatic relations were established with Brunei, Indonesia, and Singapore. The common element in all these political changes is the search for prosperity through trade, aid, and investment rather than political and military dominance.

As long as the United States insists on retaining a western Pacific military presence, which, in turn, is welcomed within the region, these forward deployed forces will increasingly depend on part-time access arrangements in Southeast Asia and direct financial payments from Japan and the ROK in the north. Japanese and Korean subsidies for U.S. forces in their countries permit the U.S. government to make the case to Congress that it costs less to maintain these forces forward deployed in the western Pacific than to repatriate them. (In 1992, Tokyo paid almost 50 percent—$3.5 billion—of the maintenance costs of U.S. forces in Japan.)

Through the early 1990s, Washington has rebuffed Australian, Canadian, and Soviet proposals for new Asian security institutions that would replace the bilateral alliances of the Cold War era. U.S. officials have argued that differing security challenges in Northeast and Southeast Asia do not lend themselves to region-wide resolution. Proven bilateral mechanisms should continue to be used to meet specific challenges. Underlying these agreements are Japanese and U.S. concerns that multilateral arrangements will accelerate the departure of U.S. forces from the region.[4] Nevertheless, if Washington follows its EASI timetable, by the end of the decade there may be no more than 60,000 U.S. troops in East Asia. Indigenous regional arrangements may then become a necessity.

## THE NORTHEAST ASIAN SECURITY ENVIRONMENT

A volatile mix is brewing in Northeast Asia's security future. The combination of U.S. trade frictions with Japan and South Korea combined with increased demands for burdensharing, growing ROK anti-American sentiment, and the collapse of the Soviet threat all portend a breakdown in the parallel bilateral security arrangements of the past forty years. Tokyo and Seoul have relied exclusively on the United States for their defense, though not on each other. Although South Korea and Japan both feared expansionist communist neighbors, each felt almost equal antipathy toward the other, going back to Japan's brutal occupation of Korea from 1905 to 1945. If the United States were to disengage militarily from the western Pacific, Korean-Japanese relations might well deteriorate as the former foresaw the latter's hegemony. Indeed, the prospect of a militarily ascendant Japan might conceivably lead to a PRC-Korean mainland coalition to balance Japan's maritime position. The point of these ruminations is to demonstrate that there is no consensus on a revamped security network for the region because there is no commonly perceived threat. Although the United States remains generally welcome—particularly if it foots most of the bill for its own presence—it is unlikely that the region's members are willing to go much beyond their current level of financial contributions to maintain U.S. forces. At some point, using those resources to build their own defense capacities may become more cost-effective, especially since regional defense decisions in a post–Cold War setting will be made locally rather than by a global power.

Despite regional anxieties over a dominant Japanese military role sometime in the future, there is little evidence to suggest that Japanese political leaders are moving in that direction. An expansionist policy requires the ability to seize and maintain control of territory on, over, and under the sea, more than 1,000 nautical miles (nm) from Japan, for an extended period. The Japanese Self Defense Forces (JSDF) would also have to transport a significant military force, undertake an opposed landing, and support that force during subsequent action and occupation. In fact, the JSDF is not equipped for any of these tasks. Nor are there plans to build or acquire the equipment to effect them.

Rather, aircraft acquisition plans for the 1990s are designed to enhance Japan's capability for successfully fulfilling its 1980s commitment: to defend the sea and air lanes within 1,000 nm of the home islands. New fighters (FSX) and antisubmarine warfare (ASW) aircraft, as well as tankers for inflight refueling, will all add to sea patrol and attack capabilities. Neither bombers nor fixed wing aircraft carriers nor amphibious forces are in Japan's future—all of which would be required for a power projection capability. The Japanese navy's mission continues to be sea lane protection in collaboration with the U.S. Seventh Fleet.[5]

U.S. forces in Japan, meanwhile, no longer serve to protect Japan from attack but rather as the primary location for U.S. forward deployment in the western Pacific, particularly with the closure of facilities in the Philippines. In the immediate future, these forces provide for contingencies that could grow from the turmoil in the Russian far east or the possibility of war on the Korean peninsula. However, internal Japanese politics could accelerate the reduction of some of these forces. It is unlikely that 20,000 U.S. Marines will remain much longer in Okinawa. Because the U.S. presence has been a source of tension between Okinawa and Japan's main islands for years, the new governor of the Ryukyus has demanded for the first time a U.S. withdrawal. If withdrawal is effected, a base would be eliminated from which the Marines traveled to the Persian Gulf during Desert Storm.[6] However, Japanese officials more generally continue to insist that the Japan-U.S. security arrangement is "the mainstay" of the relationship and "the anchor of peace and stability" in the Asia-Pacific region.[7]

To demonstrate its commitment to U.S. regional interests, Japan has also downplayed the prospect of an Asian economic grouping under Tokyo's auspices. After months of hesitation, Tokyo rejected Malaysia's offer of membership in a proposed East Asian Economic Group (EAEG) because it excluded the United States. By this action Japan demonstrated its continued willingness to subordinate its relations with other Asian countries to its predominant U.S. ties. As Chief Cabinet Secretary Koichi Kato explained, the United States should not be excluded from any region-wide economic arrangement because of its important regional security role.[8] In effect, the U.S. role as a security guarantor should entitle it to participate in any Asian economic group it desires.

Nor has Japan displayed any interest in incorporating Soviet successor authorities into a new regional security regime. Russian President Boris Yeltsin has been no more forthcoming on the return of the southern Kurile islands than was former President Gorbachev. Undoubtedly constrained by the negative views toward reversion of Sakhalin *oblast* officials who include the Kuriles within their jurisdiction, Yeltsin has devised a complex, drawn out, five-stage negotiating plan. The pace of its implementation may depend on how much aid Japan is prepared to provide Russia. Even if some agreement can be reached on the islands' return, the future of some 30,000 Russian residents would also have to be resolved.[9]

Assuming Russian continuation of Soviet East Asian policy, Moscow will probably persevere in suggesting Asian collective security accords along the lines of the Conference on Security and Cooperation in Europe (CSCE). A region-wide gathering of states, including Russia, would reassert the latter's legitimacy as an Asian actor and serve as a forum to bring pressure on both the United States and Japan for a new understanding on the deployments of naval and air assets around Russia's Asian coast.[10] An understanding that could lead to a reduction of U.S. and Japanese ASW deployments in the northern Sea of Japan would, in turn, permit Russia to continue to lower its military budget and deployments while insuring the safety of its reduced ballistic missile carrying submarine (SSBN) second strike capability in the Sea of Okhotskh.

As the former Soviet Union recedes from the position of adversary, Japan-ROK relations may become more tense. Thomas Wilborn of the U.S. Army War College's Strategic Studies Institute found in recent interviews with PRC and South Korean defense intellectuals that Japan was now perceived as a potential new threat to their nations' security.[11] Seoul has gone so far as to identify Japan officially in the ROK 1991–92 National Defense White Paper as bent on developing offensive forces. Although Tokyo has tried to reassure the Koreans that the JSDF possesses neither offensive capabilities nor intentions, the ROK nevertheless expressed concern over the prospect of Japanese forces participating in UN peacekeeping operations. The ROK Defense Ministry also claimed that by the end of the 1990s, Japan's defense capacity at its present rate of growth will exceed force levels necessary merely to defend the home islands.[12]

## THE KOREAN PENINSULA AS A NEXUS FOR NORTHEAST ASIAN SECURITY

The security concerns of the United States, China, Japan, and the former Soviet Union all converge on Korea's future. Moscow has virtually ceased military and economic aid to Pyongyang and since 1989 has been busily promoting economic and/or political ties with Seoul, Taipei, and the ASEAN states. Although Russia has not yet articulated its own East Asia policy, one of Gorbachev's last major proposals for the region was delivered during his April 1991 visit to Japan. At that time, he suggested a five-power collective security system in Asia composed of the United States, the Soviet Union, China, Japan, and India—presumably to replace the bilateral treaty arrangements of the Cold War. Gorbachev offered an additional suggestion—the creation of a Northeast Asian economic development arrangement among the countries bordering the Sea of Japan that could marry Japanese and South Korean capital, management, and technology to North Korean and Chinese labor, and Russian industrial capabilities.[13] The latter has elicited some interest from South Korea as a means of further committing Beijing and Moscow to Seoul's continued political progress, but none of the other putative members has responded.

The arms control issue that has most occupied the minds of those states adjacent to Korea has, of course, been the future of nuclear weapons on the peninsula. The threat of an autonomous North Korean nuclear weapon capability has been the focus of concern by Pyongyang's friends and foes alike.[14] The development of these facilities was accelerated in the last half of the 1980s, possibly because of a belief that neither the Soviet Union nor China were reliable backers any longer of the North's unification hopes. Kim Il-song's regime may have concluded that only its own nuclear weapon would be both a sufficient deterrent against an attack from the South—when the latter achieved military superiority sometime early in the next century—and a bargaining lever to exact concessions from all its neighbors to improve its economy and sustain its political independence.

Both China and Russia have more to gain from access to South Korean capital and trade from backing an anachronistic Stalinist ideologue in the North. Korea's future could become the basis for a multilateral collaborative arrangement through which the peninsula's neighbors and the United States underwrite a series of confidence-building measures that lead to arms reductions and, in time, reunification.[15] The initiative must, however, come from the two Koreas. Indeed, North Korea's apparent compromises during the 1991–92 Korean prime ministerial negotiations demonstrated that the Korean impasse could be broken before most analysts had thought possible.

The reasons for Pyongyang's sudden flexibility are complex. They may have included an assessment of the performance of U.S. air power and precision-guided munitions in the Persian Gulf that could also be employed against North Korean forces from offshore locations. They may also have grown from the realization that the North's economy could collapse with cataclysmic political results unless outside assistance is obtained. In any event, the December 1991 draft treaty of reconciliation and nonaggression was a precedent-setting event on the peninsula. It will reopen telephone and postal communications between the two states and provide some economic interaction as well. Railroad and road links are also to be constructed across the border. Perhaps most significant of all, Pyongyang and Seoul agree to forswear all acts of terrorism or any effort to overthrow the other.[16]

Undoubtedly, Kim Il-song would prefer to accelerate a U.S. military exit from South Korea along with the abrogation of U.S. extended deterrence. Significantly, neither of these stipulations is found in the draft treaty. Successful implementation of the accord may well accelerate the timetable for withdrawal of U.S. forces from Korea, however, as well as the transfer of command from U.S. to ROK officers.[17]

It is interesting that Washington has pressured the North to accept International Atomic Energy Agency (IAEA) inspection of its nuclear power facilities by threatening to postpone the drawdown of U.S. forces from the South and by increasing the potential lethality of joint ROK-U.S. exercises such as the annual Team Spirit. With respect to the latter, Washington has offered to sell Seoul several Patriot missile batteries and to add F–117 Stealth fighters and airborn warning and control (AWACs) aircraft to the 1991 exercise. As a carrot to the North, the United States has agreed to open U.S. bases in Korea to international inspection, though it should be noted that North Korea would still be within easy range of U.S. nuclear submarines.[18]

In effect, the North has few strategic options: The Gorbachev-Deng summit of May 1989 combined with Soviet-U.S. rapprochement has removed whatever leverage Pyongyang may have had with its backers. Indicative of the North's weak position are reports that the Soviet Union has not exercised with North Korean forces nor supplied additional modern aircraft (Mig–29s and Su–25s) since 1989 and that Moscow is now demanding immediate payment in hard currency for any new weapons sales.[19] Moreover, without Soviet logistics assistance, there is some question about whether these modern systems will remain workable.

Arms control makes sense for North Korea. Since it was abandoned by the former Soviet Union, the cost of maintaining an army of one million in one of the world's poorest economies has exhausted the Democratic People's Republic of Korea (DPRK). Facing external debts estimated to be $5 billion, stagnant foreign trade, and with a GNP of only $47 billion, the South's economic, population, and technological superiority will prevail over time if the current confrontation continues. The North needs a respite if its regime is to survive.

The Autumn 1991 decision by the United States and ROK to withdraw

U.S. tactical nuclear weapons from the South offered the DPRK a way to reciprocate through IAEA inspections without losing face. When President Roh Tae-wu promised the North that the ROK would never develop nuclear weapons on its own, a path was opened for both governments to permit international inspection of their respective nuclear facilities. As an additional incentive, President Bush, in his January 1992 visit to Seoul, offered to cancel Team Spirit exercises for that year if the North opened its nuclear plants to international scrutiny.[20] The only caveats to these promising developments are the possibility that the North has already produced and hidden enough plutonium to produce one or more bombs and that the IAEA experience in Iraq provides little assurance that international inspectors can locate all facilities designed for the production of nuclear weapons materials if the host government chooses to hide them.

Defense ties between the United States and South Korea have expanded into burden sharing and joint production over the past decade. Seoul has agreed that by 1995 it will provide about one-third of the won-based costs of maintaining approximately 31,000 U.S. forces on the peninsula. That would amount to about $300 million annually.[21] Nevertheless, there are both political and economic limits to this relationship.

Given an increasingly open democracy in the South and declining tension with the North, political priorities will change. Resources will be shifted from the defense budget to welfare expenditures. The termination of the National Defense Tax in 1990 may be the harbinger of a new age.[22] Although the United States has agreed to coproduction in the $4 billion General Dynamics F–16C/D contract, the U.S. aerospace industry is beginning to have the same kinds of concerns about future Korean competition that it has had for some time about Japan. ROK officials have complained that the United States has been reluctant to transfer defense technology despite a memorandum of understanding signed in 1988. The ROK has posited a turn to Europe or Russia as an alternative if Washington continues to hold back on coproduction arrangements and technology transfer. In military trade for 1990, the ROK ran a $1.6 billion deficit with the United States.[23]

In sum, the end of the Cold War, the prospect of detente on the Korean peninsula, growing democracy and anti-American sentiment in the South, as well as bilateral trade frictions, do not portend a continued smooth U.S.-ROK relationship. South Korea lacks an obvious resource asset such as oil. Under these conditions, Korean political leaders may reasonably ask what long-term stake the United States has in their country's future for the post–Cold War era other than strategic denial and the protection of Japan—both increasingly outdated objectives.

## TRANSITIONAL ARRANGEMENTS FOR SOUTHEAST ASIA

Southeast Asia's strategic importance to the United States during the Cold War was based on its location astride the sea lanes between the Indian

Ocean/Persian Gulf and the northwest Pacific. The Philippine bases provided U.S. naval and air forces with a surge capability in either direction. As in Northeast Asia, U.S. defense relationships have been bilateral with the Philippines and Thailand, though the Five Power Defense Arrangement (FPDA) incorporates Malaysia and Singapore with Great Britain, Australia, and New Zealand in a parallel security structure.

The future of these arrangements is increasingly problematic, however, as the former Soviet naval and air forces withdraw from the region and Vietnamese troops leave Cambodia. In a more relaxed security environment, U.S. forces will serve less as primary defender of the region and more to reassure and share in the burden of promoting its defense. Equally important, Southeast Asian states want to insure that the United States remains involved economically as an important trade and investment partner.

Indicative of this new, reduced role has been Washington's acquiescence to the closure of the Philippine bases by the end of 1992. Although it was hoping to keep the bases open until 1994, the United States preferred a rapid phaseout to the prospect of Philippine control over the exit. Once they no longer have access to the bases' superb location and repair facilities, there is no doubt that the size and duration of U.S. deployments in Southeast Asia will be reduced as forces are relocated to the mid-Pacific, Japan, and Alaska. Nevertheless, in all probability these forces would have been diminished even if the Philippine bases remained in operation because of the altered threat environment and Defense budget cutbacks.

The United States is searching for facilities to replace Subic Bay's ship repair and Crow Valley's air-ground training range. Their loss affects not only U.S. forward deployed forces but also those of a number of Southeast Asian states that trained at the Philippine facilities. Navy officials have been negotiating with Malaysia, Indonesia, and Brunei for training, repair, and access arrangements. These prospects include ship and aircraft maintenance on a commercial basis in Surabaya in Indonesia and Lumut on Malaysia's peninsular west coast. Indonesia and Singapore have proposed the construction of a new Air Combat Range on Sumatra that could be ready by 1995 and available to other regional air forces.[24] Malaysian authorities, meanwhile, have stated that repair arrangements at Lumut could provide employment for Subic Bay's skilled Filipino workers if Malaysians lack sufficient expertise.[25]

As the United States reduces its regional presence, ASEAN militaries are increasing their own capabilities for external defense, expanding beyond their traditional counterinsurgency orientation. Least able to undertake this new task is the Philippines. Its armed forces had estimated it would take $7 billion in new appropriations for modernization over a ten-year period that would cover the gamut from fast patrol craft to interdict smuggling to armed helicopters for counterinsurgency and combat aircraft and airlift capacity to defend the islands' air and sea space as well as its claims in the

Spratly chain. With the U.S. exit, however, the resource base for these modernization plans also disappears.[26]

Other more affluent ASEAN states fare better in their modernization plans. Tiny Singapore is acquiring new missile corvettes to better defend adjacent sea lanes. Its air force includes eight F–16s and a much larger number of A–4 Super Skyhawks that have been upgraded with new engines and avionics. Particularly significant are Singaporean plans to acquire new radars for an enhanced $C^3I$ capability. When these are integrated with command and control centers, Singapore will be able to monitor traffic along the Malacca Strait and out into the South China Sea.[27]

Thailand, too, is seeking to develop a greater maritime capability along both its Gulf and Andaman Sea coasts. To enhance its coastal patrol and oil rig defense, the Thai navy is acquiring four Chinese frigates, which although equipped with only 1950s technology should be adequate for surveillance. (The four Chinese ships cost the equivalent of one modern European vessel.)[28] Thailand is also buying P–3 aircraft through the U.S. Foreign Military Sales program. This naval upgrade will enhance Thailand's ability to operate along both its coasts while still leaving outer Gulf and South China Sea sea-lanes of control (SLOC) defense to the U.S. Seventh Fleet.[29] Thailand's continued security cooperation with the United States was revealed when former Prime Minister Chatichai Chunhawan acknowledged that his government permitted U.S. planes to use U-Tapao air base as a staging point in the Gulf War.[30]

Malaysia plans to allocate $2.2 billion to defense between 1991 and 1995, 11 percent of its budget. This is a 400 percent increase over its previous five-year plan. Under a 1988 agreement with Great Britain, most of these funds will go for 28 Hawk aircraft, two missile corvettes, the construction of new bases, and possibly the purchase of two submarines.[31]

Enhanced regional defense cooperation is also planned. The FPDA is expanding its integrated air defense system to include east as well as west Malaysia. Brunei has been asked to join. Malaysia and Indonesia have begun joint surveillance of the Malacca Strait. And U.S. officials have proposed greater access for their ships and aircraft on a temporary basis to increase joint training exercises.[32] None of this portends a precipitous U.S. withdrawal from the western Pacific even without the Philippine bases, though plans do suggest more intermittent deployments.

## WHY NO ASEAN DEFENSE COMMUNITY?

A number of ASEAN leaders in recent years have speculated about the prospects for region-wide defense cooperation. Interest in expanding bilateral defense exercises has grown as ASEAN states acquire more power projection capabilities and as the former Soviet Union and the United States reduce their forces in the area. Although ASEAN may be a *security com-*

*munity* in the sense that no member would seriously consider the use of force against another to settle disputes, it has not and will not become a *defense community.* Common cultural, ideological, and historical experiences are absent; and most important, there is no common threat. The benefits ASEAN has achieved—relative peace, stability, and security—do not form the base for wider military collaboration. Rather, they allow each state to pursue an independent path.

Despite parallel efforts to increase their external defense capabilities, ASEAN leaderships continue to define their security futures through economic development and cooperation rather than through a military pact. In the 1970s and 1980s, a common defense arrangement was rejected for fear that it would only encourage countermeasures by Vietnam and the Soviet Union and that external defense was irrelevant for addressing internal threats of insurgency, ethnic separatism, and political dissent. Moreover, the overall military weakness of the ASEAN states made them dependent on Western security guarantees. A mutual defense pact would have had little deterrent value.

In recent years, although the security environment has changed radically, interest in a defense pact has not increased. Communist insurgencies have collapsed in Southeast Asia (with the partial exception of the Philippines). Joint exercises and training on a bilateral basis emphasizing conventional military threats have increased. However, there is little impetus from the regional environment to move beyond these modest informal arrangements. The naval and air forces of the former Soviet Union are moving back to the North Pacific. Moscow's alliance with Vietnam has all but ended, with Hanoi now seeking political and economic cooperation with ASEAN rather than confronting the region militarily. China, too, has normalized relations with both the ASEAN states and Indochina. In sum, Southeast Asia's security environment has never seemed more benign.

Small wonder, then, that there is scant interest among the ASEAN states to remedy the lack of interoperability in their armed forces because of differences in doctrine, language, training procedures, and logistics systems. Divergent strategic priorities between, for example, Singapore's forward defense out to the South China Sea and Indonesia's defense in depth or Thailand's primary orientation toward land-based threats versus Malaysia's maritime focus render multilateral cooperation problematic at best.[33]

Under these conditions, no ASEAN state perceives indigenous cooperative defense arrangements as preferable to the maintenance of external ties through the FPDA, the Manila Pact, and in the case of Thailand, continued links to China. Malaysia's Defense Minister has noted that his country and Singapore have been able to exercise effectively and develop common procedures through the FPDA. That capability might not have emerged in the absence of outside arrangements. On the other hand, a trilateral straits defense regime among Singapore, Malaysia, and Indonesia could have the negative effect of dividing ASEAN into maritime and land-oriented subgroups. Minister Mohammed Abdul Rajak also foresaw the prospect of greater Chinese, Japanese, and Indian naval activity in Southeast Asia as a reason why the ASEAN states should retain their own linkages to external guarantors.[34] Moreover, should Vietnam and the other Indochina states affiliate with ASEAN by the end of the decade, association-wide defense collaboration would seem even more unwieldly.

Although defense collaboration with Vietnam would appear out of the question, its contribution to ASEAN's economic diplomacy could be considerable. Vietnam's membership could also facilitate a peaceful resolution to overlapping economic exclusion zones (EEZs) in the South China Sea. Continental shelf disputes could be settled comprehensively, not just bilaterally. Also, an ASEAN that included Vietnam could enhance Southeast Asia's bargaining position in dealing with the regionalization of the global economy.

Finally, it should be noted that even in a post–Cold War world, new regional tensions arise. China's involvement in supporting the repressive military regime in Burma is a case in point. Burma's army is entirely dependent for its equipment on Beijing; and northern Burma's economy is reportedly under China's domination. PRC aid to Rangoon's military leaders could add to Southeast Asian security problems by exacerbating refugee flows into Thailand and Bangladesh.[35]

## CONCLUSION

Forecasting regional security arrangements in Asia is a speculative enterprise indeed. On the one hand, political inertia and past sunk costs in military investment (represented, for example, by U.S. carrier battle groups) suggest the continuation of forward deployed U.S. naval and air forces. These forces would be assisted through access arrangements with a number of friendly states along the Asian littoral. On the other hand, modern-day elements of power are increasingly based on economic performance, technological know-how, and capacity for innovation. Military capabilities play a secondary role in this new environment. In fact, high levels of military investment may actually slow a country's general economic growth and harm its competitive performance. The irony of these conditions for U.S. policy in Asia is that although most members of the region will continue to welcome a U.S. presence that contributes to stability by dampening indigenous arms races, the United States itself has concluded that its deployments must be reduced as part of an overall revitalization of the U.S. economy.

The Soviet Union's collapse has meant that the ideological basis for U.S. commitments in Asia has evaporated. Although regional conflicts remain in Korea, between Japan and Russia, between China and Taiwan, and among the Southeast Asian states over boundaries and maritime development zones, these disputes are endemic and do not require the intervention of external powers for resolution. Nor do they threaten vital U.S. interests. Regardless of their outcomes, no new regional hegemon will emerge that may threaten international commerce or block U.S. investments.[36]

This is not to deny that residual U.S. commitments to Korea should be abrogated while the Stalinist Kim Il-song regime survives. By the end of the decade, however, rapprochement between the two Koreas and/or drastic political changes in the North attendant upon a successor regime or economic collapse could lead to new arms control measures that would greatly alter the need for U.S. forces. Should Korea be unified by the century's end, it may still desire a U.S. presence to protect against a rearmed Japan. The same reasoning suggests that both China and Korea would prefer the continuation of U.S. bases in Japan rather than the latter's development of an autonomous naval and air power projection capability.

In Southeast Asia, even though the Spratly islands remain a potential flashpoint, resolution through armed hostilities seems improbable. A joint development regime involving all claimants may be on the horizon—or, at minimum, separate national consolidations of each country's holdings. Even were China to decide to acquire the Spratly islands through naval and air attacks (an unlikely prospect), the ASEAN states possess neither the capability nor training to repulse them. Although collective military action would not occur, collective diplomacy, based on the Cambodian experience, probably would. ASEAN's past diplomatic successes will sustain its political cohesion for some purposes, while security cooperation operates at a lower level—between and among contiguous states.

Vietnam could affiliate with a loose ASEAN political group, adding to regional reconciliation. It is improbable, however, that Vietnam will become a full member of ASEAN while the Socialist Republic of Vietnam (SRV) remains a Leninist state with a centrally planned economy. Compatible political and economic values would simply be lacking. More probable will be Vietnam's participation in a Southeast Asian balance of power that would place it as the northern continental pole opposite Indonesia at the southern flank.[37] Moreover, with the cessation of Soviet military aid to Vietnam, its military's deterioration will degrade Hanoi's threat potential in the region over time.

In sum, ASEAN defense cooperation will remain at the level of regular consultations and the exchange of intelligence and some training among its members; joint exercises among neighbors primarily for border control, anti-piracy, and anti-smuggling purposes; notification of national exercises particularly in border regions; and the development of border agreements to cope with both land- and sea-based illegal labor movements and contraband. Southeast Asian defense, then, will remain at the state rather than regional level. In an environment no longer dominated by Cold War ideological conflicts and extraregional alliances, the impetus for regional defense collaboration atrophies. Although ASEAN will continue to function as a regional political and economic consultative mechanism, it should not be expected to become Southeast Asia's NATO or even its Conference on Security Cooperation.

The foregoing assessment of regional security for Asia in a post–Cold War environment yields several conclusions about the future of collective security and U.S. forward presence:

1. No collective security pact for either Northeast or Southeast Asia is on the horizon, much less an Asia-wide organization. For the foreseeable future, no single Asian state or combination of actors is perceived to threaten either the territorial integrity of others or international sea lanes. The absence of any clear threat, then, precludes the necessity for new, multilateral defense arrangements.

2. Nevertheless, security problems will persist in overlapping EEZs, competitive claims to the Spratly islands, illegal migration, and maritime resource disputes, as well as in the uncertainty over Korea's political future and the prospect of nuclear weapons development on that peninsula. Most of these issues are exclusively local and can only be resolved by the affected states. Outside powers have little substantive interest in them—with the exception of Korea—unless an outbreak of hostilities would threaten international commerce. A continued U.S. naval and air presence, then, can no longer be justified by reference to an overarching great power menace.

3. Rather, the maintenance of reduced U.S. air, naval, and army deployments in Asia will depend on a series of mutually beneficial bilateral agreements that also have the concurrence of neighboring states. Periodic access, prepositioned supplies, and regular joint exercises will probably characterize U.S. arrangements in Southeast Asia, initially with Singapore, Thailand, and Brunei. Over time, similar agreements might be reached with Malaysia and Indonesia—incentives for Kuala Lumpur and Jakarta being additional business for some of their shipyards. These exercises should focus on assisting regional armed services in developing their own capacities to monitor and defend their maritime and air spaces. The broader U.S. role would be one of patrolling the international waters and air spaces along the western Pacific littoral in collaboration with the region's members.

4. Finally, a sustained though reduced U.S. presence in Japan, Korea (for the time being), and along the sea and air routes of Southeast Asia probably inhibits efforts by Japan, China, or India to move their forces into the region to meet their own extended security needs. That is, reliance on a U.S. presence dampens the prospect of a regional arms race and reduces the probability that Japan might add a military dimension to its economic dominance in Asia.

A nagging question remains: Can the United States afford this new *constabulary* role? In all probability, only if those states involved in these relationships are willing to share some of the burdens. Both Korea and Japan already provide direct financial subsidation for U.S. forces in their countries. Although the Southeast Asian states are less affluent, if they are willing to provide access arrangements without rental costs, that, too, would be a form of burden sharing and would assist the United States in helping the Asian littoral to promote international stability through this transitional era in world politics.

The era of *Pax Americana* has ended in Asia. New collaborative arrangements can, however, foster an international environment conducive to trade, investment, and economic growth. As a dominant trading state, the United States should be an integral part of these new arrangements, though it may no longer dominate them.

## NOTES

1. For a discussion of the components of U.S. Asian strategy during the Cold War, see Lawrence E. Grinter, *East Asia and the United States into the 21st Century* (Maxwell Air Force Base, AL: Air University Press, 1991).
2. Quoted in Susuma Awanohara, "Double Standards," *Far Eastern Economic Review*, October 24, 1991, p. 26.
3. See the statement by Yikio Satoh, an official of Japan's *Gaimusho* (Ministry of Foreign Affairs), quoted in Michael Richardson, "Mixed Views on 'Pax Americana'," *Asia-Pacific Defense Reporter*, September 1991, p. 33.
4. Michael Richardson, "Quest for Cooperative Effort," *Asia-Pacific Defence Reporter*, September 1991, p. 32.
5. A. W. Grazebrook makes a persuasive argument for the JSDF's continued defensive orientation in "Maritime Potential No Cause for Concern," *Asia-Pacific Defence Reporter*, September 1991, pp. 27–28.
6. "Japanese and Americans Struggling to Overcome Their Mutual Resentment," *The New York Times*, December 3, 1991.
7. Statement by Vice Foreign Minister Hisashi Owada carried by *Kyodo*, November 18, 1991, in *Foreign Broadcast Information Service* (*FBIS*), Daily Report—East Asia, November 18, 1991, p. 2.
8. *Kyodo*, November 12, 1991, in *FBIS*, Daily Report—East Asia, November 12, 1991, p. 3.
9. *New Times* (Moscow), November 5–11, 1991, in *FBIS*, Daily Report—Soviet Union, December 5, 1991, p. 54. For a Japanese view, see Hiroshi Kimura, "Gorbachev's Japan Policy: The Northern Territories Issue," *Asian Survey* 31, No. 9 (September 1991), pp. 798–815.
10. For a discussion of Gorbachev's East Asian strategy, some of which may be adopted by Yeltsin, see Stephen Blank, "Soviet Perspectives on Asian Security," *Asian Survey* 31, No. 7 (July 1991), pp. 646–661.
11. Thomas L. Wilborn, *How Northeast Asians View Their Security* (Carlisle Barracks, PA: U.S. Army War College, Strategic Studies Institute, 1991), especially Chapters 2, 4, 5.
12. *Yonhap* (Seoul), October 28 and December 3, 1991, in *FBIS*, Daily Report—East Asia, October 28 and December 3, 1991, pp. 32 and 18, respectively. Japan's response is carried by *Kyodo*, October 29, 1991, in *FBIS*, Daily Report—East Asia, October 29, 1991, p. 1.

13. Soviet policy toward Korea is analyzed by Byung-joon Ahn in "South Korean–Soviet Relations: Contemporary Issues and Prospects," *Asian Survey* 31, No. 9 (September 1991), pp. 816–825.

14. For a thorough discussion of arms control issues on the Korean peninsula, see the special issue on arms control, *The Korean Journal of Defense Analysis* 3, No. 1 (Summer 1991).

15. William T. Tow, "Post–Cold War Security in East Asia," *The Pacific Review* 4, No. 2 (1991), pp. 97–108.

16. The draft treaty's provisions may be found in *The New York Times*, December 13, 1991.

17. A good, brief review of South Korea's foreign policy is found in Byung-joon Ahn, *South Korea's International Relations: Quest for Security, Prosperity, and Unification* (New York: The Asia Society, September 1991), passim.

18. David E. Sanger, "Cheney Calls Halt to Korea Pullout," *The New York Times*, November 21, 1991. Also see *Yonhap* (Seoul), December 12, 1991, in *FBIS*, Daily Report—East Asia, December 12, 1991, p. 23.

19. *Chungang Ilbo* (Seoul), October 30, 1991, in *FBIS*, Daily Report—East Asia, October 30, 1991, p. 18. Also see the articles by Gary Klintworth, "Arms Control and Great Power Interests in the Korean Peninsula," *The Korean Journal of Defense Analysis* 3, No. 1 (Summer 1991), pp. 155–219; and by William T. Tow, "Reassessing Deterrence on the Korean Peninsula" in the same issue.

20. *The New York Times*, January 6, 1992.

21. *The Korea Herald*, November 23, 1991, in *FBIS*, Daily Report—East Asia, November 25, 1991, p. 17.

22. Chung-in Moon, "The Political Economy of Defense Industrialization in South Korea," *The Journal of East Asian Affairs* 5, No. 2 (Summer/Fall 1991), especially pp. 462–465. Also see *Jane's Defence Weekly*, December 7, 1991, p. 1120.

23. *Yonhap*, November 18, 1991, in *FBIS*, Daily Report—East Asia, November 18, 1991, p. 16.

24. Michael Vatikiotis, "Spreading the Load," *Far Eastern Economic Review*, November 7, 1991, p. 35; and Michael Richardson, "Asia Adjusts to U.S.-Philippine Bases Deal," *Asia-Pacific Defence Reporter*, September 1991, p. 10.

25. *New Straits Times* (Kuala Lumpur), November 1, 1991, in *FBIS*, Daily Report—East Asia, November 4, 1991, p. 27.

26. Quezon City, GMA 7 Radio-Television Arts Network, December 11, 1991, interview with PAF Chief-of-Staff General Lisandro Abadia, in *FBIS*, Daily Report—East Asia, December 11, 1991, p. 43.

27. Interviews with the commanders of the Singapore Air Force and Navy, *Jane's Defence Weekly*, October 12, 1991, p. 684, and November 9, 1991, p. 926.

28. Robert Karniol, "Thais Defend Frigate Buy," *Jane's Defence Weekly*, October 19, 1991, pp. 724–725.

29. Interview with Thai Navy Commander-in-Chief Admiral Vichet Karunyawanit, *Bangkok Post*, October 11, 1991.

30. *Bangkok Post*, December 16, 1991.

31. *Far Eastern Economic Review*, November 7, 1991, p. 53.

32. Michael Richardson, "Filling the U.S. Gap," *Asia-Pacific Defence Reporter*, July 1991, p. 8.

33. See the discussion in Amitac Acharya, "The Association of Southeast Asian

Nations: 'Security Community' or 'Defense Community'?" *Pacific Affairs* 64, No. 2 (Summer 1991), pp. 159–178.

34. Michael Richardson, "Tightening Security Bonds: A Malaysian View," *Asia-Pacific Defence Reporter*, August 1991, pp. 18–19.

35. Muthiah Alagappa, "Confronting the SLORC," *Far Eastern Economic Review*, November 29, 1991, p. 28.

36. This argument is persuasively made by Edward Olsen in *The Evolution of U.S. Maritime Power in the Pacific* (Monterey: Naval Postgraduate School, October 1991).

37. Donald Weatherbee, "ASEAN and Indochina: The ASEANization of Vietnam," in *East Asian Security in the Post–Cold War Era*, ed. Sheldon W. Simon (Armonk, NY: M. E. Sharpe, 1992).

# 16

# Reconciling Alliances, Coalitions, and Collective Security Systems in Post–Cold War Europe

*Douglas T. Stuart*

This chapter represents a self-conscious intrusion into the territory staked out by Inis Claude in Chapter 14. I enter this territory with more than a little trepidation, and with justified humility, because Professor Claude is the closest thing that the international relations community has to a "definitive source" on issues relating to collective security and collective defense. I nonetheless feel that I have no choice but to confront these concepts directly in order to consider the prospects for European security in a post–Cold War world.

The title of my chapter conjoins two terms—*coalition* and *alliance*—that are not identical. A coalition is a temporary and conditional form of mutual defense agreement between governments, based upon "momentary convenience or necessity," which may or may not be formalized in a treaty between the participants.[1] By contrast, Warren Kimball defines alliances as "formal agreements between nations which call for specific joint action and responses to a given political situation."[2] Kimball emphaizes the greater reliability, clarity, and endurance of alliances in comparisons to coalitions. To illustrate: I consider the anti-German pact of World War II to be a coalition and I consider NATO to be an alliance. This small distinction is worth making at the outset, because in the post–Cold War situation we are likely to see a resurgence of coalition politics in Eastern Europe at the same time that Washington is engaged in discussions with key West European governments about the future of the NATO alliance.

I consider both coalitions and alliances to be forms of *collective defense* or *collective self-defense*, which I take to mean an outward-looking agreement for mutual security between two or more governments in which the threat from outside may or may not be explicitly named. I will be contrasting all of these concepts with the idea of *collective security*, which I take to mean an inward-looking agreement by more than two governments to preserve peace. Professor Claude dates the concept from the League experiment after World War I and notes that in its original form it was envisioned as

> a complex scheme of national commitments and international mechanisms designed to prevent or suppress aggression by any state against any other state, by presenting to potential aggressors the credible threat and to potential victims of aggression the reliable promise of effective collective measures, ranging from diplomatic boycott through economic pressure to military sanctions to enforce the peace.[3]

To illustrate: I consider Articles 39 through 50 of the Charter of the United Nations as a model commitment to collective security.

## BACKGROUND

The anti-communist containment system of the Cold War was the most successful experiment in collective defense in the history of international relations. It was a particular form of collective defense, and it operated under particular conditions, which had much to do with its success. The defining characteristic of the system was a network of bilateral and multilateral alliances that were essentially U.S. protectorates. At the core of this network of protectorates was U.S. military power, and in particular the U.S. nuclear deterrent. For a period of over four decades it succeeded in guaranteeing the security of the United States and the principal members of the Organization for Economic Cooperation and Development (OECD) community while wearing down the Soviet Union and ultimately contributing to its collapse. It is worth reminding ourselves of how close both the process and the outcome were to the ideal vision of containment that was articulated by George Kennan in the formative period of the Cold War. Kennan's frequently quoted call for "long-term, patient but firm and vigilant containment of Russian expansive tendencies" was based upon his assumption that such a policy would lead ultimately to "either the break-up or the mellowing of Soviet power." Kennan argued that this goal could be achieved without an East-West war, because the Soviet Union could not "face frustration indefinitely without eventually adjusting itself in one way or another to the logic of that state of affairs."[4] In spite of the periodic excesses and aberrations of containment, and notwithstanding Kennan's own revisionism, few critics today can find fault with either the logic or the consistency of the overall U.S. strategy of collective defense during the Cold War.

It is also worth reminding ourselves of how different this arrangement was from the system of international security formulated by Washington, London, and Moscow during the latter stages of World War II. Roosevelt, Churchill, and Stalin were all, to varying degrees, supportive of a worldwide system of collective security. After much intra- and intergovernmental haggling, all three agreed that the new global order shall take precedence over, but not block the creation of, regional approaches to security. Churchill and Stalin had initially preferred a system that accorded more status and influence to regional security arrangements—because they believed that a regionalized system would be more conducive to the establishment of British and Soviet dominance over Western and Eastern Europe, respectively. Under pressure from Washington, however, London and Moscow accepted a universalist approach in which regional security arrangements were to play a (vaguely defined) subsidiary role.

Roosevelt's opposition to a region-based system was greatly influenced by his Secretary of State, Cordell Hull. Hull's reasons for opposing regionalism are worth mentioning because they may prove to be prophetic in a post–Cold War setting. The Secretary of State warned that a regionalized world order would encourage the creation of continental blocs over which the United States would have limited influence; create a situation in which inter-regional conflicts might arise; invite the scramble for regional dominance by local powers; and lead to a sense of frustration in the United States that would fuel isolationist impulses.[5]

In any event, the universalist system of collective security that was institutionalized in the United Nations was rapidly eclipsed by the reality of bipolar collective defense. The transition from collective security to collective defense was epitomized by the creation of NATO in 1949—officially under the auspices of the United Nations, but in reality independent of, and stronger than, the UN. In the words of Robert Hildebrand:

> The vocabulary of peace, so often employed during the war, had been replaced by the language of national security. . . . With NATO, as opposed to the United Nations, the conflicting security needs of the United States and the Soviet Union would no longer be a problem. . . . [T]he contradictions posed by the need for cooperation between two such different systems were resolved by institutionalizing the conflicts between them.[6]

Thus, the Cold War was characterized by a de facto system of collective defense that took precedence over the de jure commitment to collective security. At times, such as during the Suez Crisis of 1956, the two approaches to peacekeeping came into conflict. But the Western allies never lost sight of the priority that they accorded to collective defense. The Cold War was also characterized by a de facto form of regionalism that took precedence over the de jure commitment to universalism. In spite of the rhetoric of global anti-communist containment, the U.S.-sponsored security network was essentially regionalized, with Europe representing the most fully developed and most important regional component.

Washington did dabble from time to time with the idea of transregional security linkages. Three examples were (1) the attempt to create a Middle East Defense Organization (MEDO), which would ultimately be linked to NATO; (2) plans for using Turkey as a strategic bridge between NATO and the Baghdad Pact [subsequently Central Treaty Organization (CENTO)]; and (3) discussions with London, Canberra, and Wellington about the practicality of linking NATO to the Australia, New Zealand, United States alliance (ANZUS).[7] In general, however, it was politically, militarily, and administratively easier for Washington to develop bilateral or regional security arrangements that were complimentary but not combined. This regionalization is best illustrated by the history of NATO "out-of-area" disputes—disagreements between NATO allies over issues beyond the established treaty area. These disagreements about extra-European issues were often intensely recriminatory, but they were never allowed to disrupt the regional collective defense agreement between Washington and its North Atlantic allies.[8]

By the mid–1980s, however, the trans-Atlantic bargain was exhibiting strains that seemed to portend a crisis. First, and most importantly, the U.S. nuclear guarantee, which had been the core of the bargain since 1949, had become increasingly suspect since the late 1960s—when the Soviet Union reached its goal of rough strategic parity with the United States. Nothing that Washington could do from that point onward, short of the unacceptable option of giving the European allies positive control over the U.S. nuclear decision, could reassure Washington's allies. This was an *absolute* measure of U.S. decline in the international system. Second, Washington's status and influence within the NATO alliance was undermined by its *relative* economic decline, which was exacerbated in the early 1980s by the Reagan Administration's ambitious program of defense spending. Thus, burden sharing, which had become the most divisive issue within NATO by the mid–1970s, took on a more serious and more threatening tone by the mid–1980s. As a result of these and other structural changes within the alliance, Washington's allies were actively searching for alternatives to NATO by the mid–1980s.

Concern about the long-term reliability of the NATO alliance was strongest in Germany, which had the most to lose by failure of the U.S. deterrent and the most to gain by an end to the Cold War. Small wonder, then, that the Soviet vision of a "common European house" advanced in the mid–1980s generated more excitement in Germany (a "Gorbasm," according to *Economist* magazine) than in any other West European country. By this time, Bonn was already pretty far along the road toward redefining its security relationship with Washington and with NATO. In particular, the Germans worked closely with the French during the 1980s to resuscitate the moribund Western European Union (WEU) and to use it as a U.S.-approved umbrella under which Paris and Bonn were able to work out new plans for bilateral defense cooperation. Bonn also began to take greater responsibility for its fate within NATO itself, as illustrated by its more assertive voice within the alliance and its campaign to place Manfred Worner in the position of NATO Secretary General. This new German assertiveness within NATO (and the EC) generated concern and resentment among many constituencies in Western Europe.

For its part, Paris was anxious to collaborate with Bonn on defense issues in the mid–1980s not only out of concern about the long-term reliability of NATO but also out of a desire to increase its influence over German defense decisions at a time when Germany was becoming increasingly restive. These considerations were sufficient to convince François Mitterrand to place in question one of the basic tenets of Gaullism, the indivisibility of the nuclear decision, by agreeing in 1986 to consult with Bonn before employing French tactical nuclear weapons on German soil.[9]

Evidence of a developing Franco-German axis fueled suspicions in London and Washington about the direction that European foreign and defense cooperation appeared to be taking. The concept of a European pillar had been publicly applauded by these governments throughout the Cold War, precisely because its implications were vague and its prospects remote. By the mid–1980s, however, the European pillar had begun to take form and the Anglo-Saxons had begun to take notice. Fortunately, the allies were spared a confrontation by the collapse of the Soviet bloc.[10]

## EUROPE'S FUTURE: BETWEEN "EUROPAX" AND HOBBESIAN ANARCHY

This brief survey of the last years of the Cold War illustrates that fundamental aspects of the current trans-Atlantic security debate preexisted by several years the collapse of the Berlin Wall. But this is not to imply that there is nothing unique about the post–Cold War era. The end of the Cold War has done more than accelerate the process of construction of a European pillar. It has transformed the intra-European debate about the risks involved in transcending NATO and about the preconditions for the success of any new institutional arrangement.

The wave of Europhoria that swept the continent after the collapse of the Soviet bloc encouraged journalists and policymakers to exaggerate the prospects for peace in a post–Cold War world and to downplay the costs and risks. During this early celebratory stage, very few magazines or journals shared *Economist*'s curmudgeonly perspective that "The dream of Europax" was only for the "wishful minded" and that "Europe and peace have not been words that naturally run together."[11] As reality has descended upon the continent, however, there has been an overreaction. Extreme pessimism has replaced extreme optimism in many journalistic analyses of the prospects for peace in Europe.

Fortunately, most of the scholarly discussions about Europe's future falls between these two extremes, and the principal points of reference in this discussion are institutions. A strategy for successfully combining these institutions will have to be based upon two things: an appreciation of the potential for mutual reinforcement and mutual antagonism between and among these institutions, and an appreciation of the relative merits of collective defense and collective security as guides in the formulation of an architectonic vision.

Four institutions are usually mentioned in any discussion of the prospects for a future European order: NATO, the European Communities (EC), the WEU, and the Conference on Security and Cooperation in Europe (CSCE). I will add the United Nations to this list, because it provides the legal framework for all these institutions and, more important, because it is likely to play a much more direct and influential role in European affairs in the future.

## NATO

NATO deserves to be considered first, because it is still the cornerstone of European security. Support for the preservation of NATO extends well beyond the current membership of the alliance. Indeed, some members of the former Warsaw Pact have expressed a desire to join NATO in order to bolster their security and cement their ties with the Atlantic Community. The most obvious reason for NATO's current popularity is that it has provided reassurance to European governments confronted with a major war in the Persian Gulf and the instabilities associated with the collapse of the Soviet Union and Yugoslavia.

NATO has also performed two less visible functions. First, it has provided an institutional framework for continued ties with an increasingly frustrated Turkey. Since the end of the Cold War there has been a tendency on the part of several European governments to distance themselves from Turkey, because they have too many other issues to deal with and because Turkey is seen as an "inconvenient" ally. It is a very large (58 million) and relatively poor ($1,350 per capita GNP) nation with an abysmal record in the field of human rights. Despite nearly seventy years of secularization, it has a population that is 98 percent Moslem. As long as the Soviet threat persisted, Turkey was welcomed into the Atlantic Community and encouraged to believe that its contribution to the common defense would ultimately be rewarded by full membership in the European Community. Now that the Soviet threat has evaporated, key European governments are reconsidering the prospect of Turkish membership in the EC or else are seeking to skirt the issue altogether. Worse, from Ankara's perspective, these governments are consolidating Greece's participation in the EC, including Greek participation in new arrangements for foreign and defense policy coordination. Thus, Turkish policymakers foresee a time in the not too distant future when disagreements between Greece and Turkey will become disputes between the EC and Turkey, to the considerable disadvantage of Ankara. For the present, at least, NATO provides an alternative to this situation, and by doing so it has helped to calm Ankara's fears and discourage radical tendencies within the domestic politics of Turkey.[12]

Second, the alliance has provided the context within which Europe has adjusted to the process of German unification. As previously mentioned, European concern about the growth of German power began to surface well before the Cold War ended. But once the process of East-West German reconciliation got under way, old fears and resentments returned with a vengeance. One need only consider the initial overreaction of many East and West European governments to Helmut Kohl's waffling on the issue of the Polish-German border to realize that Germany is still considered a suspect nation on the continent. More recently, Germany has been pilloried for taking the lead on the question of recognition of Croatia and Slovenia, in spite of the fact that the Germans have gone out of their way to demonstrate their commitment to European cooperation—not only in the field of economics but in foreign and defense affairs as well. NATO has been indispensable in keeping such reactions under control by keeping the United States politically and militarily involved in European affairs, and by providing Bonn with a forum for discussion and coordination of its policies. It is safe to say that both the process of unification and the subsequent process of German self-definition within Central Europe would have been more difficult and tendentious without the NATO alliance.

For these and other reasons, no European governments are anxious to see NATO disappear soon. In fact, to judge by new applications for membership, NATO has never been more popular. This is why George Bush had no reason to be concerned when he made his "love us or tell us to leave" speech to the NATO allies during the November 1991 summit in Rome. It remains to be seen, however, whether the new U.S. President, Bill Clinton, will get the same reassuring response from all NATO allies. Since the answer to this question will be largely determined by the alternatives available to European governments, I will return to it after surveying the other institutions mentioned earlier.

## THE EC AND THE WEU

One of the most common criticisms of NATO is that it is an artifact of the Cold War and therefore is inappropriate for the politics of the "common European house." What is less appreciated, however, is the extent to which the European Community is no less rooted in the Cold War era. The EC benefitted from the artificial, hothouse environment provided by the Atlantic Community. The normal workings of the security dilemma were suppressed in Western Europe by both U.S. hegemony and Soviet intimidation. For the

EC this meant that economic and political cooperation was encouraged by U.S. sponsorship and by the absence of intra-European disputes and suspicions over relative defense budgets. Furthermore, U.S. anti-imperialism and exclusionary unilateralism in the Third World combined with Soviet domination of the Warsaw Pact community to foreclose traditional areas of West European competition—Central Europe, the Balkans, and the southern littoral of the Mediterranean. The result was an unnaturally introspective Western Europe, which concentrated most of its political and economic attention inwardly.

The end of the Cold War has eliminated these artificial barriers. West European governments are rediscovering traditional interests and concerns beyond the European Community. The Gulf War was the first intimation of this changed situation. Since the Gulf War, France has begun to get the message in the wake of the victory of the Islamic Salvation Front (FIS) in Algeria, and all EC members have been shaken by developments in the Balkans, in Central Asia and in the Horn of Africa. As Europe adapts to its new geographic identity, Germany's location insures that it will be far ahead of its EC partners in economic and political relations with Central and Eastern Europe. Likewise, Italy's location insures that it will be more involved than other EC governments with developments in the Eastern Mediterranean and the Balkans.

These centrifugal pressures are already being felt by the EC, and they will become stronger in the next couple of years. But they are not likely to lead to the collapse of the EC experiment, because the process of West European economic integration is already too far along. The hothouse has disappeared, but the EC has already developed into a strong and productive economic entity that can survive in the new environment. Even Britain, which has been a disgruntled member of the EC since it joined in 1973, is too far down the road toward European economic union to gamble on an alternative.

But EC governments did more than accelerate the process of economic cooperation at Maastricht. They committed the Community to move toward "the eventual framing of a common defense policy" and the creation of a new EC foreign policy secretariat in Brussels as a step toward an institutionalized common EC foreign policy. Here, the Community is moving into new territory and may fall victim to fissiparous forces. Some experts and policymakers have argued that there is an inevitable spillover from close economic integration to close cooperation in the fields of foreign policy and defense. But there is no empirical evidence to support this claim (which is understandable in view of the fact that the EC is an unprecedented experiment in international cooperation).[13] It seems more likely that West European governments will settle for a flexible system of consultation and coordination on issues of foreign policy and defense, a system that permits common action on the basis of consensus without doing violence to the residual sovereign control that the separate Community members currently exercise over these issues. This would be a more efficient version of what currently exists within the EC, rather than a qualitatively different and more supranational arrangement. It envisions not a Europe in which progress in economic integration gradually pulls EC members toward political and defense cooperation, but rather a Europe in which management of the tension between close economic integration and more conditional cooperation in foreign and defense affairs becomes the defining characteristic of intra-Community relations.

The WEU is the institutional framework within which EC governments intend to coordinate their defense policies in the future. WEU Secretary General Willem van Eekelen and his predecessor, Alfred Cahen, deserve much of the credit for having positioned this institution to play a central role in European security. Indeed, the WEU is the greatest bureaucratic success story of the last few years. Less than a decade ago it was a footnote in the almanac of European institutions. But by making itself useful—as an umbrella for Franco-German defense discussions in the late 1980s, as a forum for European consultation and coordination in support of both the 1987–88 Persian Gulf Armada and the 1990–91 Operations Desert Shield and Desert Storm, and, in particular, as an active participant in the naval blockade against Serbia—the WEU gained considerable respect and influence. The price of success has been visibility, however, as both NATO and the EC (or, more precisely, Washington and Paris) have begun to struggle for control over this bit of institutional turf. But the EC has a natural advantage in the tug-of-war because the WEU is by definition a "European pillar" organization. Washington would be well advised to accept this fact and support the growth of the WEU within the EC framework.

As the European pillar evolves, it is likely to become harder to make the case for the indispensability of NATO, particularly if the WEU begins to develop a record of success in the defense field. NATO governments will have to give the alliance some new roles and responsibilities. Before considering this challenge, however, it is necessary to examine the other candidate for the title of institutional guarantor of European order—the CSCE.

## THE CSCE: VICTIM OF CIRCUMSTANCE

Of the institutions discussed in this chapter, only the CSCE can claim to be a truly post–Cold War organization. Although it has been around since 1973, its membership is pan-European and its structure is multilateral rather than bloc-to-bloc. For this reason, as the Cold War system began to collapse there was considerable interest in the CSCE, particularly among governments that were situated along the fault lines of the old order (Germany and the nations of Central Europe). The campaign to build up the CSCE was smothered, however, by U.S. ambivalence (because it saw the CSCE as a threat to NATO) and by French reticence (because it preferred to sponsor the EC as the cornerstone of the new European order). As a result, the CSCE has acquired a minimal institutional identity since the collapse of the Berlin Wall, and by contract to the WEU and NATO, it has made only an indirect and very modest contribution to the resolution of European security problems. This is most apparent in the challenges posed by the implosions of Yugoslavia and the U.S.S.R. Arguably, both these issues could have been ideal opportunities for the CSCE to begin to establish itself as a valuable part of the European peace system, because its purview extends to such issues as the validation of frontiers, conflict prevention, confidence and security building, and the protection of human rights. Furthermore, at the same time that the CSCE was demonstrating its irrelevance to these serious problems, NATO was beginning to adjust both its geographical and its functional identity in ways that made the CSCE look more and more dispensable. NATO's November 1991 Rome Declaration paid considerable lip service to the CSCE, while at the same time committing the alliance to such activities as "dialogue," "cooperation," and "management of crises and conflict prevention" anywhere in Europe. The allies also created a new North Atlantic Cooperation Council (NACC) as a forum for confidence building and consultation between NATO governments and the members of the former Warsaw Pact. Not to be outdone, the EC has also begun to cut into the defining responsibilities of the CSCE by establishing standards for recognizing new states and by involving itself directly, if haltingly and belatedly, in the Yugoslavian crisis. Under these circumstances even the most ardent supporters of the CSCE, such as President Vaclev Havel, have begun to lose interest in this institution.

It can be argued that the future of European security would be more secure if a strong CSCE had come into existence as soon as the Berlin Wall came down. But this no longer appears to be a possibility. What is more likely now is that the CSCE, the only truly post–Cold War European security institution, will play only a very marginal role in Europe's future, while NATO and the EC/WEU (the leading residual Cold War institutions) compete, or cooperate, to shape the post–Cold War European system. We can now turn our attention to this problem.

## REDEFINING NATO AS A PAN-EUROPEAN INSTITUTION

My analysis of the evolving security situation in Europe has highlighted four points. First, NATO is currently enjoying wide popularity. Second, the debate about "ownership" of the WEU is likely to increasingly favor the EC over NATO, with the result that a stronger European defense identity will take shape. Third, as a European pillar of defense develops, NATO governments will have to find new rationales for preserving the alliance. Fourth, the first tentative steps in this direction have already been taken at the 1991 Rome Summit, where NATO governments decided to extend the alliance's political purview into Eastern Europe and to intrude into some of the CSCE's areas of responsibility. Under these circumstances, the proper course of action for NATO would seem to be to push forward with the preemption of the CSCE and to replace it as the preeminent pan-European institution for political cooperation, collective security, pacific settlement, and peaceful change. For purposes of discussion, these new functions might come under the auspices of the recently created North Atlantic Cooperation Council. While preserving its core of members committed to collective defense, NATO could offer membership in the NACC to all nations of the CSCE and establish guidelines (similar to those recently developed by the EC) for the recognition of new states and their inclusion in this larger NACC system. A side benefit of distinguishing between the NATO core and the new NACC system is that there will be no need to confront the problems associated with changing the NATO treaty or changing NATO's established geographic boundaries. The new NATO/NACC would be developed within the context of the United Nations as a pan-European peacekeeping organization. NATO already derives its legitimacy from the UN, as reflected in the Preamble and Articles 1, 5, and 7 of the NATO treaty. This strategy would help to close the gap between rhetoric and reality. Furthermore, although the NACC's primary responsibility would be pan-European peacekeeping, it would also be available to respond to requests by the UN Security Council for extra-regional collective security action or humanitarian assistance.

This implies three areas of NATO responsibility: the Atlantic Core, the expanded NACC region, and a third area of potential responsibility beyond the European theater. Ironically, this arrangement has some similarities to George Kennan's 1948 proposal for a "three-tiered" NATO membership system (described by Robert Lovett as a system of "resident members, nonresident members and summer privileges").[14] It is instructive that Kennan backed away from this idea because he recognized that NATO had to be primarily a collective defense arrangement that would have a tenuous relationship with the United Nations. He concluded, therefore, that the alliance stood its best chance of avoiding conflict with the UN if it remained geographically confined.[15]

Three tiers of NATO responsibility will be problematic, of course, if it engenders resentment on the part of those Eastern European governments that are members of the NACC but not within the collective defense perimeter of the residual NATO treaty. The nations of the former Warsaw Pact would nonetheless recognize that this arrangement is a considerable improvement over the current situation of an eviscerated CSCE and no firm commitments from the members of the Atlantic Community.

Redefining NATO as a more political organization with an expanded membership should help to ease the tension between the alliance and the

EC/WEU. Ideally the EC/WEU group will find it easier to work within this larger NATO forum, as a true European pillar. A larger and more political NATO will also be easier for France to live with, thereby helping Paris to get rid of some of the old Gaullist baggage that serves neither Atlantic nor French interests. Finally, a pan-European NATO would still be a forum for preserving a U.S. seat at the European table, for adjusting to the reality of German power in Central Europe, and for preserving a link between Europe and Turkey.

For its part, Washington should not assume that by adapting NATO to a stronger European pillar it is setting the stage for U.S. eviction from the continent. First, as previously mentioned, the EC is not likely to achieve the degree of cooperation in foreign and defense affairs that it has achieved in the economic realm. Thus, there will be ample opportunities for Washington to advance and protect its interests in bilateral and multilateral arrangements within the new NATO forum. Furthermore, there is more substance than many people realize in the idea of an Atlantic Community. Over the last four decades NATO has evolved into what George Liska has called a social institution—a community of democratic values and fundamentally compatible national interests.[16] Washington must be prepared to believe its own rhetoric in this regard and trust in the ability of that community to withstand the changes that are taking place.

Finally, with regard to force structure, it would seem that the changes currently taking place—downsizing of national contingents and the development of a force that will have both "immediate and rapid reaction elements able to respond to a wide range of eventualities" seem appropriate to the demands of a more political and pan-European NATO.[17] The size of the U.S. contribution to this force should be determined by operational requirements rather than by some politically motivated U.S. formula that equates the number of U.S. troops on the continent with the level of U.S. influence over allied policies.[18] This formula was valid during the Cold War but is inappropriate and counterproductive today.

## CONCLUSION

There are several risks involved in a strategy of positioning NATO between the UN and the EC/WEU as the paramount organization for pan-European political cooperation and peacekeeping. Two deserve special mention. The first risk is that these changes will facilitate the development of a stronger West European defense identity within NATO that will undermine the basic trans-Atlantic bargain. I see this not as a reason to resist organizational change in NATO but rather as an argument in support of structural change as soon as possible. Further progress in the field of West European foreign and defense cooperation seems to be inevitable in any event, even though it is unlikely to lead to the development of any EC army or an EC foreign ministry with real supranational authority. NATO must not be seen as a roadblock to this progress. Otherwise, when a future U.S. President says "love us or tell us to leave," he or she will receive a very different answer than the one that Mr. Bush received in Rome in November 1991. On the other hand, West European governments are likely to welcome, and rely upon, an expanded NATO capable of performing new pan-European political and peacekeeping functions, primarily if the CSCE continues to be perceived as impotent, and they are likely to accord Washington a good deal of status and influence within such an organization.

This may not be enough for the United States. The risk that the United States will lose interest in a Europe that it can no longer control is greater than the risk that Europe will ask Washington to leave. Harking back to the concerns expressed by Secretary of State Cordell Hull during World War II, there is a real danger that Americans will not support U.S. participation in a pan-European institution that is redesigned to facilitate political cooperation and serve the demands of the United Nations on the continent. It is certainly easier to sell the American people a full-blooded collective defense system against a clear and present danger than it is to sell a system that is committed to such murky premises as collective security and humanitarian assistance. But NATO already faces this problem, as a result of its decision to take on new missions such as "dialogue," "cooperation," and "crisis management and conflict prevention." It will not be long before the neo-isolationists in the United States recognize that NATO is backing into the role of European handmaiden of the United Nations. Redefining NATO now would at least provide a conceptual framework for the changes that are taking place and perhaps make it easier to rebuff the forces of isolationism.

Reference to the murky premises of collective security and humanitarian assistance leads me to the second major risk associated with my proposal for redefining NATO. Considering the record of the United Nations and the League of Nations, there is little reason to be optimistic about the effectiveness of NATO as a pan-European security organization. Nor is the picture more encouraging if we consider the records of the leading Cold War experiments in regional peacekeeping—the Organization of American States (OAS) and the Organization of African Unity (OAU). A redefined NATO will inevitably confront all the defects that writers such as Inis Claude and Gerhart Niemeyer have associated with international experiments in peacekeeping.[19] In particular, a pan-European NATO will confront the conflicting demands of collective security and mediation and the peaceful resolution of disputes—what Claude refers to as the tension between "the use of military might for order-keeping purposes" and the "soft, anti-military approach to international relations."[20] This is why NATO must preserve its core identity as a collective defense organization and preserve the requisite military capability to back up the collective defense commitment as a form of insurance.

But the Cold War era is over, and the politics of collective defense that characterized that era will no longer be sufficient to ensure security or stability on the continent. It is neither realistic nor morally justifiable for the nations of the Atlantic Community to seek to isolate themselves from the problems that are already visible beyond the rubble that used to be the Berlin Wall. The alternative is a gamble on a new system of international peacekeeping. That gamble is most likely to work if the new system can be built around NATO.

## NOTES

1. The *Encyclopedia of the Social Sciences*, vol. 3 (New York: Macmillan Publishers, 1930), p. 600.

2. Warren Kimball, "Alliances, Coalitions and Ententes," in *Encyclopedia of American Foreign Policy*, ed. Alexander DeConde, vol. 1 (New York: Charles Scribner's Sons, 1978), pp. 1–2.

3. Inis Claude, Jr., *Swords into Plowshares: The Problems and Progress of International Organization*, 4th ed. (New York: Random House, 1971), p. 247.

4. Excerpts are from Kennan's "X" article, as discussed by John Lewis Gaddis, "Mr. 'X' is Consistent and Right," in *Decline of the West?*, eds. George Kennan et al. (Washington, DC: Ethics and Public Policy Center, 1978), pp. 138–139.

5. See Robert C. Hildebrand, *Dumbarton Oaks: The Origins of the United Nations and the Search for Postwar Security* (Chapel Hill: University of North Carolina Press, 1990), p. 25.

6. Ibid., p. 256.

7. All these schemes are discussed by Douglas Stuart and William Tow in *The Limits of Alliance: NATO Out-of-Area Disputes since 1949* (Baltimore, MD: Johns Hopkins University Press, 1990), passim.

8. Ibid., passim. See also Elizabeth Sherwood, *Allies in Crisis* (New Haven: Yale University Press, 1990); and Joseph Coffey and Gianni Bonvicini, eds., *The Atlantic Alliance and the Middle East* (London: MacMillan, 1989).

9. For analysis and discussion, see Douglas Stuart, "France," in *Politics and Security in the Southern Region of the Atlantic Alliance*, ed. D. Stuart (London: Macmillan, 1988), pp. 46–67.

10. These arguments are developed in more detail by the author in "NATO in the 1980's: Between European Pillar and European House," *Armed Forces and Society*, Spring 1990, pp. 421–436.

11. "The Dream of Europax," *Economist*, April 7, 1990, p. 14.

12. For an analysis of the Turkish situation, see Bruce Kuniholm, "Turkey and the West," *Foreign Affairs*, Spring 1991, pp. 34–48.

13. Various authors have looked to the U.S. and Swiss federative experiences for encouragement, but the EC experiment is better understood as sui generis because key participants in the EC are major international actors with long historical experience in the exercise, and protection, of sovereignty. For some representative

federalist arguments, see Clifford Hackett, *Cautious Revolution: The European Community Arrives* (New York: Praeger, 1990), pp. 14–15.

14. "Minutes of the Fourth Meeting of the Washington Exploratory Talks on Security" (July 8, 1948, 10 A.M.), *Foreign Relations of the United States 1948*, vol. 3, "Western Europe" (Washington, DC: Government Printing Office, 1974), pp. 165, 168.

15. See Stuart and Tow, *The Limits of Alliance*, pp. 32–34, 322.

16. George Liska, *Nations in Alliance: The Limits of Interdependence* (Baltimore: Johns Hopkins, 1968), p. 61.

17. *The Alliance's New Strategic Concept* (Agreed upon by the Heads of State and Government Participating in the Meeting of the North Atlantic Council in Rome on 7–8 November 1991), reprinted in *NATO Review* 6, No. 39 (December 1991), p. 30.

18. For further elaboration, see the article by NATO SACEUR General John Galvin, entitled "From Immediate Defence towards Long-Term Stability," *NATO Review* 6, No. 39 (December 1991), pp. 14–18. This article discusses in very general terms the military requirements for a new NATO force "capable of several missions, including deterrence and support for crisis management, peacekeeping, humanitarian assistance and, as before, the defence of Alliance territory" (p. 15).

19. See, for example, Inis Claude, *Power and International Relations* (New York: Random House, 1962), Chapters 4, 5; and Gerhart Niemeyer, "The Balance Sheet of the League Experiment," reprinted in *Crisis and Continuity in World Politics*, eds. George Lanyi and Wilson McWilliams (New York: Random House, 1966), pp. 341–352.

20. Inis Claude, *American Approaches to World Affairs* (Lanham, MD: University Press of America, 1986), pp. 56–57.

# Conclusions: The Strategy Paradigm versus the Political Paradigm

The search for strategy requires strategic vision and political consensus in the calculation of ends, ways, and means. This book has attempted to show why the process is so difficult. Managing national security strategy in a democracy inevitably produces conflict between the ideal strategy paradigm and the normal political process. Figure C.1 illustrates the ideal model; Figure C.2 illustrates the conflict proposed by fragmented political authority and competing visions. Historically, only a crisis precipitated by clear and present dangers or leaders with compelling visions have been successful in uniting the two paradigms.[1] Even then, unity has been short-lived.

Structural obstacles to strategy formulation are inevitable, but recognition of three related problems may improve the fractious process of translating ends and means into coherent concepts for action. First, strategic vision during periods of historic transformation need not require a detailed or perfect road map to the future. The post–Cold War period, for example, is too much in flux for that. Having vision can also mean acknowledging that historic changes have taken place as the result of our sudden victory in the Cold War, giving voice to their impact, and galvanizing—even jawboning—the bureaucracy, the Congress, and the nation to debate new issues and challenges. Strategic vision can be initiated by asking the right questions as much as by promoting preferred solutions.[2]

Articulating strategic vision, however tentative the vision may be, is related to a second problem. That is the unrealistic American concept of victory. Victory connotes that both a struggle and U.S. involvement have ended, preferably in some unconditional and final form. Military victory, for example, is symbolized by Marines raising the flag on Mt. Suribachi or

**Figure C.1**
**The Strategy Paradigm**

by dictators signing the documents of unconditional surrender on the decks of U.S. battleships or in remote desert bases surrounded by victorious allied forces. Victory in hot wars or cold ones means that we can withdraw, that our responsibilities have ended, and that our interests are secure.

Good strategy does not recognize the concept of victory. There are no victories; there are only phase lines in a permanent struggle to promote and defend our national interests. The point is illustrated in Figure C.3. At each phase line threats are defeated or recede; the international system reconfigures as old powers decline and new powers rise; and at home, resources are redistributed in support of new priorities and new strategies. But neither the international nor the domestic political systems are static. Only the nation's interests remain relatively constant, requiring new strategies for their promotion and defense.[3]

National security strategy requires the permanent management of the nation's interests through the planning and application of political, economic, and military strategies. Collectively they constitute grand strategy. Grand strategy relates to the third problem in uniting the strategy and political paradigms into a coherent plan of action. The concept of victory as an end state feeds the natural tension between domestic and foreign policy. This tension manifests itself in the debate for resource allocation.

**Figure C.2**
**The Political Paradigm**

Simply stated, every dollar invested in external security is a dollar not available to meet a domestic requirement, and vice versa.[4] This attitude is, to a large degree, the fault of strategists themselves who traditionally promote *threat-based* rather than *interest-based* strategies.

A comprehensive interest-based strategy recognizes that grand strategy bridges the gap between foreign and domestic policies in a world in which domestic prosperity is directly linked to global activism and status. Grand strategy recognizes the organic relationship between foreign and domestic interests and coordinates political, economic, and military power in the pursuit of those interests. Chapter 1 by David Jablonsky describes this process in detail. He also gives the reader a guide for recognizing when the consensus required to coordinate the strategy and the political paradigms is broken. The most telling symptom is a debate that puts domestic and military spending on a zero-sum collision course. By contrast, strategic vision is the ability to articulate grand strategy and coordinate the allocation of resources to all elements of power—political, economic, and military.

Articulating a strategic vision and mobilizing support on its behalf are not panaceas to the problems described here, but they can minimize the harmful effects to a nation that may be drifting toward political isolationism, militant economic protectionism, or military unpreparedness. These ex-

**Figure C.3**
**The Permanency of Strategy**

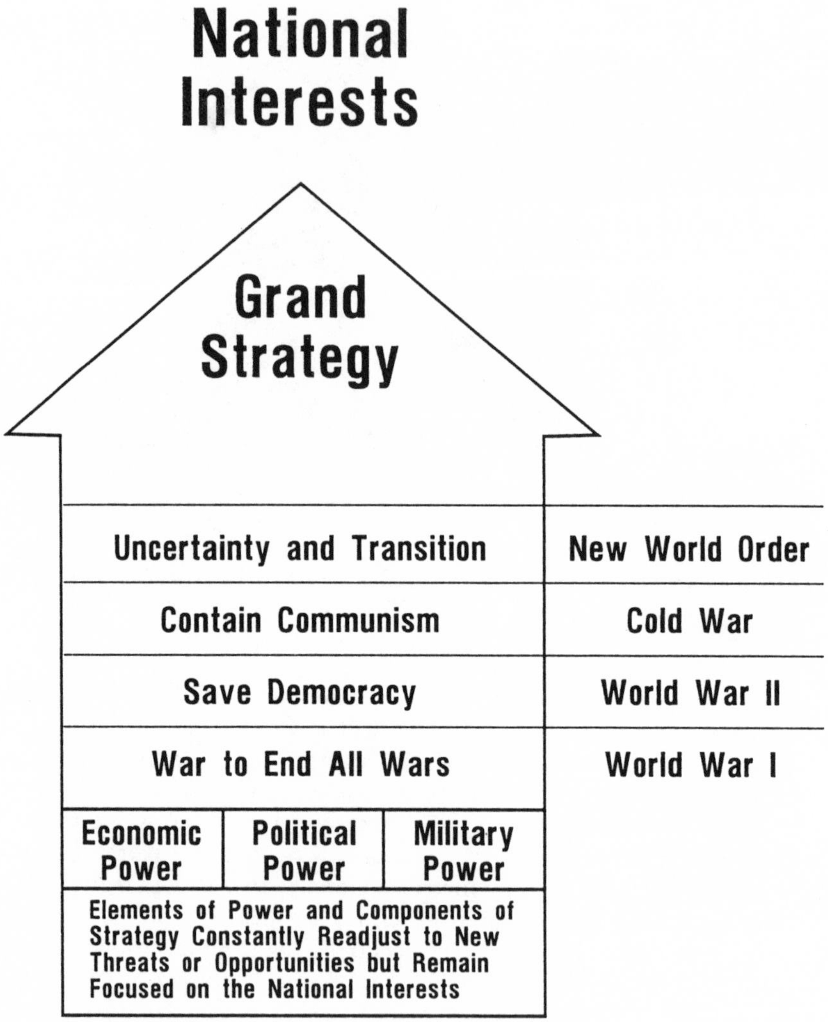

National Interests

Grand Strategy

| | |
|---|---|
| Uncertainty and Transition | New World Order |
| Contain Communism | Cold War |
| Save Democracy | World War II |
| War to End All Wars | World War I |

| Economic Power | Political Power | Military Power |
|---|---|---|

Elements of Power and Components of Strategy Constantly Readjust to New Threats or Opportunities but Remain Focused on the National Interests

tremes are the antithesis of strategy and can result in tragic intervals of conflict.

The search for strategy has consequences that are vital to the nation. This volume is not intended to provide *a* strategy for the new world order, or even an ideal process for formulating strategy. Its purpose is to emphasize that the search itself is important and worth our best efforts and attention at a time when familiar landmarks have vanished and no new strategic vision has attracted a national consensus.

## NOTES

1. Roosevelt and Churchill are examples of wartime leaders. Truman "scared hell" out of the Congress to get the first postwar appropriations to support containment in Greece and Turkey. Arguably, Nixon's China initiatives and detente with the Soviet Union were classic examples of balance of power politics and strategy until his authority and leadership were undermined by domestic scandal.

2. Also discussed in an essay by Thomas L. Friedman, "U.S. Policy Stands Still," *The New York Times*, March 15, 1992, Section 4, p. 2.

3. I am indebted to Colonel David Ingle for the concept illustrated in Figure C.3.

4. "Strategic overreach" and its negative impact on domestic strength is the thesis popularized by historian Paul Kennedy in *The Rise and Fall of the Great Powers: Economic Change and Military Conflict from 1500 to 2000* (New York: Random House, 1987). Kennedy's thesis is countered by Joseph Nye, Jr., in *Bound to Lead: The Changing Nature of American Power* (New York: Basic Books, 1990).

# Index


A-6 aircraft, 119 n.39, 195
A-10 aircraft, 195
A-12 aircraft, 183
AAAM missile, 183
adaptive planning, 61
ADATS air defense system, 183
aerospace industry, 280
aircraft, 106, 111, 112, 183, 195, 203
air defense, 181, 183, 191–92
Air Force: 102, 105, 106, 107, 118 n.29, 140, 143; force planning, 162; program terminations, 183; T-46 trainer program, 111; technological weaknesses, 195
air warfare: air superiority, 161; beyond visual range, 191; command/control problems, 139–40; counterforce targeting, 172; countervalue punishment, 132, 134–35; lift capability, 194; limited war, 135; surgical strikes, 142–43, 190
Algeria, 225, 234–35, 297
alliance: defined, 290. *See also* collective security
Allison, Graham, 38
all-weather warfare, 192
Angola, 224
Anti-Ballistic Missile (ABM) Treaty, 75, 76, 79
Apache helicopter, 183
appeasement, 31, 122
Appropriations committees, 108, 109, 118 n.29
Arab-Israeli conflict, 16–17, 145, 202, 224
Argentina, 235–36, 237 n.9
armed forces: in Asia, 274, 275–76, 279, 281, 284, 286; Base Force, 61–63, 66, 79, 85–87, 102, 125, 182; Congressional relations, 110, 111; downsizing, 28–30, 31, 36, 64, 102, 103, 113, 125, 181, 182; interservice disputes in, 89–90, 105–7; joint duty, 84, 91–92, 106; lack of integration, 83; overseas deployment of, 72–73, 75, 76–78, 136, 153, 154, 170, 274, 275–76, 279, 281, 284, 286; peacekeeping role of, 76; professionalism of, 20–21; readiness for combat, 83, 87, 125; reconstitution capability, 59, 79–81; reinforcement capability, 78; reorganization of, 19–20; Reserve forces, 29, 35, 60, 119–20 n.44, 194; servicism, 83–84; Soviet threat and, 100–102; spending by services, 82–83; as stabilizing force, 77; standing army, 19; tasks of, 160–61

Armed Services committees, 108, 109, 117–18 n.29
Armey, Richard, 119
armored forces, 193, 194, 195
arms. *See* arms limitation; munitions; nuclear weapons; technology, military; weapons
Arms Export Control Act of 1976, 239
arms limitation: arms transfer restraints, 240–45, 248–50; nuclear nonproliferation, 74–75, 93 n.5, 173, 176 nn.10, 11, 177 n.17, 222–25, 228–30, 279–80; START treaty, 92–93 n.3, 173
Army, 102, 105–6; force planning, 162; program terminations, 183; technological weaknesses, 194, 195
artillery antitactical missiles (ATACMs), 195
Art, Robert, 18
Asian security: change in security environment, 273–75; defense cooperation and, 282–84, 285–86; northeast, 275–80; southeast, 280–84, 285–86; U.S. role and, 272–73, 275–76, 284–85, 286–87
Aspin, Les, 44 n.91, 118–19 n.36, 127 n.7
Assistant to the President for National Security Affairs (APNSA), 49
Association of Southeast Asian Nations (ASEAN), 273, 274–75, 278, 281, 282–84, 285–86
atomic bombs, 221
*August 1914* (Solzhenitsyn), 11
Augustine Curve, 203
Australia, 274, 275, 281, 293
AX attack bomber, 106, 186, 195

B-1 bomber, 112
B-1B bomber, 111, 186
Bacon, Roger F., 106
Baker, James, 80, 242
balance of payment deficit, 273
balance of power policy, 80, 273, 309 n.1
Baldwin, Hanson, 10–11
ballistic missiles: defense, 75–76, 78–79, 171, 196–97; proliferation of, 59, 93 n.4, 140, 222, 240; reduction of, 93 n.3
Bartholomew, Reginald, 245
Base Force, 61–63, 66, 79, 85–87, 125, 182
battle management, 168, 191
Beirut, 88–89, 145
Benjedid, Chedli, 228
beyond visual range air-to-air combat, 191
Biden, Joseph, 243, 246
Biological Weapons Convention (BWC), 239
Block III tank, 183
Boer War, 9
border conflicts, 189–90
Bradley, Omar, 22
Brazil, 235, 237 n.9
Britain, 11, 205, 213, 281; anti-military tradition in, 19; civil-military relations in, 21; deterrence and, 132–33, 134, 135, 137–38, 139; and nuclear nonproliferation, 222; as nuclear power, 220–21; strategic consensus in, 31; strategic culture of, 37; strategic vision of, 67
Brodie, Bernard, 14
Brunei, 275, 281, 282, 286
Buchanan, Patrick, 32, 122
Buckley, James L., 239–40
Budget and Impoundment Act of 1974, 109–10
Budget committees, 108–9
budget deficit: defense budget and, 27, 28, 100, 104–5, 122; entitlements explosion and, 27–28
Budget Enforcement Act of 1990, 86
Burma, 284
Bush, George, 75, 113, 141; and arms transfers, 242–43, 245, 246, 248; and collective security, 256, 267; defense budget (1992) of, 182, 183; and defense strategy, 71, 92 n.1; *National Security Strategy* reports, 47, 51, 57; and NATO, 296, 302; and nuclear nonproliferation, 173, 176 n.11, 177 n.17, 224, 228, 280;

peacetime engagement policy of, 163 n.2; and Persian Gulf War, 262, 263, 264, 265, 267

$C^3I$/BM, 185, 189, 194, 196
Cahen, Alfred, 298
Cambodia, 273, 274, 281, 285
Canada, 132–33, 138, 211, 275
Carlucci, Frank, 49
Carnot, Lazare, 9–10
Carter, Jimmy, 112, 117 n.22
casualties, assessment of, 194
Central Treaty Organization (CENTO), 293
Chairman Joint Chiefs of Staff (CJCS), 64, 65, 66, 67, 68, 72, 82, 84, 86, 90, 91, 106, 177 n.14
Chairman's Guidance, 65–66, 68
chemical/biological weapons, 141–42, 143–45, 190, 197, 224
Chemical Weapons Convention (CWC), 239
Cheney, Richard, 36, 78, 85–88, 91, 92 n.1, 244, 245, 247, 267
China. *See* People's Republic of China (PRC); Taiwan
Churchill, Winston, 37, 39 n.8, 291–92, 309 n.1
Cincinnatus, 30
civil war, 189, 270
Civil War, U.S., 10
Claude, Inis, 290, 291, 302
Clausewitz, Karl von, 4, 5, 6, 7–8, 9–10, 11, 14, 23, 25, 30, 68, 121
Clausewitzian trinity, 6–7, 9, 11, 17, 23, 24, 25, 30, 31, 36, 121
Clemenceau, Georges, 25
Clinton, Bill, 250, 296
coalition, defined, 290
Cold War. *See* military strategy, Cold War
collective engagement, 80
collective security, 29; in Asia, 272–87; coalition *vs.* alliance in, 290–91; conventional deterrence and, 169–70; defined, 255–56; in Europe, Cold War, 291, 292–94; in Europe, post-Cold War, 294–303; forward presence and, 170; last resort concept of war and, 262–64; leadership of, 265–67; military objectives of, 264–65; peacetime decline in, 259–61; in Persian Gulf War, 261–64, 265, 266; predicament wars and, 270; selective approach to, 267–69; United Nations and, 256, 257–59, 262, 291, 292; in World War II, 291–92
Comanche RAH-66 helicopter, 183, 195
Commander in Chief, Europe (CINCEUR), 89
Commanders-in-Chief (CINCs), 20, 83, 84, 88, 89, 90, 91, 106
committees, Congressional, 108–9, 118 n.31
communications, mass, 8, 24
component upgrades, 169
Conference on Security and Cooperation in Europe (CSCE), 77, 277, 295, 298–99, 300, 302
Congress, and military, 15, 23–24, 47, 82, 100; arms transfers and, 242–43, 244, 246, 249; defense budget in, 18, 21–22, 27, 28, 104, 107–13, 182, 184; ground-based defenses and, 75; national consensus and, 25, 26; powers of, 17, 20–21, 124; relations with military, 22; relations with president, 17, 48–49, 50
Congressional Budget Office (CBO), 104
Congressional Research Service (CRS), 109, 246
Constitution, U.S., 20, 21
containment, 16, 17, 26–27, 47, 58, 105, 122, 152–53, 291
continental U.S.-based forces, 158
contingency planning, 188–91
conventional deterrence, 131, 152–63; chemical weapons and, 141–42, 143–45; by denial, 132; effectiveness of, 138–39; in multipolar system, 147–48; nuclear role in, 172–75; requirements for, 157–63, 167–71; response to critics of, 166–67;

strategy, 152–57, 171–72; surgical strikes and, 142–43; theoretical foundations of, 148–52
Corbett, Julian, 133–34, 145
Cordesman, Anthony, 168
Cranston, Alan, 111
crisis response, 59, 78
Croatia, 296
cross-border invasion, 161
Crowe, William, 86, 91
Cuba, 189
Czechoslovakia, 77

Dahlerus, Birger, 135
damage assessment, 194
decisive force concept, 60, 61
defense budget, 18, 21–22, 83; areas of, 87; balanced spending, 82–83, 87–88; Base Force in, 86; in Cold War period, 98–99, 204–5; Congressional politics and, 18, 21–22, 27, 28, 104, 107–13; deficit pressures on, 27, 28, 100, 104–5, 122; increase in, 88, 104, 115 n.5, 183, 209; interservice rivalries, 105–7; "liar's contest" syndrome and, 184; procurement in, 182–83; reduction of, 28, 86, 87, 99, 182–83, 195, 205; transfer pressures on, 27–28, 103, 104, 107, 122–23
Defense Department (DoD), 18, 29, 64, 75, 100, 201; bureaucracy, 99, 115 n.4; Cheney-Powell management style, 85–90; Cheney-Powell strategy, 78–81, 102–3; and Cold War, 82–84; Congressional relations, 111, 112; and defense industry, 209; and East Asian Security Initiative (EASI), 273–74, 275; management tools of, 81–84; military-industrial complex and, 98, 111; national strategy defined by, 12, 15; reorganization of, 20, 47, 72, 84–85, 89, 90–91, 106. *See also* defense budget
defense industry, 98, 111; contribution to strategy, 201–2; efficiency of, 203–4; flexibility of, 204–6; foreign participation in, 212–13; innovation in, 207, 208–10; profit decline, 209–10; quantity *vs.* quality and, 206–8
Defense Planning Guidance (DPG), 85, 86
defense policy. *See* military strategy; military strategy, Cold War; military strategy, post-Cold War
defense policy groups, 110
Defense Reorganization Act of 1986 (Goldwater-Nichols), 15, 20, 47, 48, 64, 71, 72, 82, 85, 88, 89, 90, 91, 106
Defense Security Assistance Agency (DSAA), 239
defensive weapons, 9
Desert Shield/Desert Storm. *See* Persian Gulf War
deterrence, 14, 37; during Cold War, 147, 150; components of, 149; criticism of, 150–51; by denial and punishment, 131–35, 138, 145, 153, 172; extended, 29, 30, 74, 75, 136–39, 150; failure of, 30, 31, 126, 134–36, 151, 154, 167; homeland, 73–74; immediate *vs.* general, 149; nuclear, 73–75, 92 n.2, 132, 136, 137, 139, 150, 151, 157, 172, 218, 226; peacemaking and, 76–77; rationality concept and, 164 n.9; strategic, 59, 78. *See* also conventional deterrence
Dodd, Christopher, 111
Douhet, Giulio, 132, 139–40
Dresden air raid, 140
Dreyfus Affair, 9
dual-capable aircraft (DCA), 173
Dupuy, Trevor, 207

E-2C amphibious ship, 183
Earle, Edward Mead, 15
East Asian Economic Group (EAEG), 277
East Asian Security Initiative (EASI), 273– 74, 275
Eccles, Henry C., 12, 17
economic exclusion zones, (EEZs), 284, 287

Economist, 293, 294
Eekelen, Willem van, 298
Egypt, 17, 145, 246
Eisenhower, Dwight, 24, 105, 120 n.45
Elliott, J.H., 27
ends-ways-means paradigm, 3, 4, 5, 11, 32, 38
Energy Department (DoE), 118 n.30
ethnic warfare, 188, 270
Europe: collective security in, Cold War, 291, 292–94; collective security in, post-Cold War, 294–303; extended deterrence in, 77, 139, 153; threat to, 188, 296. *See also* North Atlantic Treaty Organization (NATO); World War I; World War II
European Community (EC), 76, 296–98, 301–2
executive branch, and military strategy: bureaucracy of, 18; failure to produce peacetime strategy, 18–19; National Security Strategy report and, 49; powers of, 17, 20–21, 22, 124; strategic planning, 53, 54–55. *See also* president

F-14 aircraft, 112, 195
F-14D aircraft, 183
F-15 aircraft, 183, 195, 245, 250
F-15E aircraft, 183, 195
F-16 aircraft, 183, 195, 245, 246, 250
F-18 aircraft, 195
F-18F aircraft, 195
F-111 aircraft, 195
F-117 aircraft, 151
Fairchild Republic Company, 111
Falkenhayn, Erich von, 145
Fascell, Dante B., 249
Finland, 139
fiscal policy, military strategy and, 99
Five Power Defense Arrangement (FPDA), 281
force multiplier, 185–88
foreign dependence, technological, 210–13
Foreign Relations Authorization Act, 249–50
forward presence, 30, 59, 78, 155, 170
France, 11, 31, 248, 297; and extended deterrence, 136–37; German relations with, 293, 294, 298; and nuclear nonproliferation, 222; as nuclear power, 220–21; offensive strategy of, 9
Franck, Thomas, 268
Frederick the Great, 4
French Revolution, 5–6
Friedberg, Aaron, 15
friendly fire, 196
Future Years Defense Plan (FYDP), 183, 194

Gaddis, John Lewis, 16
*Gaither Report*, 105
Gates, Robert, 101–2, 164–65 n.18, 176 n.6
General Accounting Office (GAO), 109
General Dynamics, 280
Germany, 8, 9, 31, 38, 64, 74, 77–78, 143, 297; chemical warfare of, 144; defense manufacture in, 205; deterrence and, 134–35, 137; French relations with, 293, 294, 298; military technology of, 207; and NATO, 293–94, 296; unification of, 296
global protection against limited strikes (GPALS), 78, 79, 171
Goldwater-Nichols Act. *See* Defense Reorganization Act of 1986 (Goldwater- Nichols)
Gorbachev, Mikhail, 256, 277, 278, 279
Gramm-Rudman-Hollings Deficit Reduction Act of 1985, 100, 104, 115 n.6
grand strategy, 306
Great War. *See* World War I
Greece, 295–96
Grenada invasion, 83

Haass, Richard N., 244–45
Hale, Robert, 88

Hamburg air raid, 140
Hamilton, Alexander, 21
hard target killing, 192
HARM missile, 183
helicopters, 183, 187, 195
Hildebrand, Robert, 292
Hiroshima bombing, 142, 143, 221
Hitler, Adolf, 134, 139, 143
Hobbes, Thomas, 35
Howard, Michael, 10, 68
Hughes, Arthur H., 247
Hull, Cordell, 292, 302
humanitarian aid, 44 n.91
Hungary, 77
Huntington, Samuel, 21, 23, 36, 83, 94 n.17
Hussein, Saddam, 77, 141, 142, 159–60, 161, 218, 227, 241, 242, 248, 263, 264
Hyland, William, 27, 122

Ikle, Fred, 38, 175
Ikle-Wohlstetter Commission of 1988, 54
India: extended deterrence in, 138; nuclear capability of, 221, 222, 223, 224, 225, 231–32, 236 n.4, 237 nn.10, 12
Indonesia, 275, 281, 282, 283, 286
industrial base. *See* defense industry
Industrial Revolution, 6–8
integrated circuits, dependence on foreign sources for, 211
Integrated Strike Employment Plan (ISEP), 173–74
intelligence, 191, 194
International Atomic Energy Agency (IAEA), 222, 223, 228, 229, 230, 237 n.9, 238 n.20, 279, 280
Iran: arms sales to, 246, 248; -Iraq War, 238 n.17, 240; nuclear capability of, 223, 225, 226, 229, 234
Iraq: arms sales to, 241, 248; attacks on nuclear reactor of, 226, 227, 238 n.17; contingency planning and, 189; nuclear capability of, 219–20, 223, 225, 227, 229, 230, 233–34; war with Iran, 238 n.17, 240. *See also* Persian Gulf War
Islamic Salvation Front, 297
isolationism, 103, 121–22, 148
Israel: -Arab conflict, 16–17, 145, 202, 224; arms sales to, 246; attack on Iraqi reactor, 226, 227, 238 n.17; nuclear capability of, 221–22, 223, 224, 225, 231, 236 nn.3, 5, 236–37 n.6
Italy, 297

James, William, 10
Japan, 74, 77–78, 205, 211; Korean relations with, 228, 275, 277; and regional economic group, 276–77; and regional security, 273, 274, 276, 277, 286; Soviet relations with, 274, 277; and U.S. deployment, 275, 276; World War II bombing of, 142, 143, 221
Joffre, Joseph, 9
John Paul II, Pope, 263
Johnson, Lyndon, 120 n.45
Joint Chiefs of Staff (JCS), 22, 61–62, 188; Chairman's Guidance, 65–66, 68; joint planning system, 64–68, 86–87; powers of chairman, 82, 84, 86, 90, 91, 106; presidential policy support by, 120 n.45; threat scenario of, 125
joint duty, 84, 91–92, 106
Joint Military Net Assessment, 188
Joint Strategic Capabilities Plan (JSCP), 65
Joint Strategic Planning System (JSPS), 19, 64–68, 86, 87
Joint Strategic Target Planning Staff Advisory Group, 173
joint surveillance target attack radar system (JSTARS), 186
Jomini, Henri, 3–4
Jones, David C., 106
jungle warfare, 196

Kato, Koichi, 277
Kaufmann, William, 87–88
Kennan, George, 291, 300

Kennedy, John F., 25, 93 n.4
Kennedy, Joseph, 37
Kennedy, Paul, 27, 68
Kim Il-song, 278, 279, 285
Kimball, Warren, 290
King, Coretta Scott, 263
Kissinger, Henry, 19–20
Kohl, Helmut, 296
Korb, Lawrence, 116–17 n.20, 120 n.45
Korea. *See* North Korea; South Korea
Korean War, 23, 24, 100; collective security in, 260, 264, 265, 272; national interests and, 16, 122
Krauthammer, Charles, 32
Kuala Lumpur, 286
Kuhn, Thomas, 151
Kurile islands, 277
Kuwait: arms sales to, 246, 247; Iraq invasion of (*see* Persian Gulf War)

League of Nations, 256, 260, 291
Lebanon, 89–90
Lee Jong Koo, 226
Libya: nuclear capability of, 223, 225, 226, 234; Scud missile attack, 237 n.16
Lippmann, Walter, 26, 37
Liska, George, 301
literacy, mass, 8
Lithuania, 177 n.14
LMAP H landing craft, 183
loiter sensors, 192
Long Commission, 88–89
LOSAT missile, 183
Lovett, Robert, 300
LSD-41 amphibious ship, 183
Luttwak, Edward, 248
Lykke, Arthur, 3, 69 n.2

M-1 tank, 112, 183
MacArthur, Douglas, 20, 22
McCain, John, 246
Mackinder, Halford, 138, 139
McNamara, Robert, 19–20, 116 n.17
Madison, James, 19
Mahan, Alfred Thayer, 3–4
Malaysia, 277, 281, 282, 283, 286
maneuverability, 192
Manila Pact, 283
Marathon, 30
Marine Corps, 102, 105–6; force planning, 162; technological weaknesses, 194, 195; V-22 Osprey, 107, 112
Mearsheimer, John, 155
media, defense coverage of, 110
Middle East Defense Organization (MEDO), 293
military bases, 110–11, 155, 281
military-industrial complex, 98, 111
military spending. *See* defense budget
military strategy: ends-ways-means paradigm, 3, 4, 5, 11, 32, 38; French Revolution impact on, 5–6; Industrial Revolution impact on, 6–8; interest-based *vs.* threat-based, 306–7; national, 10–14, 15–19; offensive *vs.* defensive, 9; political ends of, 4–5, 99, 307; presidential statement on, 15–16, 17, 47–52; as science *vs.* art, 3–4. *See also* collective security; deterrence; technology, military; war
military strategy, Cold War, 14–15, 25–26, 98, 202; in Asia, 272–73; defense acquisitions, 204–5; deterrence and, 147, 150, 152–53, 157; force structure, 100–101; and global commitments, 122; government role and, 15–19; military establishment and, 19–23; national consensus on, 23–25, 31–32; organizational structure and, 84–84; unilateralism in, 80
military strategy, post-Cold War, 99–100; arms sales policy and, 245–48, 250; budget deficit impact on, 27–28, 122; collective security and, 260–67; comprehensive, 63–64; concepts of, 59–61, 167–71; controlled builddown, 28–30, 31, 64, 102–3, 113; debate over, 102–3; domestic missions of, 34–35; domestic priorities and, 26–27, 122–24; elements of, 73–78; failure of

deterrence, 30, 31; flexibility of, 64; force structure, 61–63, 103, 155, 162, 168; formulation of, 64–68; goals of, 57–59, 72–73, 158–59; interest-based, 126; lack of consensus on, 26, 29, 31, 52–53; lack of long-range planning for, 53–55; leadership role in, 80; National Security Strategy (NSC) reports on, 51–52; need for consensus on, 31–33; nuclear-armed radical states and, 226–31; organizational structure and, 84–85; Pentagon proposals, 78–81; regional crisis response, 28–29, 52, 55, 58–59, 218–20; risk/benefit calculus in, 218–20; strategic culture and, 37; strategic vision in, 33–36, 37, 66–68, 124, 305–8; technological adaptation and, 181–99; technological dependence and, 202–210. *See also* arms limitation; conventional deterrence
Milward, Alan S., 204
mine warfare, 194
Missile Defense Act of 1991, 75, 94 n.15
missiles. *See* ballistic missiles
Missile Technology Control Regime (MTCR), 241, 249
Mitchell, George J., 265
mobility, 193
Mobilization Concepts Development Center (MCDC), 211–12
Moran, Thomas, 212–13
Morgan, Patrick, 163–64 n.8
Morgenthau Prize, 38
multilateralism, 265, 266
multilaunch rocket system (MLRS), 186, 195
multinational corporations, 273
munitions: funding cuts, 195; lethality of, 192, 196; precision-guided (PGMs), 211

Nagasaki bombing, 143, 221
Namibia, 224
Napoleon, 10, 11
National Command Authority, 64
National Defense Tax, 280
National Guard, 22, 23, 119–20 n.44, 194
national interests, 16, 67, 113
nationalism, rise of, 8
*National Military Strategy* document (NMSD) 1992, 57–58, 59, 65, 86–87, 172, 175 n.1, 176 n.4
national security: defined, 41 n.41, 52; goals of, 158
National Security Act of 1947, 15, 90
National Security Council (NSC), 48–49
national security decision directives (NSDD), 50
National Security Division, 110
national security state, 98
*National Security Strategy* reports, 15–16, 17, 46–47, 57–58, 65; 1987, 50; 1988, 17, 50–51; 1990, 51; 1991, 51–52; political context of, 47–50
national strategy, 10–14, 15–19
national will, 10
naval warfare: countervalue punishment in, 132, 133, 134, 138; fire support, 194; nuclear, 172–73
Navy, 102, 105, 107, 138; force planning, 162; program terminations, 183; submarines, 106, 111; technological weaknesses, 194, 195
New Zealand, 281, 293
Niemeyer, Gerhart, 302
night warfare, 192
Nitze, Paul, 155
Nixon, Richard, 25, 120 n.45, 177 n.17, 309 n.1
Nixon Doctrine, 272
Nolan, Janne E., 249
Non-Proliferation Treaty (NPT), 93 n.5, 173, 222–23, 228, 239
North American Defense Industrial Base Organization (NADIBO), 216 n.23
North Atlantic Cooperation Council (NACC), 94, 299, 300
North Atlantic Treaty Organization (NATO), 77, 94 n.13, 133, 136,

153, 177 n.14, 196, 218, 256, 290, 292; functions of, 295–96; long-term reliability of, 293–94; and out-of-area disputes, 293; redefining, 299–301
North Korea, 77, 273; arms sales to, 279; force-sizing contingencies and, 189; nuclear capability of, 223, 225, 226, 228, 232–33, 278, 280; and nuclear nonproliferation, 228–30, 279–80; and reunification, 278–79, 285
NSC-68, 16, 105, 153
nuclear delegitimization, 74, 75
nuclear reactors, attacks on, 226, 227, 237–38 n.17
nuclear umbrella, 74, 75, 93 n.4, 171, 226
nuclear weapons, 23, 187, 190; in conventional force-dominant deterrent, 172–75; deterrent force of, 73–75, 132, 136, 137, 139, 150, 151, 157, 172, 218, 226; direct retaliation and, 174; forward deployment of, 101, 136, 137; freeze, 224, 230; inspections, 229, 230, 238 n.20, 279, 280; Iraq's capability, 219–20; military force against installations, 226–27, 237–38 n.17; nonproliferation, 74–75, 93 n.5, 173, 176 nn.10, 11, 177 n.17, 222–25, 228–30, 279–80; proliferation, 74, 78, 79, 100, 139, 140, 156, 171, 175, 217–18, 220–22; reduction of, 74–75, 92–93 n.3, 93 n.5, 173, 174, 176 nn.10, 11, 177 n.17; signaling function of, 172–73; size criteria for, 92 n.2; targeting, 173–75; testing, 221; and threshold states, 221–22, 223, 224–36, 278, 279–80
nuclear winter, 142
Nunn, Sam, 28

offensive strategy, 9
Office of Management and Budget (OMB), 108
Office of Technology Assessment (OTA), 110
Office of the Joint Chiefs of Staff (OJCS), 124
Office of the Secretary of Defense (OSD), 83, 87, 124
Office of the Undersecretary of Defense, 86
Okinawa, 276
Oman, 246
O'Neill, Thomas "Tip," 122
*On War* (Clausewitz), 23
Organization for Economic Cooperation and Development (OECD), 291
Organization of African Unity (OAU), 302
Organization of American States (OAS), 302

Pakistan: nuclear capability of, 221, 222, 223, 224–25, 232; and nuclear nonproliferation, 225, 237 n.10
Patriot missile, 248, 279
peacekeeping role, 76
peacemaking role, 76–77
peacetime engagement policy, 163 n.2
Pentagon. *See* Defense Department (DoD); Joint Chiefs of Staff (JCS)
People's Republic of China (PRC): and Asian security, 272, 274–75, 278, 283, 284, 285; ballistic missile threat of, 76, 222; and nuclear nonproliferation, 222, 224, 230; as nuclear power, 220–21, 231, 232, 234, 235; tactics in Tiananmen uprising, 144; and U.S. forward deployment, 77
Perm Five: and arms transfer restraints, 243–44; Cambodia plan of, 273, 274
Permissive Action Links (PAL), 140
Perry, William, 159
Persian Gulf War, 28, 29, 51, 61, 77, 79, 90, 91, 106, 126, 226, 276, 297, 298; air superiority in, 161; arms transfers as cause, 241; chemical weapons and, 236 n.1; collective

security and, 261–64, 265, 266; conventional deterrence in, 138, 141–42, 151, 159–60, 161–62; foreign technology dependence and, 211; friendly fire in, 196; lessons of, 189; military conduct of, 88–89, 207–8; nuclear installations in, 227; opposition to, 263; risk/benefit calculus and, 218–19; technological superiority in, 181, 183, 207, 242; theater strategic targeting in, 172; vulnerabilities of U.S. forces in, 193, 195, 196

petroleum: in Persian Gulf, 240; stockpiles, 211

Philippines, 274, 281–82, 283

Planning, Program, and Budgeting System (PPBS), 19, 84, 86

Poland, 77, 137, 296

police action, 160–61

population, increase in, 8

Powell, Colin, 29, 49, 57, 62, 78, 85–88, 91, 92 n.1

power projection capability, 29–30

precision-guided munitions (PGMs), 211

preemptive attack, 80–81

president: Congressional relations, 17, 48–49, 50; defense budget and, 112–13; *National Security Strategy* report of, 15–16, 17, 47–52; State of the Union address, 50. *See also* executive branch; *names of specific presidents*

Pressler Amendment, 224

*Primas der Aussenpolitik*, 8

procurement: budget reduction, 182–83; goals of, 187

Prussia, 8

public opinion, domestic priorities of, 122– 24

punitive raid, 160

railroads, 8

Rajak, Mohammed Abdul, 284

RAND Corporation, 213

rationality, concept of, 164 n.9

Reagan, Ronald, 52, 80, 88, 99, 224; and arms transfers, 239–40; defense budget of, 104, 105, 112–13, 117 n.22, 183; national security strategy of, 32; *National Security Strategy* report, 17, 47, 50

*Realpolitik*, 8

rear areas, 193

reconstitution capability, 59, 78, 79–81

Reed, Thomas C., 173

reinforcement capability, 78

"Relating Means to Ends: An Economic Agenda for the 1990s," 16

research and development (R&D), 34–35, 182, 186, 202

Reserve forces, 29, 35, 60, 119–20 n.44, 194

return on fixed assets (ROA), 209

Revolutions of 1848, 8

Rice, Condoleezza, 14–15

Roh Tae Woo, 228

Rome Declaration, 299

Roosevelt, Franklin D., 206, 291–92, 309 n.1

Roosevelt, Theodore, 36

Rowen, Henry, 117 n.21

Russia, 9, 11. *See also* Soviet Union/ former Soviet Union

Russo-Japanese war, 9

Sadat, Anwar, 17

Safety, Security, and Dismantlement of Nuclear Weapons (SSD) talks, 177 n.13

Salisbury, Lord, 25, 35

Saudi Arabia, arms sales to, 245, 246, 248, 250

Scherer, Frederick M., 208

Schlesinger, James, 26

Schlieffen Plan, 9

Schumpeter, Joseph, 208

Schwarzkopf, Norman, 88, 89

Scud missiles, 237 n.16

*Sea Power*, 240

Secretary of Defense, 72, 82, 83, 84, 87, 90, 106, 108

Security Council, U.N., 243, 257, 258, 261, 265. *See also* Perm Five
separation of power, 21, 23
Serbia, 298
servicism, 83–84
Shaposhnikov, Boris, 174
Sherman, William Tecumseh, 30
show of force, 160
Singapore, 275, 281, 282, 283, 286
Single Integrated Operation Plan (SIOP), 151, 173
Slim, Sir William, 37
Slovenia, 296
Smith, Perry, 66
Snyder, Glenn, 131–32
Solomon, Richard, 274
Solzhenitsyn, Alexander, 11
South Africa: nuclear capability of, 221, 222, 232; and nuclear nonproliferation, 222–23, 227, 230
South Korea: arms sales to, 279; Japanese relations with, 228, 275, 277; and nuclear nonproliferation, 223, 226, 227, 228–30; and reunification, 278–79, 285; U.S. relations with, 74, 77, 137, 189, 273, 275, 279, 280, 285
Soviet Union/former Soviet Union, 58, 61, 62, 64, 73, 80–81, 100, 275; and Asian security, 277, 278, 283; Cold War strategy of, 14; containment of, 16, 17, 26–27, 47, 58, 105, 122, 152–53, 272, 291; deterrence and, 135, 136, 150; internal conflicts in, 188–83; and Japan, 274, 277; as military threat, 100–101, 139, 174, 177 n.14, 188, 202, 274; and nuclear nonproliferation, 92–93 n.3, 173, 222, 224, 230; as nuclear power, 79, 140, 220–21; regional conflicts and, 60, 262; strike options against, 173–74
space-based defense system, 75, 78–79, 171
Spratly islands, 285, 286
SQY-1 ASW combat system, 183
Stalin, Joseph, 291–92
State Department: on arms sales, 246; Office of Defense Trade, 239
State of the Union address, 50
Steinbruner, John, 32–33, 87–88
strategic agility, 60–61, 170
Strategic Arms Limitation Talks (SALT), 177 n.17
Strategic Arms Reduction Treaty (START), 92 n.3, 173
strategic defense concept, 59
Strategic Defense Initiative (SDI), 72, 75, 171
strategic deterrence concept, 59
strategic planning: adaptive, 61; joint, 64–66; lack of, 53–55; reorganization of, 86
strategic targets, soft, 192
strategic vision, 33–36, 37, 66–68, 124, 305–8
strategic warning, 60
strategy. *See* military strategy
submarine-launched ballistic missile (SLBM), 140, 176 n.11
submarines, 106, 111
Suez Crisis, 292
Sumatra, 281
Summers, Harry, 35
surge requirements, 202, 204
surgical strikes, 142–43
sustainability, 192, 195
Syria, 235, 246

T-46 trainer program, 111
table of organization and equipment (TO&E), 195
Taft, Robert, 22
Taiwan, 223, 227, 236, 245, 250
Task Force Smith, 31
technology, military: application to domestic problems, 34–35; contingency planning and, 188–91; dependence, 202–10; dependence, on foreign sources, 210–13; force multiplier effect and, 185–88; force-on-force priorities, 197–99; future of, 214; impact on national consensus, 23–24; impact on war, 8–9, 10, 11; and industrial base (*see*

defense industry); Industrial Revolution and, 6–8; laws of effective use, 185; limitations on, 14; prioritization, 184; procurement funding, 182–83; procurement goals, 187; superiority, 168–69, 181, 202, 206–8, 210; weaknesses of threat forces, 191–93; weaknesses of U.S., 193–97. *See also* arms limitation; nuclear weapons; weapons
Thailand, 274, 281, 282, 286
theater defenses, 75, 171
theater missile defense (TMD), 75
Tokyo air raid, 140, 143
Tomahawk Land Attack Missiles (TLAM), 173
TOW sight improvement program, 183
transportation, 7, 8
trip-wire theories, 155–56
Truman, Harry, 20, 26, 120 n.45, 122, 309 n.1
Truman Doctrine, 26
Tucker, Richard, 32
Turkey, 293, 295–96

UAV killers, 192
unilateralism, 80, 265
United Arab Emirates (UAE), 246
United Nations: arms trade register of, 249; and Cambodia, 273; and collective security, 256, 257–59, 262, 265–66, 270, 291, 292, 302; nuclear inspection by, 227, 238 n.20; peacemaking operations of, 76–77; and Persian Gulf War, 261, 262, 264, 265. *See also* Perm Five; Security Council
urbanization, 8
urban warfare, 188, 195–96

V-22 Osprey, 107, 112
Vanunu, Mordechai, 221–22
victory, concept of, 305–6
Vietnam, 274, 283, 284, 285
Vietnam War, 18, 24–25, 31, 32, 124, 137, 202, 207, 272
vital interests, 16
Von der Goltz, August, 133–34
Von Hippel, Eric, 208–9
Von Roon, Albrecht, 8
Vuono, Carl E., 240–41

war: American dislike of, 116 n.13; border conflicts, 189–90; chemical, 143–45, 190; civil, 189, 270; Clausewitz on, 4, 5, 6, 14, 23, 25; countervalue aspects of, 132, 133–34; ethnic, 188, 270; global, 59, 60, 61, 79–81; last resort concept of, 262–64; limited, 14, 135; low-/mid-intensity, 186–87; parallel, 161; peacetime planning for, 10, 15, 36–37, 68; people's, 6; predicament *vs.* policy, 270; regional, 79, 217, 218–20; rough terrain, 196; technological advances and, 8–9, 10, 11; total, 10–14; urban, 188, 195–96. *See also names of specific wars*
Warnke, Paul C., 248
War of 1812, 138
War Powers Resolution of 1973, 25
Warsaw Pact, 64, 100–101, 198, 295, 297
Wavell, Archibald, 40 n.22
weapons, 7; breech-loading, 8; chemical/biological, 141–42, 143–45, 190, 197, 224; Congressional politics and, 110–11, 112; conventional, 138–39, 140–45, 151, 166, 169, 172, 239–50; crew-sized heavy, 195; defensive *vs.* offensive, 9; efficiency measurement, 203–4; ground-based defense, 59, 75–76, 94 n.15; mass production of, 8; modernization, 87, 88; program terminations, 183; sales, 239–50, 279, 282; space-based defense, 75, 78–79, 171; undeployable, 186. *See also* munitions; nuclear weapons; technology, military
Weinberger, Casper, 91, 116 n.17, 117 n.22
Weinberger Doctrine, 25
Weiner, Sharon, 85
Western European Union (WEU), 293, 298, 301

Wilborn, Thomas, 277
Wilson, Henry, 67
Wilson, Woodrow, 255
World War I: chemical weapons in, 144; collective security after, 255–56, 260, 291; deterrence in, 132, 134, 135, 145; isolationism after, 121–22; military technology in, 207; national strategic problems after, 31; national strategy in, 10–12; offensive strategy in, 9, 145
World War II, 38, 103, 122; collective security in, 291–92; deterrence in, 132, 134–35, 141, 143; limited air war, 135; military technology in, 205–6, 207; strategic culture in, 37
Worner, Manfred, 294
Wylie, J.C., 4, 42 n.59, 61

Yeltsin, Boris, 173, 176 n.11, 177 n.17, 277
Yom Kippur War, 17
Yugoslavia, 76, 296, 298, 299

# About the Contributors

GORDON ADAMS is the founder and director of the Defense Budget Project. He is a member of the Council on Foreign Relations and the International Peace and Security Committee of the Social Sciences Research Council, and a Senior Fellow of the Center for the New West in Denver, among other affiliations. He is the author of over 100 books, reports, and articles on the defense budget and national security, including *The Politics of Defense Constructing: The Iron Triangle*, and *Defense Spending and the Economy: Does the Defense Dollar Make a Difference?*, with coauthor David Gold.

ROBERT J. ART is the Christian A. Herter Professor of International Relations at Brandeis University, and Research Associate, Center for International Affairs, Harvard University. He has published in the field of national security affairs and U.S. foreign and defense decision making. His most recent publications are "A Defensible Defense: U.S. Grand Strategy after the Cold War," in *International Security*; and with Seyom Brown, ed., *America's Foreign Policy after the Cold War*. He is currently working on a book for the Twentieth Century Fund entitled *The Purposes of Power*.

JAMES BLACKWELL is a Senior Fellow at the Center for Strategic and International Studies, where he is Director for Political-Military Studies. A specialist in military technology, doctrine, and operations, he served in the U.S. Army and taught at the U.S. Military Academy at West Point. He is currently co-chair of the Project on Persian Gulf War Military Lessons Learned. He has authored *Thunder in the Desert: The Strategy and Tactics of the Persian Gulf War*. His articles have appeared in *Parameters*, *Military Technology*, *NATO's 16 Nations*, and *National Defense*, and he has contributed to numerous books and edited volumes. He is coeditor, with Barry Blechman, of *Making Defense Reform Work*, published in 1990. He served as CNN's military analyst during the Persian Gulf crisis.

INIS L. CLAUDE, JR., is Professor Emeritus at the University of Virginia. He is an internationally respected scholar on international organization and collective security. His books include *Swords into Plowshares: The Problems and Progress of International Organization*; *Power and International Relations*; *The Changing United Nations*; and *States and the Global System.*

ANTHONY H. CORDESMAN is Adjunct Professor of National Security Studies at Georgetown University. He is actively involved in legislation to control the proliferation of biological, chemical, and nuclear weapons and the proliferation of long-range missiles. He has written and lectured extensively on the Middle East and the Gulf, the U.S. and Soviet military balance, and the lessons of war. He is the author of nine books, including *The Iran-Iraq War: 1984–1987*, *The Gulf and the West*, and *Lessons of Modern War.*

GARY L. GUERTNER is Director of Research at the Strategic Studies Institute, U.S. Army War College. A former Marine Corps officer and veteran of Vietnam, he has also served on the staff of the U.S. Arms Control and Disarmament Agency and as Professor of Political Science at California State University, Fullerton. His latest book is *Deterrence and Defense in a Post-Nuclear World.*

ROBERT P. HAFFA, JR., is a Senior Analyst with the Northrop Corporation in Washington, DC. Assignments during his Air Force career included operational tours in Vietnam, Korea, and Europe; Professor and Acting Head of the Political Science Department at the U.S. Air Force Academy; Chief of the Long Range Planning Division at Headquarters, U.S. Air Force; and Chief of a Staff Group supporting the Air Force Chief of Staff. A graduate of Air Command and Staff College and the National War College, he was a Senior Fellow at the National Defense University. As a lecturer in international politics at the Nitze School of Advanced International Studies, the Johns Hopkins University, Dr. Haffa teaches courses in U.S. defense policy and force planning. He is the author of two books, *The Half War* and *Planning U.S. Forces*, and numerous articles and book reviews.

DAVID JABLONSKY is Professor of National Security in the Department of National Security and Strategy of the U.S. Army War College. His last position on active duty was Chairman of the Strategic Research Department of the College's Strategic Studies Institute. He is a graduate of the Army Command and General Staff College and the U.S. Army War College, and he has served in a variety of assignments in Vietnam, Europe, and the United States. He was a member of the Army Chief of Staff's Warfighting Study Group in 1985–86. He is the author of three books, including *Churchill: The Making of a Grand Strategist* and *Churchill, The Great Game and Total War*.

MICHAEL T. KLARE is the Five College Associate Professor of Peace and World Security Studies and Director of the Five College Program in Peace and World Security Studies (PAWSS). He is also the Defense Correspondent of *The Nation* magazine. He is the author of several books, including *Beyond the "Vietnam Syndrome"* and *American Arms Supermarket*. He is also coeditor of *Low-Intensity Warfare, Peace and World Order Studies: A Curriculum Guide* and *World Security: Trends and Challenges at Century's End*. His articles on international affairs and defense policy have appeared in such journals as *Foreign Policy, International Security, World Policy Journal, Harper's, The Bulletin of Atomic Scientists, Arms Control Today*, and *Technology Review*.

GEORGE H. QUESTER is Chairman of the Department of Government and Politics at the University of Maryland, where he teaches courses on defense policy, arms control, and U.S. foreign policy. He is the author of numerous books and journal articles on international politics and international security.

HARRY E. ROTHMANN is currently Chief, Strategy Application Branch, Strategy Division, J–5, Joint Staff, Washington, DC. He was commissioned in the infantry upon graduation from the U.S. Military Academy. His major previous assignments include Company Commander, 3d Battalion, 506th Infantry, 101st Airborne Division (Airmobile), Republic of Vietnam; Company Commander, 2d Battalion, 39th Infantry, 9th Infantry Division, Fort Lewis, Washington; Associate Professor, Department of History, USMA, West Point, New York; Operations Officer, 3d Brigade, 101st Airborne Division (Air Assault), Fort Campbell, Kentucky; Action Officer, War Plans Division, Office of the Deputy Chief of Staff for Operations and Plans, Washington, DC; Executive Officer, 2d Brigade, 101st Airborne Division (Air Assault); and Commander, 3d Battalion, 502d Infantry. He is a graduate of the Infantry Officer Advanced Course and the Naval War College.

SHELDON W. SIMON is Professor of Political Science and Faculty Associate of the Center for Asian Studies at Arizona State University. A specialist on Asian security, he is the author or editor of six books and more than seventy scholarly articles and book chapters. Dr. Simon has served as a consultant to the U.S. Information Agency, U.S. AID, the State Department, and the Defense Department. His most recent book is an edited study, *East Asian Security in the Post–Cold War Era.*

DONALD M. SNIDER is Deputy Director, Political Military Studies, at the Center for Strategic and International Studies (CSIS). He joined the Center in March 1990 when he retired from active duty. Since 1980 he had specialized in assignments related to military strategy and defense policy, serving consecutively as Chief of Plans for the Theater Army in Europe; Joint Planner for the Army Chief of Staff; Deputy Director of Strategy, Plans, and Policy on the Army General Staff; and Federal Executive Fellow at the Brookings Institution. He then joined the staff of the National Security Council in the White House in 1987 as Director, Defense Policy, serving in both the Reagan and Bush Administrations. Within the Center, he specializes in national security strategy, defense policy and programs, military strategy, and European security issues. His publications include a CSIS Panel Report, "A New Military Strategy for the 1990s: Implications for Capabilities and Acquisition," and "The Gulf War: Military Lessons Learned."

LEONARD S. SPECTOR has been active in the nuclear nonproliferation field for over ten years, working first at the Nuclear Regulatory Commission and later as Chief Counsel to the Senate Energy and Nuclear Proliferation Subcommittee. While he was with the Subcommittee, Mr. Spector assisted in drafting the 1978 Nuclear Nonproliferation Act, the basic law governing U.S. policy today. Since 1984 he has been a Senior Associate at the Carnegie Endowment for International Peace and Director of its Nuclear Nonproliferation Project. He is the author of the Endowment's five annuals on the spread of nuclear weapons, *Nuclear Proliferation Today*, *The New Nuclear Nations*, *Going Nuclear*, *The Undeclared Bomb*, and (with Jacqueline R. Smith) *Nuclear Ambitions.*

DOUGLAS T. STUART is Professor and Director of International Studies at Dickinson College in Carlisle, PA. He is a former NATO Fellow and Visiting Scholar at the Brookings Institution in Washington, DC, and a member of the NATO Fellowships Review Committee for the Council for International Exchange of Scholars (CIES). A specialist in NATO affairs and northeast Asian security, he is the author, coauthor, or editor of four books and over twenty published articles. His most recent book, with William Tow, is entitled *The Limits of Alliance: NATO Out-Of-Area Problems since 1949.*